THE ROBERT SHAW READER

THE

ROBERT SHAW

READER

Edited by

ROBERT BLOCKER

Yale University Press

New Haven & London

Published with assistance from the Kingsley Trust Association Publication Fund
established by the Scroll and Key Society
of Yale College.

Set in Minion type by Keystone Typesetting, Inc.
Printed in the United States of America.

Library of Congress Control Number: 2004046538
ISBN: 0-300-10454-5 (cloth: alk. paper)

A catalogue record for this book is available from the Library of Congress
and the British Library.

The paper in this book meets the guidelines for permanence and durability
of the Committee on Production Guidelines for Book Longevity
of the Council on Library Resources.

10   9   8   7   6   5   4   3

CONTENTS

PREFACE

Most people who knew Robert Shaw first met him through his music. Some were acquainted with him only in this way, while others had the experience of knowing him as friend, or conductor, or cultural leader, or educator, or raconteur—or more than one, or even all of those roles he embodied. As a musician, however, he belonged to the world. His musical signature was—and still is—an extraordinary sound that touches one's deepest emotions.

His thoughts and words also belong to all humanity. In letters, lectures, and addresses, a plethora of musical topics are explored alongside Shaw's philosophical musings on other subjects. For many years Shaw spoke of a book he contemplated, and this was certainly not surprising in view of the fact that he organized a complete conservatory curricula for the Collegiate Chorale. His commitment to education was unwavering throughout his career, for Robert Shaw was the perpetual student. His intellectual curiosity was insatiable, and he continued to seek answers about questions most musicians had dismissed as inconsequential.

This is Robert Shaw's book. Each word is his—wisdom, wit, and immediacy from a treasury of writings and musings. It is a volume that reflects the unique perspective he brought to the podium. While a body of information can be drawn from the letters, the detailed analyses of several major works provide unusual insights. Addresses on the general theme of "The Role of Worship and the Arts" show yet another dimension of his personal credo that "the Bible teaches of a divine miracle when the Word became flesh. Is it no less a divine miracle when the flesh—the arts—become word?" The humanity of Robert Shaw is also fully revealed in his eulogies for national leaders and personal friends.

The Robert Shaw Reader attempts to record the primary themes of his musical journey and the manner in which a larger-than-life personality shared life with "his people." The efforts of many associates contributed to Shaw's book, but the devoted work of Eddie Barrus and Nola Frink is paramount in this regard. During the Atlanta years, Miss Frink ensured the legacy of his archival papers and scores with consummate administrative skill. To her we owe a great debt of gratitude.

Many others gave immeasurably to this volume. We can be certain that Robert Shaw's talent was nurtured lovingly by his family—Caroline, Alex, and Thomas—as well as by his many choristers, orchestra members, administrators, and assistants. Norman Mackenzie, Ann Jones, Nick Jones, and Jeff Baxter readily come to mind.

In the preparation and distillation of these materials, many of my colleagues have provided assistance and counsel. Harry Haskell and Lauren Shapiro of Yale University Press have been superb editors, and both possess deep reservoirs of patience. James McElroy, as my associate editor, has brought his excellent literary and technical skills to this task. William Thomas served as assistant editor for part II, and his insights were invaluable. Steven Hegarty lent his graphics expertise to help render Shaw's sprinkling of musical notations throughout his letters. Rosamond Hamlin and Eileen Kim have been invaluable administrative assistants, and others too numerous to name have offered counsel.

Finally, I thank my wife, Serena, for her encouragement, wisdom, and love.

Robert Blocker
New Haven, Connecticut

INTRODUCTION

Over the course of his long career, Robert Shaw must have raised more than a million voices in song—voices young and old, trained and untrained, in classrooms, churches, and concert halls across the country. He was equally at home with spirituals and symphonies, with Stephen Foster melodies and Paul Hindemith premieres, all of which he conducted with the same inspired—and inspirational—energy.

When Shaw was on the podium, he came across as somebody who had discovered exactly what he was put on the planet to do and was doing exactly that. With a motion of his hand, he could take a chorus of fifteen or five hundred from the tiniest of whispers to the most jubilant of shouts. His performances were remarkable for their energy, articulation, and sheer sonic grandeur.

Fortunately, Shaw left an impressive legacy—numerous recordings, some wonderfully instructive filmed workshops, and the mixture of articles, speeches, letters, and spontaneous jottings that make up the volume you hold in your hands. Robert Blocker has sifted through the magnificent and daunting piles of Shaw material in Atlanta and New Haven, and *The Robert Shaw Reader* is one of those rare musical compilations aimed at just about everybody—scholars, conductors, and choristers, of course, but also the fabled "general reader" with an interest in music and a respect for clear, vigorous prose.

From the very first page, there is no mistaking Shaw's sense of moral mission. It was bred into him from earliest childhood, for he was the son of a minister, Shirley Richard Shaw, and his wife, Nellie Mae Lawson Shaw, who was usually the leading vocalist in her husband's church choirs. Imbued with an evangelical spirit, Shirley Shaw changed pulpits so regularly that every one of his five children was born in a different California town. Robert Lawson Shaw, who entered the world in Red Bluff on April 30, 1916, was the oldest son and regularly helped his father with his musical duties. As a result, the young man was already an experienced choral conductor before he was in his teens.

It was Fred Waring, an enormously popular songwriter and bandleader, who led Shaw into professional music making. Shaw was then a member of the Pomona College Glee Club, and when Waring came to town with a variety show and invited the club to participate, he was so impressed that he offered Shaw a job.

Shaw turned him down. "I was studying comparative religion and English literature and I planned to go into the ministry," he explained in 1998. A year later, he changed his mind, moved to New York and assembled the Fred Waring Glee Club. Before long, Shaw had founded his own ensemble, the Collegiate Chorale, an amateur chorus with two hundred singers, which made its debut at Carnegie Hall in 1942.

That same year, he attracted the attention of Arturo Toscanini, who was then at the height of his fame and influence and perhaps the most admired musician in the world. "There were all sorts of stories about the Toscanini temperament, but I always found him very kind and very modest," said Shaw. "We met to prepare a performance of Beethoven's Ninth Symphony, and he seemed gloomy about the prospects. 'Oh, Maestro,' he said—here I am in my early twenties and Toscanini is calling me Maestro!—'Oh, Maestro, I've never heard a good performance of this work. The soloists are always wrong, the chorus is never quite precise, something always goes wrong.'"

But Toscanini was thrilled with Shaw's preparation of the highly difficult choral music. He released a statement to the press—"I have at last found the maestro I have been looking for"—and worked with him thereafter whenever he could. The two men went on to record the symphony and the *Missa Solemnis* for RCA Victor—classic interpretations that have hardly been out of print for a moment during more than half a century.

Some of Shaw's other early performances were recorded with his own Robert Shaw Chorale, which could deliver nuanced and exciting renditions of everything from Masses by Poulenc and Mozart through Broadway show tunes, Christmas carols, and, of course, the hymns with which the conductor had grown up. For two decades, the Robert Shaw Chorale was the country's premier touring choral group and was sent by the U.S. State Department to thirty countries in Europe, the Soviet Union, the Middle East, and Latin America.

By the early 1950s, Shaw was without doubt the most famous of American choral conductors. He appeared regularly on radio and television and brought much of his father's evangelism to the propagation of choral music throughout the country. But he was increasingly interested in symphonic conducting as well, and held posts with the San Diego Symphony and the Cleveland Orchestra (where he served as associate conductor under George Szell). Ultimately, he became the music director of the Atlanta Symphony, where he led the orchestra from 1967 to 1988.

Thereafter, Shaw appeared regularly as a guest conductor throughout the world. He was a champion of contemporary music and led first performances of works by such composers as Aaron Copland, Benjamin Britten, Samuel Barber, Charles Ives, Darius Milhaud, and Philip Glass. In 1991, he was a recipient of one of the Kennedy Center Honors, and the following year he was awarded the National Medal of the Arts in a White House ceremony. He died on January 25, 1999, in New Haven, Connecticut, at the age of eighty-two.

It is only proper that Shaw's thoughts on the volunteer chorus should open the book. The letters he wrote to the Collegiate Chorale are not only full of what Glenn Gould called "those home truths that you never actually get at home" but engaging musical history as well. Like Jay Gatsby, Shaw may be said to have sprung from his own Platonic conception of himself, and it is exhilarating to relive those formative days with him, as he rushes from project to project, testing limits, setting down rules, creating a place at the table for himself in the musical hierarchy of long-ago Manhattan.

From the beginning, Shaw displayed a welcome American practicality in his music making. Nowhere was this more obvious than in the way he prepared rehearsals. "I bring in text, rhythm, dynamics and intonation one element at a time," he once explained. "We might sing the text on a monotone until it's fully learned. And we will rehearse at a speed where it is all but impossible for anybody to make a mistake. That way, nobody can memorize errors. If you prepare this way, you will ultimately end up with a steady, unified, assured and beautiful sound." In short, he took the music apart and found out how it worked, rather in the manner of the legendary little boy with the alarm clock. But there was one important difference: when Shaw put everything back together again, it was better than ever—indeed, better than his musicians ever thought it could be.

Shaw's marvelous general prefaces to Bach's Mass in B Minor, Beethoven's *Missa Solemnis*, the Berlioz Requiem, and several other works makes one regret that he never undertook a full-scale introduction to the choral literature. Especially in the *Missa* essay, Shaw gives us not only the forest and the trees but also the bark and its lichen, as he takes us through this great and difficult music, measure by measure, illuminating tiny beauties that others have neglected.

Well though he knew these pieces, Shaw never stopped learning. "The real joy in working on the *B Minor Mass* is that there is absolutely no end to the refinement which the work inspires and commands. One cannot live long enough—or encounter so frequently conditions appropriate to its performance—that one exhausts it or becomes immune to its marvels."

Shaw's wry and sometimes agreeably ribald wit finds full play in his letters. During one Atlanta Symphony concert in Montgomery, Alabama, a stage manager seems to have been watching a televised baseball game in the wings. Unfortunately, the television set was well within the orchestra's line of vision, leading to some predictable distraction and at least one furious letter. While apologizing wholeheartedly ("I cannot believe I should have missed the television's presence and potential hazard"), he took a humanist view of the matter: "If [the set] was positioned on an elevated light platform off-stage and tuned to the game, it seems to me as naive to expect orchestra brass players to avoid looking as it would be to expect a troop of Boy Scouts marching past a nudist colony to look only at their Scoutmaster."

It is sometimes said that geniuses are just like everybody else, only more so. Shaw the heaven-storming Maestro was also Shaw the earthy raconteur. Within these covers you will find high solemnity—and even higher aspirations—set cheek by jowl with endearingly awful jokes and Shaw's own inimitable brand of doggerel verse. "Who touches this touches a man," Walt Whitman, who provided texts for so many sumptuous choral works, once observed of his own *Leaves of Grass*. Much the same may be said for *The Robert Shaw Reader*.

Tim Page
Washington, D.C.

We believe . . .

that in a world of political, economic and personal disintegrations *music is not a luxury but a necessity*—not simply because it is "therapeutic," nor because it is the "universal language," but because it is the persistent focus of man's intelligence, aspiration and goodwill.

We believe . . .

that music is always a community enterprise. The solo performance does not exist. Even its creation is an attempt to communicate, and every performance an effort to unite the minds of men even of different generations.

We believe . . .

that music . . . is *one* art. The chorus, the symphony orchestra, the virtuoso recitalist and the string-quartet are not competitive "attractions" for the public fashion in patronage, but are instruments of a single craft with similar responsibilities.

We believe . . .

that music is peculiarly a *doer's* art, and its benefits are in direct proportions to active participation.

We believe . . .

that it is the performer's business to get out of the way of music. His craft is to "reveal—not to interpret."

We believe . . .

that the choral art stands in a unique position to be of service to man and music because it offers the most immediate and accessible avenue of active participation.

And we believe . . .

that the choral instrument should assume a position of respect and musical responsibility commensurate with the distinction of its literature and comparable to that of the major professional.

—Creed of Collegiate Chorale, early 1940s

PART I

ORGANIZING AND SUSTAINING
THE CHORUS

March 4, 1964

Half-ideas are transient-shaped
Or else they must dissolve somehow each into each.
If only they would stand completely still
Until one found the words their size.
"I see, your measurements are thus and thus –
That's clear enough."
You inventory your entire stock
"Now this should fit"—and turn to find
It really doesn't fit at all.
You have a cubed suit
For a sphered thought.

You were sure that thought had corners.

I tried to get down on paper some of the things that are jamming my mind with reference to music and the spiritual qualities.

We have, almost from the beginning of the COC, assumed the function—if not the particularized truths—of that relationship, and now with a frightening clarity and in a flood of specific detail I begin to understand that music is spirit.

I guess the first Bible verse I learned "by heart" in the Beginner's Class at Sunday School was "God is love." It must have been at least twenty years later that it occurred to me that what it probably meant was "You know what God is—Love." And the same thing happens now with "Music is spirit"—but this time in overwhelming detail.

We began years ago by assuming that song was a story—it had a tale to tell, an argument to deliver, or a mood to convey. Its function was dramatic. Song was drama. Our first understandings of spirit in music were limited then to understandings of the text; and our techniques centered around systems of enunciation and a practical speech discipline, if also text was seen to qualify tone and sonority.

We understood spirit, too, as synonymous with our own corporate enthusiasm for the music we sang. It was very evident in concert performance that here was a group of people who loved to sing together and who somehow believed their song.

But at this point and from this time on the Cleveland Orchestra Chorus begins. I have never felt so sure of anything in my life. The ends for which we have assembled take shape; the pace and manner of their achievement grows more conscious and clear.

I believe that the essential musical properties—harmony, melody, rhythm, tone, and dynamics—under whatever critical microscope—are to be understood finally only as relations of qualities.

I believe that the relation of a note to its octave is the relation of one-ness to two-ness (which it is in terms of vibrations per second) and that at the same time the fact of their recognizable unity is a qualitative symbol knowledgeable only to men's spirits.

I believe that when voices switch functions for even the span of two notes, so that one voice sings what the other sang and what the second sang the first now sings the human spirit is involved. And the fact of a fugue wherein voices propose identity in alteration is a spiritual phenomenon.

I believe that form in music is a symbol of relations and values, not a blueprint of construction technique.

I believe that intervals have quality; that good intonation is the result of sensitivity to truth and untruth in tonality.

I believe that the voice is fantastically responsive to musical understanding, and that in every instance the sense of What must be precedes the How.

And I am no longer so concerned about the inability of any choir (including the COC) to master the long line of a long piece in a single sitting; for there are a hundred miracles in every measure worthy of the whole of a man's understanding.

I believe, then, that spirit in music is not the wholesale emotional orgasm that weeps appropriately in public, but rather the marshalling of one's keenest, most critical intellectual and moral forces to the point of complete conscious-ness—'til one hears in terms of values and the movements of values, until the most pedestrian minutiae of pitch and rhythm are heard inwardly in relation to adjacent minutiae; and finally in relation to wholes of form, tonality and intent.

I believe that we are only at the beginning. I believe we can scale and direct every rehearsal to this end, and that in those hours will lie the "life we have lost in living—the wisdom we have lost in knowledge—the knowledge we have lost in information."

December 2, 1948

In the last three weeks I've been reminded of the importance of the time-consuming non-musical mechanics of building and maintaining a chorus. Chief case in point would be this business of increasing membership, and the operation is as far removed from the golden glow of art as one could get. You need fifty new members—mostly men; so you send out 1,500 letters with 3,000 announcements knowing a few hundred will find a small response, you send announcements to 7 newspapers knowing 2 or 3 will find space for it, you post 80 or 90 posters understanding that they may be taken down in twenty-four hours; and from all this you get 30 to 40 hours of auditions, of which a fourth to a third are men. During the auditions it seems like it's women, women, and more women; but at the end of the day, you discover you've found 3 baritones and 2 tenors— and it's all worth it. – Because all the noble musical dreams don't make a choir. People make a choir. If you have people, you sing.

On the road this fall, it seems to me that I did my most important work not conducting but during the 3 or 4 hours before every concert setting the stage— moving platforms, improvising ceilings, back-drops and walls, setting up chairs, altering seating arrangements.– More productive, I'd imagine, than dreaming beautiful sounds and admiring the dream.

So also it is with all of us in the Chorale. All of us have unromantic and nonartistic responsibilities, things that have nothing to do with the music—but there's no music if they don't happen. The first one would be the simple legwork of rehearsal attendance. I've known many of our people to come to rehearsal when they couldn't sing a note—laryngitis or something. Well, that makes sense in ways other than the possibility of learning while listening. All of us are disturbed by empty chairs. If the room is packed, we know we're ready for work. At least we have 11 men on the field.

I have an idea also that if, say, even 80% of us were in our seats by 7:30, it would save us close to 30 minutes of rehearsal time. It's not only the time lost before beginning, it's the time half-used trying to get under way. Now, that's an unaesthetic mechanical angle if there ever was one; but I bet there aren't a dozen of us who couldn't be at rehearsal at 7:15 as easily as 7:35. And I know we could get more done in the first 15 minutes of rehearsal under those circumstances than we could in 30-plus at 10:15 or 10:30. Being there, and being a few minutes ahead of time—mechanics and leg-work—but it makes choirs.

Here's another angle. Group sense is a fine thing, and it has a host of implications for choral tone, rhythm, enunciation and intonation. But there's something that's more important. That's individual sense and individual responsibility. I'm speaking musically now. A lot of us relax into our section and into the huge choral sound. That's dangerous. What we need to do is sharpen our own critical individuality: That is, listen each one to himself, each one deciding how intense and controlled his tone is, how secure his rhythm, how precise his articulation. In this respect a group of soloists does make a chorus. If we can arrive at that state within the next two weeks it will be a great concert.

Looking forward to seeing you Saturday, (some) Sunday and Monday. Remember—left-foot, right-foot—be there—and we'll make music.

Bob

January 29, 1949

To members of the Juilliard Chorus:

I'm going to try another letter—in an attempt to straighten out some things before Tuesday's rehearsal. It appears to be a dangerous procedure, judging from the reaction to the last one. Anyway, let's dispense with the Juilliard letter-head, and make it person-to-person. If it were possible to write one hundred twenty-two individual letters, that could obviate the mimeographed form. – But it isn't—so this is.

In the first place, I regret greatly my inability to attend Thursday's rehearsal. People sometimes get sick—and I had two days of it.

In the second place, let's review that note of last-week. It said three things: one and obviously, that the Rogers *Passion* can't be prepared by a "part-time chorus"; two, it said "thanks to all who have been active and regular"; and three, it said that "dilettantes and absentees" might expect "full penalties." Evidently the last line of the letter got no laughs at all.

Now my thinking runs along these lines:

First, I would have expected the majority of people in the chorus to have been pleased and gratified, to have reacted with, "It's about time somebody cracked down on absentees. The habitually absent are the ones who slow down rehearsals, and the piece is certainly tough enough without having to re-rehearse it for those who attend haphazardly."

Second, I admit that I am very much perplexed by the non-professional habits of a large percentage of those enrolled in a presumably professional school. This really is difficult to understand. Digest this fact: there are eight persons in the Juilliard Chorus I *know* to be qualified for professional work. (There undoubtedly are more, but these I know well; some of them have worked with me professionally for as much as three years.) These *eight* persons had a total of *four* unexcused absences for the first semester. One-half [the] absences per person for those who probably have least to gain from rehearsal, who know the work best, and who certainly carry the heaviest vocal load. Not one of these persons was absent from last Thursday's rehearsal—when there were 25 absent and 10 tardy out of a total of 122 enrollment.

I just don't understand that. Here are some more figures: 82 members of the chorus have had a total of 160 unexcused absences—which certainly is fair enough; but the remaining 40 have had a total of 245 absences—which isn't at all fair. (If I were one of the 82 I'd kick.) And if you take into account the excused absences the overall is a hard average to cope with in the preparation of a difficult work like the Rogers.

The problem of discipline in a school situation is a thoroughly confusing one. Somehow, both professional and completely amateur regimens are easier to handle. The professional's pay stops, and the amateur simply drops out. But a school is more complex. One contracts to take certain courses, and if they are ensemble courses with performance as their objective, then attendance must be counted one of the contractual obligations. (One cannot balance an unbalanced group, for instance, when the conditions of imbalance alter from week to week.) And it seems reasonable to me that those who break that contract-of-sorts should not expect the benefits of credit and/or performance. If that is unfair, I'd like to know it. – And you'll just have to take my word that it is not representative of ill will.

I happen to believe in the Rogers *Passion*. I feel a little lonely, but I feel less lonely having heard what some of the soloists are making of this music when placed within the orchestral frame. Any time that the orchestra has played what Rogers intended, this work has proved its right to be heard and respected and loved. There is no lack of craft or heart on Rogers' part. The weaknesses are ours—conductor's (most of all), then instrumentalist's and singer's. The only question is whether we have—or can acquire in the next three weeks—musicianship sufficient to the music.

I'm certainly going to try, and it would be nice to know that you were also.

R. S.

September 1960

Dear Sir:

The Cleveland Orchestra Chorus is again announcing its annual auditions for membership.

This particular letter is addressed to educational, industrial and social institutions throughout the city.

It may well be that your organization already sustains a musical program for its members; and we would not like to offer it in competition in any matters of time, energy, or attention.

If such is not the case, however, and if members of your organization might enjoy association with the musical program of the Cleveland Orchestra, or if—as is felt by some—such association might increase their value to your own musical program, we should be grateful if, through your customary media, you could bring announcement of our auditions to their attention.

Scheduled for this season are:
Brahms—*A German Requiem*
Barber—*Prayers of Kierkegaard*
Bach—*Magnificat*
Schubert—*Mass in G*
Christmas Festival Program
Beethoven—*Symphony No. 9*

Interested persons may phone or write for audition appointments to: The Cleveland Orchestra Chorus, Severance Hall, Cleveland 6, Ohio or telephone CEdar 1-7300.

With deepest thanks for your courtesy and attention in this regard.

Cordially,

Robert Shaw, Director
The Cleveland Orchestra Chorus

September 21, 1960

Dear friends –

It is my unpleasant duty to inform you that your re-audition for the Cleveland Orchestra Chorus has been successful, and you may expect to resume orbit sometime between 7:30 and 7:45 P.M. next Monday, September 26.

You may wish to know some of the considerations which have guided our evaluations and have qualified you for re-admission. Believe me, it ain't been easy.

Number One: Any good-looking woman was admitted *ipso facto* and *sans souci*. This might sound to you like a pretty personal way to go about this sort of thing—but I assure you that George and I had either (1) to agree, or (2) voluntarily disqualify ourselves before a decision was reached and as George says, "A chorus is a pretty personal sort of instrument—let's keep it that way."

Number Two: Anybody who was really scared made it. I mean *really* scared. George and I get a big kick out of seeing some of you who *really* suffer: you know—clammy hands, all choked up in the voice, stomach muscles shaking like crazy, stumble up the steps or trip over the electric fan, start sight-reading from right to left and all that—anybody who gave old George and me a sort of pin-the-butterfly chuckle had it made.

Number Three: Anybody who had a cold got in. Almost all the great singers we know are hypochondriacs—and we didn't feel we could afford to pass anybody up here. (I remember one person who's had throat trouble at every audition since 1956, and that's the kind of sensitive person we like to have around.)

Number Four: There are always a few special rules for tenors. For instance, their reading test would be a little more accurately described as "sight improvising." I ask them to make up a note and hum it—and if George can find it on the piano, they're in. (I try not to look when these things are going on because I don't want to be unduly influenced by appearances or things like that, and George says three tenors made it this year just by blowing their noses.)

Number Five: Husband and wife teams stood a good chance this year, particularly when one partner to the marriage (and here we accept their word completely) was a bass or a tenor. This is a sort of insurance policy. Remember last year when the churches got mad because we had scheduled a *St. Matthew Passion* for Easter Sunday—well, suppose one of our concerts happens to fall on Mother's Day! From here on we have our own built-in mothers—and fathers—and anyway like George says you can't win 'em all.

These things—plus little things like giving preference to people who were studying medicine or engineering or math—because they'd have lots of free time and could make extra rehearsals, or to folks who lived fifty or one hundred miles from Cleveland—so that their families could learn independence—these are the things my friends and fellow-Americans which lead me to believe that this year's chorus will be the chorus of 1960–61, and I'm sure we all know how we all feel about all that.

Pox nobiscum,

R. S.

February 11, 1954

I

Whereas, it's the only way choruses can be understood, and
Whereas, it settles half the problems of intonation, color, balance, and phrasing, and
Whereas, I'm going to keep on hollering 'til it's settled
Be It Resolved: Leave us save our ears and voices a helluva beating.
Leave us –

(1) Exaggerate the duration and loudness of consonants having pitch: like M's, N's, NG's, L's, B's, G's, D's and J's.
(2) Exaggerate the duration and loudness of the maker-uppers of diphthongs and triphthongs: like say-ee for say, so-oo for so, lah-ood for loud, bah-eet for bite, ee-oo for you, oo-awk for walk, fee-uh for fear, vaw-ees for voice.
(3) Phrase ideas as well as melodies, breathe according to sense, not whimsy.

Meld words together; tie final consonants across to the next word. Leave us have no solo sibilants.

Practice by reading any newspaper paragraph in a monotone, steady, sustained, no breaks except at ends of sentences.

II

I've written and talked a lot about the Timeness of Music and the wonderful directives to choral singing which derive from that awareness. Time providing Music its medium, its "matter" to be shaped—not doubling back on itself fresh every instant, each song a new song, and every performance a first performance . . . the here-nowness of Music, its Going Somewhere-ness.

If any stray soul has missed those eternal verities send a stamped, self-addressed envelope to *And The Truth Shall Make You Inc.* (same address).

Anyway, I've got another pearl –

Department of Antithesis:

Time's contradictory quality is that of *Recurrence, Pulse, Rhythm.* It's the extension into Music of the heart-beat, the seasons, the tides, the biped, gestation, and when you get right down to it—whether by confirmation or denial—most of man's religious mysteries. It's the beat the beat the beat! It's the here it comes again-ness.

What it boils down to for members of the COC is that we don't sit around listening to our beautiful voices when we're supposed to be in the next bar. Time's tides move right along, and we move along with them. *"Rests"* are not what comes after *releases*—rests are what comes *before attacks*. – And both releases and rests are dramatic *accents*. It is *rhythmic integrity* which gives motion and vigor to music. We're going to shade and color within that frame, not without it. Here comes that brass ring again—get ready *now*.

R. S.

March 10, 1964

I

It is perfectly possible to have vowel definition without grotesque facial contortion and the fracture of vocal line. The vowels are formed at the "voice box" (or whatever you want to call it), not by the teeth, nose or position of the tongue in the mouth. Their chief resonator is the throat column directly adjacent to their point of origin; and though in particular instances the mouth and jaw may aid clarity and facility (as in the difference between OH and OO; or prestissimo, pianissimo passages of calculated dexterity) the fundamental voweling area is before the mouth. Try it. Put your hands up alongside and forward of the hinges of your jaw. Drop your jaw slightly and naturally. Now say all the vowel sounds you can think of. Note how firm, full and virile they sound. For contrast's sake try to form them by facial gesticulation; try to cut off all resonance before the mouth. Note how whiney, thin, reedy and emasculate they become.

Actually—all it takes is a little mind.

II

We will exaggerate the intensity and the duration of the distinct vowel sounds in diphthongs and triphthongs. We'll sing them louder and longer and more clearly. We will never—never sing one vowel sound where two belong.

Always for "ay" (as in *say*) we will sing "ay" (almost "eh") and "ee."
Always for "ow" (as in *cow*) we will sing "ah" and "o."
Always for "oy" (as in *boy*) we will sing "aw" and "ee."
Always for "I" (as in *sky*) we will sing "ah" and "ee."
Always for "yoo" (as in *yoo-hoo*) we will sing "ee" and "o."
Always for "ear" (as in *ear*) we will sing "ee" and "uhr."

Note that this holds no matter how fast the tempo, or whatever the duration of the diphthong. Break it up; sing both parts separately and distinctly.

III

We will exaggerate the intensity and duration of the consonants that have pitch. We will sing M's, N's and NG's longer and louder.

A—If the hummed consonant is an initial consonant and preceded by a vowel (as in "new Masses") (what a lyric!) we will sing the "m" as though it belonged to both words, thus "newM-Masses."

B—If the hummed consonant is a final consonant and followed by a vowel (as in "I'm asleep") we will sing the "m" as though it belonged to both words, thus "I'm-masleep."

C—We will be conscious of the fact (chiefly for the sake of intonation) that the "sub-vocal" consonants have an initial pitch, and that they are to be sung on the pitch they are supposed to be sung on. Thus B, D, J, G, L, V, Z all have a fragmentary initial pitch. Sing it.

IV

All explosive and sibilant consonants will be pronounced as though they began syllables, not as though they ended them. Thus, "what is this all about anyway" becomes "hoouh-ti-zth-saw-luh-bahoo-tehn-nee-ooayee."

V

We will give always *proportionate* (that is, rhythmic) time value to the various portions of speech sound that make up a word. That is to say, hummed consonants and the final vowel sounds in diphthongs will always have an actual rhythmic allotment, varying up to ½ of the full time value, and depending upon tempo and style.

This is hard to illustrate, but suppose you had the word "home" on a half-note in fairly rapid time. We would sing the first quarter-note value "Ho" and the next quarter-note value "oom," coming immediately to the M. Thus, count "one-two, one-two," "Ho-oom, Ho-oom." Or take the opening line of the "Star Spangled Banner." Now, instead of quarter-note values on "Oh, say can you," think eighth-note values on "Oh-oo say-ee ca-aN-you-oo."

There is one further refinement of this; and it's also tough to put on paper without musical notation. It is that hummed consonants and the final vowels of diphthongs do not fall (except in very fast tempi or short note values) exactly on the rhythmic sub-division.

For example, sing to yourself in a slow tempo, "Oh come all ye faithful." Now, instead of half-notes on "come" and "faith," think quarter-notes on "Kuh-uhM" and "Fay-ayEM." Note that if we sang "Kuh-M" and Fay-EE," it would sound quite artificial, but if, on the second-quarter value, we preface the M and the EE with just a fragment of the main vowel sound, most of the angularity and artificiality disappears. This allows then an enlarged duration for the secondary vowel or hummed consonant, but maintains the normal accent of the primary vowel. OK?

Enunciation –

I.   Pure, vigorous vowels.
II. Carefully broken-up diphthongs.
III. Long and intense hummed consonants.
IV. Explosive consonants always exploded as though they began a syllable.
V.   Rhythmic, proportionate allocations of hummed consonants and secondary vowels.

Now what all this issues in is –

1. Musically, the legato phrase, which is the substance of melody.
2. Dramatically, a continuous intensity of mood and sense. There are no spasmodic, diverting interruptions of the song's story. We end phrases where it makes it make sense textually and beauty musically. If someone has to breathe, he does so in the middle of a vowel or hummed consonant, and jumps back in the middle of a vowel or a hummed consonant.
3. Uniformity and discipline. For instance, in the case of the exploded consonant, the technique of tacking it on the following syllable places it *on the beat* or sub-division thereof. So far as I can tell, that's the only instant capable of absolute definition and unanimous understanding. – And, people, that's the point of a chorus; doing the same thing together at the same time.

– Which brings us 4:00 A.M. and the Second lesson. From here on it comes slower.

A. The cardinal sin of singers and choruses is their unmusicality.
B. I've heard people quote Mozart something like this: "What is music? Music is first of all Rhythm; in the second place – Rhythm; and finally—Rhythm." *Q.E.D.*: The cardinal sin of singers and choruses is their lack of rhythm.

I'd like to be able to tell you all I feel about Rhythm and the Time-mess of music, and make it sound fresh and exciting. As a matter of fact, I've written to you so many times about it that I'm sick and tired of the whole subject. It all sounds like *slogans*. – Or the "Infatuation with the Sound of Own Words Department."

– Yet I *know* it's right. And I know it's the one absolutely necessary, basic, urgency of the choral art—(or any other musical art).

Up above it says "sick and tired of the whole subject." That's not quite true. I'm not tired of *doing* it, only tired of talking about it. It's always fresh and exciting in the music. We work always with new rhythms, new patterns, new accents. That's the wonderful invigorating part. These excerpts, analytical and critical, are awfully shy of the intense practical organic excitement that comes with actual performance; but it ought to do us good to review them.

I can think of a couple of emphases that haven't been emphatic enough up to now. The first is that little notes are just as important as big notes, that they have places, and that they should be put in their places. Sixteenths and eighths and quarters are not just things that come between bigger things. They are not "introducings" or preparations or pick-ups. I get a horrible picture from the way you sing of little, bitty eighth-notes running like hell all over the place, to keep from being stepped on. Millions of 'em! Meek, squeaky little things. No self-respect: Standing in corners, hiding behind doors, ducking into subway stations, peering out from under rugs. Refugees.

Dammit, you're all a bunch of Whole-Note Nazis. And dots! Poor little dots! Oh—(I can't stand it!) I just thought of a *double* dot!

Look, this is a democracy. Little people count. They're included in the census. Eighth-notes can vote. They carry ID cards. They belong.

Dialogue:

Sixteenth note marches up to a bar, "Gimme a glass of beer."

COC, "I'm sorry, my little man, that's only for whole notes."

Moral: Give 'im a drink.

R. S.

November 14, 1961

This letter is considerably more difficult to write than the long and arduous ones which have to do with some phase of the music we are performing or some complex matter of choral technique.

What makes it difficult is that any worthy amateur choral organization is built around only a single idea extended two ways: a mutual and high regard for the music which is being performed, and a mutual and high regard for all the people with whom it is being performed. A distinguished amateur chorus is so materially the product of devotion and self-discipline that when these cease to be present there is no chorus. They were woefully absent from the first twenty-five minutes of last night's rehearsal.

When, at a critical rehearsal of music of the stature which we faced last night, only half of the choir is present at the moment the rehearsal is supposed to begin, and when even among those present there is inattention and persistent chatter then there is no Cleveland Orchestra Chorus.

I am not unaware that the previous week's schedule had been a demanding one, nor that performances had been on a high level. These have no effective bearing on the childish and destructive lack of responsibility of Monday night. We have had better and more prompt attendance during blizzards. Given that wasted time Bach's *Dona Nobis Pacem* might have been a truly affecting prayer rather than a damnable gamble.

I believe that the quality of this chorus' musical aspiration and the quality of its performance justify devotion and responsibility from its members, and I believe there are two hundred people in this area who would go along with that. All we have to do is find them.

This chorus has been and will continue to be understanding [of] and sympathetic to occasional and unavoidable absence. – But it cannot tolerate tardiness and inattention and remain true to its aspiration, or valuable to the probable majority of its members to whom the experience has some meaning.

A little tardiness is inexcusable. – And since it is also lethal—as witness Monday evening—it merits the most stringent of remedies and penalties.

It takes a certain amount of time to prepare one's own mind for the artistic and technical responsibilities of rehearsal. I cannot see that five to ten minutes prior to the beginning of rehearsal *spent in one's proper place,* reviewing or examining the materials to be rehearsed, is too much to ask, or can help but add enormously to the joy and accomplishment of rehearsal.

R. S.

October 24, 1962

It has consistently been our hope and endeavor to make the rehearsal experience as productive, interesting and exciting a part of belonging to the COC as the actual performance itself. Where much is demanded—with reason and necessity—then much is learned.

To each of you there should now have come an alertness to rehearsal techniques and procedures. These latter are short-cuts to learning: the ability to listen when other sections are rehearsing, to jump back and repeat appropriate numbers of measures without breaking tempo, to isolate rhythmic problems from problems of text and sonority; to make rhythm clean and steady, intonation true, tone both more uniform (better conceived and supported) and more responsive to variety in color.

Increasing efficiency means at least two things for our pleasure: first, we should be able to perform more of the great works in any given season; and second, I see no reason why we shouldn't build into our rehearsal sessions periods of reading for pleasure—rather than for imminent performance.

The assumption upon which all this increased pleasure is based you know probably as well as I. It is that a chorus is not a lump of human talent and energy chipped, sliced, rolled, moulded and stamped into a maneuverable manikin of the lowest common artistic denominator, but a group of unique and varied human beings, voluntarily congregated, who accept personal responsibility, and bring to a performance of the whole each his utmost endowment, preparedness and sensitivity.

Group productivity in art is not mass production.

Art by the many, perhaps like government by the many, is at its best when it not only allows but inspires the greatest possible individual participation, self-discipline and self-expression.

R. S.

Closely allied to this business of your enjoyment of the COC experience are the ground rules—practical do's and don'ts—to hang on to, to steer by, the that-which-you-can't-tell-the-play-('er, players) without.

Absences: These we hopefully will never have, but necessarily do. You are allowed four (4) unexcused absences during the season. Slips are available so that the unavoidable absences (excused ones) may be recorded before they occur. If they are unexpected and very last minute just telephone.

Guests: You are welcome to bring guests to Monday night rehearsals, but we must know in advance how many you wish to bring and on what date. Fire laws and available seating being our main concerns. We ask you not to bring, or request to bring, guests to Sunday [rehearsals]—these are the cut-'em-apart-diagnose-the-dilemma-sessions. – Nor are guests permitted at "with orchestra" rehearsals or pre-concert warm-up sessions.

On those occasions when you spy people in the auditorium it will be because management has made some special arrangement for them.

Atlanta, Georgia
January 14, 1965
¥¥¥¥¥¥¥¥¥¥¥¥¥¥¥
We might as well
get right down to
the nitty-gritty
of it. Last Mon-
day night's re-
hearsal was a de-
bacle, completely
unworthy of the
Cleveland Orchestra Chorus.
The first reading of the Britten War Requiem was superior in every way. The first rehearsal of the season --
even with the attendant disruptions of new member registration, music allotment and exchange of greetings-- was
better motivated, better mannered and more constructive.
This chorus is not a social club.
Such satisfactions as we gain because of musical excellence are
achieved through self discipline
and undivided responsibility.
The fact that we enjoy our collaborator's company is a splendid bonus, but even this would
disappear did we not address
ourselves firstly, secondly,
and throughout to the music.
/// Rehearsals of a chorus
of this calibre should not
ever be primarily a place
for note-learning. T h e
problems of ensemble are
complex enough. Most of
the note-learning should
be done at home. Monday
night should be an oc-
casion for pooling our
skills and knowledge,
not our ignorances .
/// Look at our re-
hearsal schedule.
Obviously we will
have to concentrate
on the Beethoven
Ninth Symphony. It
should be sung
from memory in
Cleveland and
New York. ///
Consider how
little time
there is fol-
lowing that to
conclude prep-
arations on
the Britten
War Requiem
-- far too
little to
allow the
lack of at-
tention
by which
l a s t
Monday
night's
rehear-
sal was
betray
ed. //
//So
there
! !
R

October 4, 1968

Friends and ASOCCiates –

I have been thinking the past two days of writing a note in confirmation of the value—and necessity—of our marking of choral scores at rehearsals; and I find myself—without going very far afield at all—examining that ancient canard about *singers* as distinct from *musicians.*

The values of personal annotation to ensemble performance are obvious, practical and immediate. No one of us can remember every musical or inter-pretative advice, caution, definition or correction. – But a note in one's own handwriting (as to duration, accentuation, enunciative device or modification of tempo or dynamics) nine times out of ten will guard us against repetitive error and the consequent danger of its memorization.

Let's examine for a moment the suppositions behind this practice of per-sonal markings: The first is that musical ensemble is *not* primarily the product of "following the conductor." Rather, it is the product of both of them *following the composer.* In thirty years of public choral performance—from professional con-certs, recordings, radio and television to amateur festivals, workshops and "clinics"—it has seemed to me essential and honorable to insist that singers work with music in front of them. It is not the conductor's prerogative to establish a willful or whimsical musical dictatorship, but rather by solid education to arrive at a satisfying and productive relationship to the composer through his printed page. Anything other than this is thin-ice morality and chaos-courting. (I give you a for instance: Try conducting an all-state high-school choral festival: 1,500 to 1,000 singers from 125 to 250 different schools, all of whom have arrived "with the music memorized"—but without the music.)

The ensemble singer's responsibilities to the score is like that of the conduc-tor, and each is further responsible to the other for visual contact at critical points of attack and release or changes of tempo or dynamics.

The second supposition upon which individual marking rests is that musi-cal notation—*at best*—is less than half-that-asked. A composer may mark "cre-scendo," but the questions remain: "*From* what level—how quickly—for how long—*to* what level?" A composer may mark "diminuendo," but in addition to the questions above must be asked: "Is it to be accompanied by a change in vocal color or texture?" The composer sets the text—"underlays" it syllable by syl-lable—but never really tells us where to put the final consonant, or how to deal with adjacent explosive consonants, or how long and/or loud to sing the hummed consonant, or what to do about diphthongs.

For years the greatest teachers of solo woodwinds have been examining the structure and scale of dynamics within the musical phrase: not merely which note of a phrase is to be the loudest, but *how loud*? And how does one get there? And how leave there?

What they've been trying to do, of course, is relate great instrumental art to great singing. – This, then, is the nitty-gritty. For it behooves us to remember that the greatest vocal artists are those who best know what they are doing. (Isn't it a strange aspect of the American political and religious heritage that it credits intuition, good intention and "dumb-luck"—all those factors in man's know-how which are easily arrived at (and fun to have)—and denigrates those elements which are hard to come by. "Intellectual" is the dirty word for November.

By constant "re-editing" of one's choral scores, each of us will add heightened consciousness—and a deeper conscience—to his solo repertoire.

See you Monday—R

December 5, 1968

At our rehearsal two weeks ago I said half-jokingly something about it being "the last time we would be together." At that moment I was not quite sure that we indeed did have another time together prior to orchestral rehearsals. – But, of course, we did, and it was last Monday night. Since when I have spent most of the day pondering my premonition, and wondering how we might have spared ourselves that experience—or reconstituted it.

Following the rehearsal two weeks before—wherein I had not known what to expect, since we had spent so little rehearsal time on *Messiah,* and even that so fragmented—I was ecstatically delighted with our choral discipline and involvement, and with the progress of the evening, feeling that they assured a beautiful and secure performance. And I laid that accomplishment to the conditions first, that *Messiah,* after all, was a familiar part of everyone's experience and second, that though we had not spent numberless hours on its particular preparation, we had spent a good many hours in the preparation and performance of other works, and probably had acquired certain common senses and sensitivities. – Which abruptly last Monday night were absensitivities.

I said at the end of that disconcerting period that "there are no bad choruses, only bad conductors," and that has to be true. It simply is the conductor's responsibility to deny lethargy access to rehearsals: This could be done, I suppose, by "overwhelming" an occasional, inexplicable, intractable group psyche or, more productively, I would imagine, by showing so clearly the *necessity* for such and such a musical procedure that apathy flees before enthusiasm "one by one by one."

Conversely, I have known occasions wherein original and equally inexplicable group enthusiasm was so strong that a conductor's fatigue and dullness simply were stripped from him, and he found himself bewilderingly alive, perceptive and persuasive. – But for the flip-side there has to be some answer beyond "Mother told me there'd be days like these."

I came across a great line quoted in a news magazine this week from a sonnet of Michelangelo; and its pertinence to our problem is eerie. "My soul can find no stair on which to climb to Heaven," he wrote, "unless it be earth's loveliness."

It accuses your conductor, I feel, of thus far being unable to convince his chorus of the *necessity* of achieving their own particular "earth's loveliness." – In this instance, the delicate fragile perfection of tone and time, of timbre and texture which make up Handel's musical language. For me, this admittedly "earthly" accomplishment is the *absolute unavoidable minimum prerequisite* for the "climb to Heaven."

I witnessed last Sunday in a televised church service something which still is hard to believe: a night-clubbed and travestied, sanctimonious but pulpitted performance of unmanly and ungodly swill entitled "When Children Pray." Considering the occasion and the place this would be difficult to match for obscenity and filth.

Perhaps eighth-notes and exactitude, and transparency and oh-so-sweet-but elusive simplicity don't matter "all that much"—*unless* one is charged with the responsibility of actually beholding and achieving "earth's loveliness," and unless his "soul can find no other stair on which to climb to Heaven."

R. S.

January 31, 1973

Dear Friends and Collaborators:

A chorus in performance is an overwhelming, apparently spontaneous, combustive unison of hearts, minds, physical energies and sound. Such spontaneity is a lie. The real reason for that fantastic eruptive communion—which for many of us has provided the central exhilarating and moving experiences of our lives—repeat, the real explanation is the week after week tenacious, restless search for discipline in rehearsals. In art, as in a good many other affairs of men, miracles don't just happen. They're earned.

The next thing I want to say is that each of you is important. "How can I possibly influence the decision—and whatthehell difference does it make?" is the inescapable consumptive plague of our time. Well, I don't know how you can help the Brothers K arrive at a decent settlement of the one- or no-world controversy, but insofar as the Atlanta Symphony Orchestra Chorus is concerned you make a difference.

You were selected for membership in this chorus because you seemed to possess talents of voice and musicianship, and—just as importantly—intellectual capacities and human sensibilities which would enable you to join with others and undertake the re-creation of certain great works of musical art—"Intimations of immortality"—unavailable to the solo performer.

The big decision in this whole audition procedure was not made by the conductor. His was secondary and independent. The big decision was, in fact, your initial decision to audition. You proposed, he accepted. This only means that all of us had common hopes and hungers before we met and began living (as in "coming to life") together rather regularly on Monday evenings, assortedly on Thursdays, Fridays and Saturdays and—'par'n 'spresshun—occasionally on Sundays.

If our net product—our performance—were arrived at by individual competition, victory and defeat, then each of us would not be so important. (This world insists on *one* winner—even between champions.) But if our product is arrived at by common effort and understanding and devotion, then all of us are diminished by the absence or weakness of each of us.

What is required of you as members of this chorus is not that you bring a standardized, prescribed and unvarying amount of voice, musicianship and mental capacity to rehearsals (music making has little in common with automatic pin-setters), but that you bring yourself—ruffed-up and idiosyncratic as that may be. No one else has that. No one else can bring it. The more varied our heterogeneity, the richer should be our community—if it happens.

What is required of the conductor is that he make available and attractive to his co-workers disciplines which educate—not simply dictate, to the end that each person ultimately is capable of accepting his own honest and entire musical responsibility. Granted, it's the conductor's job to teach "notes"; much more important is his responsibility to teach ways of learning notes. If two rehearsals on a Benjamin Britten cantata do not short-cut and simplify the problems of learning a Walton cantata, then the conductor also should leave rehearsal at intermission—and stay away.

– For at the final point music is sound, and you people make the sound. – And the most meaningful sound in music is that which is *self*-disciplined, *self*-instructed and *self*-motivated.

Do you newer members of our chorus begin to see what a maniacal musical monogamy you've contracted? And on the occasion of our *x*th anniversary, senior heads, are you once more apprised of the strength and state of the union?

In addition to the *War Requiem* just two weeks hence and the *Choral Fantasy,* in collaboration with the delightful and uniquely talented Rudolf Serkin, and the Haydn *Seasons* in the Spring. It can all be learned and joyfully performed—but only if our work is informed with constancy, free from the drip-drop erosion of tardiness, absence, inattention.

Onward and upward, men! Ladies, stamp out sloth: We have nothing to choose but our lanes.

R. S.

May 4, 1973

More rehearsals back to back like Sunday's bi-sectional and Monday's vivisectional certainly should qualify us as contenders for the crown of World's Best Losers.

Experiences like these certainly are worth a chapter or two in somebody's book of Choral Conducting. The conductor's opportunities for failure are so manifold that it scarcely is worth mentioning those of his collaborators. In the first place it is the conductor's failure if, by pre-rehearsal information and in-rehearsal procedures, he cannot produce performing skills which are *accumulative, retentive*—and, in the main, pleasurable. His also is the ultimate responsibility of transforming group lethargy and flaccidity to commitment and tonus. – So, few of you can match the conductor's failures.

Consider for a moment, however, some of the strange phenomena of choral life: Amateur choruses, however badly trained or minimally talented, *more often than not* excel themselves in contests or concerts. More often than not even talented, well-trained choruses perform better and accomplish more at a first reading than they do at a second or third rehearsal. More often than not there is a sort of law of momentum in any given rehearsal wherein success pre-disposes toward further success and error compounds error.

This latter "rule" operates, of course, among professionals also, from sports through business to the fine arts; but its scale is much more dramatic in amateur organizations—for the following reasons.

The ratio of commitment to ability *generally* is higher among amateurs than among professionals. This can be due to two factors: first, that the amateur's talent is, by comparison to his professional counterpart, generally limited; and second, that his is a recreational endeavor, undertaken to provide any one of a number of personal, non-material satisfactions, originally, at least, with high enthusiasm.

The point is that while the professional *may* lose some of his enjoyment and personal commitment to his work without *necessarily* impairing his craft to a dangerous degree, the amateur, if he loses his commitment and moment-to-moment enthusiasm and concentration is in danger of diminishing his abilities by fifty to seventy-five percent.

This is the nature of a "society" such as ours. Unless it is unremittingly committed to success it only adds failure to failure. It is commitment which discovers, enlarges and refines our capabilities—not vice versa. Since it is most of what we have it has to be practiced at every rehearsal—like scales for a Casals.

R

May 8, 1973

Dear Friends and Co-Workers –

In even the most professional of choruses the range of individual musical and vocal capabilities is staggeringly wide. There is always the question as to whether voice or musicianship should be given prime consideration. There are requisites imposed by repertoire (vocal color, size, vibrato characteristic, etc.), size of group, size or nature of performing area (recording studio vs. concert hall) and a host of associated aspects of the singer's craft.

Therefore, we must accept as one of the "self-evident truths" that the large symphonic choir encompasses even wider extremes of capability. It carries always, thereby, the potentialities of friction, fissure and disruption: some people read faster than others, some memorize more quickly or remember longer, some have better intonation—make your own list.

The only factor which makes the large volunteer chorus able to operate at all is the recurrent convincing demonstration that, whatever its heterogeneity or variety of capabilities, the final product is light years beyond what one person could accomplish by himself. In the successful chorus one learns to move with the tide, to be more tolerant of others' mistakes—and less tolerant of his own; and, if he is wise, to expect a certain number of hours of fundamentals and drudgery per annual homecoming game.

In principle I'm of the opinion that nothing in music is or need be drudgery. I think "note-learning" ought to be "love at first sight-reading." – But, humans being what they mostly are instead of what they occasionally are, into every life falls a little egg-plant. – And some of the most rewarding rehearsals I've experienced were those wherein at the start of rehearsal I had the sense to say, "Now friends, no fireworks tonight—just lots of notes. No honeymoon—let's first find out how the darn thing works."

So far as I can tell, choral conductors for years have been approaching this problem from the wrong end. Almost all of us began as cheerleaders. What we didn't know about music—which was almost everything—we attempted to make up with enthusiasm, which meant mostly, of course, enthusiasm for ourselves and our inspiring personalities, or enthusiasm for the "spirit" of the music—by way of our inspiring personalities. (One of the reconciliations that choral conductors find it so difficult to make is that "*This* is the way" is so much duller than "*I* am the way." – Which should surprise no-one willing to face the prospect that *learning* is so much more of a commitment than *leaning*.)

R (for Really)

October 16, 1974

Friends,

It's a terribly shaming thing to get mad at rehearsals. Anyone with an ounce of sense or honesty knows that music and anger don't really mix. – For two very good reasons:

First, nothing technically sick, broken or out-of-sync is cured. On some occasions (I can think of none), when skills and schooling are perfect, everyone may rave to guard against indifference or lassitude, but for the most part conductors of choruses get mad when they don't know how to fix the fool thing—so they kick its tires.

– And, of course, in the second place, anger is completely alien to the whole purpose of music—or of a chorus, for that matter. The purpose of these is communication (it does seem to me that "communion" is a more suitable word except for its religious connotations) and anger is a barrier, an isolation.

The dilemma of this particular conductor is that though the teaching (and for him, the learning) of "fundamentals" is an extraordinarily pleasurable experience—except when it gets racked up by the pressures of schedules and performances, there's really not a great deal of stimulus or "point" to learning (or teaching) a performing art unless somebody performs.

Since my failure of Monday night I've spent some hours outlining and starting to assemble a handbook, tentatively titled *Fundamentals of Choral Musicianship,* "a syllabus of drills and exercises for the choral rehearsal."

For years I've written (letters and articles) and lectured on the "principles and rules of choral technique," and tried, so long as I could stand the sound of my own tape, to apply them to the repertoire at hand. But "principles" and "rules" somehow are convincing principally and as a rule mostly to those who "invent" or "discover" them. And to become effective, efficient and dependable, they need to be isolated from other technical complexities and psychological urgencies, and repeatedly drilled, and comprehended in the "doing."

So—as your onetime choral-scout bows his way out the door with rue on wry for his inability to lead you sweetly, bloodlessly and drily across Kishon's brook—lift them eyes—O lift them eyes unto the mountains of exercises that even now begin to take shape hill by drill and from whence if any help cometh at all who can afford to say it neigh?

Au reve –

R

April 21, 1977

Friends—

On Monday I had thought to write you a letter of thanks for the performances of Friday and Saturday. Somehow that entire day went for study of this week's scores, and in the evening there was the rehearsal of the Verdi *Requiem.*

I'm glad I waited. – Not that there is anything inherently wrong with words of appreciation—except that they're habit-forming. – But more because there's even more now for which to be thankful.

It seems to me that Monday night's rehearsal was something of a breakthrough. Two things happened which never had happened before—at least to this extent and for an entire rehearsal. In the first place the reading was done *within ensemble disciplines.* So frequently when we read each person sings as though he or she were entirely alone. Our sectional disciplines are fractured and fragmented, and our learning severely impeded. The fact of the matter is that when we read with all of our "togethernesses" in full operation our total reading ability is quicker almost than that of any of us alone.

The second aspect of our reading was equally important. Somehow Monday night we read with the atmosphere and intent of trying to understand the score, rather than merely exercising the vocal muscles. This made possible an aware-ness of style and balances, and enormously speeded the learning process.

I think great orchestras read this way, but it's the first time I've experienced that so clearly with a chorus.

– And that's reason enough to risk the habit-forming dangers of thanks.

Peace,

R

Editor's note: Shaw was a demanding taskmaster, but he also made a point of acknowledging diligence and expressing his gratitude in return. The following ex-emplifies the esteem in which he held his choir members.

December 21, 1977

Dear Friends –

Idon'tquiteknowhowtosaythisbut—your commitment is showing. – Also your virtuosity.

Most of you will see the video-tape of the 11th Annual Christmas Festival on Christmas Eve. 'Do hope you enjoy—your own performance, as well as video productions, etc.

One should not overly monkey with Christmas, but I did find two weeks ago—and too late for the Eleventh—some wonderful new materials for the Twelfth Night of Christmas: that of 1978 and, hopefully, network TV.

It has occurred to me, as I have pondered from time to time the possible "exploitation" of this vessel of volunteer vocal virtuosity, that of all the voluntary wings that enable any art institution to get off the ground at all—let alone fly—ours is one of the few that returns appropriate reward. So many of the other volunteer organizations are obliged to measure their emoluments in terms as vague and vapid as "prestige" or "standing."

Ours are as real as they seem—at the time and in retrospect.

So—thank you for your labours and your love.

We hereby highly resolve to return great quantities of same in 1978.

The Shaws

March 7, 1978

Friends –

Nola and the head of our membership committee have asked that I write you concerning the events—choices and decisions—of last Saturday night, together with my feelings and judgements in the matter. Perhaps it is necessary. (At this moment I could better use the time in preparation for our Athens residency.)

There are all sorts of tangential aspects to the situation. (The facts are these: On Saturday night, March 4, the Atlanta Symphony Orchestra Chorus had a performance. On the same night Pavarotti was in Atlanta giving a vocal recital. Some of the chorus members who had rehearsed and, indeed, participated in the Thursday/Friday performance of the Berlioz *Damnation,* chose on Saturday night to attend the Pavarotti recital.)

As I say, there are a score of tangential areas, factors, accommodations and dislocations. – But the nitty-gritty of the problem is as simple as can be.

First, no one of us has the right to decide for another what that person should value most highly. I would also guess that no one of us has the right to pass judgement upon how another person considers his or her "commitment" in an undertaking such as ours. (That's between a man and his own soul and, as Charles Ives says, "I know of no place where it's likely to be lonelier.")

But, the sad fact is that an organization like ours simply has to learn— whether it likes it or not—to struggle along with those people who will show up for performances. I would not in my youth deliver to Toscanini one chorus for rehearsal and a lesser one for performance; and I cannot, being older, treat the Atlanta Symphony Orchestra or its audiences any differently.

Some have urged "sympathy" for those who no longer are members of the chorus. "Sympathy" herein is completely irrelevant. – But I do feel sorry for some people:

I feel sorry for the chorus that has to learn to get along without qualified and potentially contributive members.

I feel sorry for two-hundred-fifty-plus people on the stage at Symphony Hall who, more than any other people in Atlanta, would have enjoyed that recital.

(I even feel sorry for myself; for one of my three very dearest of friends was accompanying that recital and, except for a few choral rehearsals in recent years which we've done together "for fun"—as the saying goes—I haven't heard John Wustman since he's become the "greatest accompanist in the world.")

Mostly I feel sorry for one of our members, a teacher of voice and a professional tenor soloist who has been ill with laryngitis the past three weeks, but nevertheless drove 200 miles to and from each and every rehearsal so that he could mark his score, and as his voice improved, attended also all three performances, making a greater and greater contribution. I wish *he* could have heard Pavarotti.

– Surely, events like this are going to happen. Every day of every year there will appear some item so attractive, so alluring, even so potentially productive, that it seems to wash out the grayer values of the accustomed and the year-in-and-year-out. – At a time like this, I'd guess, one needs perspective most of all— needs to weigh very carefully a particular point of time against time's coursing.

Perhaps one of the problems is that it is difficult to feel "important" or "essential" in a 200-voice chorus.

– Now, I can't speak of your own sense of importance to yourself. But I can tell you that each of you is important to me. If, in a warm-up session, I can close my eyes and identify the row and very nearly the seat-number from which a disturbing sound is emerging, and if the sound then stops, *you* know that you can be heard and are important.

Each of you may, indeed, be more critically necessary to an eighteen-voice choir in some other situation. – And that's fine; and each of you must do—and obviously will do—what you think is most important for *you;* and that will frequently coincide with the time or event wherein you feel most important to yourself. We form our own values, and sometimes we live by them.

– But let me remind you in parting that you're also important to Beethoven and Brahms and Berlioz. They can't get along without you—or somebody in your place. Eighteen voices won't serve a *Ninth Symphony* or a Brahms *Requiem,* and eighteen voices absent will harm a Berlioz *Damnation*—even were they all as bad as mine is.

I said last week at the ACDA convention that the greatest choruses were made up of the greatest solo voices—and I believe that, and will continue to believe it until I die. – But I also have to face the fact that even *my* voice is more helpful than *no* voice.

We want for our continued growth and improvement the finest singer-musicians we can enlist. Your aid in discovering them is absolutely essential. But, let us also be sure that, having rehearsed together, and balanced and disciplined ourselves together, barring unavoidable emergencies, we'll find ourselves banded together on performance nights.

I close by recalling an earlier paragraph. I can quit my choral responsibilities—and that's an alternative. – But so long as I continue to accept them, I cannot serve up to the ASO and its audiences one chorus when Caruso is in town and one chorus when he isn't.

Peace,

R

Tuesday Morning, May 13, 1980

Ladies and Gentlemen of the ASO Chorus:

Let me begin with two sets of figures:

(1) There were 244 people in the ASO Chorus which took the trip to Carnegie Hall; there were 195 at last night's rehearsal.
(2) There are 124 measures of choral singing in the Mahler *Symphony No. 2.* Roughly one-half of these represent 20 measures repeated or slightly varied. Of the remaining 60, 10 are unison, and 45 are half- or whole-notes. There is only 1 measure of moderate metrical complexity. (It happens twice.) The harmonic language is that of the Sunday hymnal. We already have had 3 rehearsals on these 124 measures.

Questions:

(1) What does the first set of figures tell us about the "commitment quotients" of the 21% of our membership not present last night?
(2) In view of the difficulties encountered in last night's rehearsal, what does the second set of figures tell us of the "commitment quotient" of those present? Of their self-preparation?

Now, let me conclude with some personal observations:

Rehearsals which culminate in moments like that of last night are not good for the music, and obviously harm both singers and conductor. Such moments destroy music's meaning.

It is clear—by dawn's early light—that we shall have to go through with the rehearsals and performances of next week as scheduled. I will have to conduct, and you will have to sing. I am sure we can make do.

Next season (1980–81) also poses a problem; for I am already announced as conductor of the choral portions of that season, and tickets have been sold on that basis. However, I will see that you have a choral director better qualified than myself to prepare you properly and happily.

For the *B Minor Mass* there will be separate auditions, and in the event that we do not find enough people sufficiently qualified to form a chorus suitable to make the contemplated new recording, we will cancel that, and invite a university or conservatory chorus to perform the work with the orchestra.

– And by the season 1981–82 we should be able to find a conductor with whom you will be happy both to prepare and to perform.

During most seasons I perform, I suppose, with 6 to 10 choruses in addition to the ASOC. Some of them are professional, some are adult volunteer, some are student, and some are made up of professional vocal musicians in short-term study situations.

Perhaps because less is expected of them, perhaps because they are better prepared—individually or collectively—those occasions are in the main happy and productive. The singers feel they are experiencing something rather special; I feel I'm doing good work. So far, the end results have not matched what this chorus (or what it once was) accomplished in Carnegie Hall a few weeks ago. – But at least we do not abrade or demean one another: We leave rehearsals and performances happy and, as my father would have said in his pulpity pastoral-ese, "lifted up."

'Sorry that doesn't happen for us.

– But thanks . . .

R

December 1, 1982

Friends –

The nature and repertoire of this year's Christmas Festival program were influenced by two factors:

First was the hope of making a significant sum of money for the Symphony by the re-recording of Robert Russell Bennett's "Many Moods of Christmas" album and its successful merchandising thru new and "creative" channels in the Fall of 1983.

Second was the inability of the Men's Glee Club of Morehouse College to participate in this year's scheduled program.

Given the "American musical theatre" ambience of the Bennett materials, some of our traditional repertoire became inappropriate, and the Northside School of Performing Arts's Broadway-oriented Xmas style and repertoire appeared suitable and communicative—as well as a valid recognition of this institution's contributions to Atlanta's cultural life.

I tried to preserve, however, what I have always hoped would seem the four chronological and/or psychological sections of the program. They are:

I   —Yearning, Promise and Advent
II   —Nativity and the Manger
        (This, understandably, always has been the longest of the sections—
        heretofore ending with "My soul magnifies . . . " and "He, watching over
        Israel . . . ")

III —The Fun and Games Men Play
>   (This has been the catch-all for the secular carols, customs and festivities of the holiday season. At its best I have hoped it would have the character of a large family unwrapping, exciting and unexpected presents on Christmas morning.)

IV —Flight for Life and So-What
>   (In my mind, this meant a return to the manger, to the shepherds' farewell, and to a pondering of the meaning of that Child for Our Time—"a sign that is spoken against . . . that thoughts out of many hearts may be revealed.")

In my thinking the program always has ended with the *Dona Nobis Pacem;* and the *Hallelujah Chorus* or *Adeste, Fideles* (or both) are redundant and recessional—albeit conclusive. I would prefer to omit the flowers of bows and applause, but that's not an option in this situation.

This year the presence of Don Smith as producer of the telecast assures the Festival of enhanced visual presentation. It also gives those responsible for materials, both heard and seen, a chance to explore the potentials for 1983, when we return to our accustomed fare.

It ought to be said, before concluding, that the Christmas Festival repertoire, of whatever vintage, does make a unique contribution to our basic choral techniques.

Substantially all of these materials derive from carols, hymns or folk-songs. As such, they are basically strophic (have several verses) and homophonic (are harmonized so that the words occur simultaneously in all voices.)

These conditions force two technical sophistications:

First, they demand extraordinarily precise disciplines of enunciations: When text is the substance of communication—rather than its original inspiration— "words" become more important than "line."

Second, they demand a much richer and more varied vocabulary of phrasing. When the same melody and harmonies must serve two, three or more verses of text, subtle variations of accentuation and dynamics must be contrived to keep the communication clear and fresh. Moreover—and what is even more difficult—the long procession of rhythmic values must be individually and subtly stretched or compressed to accommodate and illumine word meaning.

These matters are a "natural" for the solo voice. – But even the solo quartet begins to experience difficulty. – And for two hundred people to arrive at a point where they can accomplish instant and identical emphasis is some kind of miracle.

With your affectionate commitment that miracle can still occur next week—

even though, for this year, it may occasionally smack of the Miracle on 42nd Street along with that of Bethlehem.

Peace,

R

November 9, 1983

Friends –

American democracy has a tradition that war is "too important to be left entirely to the military." (Hence, a civilian commander-in-chief.)

In a similar sense, I have felt for some years that the arts were too important to be left entirely to the professionals.

There can be no doubt that unremitting professionalism puts a strain upon the arts and artists; as, indeed, it can and does upon other human activities, however noble they may be in concept—from sports through religion to sex.

Even with the "best of intentions," the things that people do "for love" are likely to undergo modification when done only "for money." – And not the least of those modifications may be in the doer.

I'm leading up to trying to say "thank you" for all the time, energy and talent you poured into the recording of the Brahms *Requiem*—after the time, energy and talent you already had poured into its rehearsals and concert performances.

Our present choral structure is certainly not perfect. It probably is not even "right." It calls for an extraordinary "giving" on your part—as, also, on the parts of your homes, families and vocations.

Very probably, our most important institutional responsibility is to get this chorus structured so that (1), it gives to everyone as much as it receives and (2), it obliges no talented enthusiast to deny himself the joys of participation because he can't afford its rigors.

Conceivably, this could mean multiple choruses and multiple conductors. Let's get ourselves an *ad hoc* steering committee to wrestle with this problem.

But, until we can perceive and mount a safer and saner choral force, I want you to know that somebody not only feels gratitude for your gifts to the Atlanta Symphony and its community, but also is very convinced that your efforts and your attitude towards your efforts are mankind's therapy for an all-consuming, all-consumptive professionalism in the arts.

Since you sing like angels, anyway, you might as well be on their side.

R

Editor's note: Shaw produced a number of timeless recordings of choral master-works. In the following two letters, he addresses some of the particular concerns that come up when preparing a choir to record a performance.

November 27, 1985

Friends –

Whatever else can be said about recording sessions, they are certainly a fool-proof prophylactic for/against tears.

Audiences, too, can act as a sort of sterilizing or preventive agent. Although communication in the concert-hall is not specifically proscribed and may, in fact, occur, today's faddish addiction to the instant standing ovation testifies more to a listener's desire to be seen and heard than his wish to be left alone in order to hear. It is the sort of response at which the commercial/popular forms of music are frankly and specifically addressed. – As also are the balletic exag-gyrations of a fashionable school of performing concert artists so repugnant to musicians as recent—and as secure—as George Szell, Paul Hindemith and Ar-turo Toscanini.

The inherent danger to the performer in front of an audience is that he may be tempted to consider himself the message rather than the messenger.

In recording, while there may not be the asepticizing temptations to preen and prettify, there are other real hazards.

The most obvious is that a recording, far more often than not, is supposed to be a sort of "last will and testament," a fixed and final word. For instance, the chances that any of us will again have the opportunity to record the Durufle *Requiem* are very, very thin, and that all of us will have a second chance—non-existent.

This means that we cannot tolerate the inadvertent flaw, the transient blemish—because it will be perpetuated and immortalized *ad infinitum*. – And in our determination to be letter-perfect we run the greater danger of becoming word- and paragraph-sterile. Not a lot of propagation of the species would occur if the act of insemination were interrupted at the critical moment in order that only certain precise and qualified genes were allowed to proceed.

A second inhibition is simply the proscription of extraneous noise, whether it be circuit hum, rain on the roof or creaking risers. A rigid posture, for example—to forestall the third of these disturbances—simply cannot be condu-cive to free and easy vocal flow.

A third, and frightfully inhibitive, condition is the set of temporal restric-tions, however they initially were intended to provide "fair working conditions."

Artistic "inspiration" is terribly vulnerable to *musicus interruptus*. There is not a serious composer living or dead who has not worked through the night—almost without realizing it—when the ideas were flooding the mind. – Nor a serious solo instrumentalist who has not practiced, unheeding, through at least two normal meal periods, so heavy was the attention on the work itself.

Close to these latter two is a fourth hazard; it is the presence—and critical importance—of non-performing personnel. It would be unthinkable to consider recording without an "engineer" or a "producer." – But, particularly if they are concerned and talented, these persons will have their own preferences as to placement of the performers, acoustical properties and environment, and even balances, color, tempo and intonation. Recording is "a sometime thing," and producer and engineer have not lived through the building and preparing processes nor, in some instances, heard the "live" performance. It would be surprising if there were not areas of disagreement between performers and producers as to disciplines, styles and practices, between what is heard in the control-booth and what is heard in the out-of-control-hall.

But, under the contemporary procedures of recording, suggestions for "improvement of the product" have an effect upon the concentration of the performer that a music critic might have were he to interrupt a concert twenty to forty times per evening to offer his evaluation and suggest appropriate correction.

The great danger in recording, however, is the danger of fragmentation.

I doubt that there is a single person in our chorus who, during one or another of the performances or rehearsals of the Durufle *Requiem* did not encounter a tear or two of mysterious origin, but possibly "holy" water.

Not many of us can or would claim the one-to-one relationship with the text or the musical tradition that the composer knew. – Still, we all were moved by some mysterious compulsion. (This letter started out, last night, to be a consideration of the "varieties of religious experience" as encountered by the amateur chorus in the secular concert hall. – More of that later.)

My present point is that when we cut up a Durufle *Requiem* even into movements—it's really no more serious than cutting up the lives or the bodies of people into parts—like chicken at meat-counters.

So, whatever else can be said for recording sessions, they certainly are a foolproof prophylactic against tears.

Peace,

R

October 24, 1989

Friends –

Ideally, for us, the making of music is a contract between ourselves and the composer. It is an attempt—and a labor—to reach consensus with the creator. Ideally, for us, an audience does not exist. (The least important thing a listener can bring to a concert is the price of a ticket.)

By contrast, it is the specific intent of Fad-Music, by promotional and acoustical excess, to assemble, address and arouse as large a crowd as may be possible. Its success is measured precisely in multiple units of mass hysteria and psychological derangement.

Ideally, our performances should have the qualities of adult conversation among thoughtful and informed friends, whose voices may be raised for emphasis—but not for show.

Therefore, is there any situation so ideally suited to music's purposes as the volunteer adult chorus? We bring to the work and to one another the absolute limit of energy and sensitivity—not for pay, but as a gift—hoping to find and to forge a community with the spirit and the specifications of the composer, searching for the unspeakable within the singable.

– Which leads to the second of today's homey-lies: Music is a *rational* undertaking.

True, music can have extraordinary *emotional* consequences. – But, in the main, successful performance is the product of *reason*. Moreover, the tears which flow from our kinds of music are private and personal. They are not Woodstock's dreck-deck and gang-harangue.

It is precisely the careful shaping of intonation, articulation, dynamics, tempo, enunciation, balance and vocal color which releases music's mysterious communications.

Last night, upon successive repetition, there was scarcely a measure which was not shaped more expressively than almost any measures I can recall from this chorus. Obviously, two things remain: (1) Being right the first time, and (2) Being right one-thousand-two-hundred-and-fifty-four measures in a row.

Last night, also, this expressivity was achieved at the expense of a review of *Itaipu.* Will you please take ten minutes per day to review the text of *Itaipu,* in meter and approximate tempo? It need not be sung, simply spoken in tempo. This daily small fraction of an hour will make next Monday night possible and possibly even funnible.

Thank you,

R

April 16, 1991

Friends –

The basic premise of music is *communication:* communication which can leap across centuries and oceans; and communication of values and pleasures—intellectual, aesthetic, perhaps "spiritual" but certainly physiological—which seem expressible best by music or possibly even only by music.

The basic premise of *music-making* is *unity—*and *unanimity—*and, in its non-liturgical sense, *communion.* The unity is one of both purpose and product. The music-maker strives first for a unity with the composer-creator, to fulfill the composer's specifications exactly and enthusiastically. He/she strives next for an absolute unanimity of pitch, rhythm, timbre, tempo, accentuation and sonority with his/her collaborators—in order to allow a communion to take place involving all three personal elements: creator, performer and listener.

All this abstract puffery is simply to say that our first and constant attention at rehearsals is *the sound of unity—*at long last a "unison."

Choral unison can be disturbed by factors of pitch, rhythm, tempo, dynamics, timbre and enunciation. – And the denser the composer's musical texture, the more precious and critical becomes sectional unanimity as to these elements.

Our business is to see that (is it too long for a bumper-sticker?) UNANIMITY HAPPENS.

I always have felt that it was useless to command choral singers to "Blend!" In the "great" chorus, which this one certainly wants to be, singers care enough about their unanimity to accurately appraise their own contributions—or violations—as regards pitch, rhythm, tempo, dynamics, timbre and enunciation.

It could very well be that the most attractive thing about choral singing is its difficulty. "Singing in synch-" is an extraordinarily complex and difficult accomplishment. (The woods are full of bad choruses and singers who never have had—nor ever will have—any idea of how difficult it actually is.) It calls for listening and a self-criticism which most people can't face.

But, what wonderful compensations! – When we finally have asked enough of ourselves!

Recall the solid sonorities which ended last night's rehearsal: immensity with manners. When a chorus finally has the six essential disciplines working for it, it's a tough mother to smother.

Recall the clear, sweet and unified sounds which derived from even our cursory re-study of "church" Latin. The same sweetness and pliancy can characterize our German assignments (even that of Chorus I, Nos. 81–85, and Chorus 11, Nos. 114–17 and Nos. 55–60, should enough of us be moved this week to drill again at home).

The way it sorts out numerically—with three hundred twenty supernumeraries arriving Monday night—is that each of us has to accept two-and-one-half times her/his usual responsibility: one per self, one-and-one-half per "brother's keeper."

"On our way rejoicing!"

R

February 8, 1994

Friends –

Today a few sentences about *corporate* and *individual* responsibilities in choral performance –

Our rehearsal methods and disciplines have two objectives: first, in the instance of *unfamiliar* music, to *speed the learning process;* and second, in the case of *familiar* music, to *unify each section of the chorus* (and finally, of course, the whole chorus) as to pitch, rhythm, dynamics, enunciation, and vocal timbre.

Now, everyone would have to admit that a 200-voice volunteer chorus—no matter how earnestly recruited and auditioned—inevitably will represent a wide range of (1) vocal talent, (2) musicianship and (3) experience. Further—since it only takes one lousy (or lazy) voice to louse up a whole section—everyone would have to agree that the pace of the learning process has to be adjusted to the pace of those who are (1) least talented, (2) least musicianly and (3) least experienced. (In simple English this is writ: "Never allow nobody to memorize no mistakes!") You and I are obliged, therefore, to be sympathetic with those among us who have absolute pitch and degrees from Nadia Boulanger in Solfege, and who already have sung everything written for human voices and instruments since 1600 AD. 'Small wonder they lose interest and drop out of our chorus.

I am particularly mindful of this schism because of recent experience with this year's Carnegie Hall Professional Training Workshop on Benjamin Britten's *War Requiem*. Rehearsals began on a Tuesday morning at 10 AM. This first rehearsal ended at 1 P.M., and the afternoon rehearsal ran from 2:30 to 4:30. Both were substantially similar to ours last night on the *Missa Solemnis*. The difference appeared on Wednesday morning.

It became clear by a few moments into Wednesday's rehearsal that the second of our objectives was substantially accomplished, and that the first—except for a bit of proof-reading the day before—had been by-passed. The notes were remarkably clean, and the sound had been unified to the point where we were free to deal with refinements of tone colour and dynamics, niceties of language and—more importantly—pertinent intellectual aspects of motivation and meaning.

Of all symphonic choruses I have met, this is the only one which, starting from scratch, could in two rehearsals attempt "flight." From that point on all corporate embellishments and burnishings only increased private joys and understandings.

This was a group made up almost entirely of music professionals. Most were choral conductors, some were choral "nuts"—experienced and enthusiastic choral *aficionados;* and all had either performed the *War Requiem* or had done serious preparatory study. They had come from most of the United States, and the Pacific Rim, European and African countries, and they weren't about to waste their time and money.

Now, we are not that select or selective a group and, consequently, more of our rehearsal time must be spent on the first of our objectives: speeding *the learning process.* But, has it ever occurred to you that if those of us who never attended the Curtis Institute, or won the Met Auditions, or have not yet sung a half-dozen performances of the *Missa Solemnis* were to take Beethoven seriously enough to master his notes at home in private—what a great big world of understanding ours could be?

Great *corporate* sound depends upon great *individual* responsibility. Some of us read faster than others. Some of us have more voice and more beautiful voices than others. *But* there *is not a person in this chorus* who is incapable of singing the choral portions of the *Missa Solemnis* as a solo—if he or she wants to. Each of us has gifts enough for the job at hand. All that could be lacking are desire and industry.

I'll guaran-double-tee you that each hour you spend at home on any page of the *Missa Solemnis* will sharpen your intelligence, challenge your theology and exalt your humanity.

R

March 21, 1995

Friends –

The quandaries which surround the programming of religious music in secular symphonic institutions are not unlike the quandaries and range of conflicting opinions which surround the First Amendment to the U.S. Constitution regarding the "establishment of religion or . . . the free exercise thereof."

As noble a musical edifice as Bach's *St. John Passion* may be, and as "liberating" (liberalizing?) as may have been Greco-Roman influences upon its doctrine, many of us never will cease to be embarrassed by its occasional vehement-to-vicious racial attribution regarding the crucifixion of Jesus. There can be no doubt that its traditional text has added to the waves of anti-Semitism for generations and centuries since its composition.

Since Western Civilization (along with its fine arts) was dominated, undergirded, sponsored and protected by Christianity, it is not surprising that our "classical" vocal music—music with text—should share that heritage. – Or that it should share an historical, stylistic similarity to the non-textually religious music of its period.

If Bach's *Christ lag in Todesbanden* is "sacred" music, what are we to make of the daring, soloistic self-exposures of Mozart's *Exsultate jubilate,* or the New Orleans-by-way-of-Hollywood ravishments of Poulenc's *Gloria* or, for that matter, a sincerely-yours come-to-Jesus cantata by Dave Brubeck or a *How great thou art* invitation hymn by George Beverly Shea?

What makes sacred music "sacred?"

– And do any of the above belong on the annual subscription repertoire of a symphony orchestra in today's world? – For that matter, do any of them belong in a service of Christian Worship?

Well—chew on that awhile.

There's lots more.

R

October 30, 1996

Friends –

Two factors prompt this writing on the morning after the night that wasn't. First is the scent of 5,000-plus man-hours of dedicated labor going up in thin smoke. If one adds to the hours of rehearsal the hours of auditions, editing and preparation of scores and parts, administrative functions and correspondence, home study, travel-time, and the adjustments that others make to allow us our musical exercises—the smoke gets thicker.

Second is to qualify and add to my letter of last week which suggested that Bartok's *Cantata Profana,* like Bach's *B Minor Mass,* might be one of those works better served by a small chorus of uniformly gifted vocal musicians than by a 200-plus symphony chorus of volunteer singers with widely ranging personal talents. The reasoning was that the large chorus produces such a size and density of sound that it is difficult—and in some cases, impossible—to achieve lucidity of contrapuntal line, rhythmic cohesion and enunciative clarity.

Now, some of you may be old enough to remember that in my earlier years, along with a few others, I had a hand in the development of the professional touring and recording choruses in the United States. I am not unfamiliar with professional choirs—their virtues and their limitations. – And, so far as I can tell, that experience only has added to the technical proficiencies achievable by the volunteer chorus, and to the respect I have for "amateur" motivation and accomplishment in the Arts.

I cannot recall if it was A. Lincoln who said that "war is too important to leave to the generals," but that is certainly the rationale for having a civilian "commander-in-chief." – Not that civilians should be responsible for war's tactics and techniques, but rather for its proprieties and purposes.

To borrow the metaphor, this morning's topic is: "The *Arts*—like *Sex*—are too important to leave to the professionals."

"Amateur" is not a dirty word. Its lineage is (Latin) "*amare*, to love; *amator*, a lover."

Now, one should not for a moment infer that "professionals" cannot also be *amators*. The greatest "lovers" of music in my experience have been Rudolf Serkin—who poured both his love and his fortune into Marlboro's (Vermont) incomparable summer Festival/Study Program of chamber music, and Pablo Casals, whose entire professional life of more than 75 years (he lived to be 97) was an unending testament to individual liberty, political freedom, racial and economic justice, "universal peace" and the "brotherhood of man."

Similarly, we must never forget that the "professionals" of our closest acquaintance—even those with whom we occasionally "make" music—when they chose music as their "life-work" had the same "stars in their eyes" that we experience working on a Brahms *Requiem* or a *St. Matthew Passion*. – The point is that it is a uniquely difficult thing to be a professional "artist." Professionalism—and its economic/institutional structures—put great strains upon the durability of *love* in the Arts. It could be that it is as difficult to be a *musical* artist—and maintain an *amator's* motivation as it would be to work as a professional *sexual* artist—and retain an *amator's* inspiration.

Let's list for a moment the virtues of volunteer symphonic choruses—the things they contribute to our lives, to our community and to man- and woman-kind.

1. First, of course, is the participant's personal joy, enlightenment and technical skills. No other art, to my knowledge, offers such immediate contact

with supreme achievements of human creativity. We get to meet Bach, Mozart and Beethoven our first day at school. Moreover, in no other collective venture that I know of is it possible to find a community of aspiration or belief without sacrificing something of personal intelligence or integrity along the way. (– As witness voting booths or the inescapable preponderance of Sabbath homi-lies.)

2. Second would by the joy, enlightenment and inspiration given to listeners— both in person and through broadcasts and recordings. In a world of mawk, muck and mock, how inspiriting must be the somebody-really-cares of Barber-Bartók-and-Vaughan Williams.

3. Third is the influence a superb volunteer symphonic chorus can have on other musical organizations in its community. The ASOC has helped to bring people like Ann Jones, Norman Mackenzie and Norma Raybon to Atlanta to live and work. Church and school repertoires, together with standards of performance, reflect your influence. – As, indeed, do other symphonic choruses, national and international.

4. – But the fourth virtue of the volunteer symphony chorus is the winner of my Consolation-of-the-Week Award. Richard Clement, who was to have been soloist of the very demanding tenor role in the *Cantata Profana,* and who, I hope, will remain available when we are able to re-schedule it, was seated in the hall during all of last Monday night's rehearsal. Prior to rehearsal we had commiserated with one another and laughed (bleakly) at the work's difficulties. After rehearsal he said in part and in parting, "I had no idea that the work was so beautiful!"

Most of us have had the opportunity to hear the work only in recordings— and it is not an easy piece to record. The orchestral materials—principally brass and percussion, but also strings and woodwinds—are woefully over-marked dynamically; and, with only one exception—which could be a slip of the pen or of memory in hasty scoring or editing—the tempi are uniformly fast, such is the way that imagination in the composer's study out-paces experience in the concert-hall with real live singers and players. So far, the recordings have not made for relaxed, Just-a-Song-at-Twilight listening.

– But the *Cantata Profana* does tell a sweet, sad story and, except for 9-Boys-Gone-a-Hunting and Big Brother's solo prophecy of Daddy's Dire Straits, the music is sweet, gently troubled and tender.

". . . no idea the work was so beautiful!" Surely, I have never found that to be true in previous rehearsal sequences and performances. What I am now saying to myself—and writing to you—is that it may be precisely because we have worked so long and so hard, and with such diversity of personal backgrounds and skills, and with no recompense but those unique to *amators,* that we now begin to fulfill what must have been Bartók's vision from the beginning. (We certainly did not come anywhere near this close at the American premiere with totally professional forces at Carnegie Hall in 1952.)

This raises the possibility that the amateur's relationship to the Arts changes not only the lover—but also the beloved.

As Pooh would say, "That's my hum for the day after. It's come different from what I thought, but there it is."

R

August 14, 1996

Friends –

> Barber, *Prayers of Kierkegaard*
> Bartók, *Cantata Profana*
> Vaughan Williams, *Dona Nobis Pacem*

Our opening program for Season 1996–1997 presents some splendid opportunities—and some just-maybe-surmountable difficulties.

Chief among the former is the opportunity to present three 20th-century works of the musical art to an audience that by custom and self-selection is a lot more comfortable with—and responsive to—the familiar and the traditional than with the innovative or experimental.

This is a strange reluctance, because a symphony audience—given the restraints imposed by economics, formalities and inconveniences of place and time—is almost certainly the best-educated, aesthetically concerned and socially committed audience assembled today anywhere in our land. It is a reluctance particularly baffling because the symphony audience is substantially that which delights also in the current theatre sensation, and which runs to the new traveling show at the museum.

I find a number of overlapping reasons for this state of affairs, none of them quite strong enough to stand on its own.

(1) Music, being uniquely an art which organizes and proportions *Time* (versus Space as in the Visual Arts—painting, sculpture, architecture and even ballet) challenges and disturbs (or coddles and confirms) a listener's "Life"-Time, in particular a person's meditative "Life"-Time. Music as disturbing

44

as Stravinsky's *Rite of Spring,* for instance, can do all sorts of weird things to a listener's breathing.

(2) While most of us may wish it were not so, the audience for symphonic music in our time is a sort of intellectual/economic aristocracy—and aristocracies have long shown a preference for the *status quo* (defined by Peanuts, W. C. Fields or Mark Twain as "the fix we's in").

(3) Listening to music—particularly *new* music—is a complex, concentrated intellectual exercise. – And it is unremitting.

One can stand in front of an entirely unfamiliar piece of visual art, and his mind—or feet—are free to roam, wander or day-dream. – One can close his eyes or, by changing his position, change the light on the object. One has control of at least the tempo of the evaluative processes.

But the new piece of music is absolutely remorseless in its demands upon one's attention. Second after second and milli-second after milli-second it hammers at the listener's perception, memory and ability to relate. One must accept unexceptionably the tempo of its flow of data. One cannot halt it for a moment to examine, cogitate or rest; consequently, if something occurs which is even momentarily un-understandable, everything which follows become less and less understandable.

(4) We may have to admit—though we would rather not—that since symphonic music calls for both experienced and aesthetically sophisticated listening, it is also sure to have a more mature (and less "participative") audience: very seldom a stampede to the stage; very few ear-stunning, mind-numbing, inhibition-crushing, rabble-rousing cliches. – Rather, a few more grey-heads and sleepy eyes (saying they can hear better with their eyes closed). Maturity, they say, is that part of life when one is better equipped to reason and evaluate—and would rather not.

– Whatever . . . There would appear to be ample opportunity in this opening program to rattle some cages.

For years I have been convinced that there are two conditions which can meet and conquer this somewhat natural apathy of the symphony audience toward new serious musical fare. The first is virtuosity. We've just had a convincing demonstration of this in Olympic athletic competition.

Very few of us have any idea of the sequence and complexity of the muscular gyrations by which a pole-vaulter can surmount a twenty-foot barrier with a 16-foot pole, or a high jumper can leap over a fence nearly two feet above his head, or a diver can manage three-and-one-half somersaults with a full twist—but we stand up and yell like mad when we see it done.

Virtuosity convinces. It does it in jazz, and it does it in the symphonic choral repertoire. Perfect balances, perfect intonation, proper tempi and superb enunciation not only evoke approval; they make it sound "easy." And "if it's easy for them to do it . . . it can't be too hard to listen to . . ."

The second condition that will lead a reluctant audience to the fountain of life is plain old-fashion passion.

Passionate conviction that "this here-now music is absolutely and unreservedly essential to your (Mr. Audience's) here-now humanity, understanding and behavior" will wash "Don' wanna!" from the crustiest ear.

Close kin to passion, perhaps even its begetter or quintessence, is energy. – And it will take a lot of that to produce virtuosity and passion by Hallowe'en.

– Which signals that we had better leave discussion of the "just-maybe-surmountable difficulties" to the next letter.

'See you soon,

R

PART II

THOUGHTS ON MUSIC, SINGING, REHEARSAL, AND PERFORMANCE

Alternating between the whimsical, the poetic, the pedantic, the preachy and the profound, these observations and reflections document the continuity of Shaw's work in Atlanta, and they provide a near codifying of his attempt to address his "greatest challenge," choral enunciation. The letters also point to the elemental truth that Shaw was first and foremost a teacher—a mentor anxious to uncover new layers of artistic, musical, and textual insight, not in order to possess them but eagerly, emphatically to pass them along to his choral charges.

These passages do not reflect a complete picture of his rehearsal methodology; there is no mention whatsoever of the mesmerizing practice of having the chorus divide a semitone into sixteen equal portions as a part of its warm-up regimen, or of the building of such a perfect unison octave that the fifths and twelfths sounding as overtones nearly match the fundamentals in clarity. The material does provide, however, an important glimpse into the deeply layered and complex thought processes that gave Shaw-trained choirs a remarkable warmth and unity of tone and a distinctive and compelling rhythmic vitality. As is the case with the work of all great conductors, much of the success of Shaw's legendary rehearsals stemmed directly from the painstakingly thorough preparation that preceded each of them. Regardless of the number of times he had conducted a piece, he saw each successive performance as a new opportunity to get closer to the truths intended by the composer.

For example, his final performances of Brahms's Ein Deutches Requiem were conducted from the last of four well-worn and well-marked orchestral scores, the first three of which could absorb no more margin notes and tempo indications. His carefully pondered research, analysis, and musical and textual insights were reflected in every aspect of the rehearsal—from the carefully adhered to, minute-by-minute rehearsal plan, to the tempo-watch-calculated variations in pulse and subpulse, and the minutely focused edits provided for the singers' scores. Shaw's oft-stated appeal for the chorus to "clean the perch so the dove (of inspiration) will have a better chance of landing" was advice that he constantly applied to his own detailed, and (though he'd deny it) devotional, approach to score study and preparation.

—William Thomas, Assistant Editor

APPROACH, ANALYSIS, PREPARATION

. . . this thing which we are trying to do together is somehow greater—more important and more rewarding—than most things which we attempt alone.

. . . in every work of what is generally assumed to be "instinctive," "unselfconscious" art, the miracle of the life-force is appreciable in even the most minute and pragmatic of details.

. . . the simple numbering of measures can be meaningful. The numbers represent not only a piling up of materials, but a passing of time.

September 13, 1978

Bruder und Schwester –

Let's talk first about rehearsal methods.

Theoretically, it seems to me, choral rehearsals should have two major premises:

1. Save the human voice! Avoid wear and waste of singers' "gold" when learning notes; invent devices which teach pitch, rhythm and text with a minimum of vocal effort.
2. Use devices which make it impossible not to hear, recognize—and correct— errors of pitch, rhythm and text. (– Like counting/singing or nonsense syllables.) Stated in flat-out technical terms, there are only five fundamentals of good (choral) singing: the proper pitch (1) – sung at precisely the proper time (2) – on the correctly isolated element of speech (3) – delivered in a vocal color (4) – and at a dynamic level (5) – appropriate to the musical style and structure, and sensitive to textual meaning and emotion.

Our underlying supposition—our "faith"—is that the great composer is also the great illuminator and communicator. – Therefore, if we wish to have our lives "touched" and "illumined" by his understanding, we need first to satisfy his technical prescriptions. At the moment we fulfill his musical instructions we receive his "message." "The message" is in *the music*—in the nitty-gritty-mini-matters of good intonation, good rhythm, good speech, good color and good dynamics.

There is one other underlying supposition that is concerned not with our relationship to the score, but with our relationship to one another. Recognizing that each of us is a product of varied intellectual, economic and social backgrounds, and a highly individual complex of musical capabilities, and native vocal endowments, we all willingly and happily agree that for this undertaking, at least, the thing which we are trying to do *together* is somehow greater—more important and more rewarding—than most things which we attempt alone. Though using the most personal and intimate of musical instruments—the human voice—choral singing (perhaps in particular, voluntary choral singing) shows music in an almost abstractly ideal form, an ensemble art which, rather than circumscribing and diminishing the individual, somehow frees, sensitizes and, it is to be hoped, enriches and occasionally ennobles.

At any rate, pulpits notwithpounding, each of us has a few moments on the other six days per week to prepare to spur rather than drag the united thrust of Monday night. Each must privately wail—for the common weal.

Freude! und Friede –

R

September 20, 1984

Dear Friends –

Let's consider—for a page or two this week—the major premises of our choral "technique." (I realize, of course, that these are personal emphases, and that other choral specialists may have their own underpinnings. – But two-thirds of us, probably, have been working together for several—or more—seasons with these principles as foundations of our rehearsal techniques and performance practices. So, in fact, by this time they may indeed be a consensus, and worth re-stating.)

The first of our foundations is that *intonation* is the *sine qua non* (without which nothing) of choral singing. It is absolutely essential that we understand that we of the present generations live constantly in a world of execrable and intolerable musical pitch.

For instance, this is the open season on the National Anthem; and we can hear it crooned, hollered, rolled and rocked, stamped on and beaten to death, with scarcely one of its hundred consecutive pitches in proper relation to a major scale.

The communicative premise of most of today's commercial music is essentially loudness. (Witness the tractor-trailer loads of amplifiers and speakers without which the present musical groups would be unable to perform.)

Even the symphony orchestra has constantly to be on guard—cautioned by principal players and section leaders—that its intonation be not subverted by concentration or sonority or coloristic effect. All of us have heard "famous" symphony recordings or broadcasts (both American and European) which are simply and shockingly "out of tune."

The instrumental music which is most vulnerable as regards intonation is, of course, chamber music: the string quartet, the woodwind quintet, etc. – And the consequent care which these players devote to playing "in tune" must equally be our guide.

As we become more sensitive to proper intonation our problems do not disappear. – For then we have to reconcile the differences which exist between "just" intonation (that based upon acoustical laws of the "over-tone" series) and that based upon the compromises of "equal temperament" (piano pitches—in which, for instance, an F-sharp has also to serve as a G-flat).

Living in a world wherein musical intonation ranges from the excremental only as far as a tolerable compromise (the well-tempered keyboard) it is a monumental accomplishment for two hundred voices to sing one note in tune— let alone eighty minutes of four- to seven-part harmony. – And it takes everybody caring every second.

Our second premise is that *time* is *divisible,* and must be particularized with a precision as inexhaustibly sensitive as that accorded to intonation.

Everyone will understand that musical time is in one sense an artifice: all of us have known "moments" that were "endless," and "hours" that "whizzed by."

– But since music proposes to organize Sound through Time, it has to assume that Time can be "measured" and proportioned.

If one recognizes the difficulty of contriving occasional simultaneity between just two persons, the brashness of proposing it for two hundred persons should scare him to death. – But that is our premise.

Not infrequently—as in some of the faster choruses of a *B Minor Mass* or a *Messiah*—we take upon ourselves the task of lining up four-parts, each with six different pitches per second. (An orchestra may have to play twelve per second.)

Our premise and intention can be realized only under two conditions—both of them extremely difficult to achieve:

First, every participant must be excruciatingly sensitive to *tempo*—the passing of consecutive and equal units of (artificial) *time;* and absolutely nothing must be allowed to change that *tempo* which is not conscious and proportioned.

Second, everyone involved must carry in consciousness at all times not only the larger unit of *tempo* (which we call *pulse*) but also its divisions and subdivisions from halves and thirds to minuscule sixths and eighths.

This is a simultaneity considerably more difficulty to achieve for a chorus than for an orchestra. It is not only that ten fingers can respond faster than two vocal cords. It is that any language and all the sounds of speech have inherent durations and rhythms which may not necessarily be (indeed, almost never are) identical with their musical allotments.

In great solo singing the sensitive artist "bends" the musical time values to allow the text to become "more expressive." But in choral singing not only do all the voices in a single section have to perform simultaneously, but all of the several sections have to achieve a simultaneity and integrity of pulse division and *tempo* in spite of having to accommodate at any given moment four or more *different texts.*

Still—it can be done (by courting self-hypnosis and schizo-phrenia).

Our third premise is that vocal tone (in addition to being capable of *absolute pitch* at an *absolute moment*) is also capable of *variety* of *dynamics* and *colors.*

To a certain small degree this runs counter to what some consider sound musical pedagogy (both for vocalists and instrumentalists). Recall, for instance, Alexander Schneider's observation that, while most solo string players labor for years to achieve "their-own" soloistic and characteristic vibrato, Pablo Casals was more interested in being able to vary his vibrato (as to speed and width). Recall that while most vocal instruction at an advanced/professional level is directed toward developing a voice of sufficient size and timbre to carry over a large orchestra, most of baroque and early classical vocal music would appear to put a higher value upon vocal agility, accuracy and compatibility with chamber music instrumentalists than upon sheer size of sound. – And the successful singer of *lieder* would add to those expertises subtle changes in vocal color and an exceptional sensitivity to text.

It is clear to anyone who has worked with choruses of both "amateur" and "professional" voices that well-taught voices can make a better choral sound than un-taught voices. (They also can make a better sound than badly taught voices.) The teaching of voice has to be one of the most difficult and complicated of musical endeavors. You can't see it, you can't touch it—and, if you're the one doing it, you have to depend upon someone else even to hear it.

One can only be grateful for those who undertake this remote and complex task, and who approach it as a means of musical-expression rather than self-exhibition.

So, in addition to micro-precisions of *intonation* and *time,* we seek a choral texture as varied as may be possible and appropriate with regard to *color* and *dynamics.* We travel ranges of "dark" to "bright," of "brassy" to "fuzzy," of "yelly" to "mumbly," of *ffff* to *pppp,* of non-vibrato to *molto*-vibrato, of wide- to narrow-vibrato, of fast- to slow-vibrato. – And we try to relate these techniques to the emotional and psychological inferences of both text and music.

There's a fourth and final premise of our choral arts. Quite simply, it is that vocal (choral) music has words—as well as pitches, rhythms and colors; and that it is possible *most of the time* to project them through and over instrumental collaboration.

We do this by concentrating not upon the words themselves, but upon the distinct and successive sounds which form those words; and by allotting to each of these sounds their precise moment and amount of musical time. Simple, ain't it?

It's not simple. There's no more complicated collaboration available to the human animal.

But, doggone! Ain't it fun!

R

October 8, 1975

Musicology for Musicians

– or Analysis for Singers (and do they need it)
– or What we don't know won't help us, either.

The information and style which constitute good program notes and make for more enjoyable listening may be of peripheral and even invigorating interest to the performer, but they won't help him get from A to B-flat any sooner or louder—if that's what the composer happens to have prescribed.

The singer faces a complexity, or at least an obscurity, not quite so constant a part of the instrumentalist's experience, basically because the singer's "instrument" is an unseeable, untouchable, complicated physiological function of his "self."

It is no wonder, under the circumstances, that vocal pedagogy—even great vocal pedagogy—must be so vague, so largely dependent upon a terminology of association rather than sensation, and no less psychic in its prescriptions than physical.

However infrequent it may be that the great voices are "made not born," voice *can* be taught. – But I mistrust a choral discipline founded primarily upon vocal pedagogy because Sometime's motherless child too frequently comes across as Madame Butterfly on the road to Mandalay.

– And history *can* be read; none of us who attempts to be a serious performer can be without its information on style and logistics. – But, to Trumanize an already mixed-up metaphor, I suspect that performance always takes place in today's kitchen, not in yesterday's ivory tower, or who left the ball game in the dressing room.

The two areas which I find enormously instructive and productive to choral performance are, first, an examination of over-all structure—what the basic and pervasive architecture is; and second an examination of the minutiae of motives, the details of dynamics and articulation which add up to phrasing, and the specifics of balance, intonation and enunciation by means of which truth puts on beauty.

The understanding of "structure" is important because all of its elements happen also to be psychically and existentially true. Most of the terms which have accrued to "explain" the nature of a work of "art" are really just somewhat inadequate academic jargon for "real" human understandings, for psychological phenomena which do in fact exist. Matters of proportion and scale, of introduction, use and recurrence play upon our minds and memories, so that even seemingly unrelated experiences are awakened and touched by the *surprise* of this "modulation," the *freshness* of that "episode" or the *reassurance* of this "recapitulation."

Similarly, in every work of what is generally assumed to be "instinctive," "un-self-conscious" art, the miracle of the life-force is appreciable in even the most minute and pragmatic of details. Perhaps even by accident one stumbles in rehearsal upon the proper tempo—or balance or quality of *pianissimo;* and, all of a sudden, the "meaning" becomes so clear that tears start. (Tears are a frequent testimony to understanding, but a questionable medium of the exchange of same since they screw up the entire vocal mechanism.)

– All of which is substantially not much more than an "introduction" or "preface."

At the same time, since what was referred to above as the most "instructive and productive" analysis probably only takes place in rehearsals where it mingles with sweat, sound and occasional sniffles, literacy—the ability to speak the right notes—becomes the absolute prerequisite to understanding.

I'll certainly try to communicate those "presences" which long hours of study can begin to divine, which are my responsibility and which you should not be expected to undertake; but if we're really going to leap, you better bring your own starting-blocks.

R

October 25, 1984

Friends —

Let's consider for a few sentences the relationship of musical analysis to musical performance.

Music is made up of elements tonal and temporal. The tonal elements are pitch (vibrations per second), color (each instrument or voice having by nature different ranges and over-tone characteristics), and amplitude (degrees of loudness—or quietness).

The temporal elements are those occasioned by the fact that music is a "time"-art. Unlike "Space"-arts of painting and sculpture, music is not assayable by contexts of "area" or "volume." It exists from now to "somewhen"; and its principal organization is that of auditory sensation *through Time.*

When pitches are sounded simultaneously, we call that prescription harmony. When pitches are sounded successively, we call that prescription melody.

In addition, there are purely temporal prescriptions of duration and accentuation which we call rhythm. Some of these accentuations are ordained simply by the choice of meter. (For whatever complex of psycho-physiological reasons, unless specifically contradicted, triple meters present themselves to the human unconsciousness as STRONG-light-light, while marches are binary in accentuation (L-R, L-R) principally, of course, because man has two legs.)

Beyond the general meter, however, the composer may prescribe a whole series of durations and accentuations which may minutely sub-divide the basic pulse of the meter, or arch over it—or both.

Musical analysis, then, is the attempt to comprehend the composer's musical language tonally and temporally. It asks: what is his vocabulary? – what are his materials? – what are the metric motifs? – what are the melodic motifs? – how does he organize those pitches which sound simultaneously? – which sound successively?—what tone-"colors" are uniquely his? – how does he deal with loudness and quietness? And, finally, what materials are "structural" (and important) and what are "accompanimental" (and subsidiary)?

"Greatness" is an infrequent guest in our lives, and it is difficult to comprehend creative virtuosity of exalted magnitude. Consequently, we tend to associate "greatness" with mysterious "gifts," voodoo or extra-terrestrial influences—as though the creator himself had no control over his creation.

What we must not forget is that the creator (in our instance, the composer) went through years of the stiffest sort of mental disciplines to arrive at "his" or "her" language. One does not "break" a compositional rule or custom (or "invent" a new one) without knowing what rules already exist. That Mozart could be an exceptional creative intelligence by the time he was ten doesn't mean that it was easy—for Mozart.

Music is "structured" intellectually, just as architecture is structured. It is not merely an emotional mystery (though, of course, it is that); it is also an intellectual achievement. Great music has order, design and balance; and these are not some cold, arithmetical or musicological trivia; they are the frame upon which all ornamental and cosmetic factors are draped.

For some of us this "frame"—the proportions and strength of the structural elements—is also the source of great music's communicable fervor and survivability.

For me, the most stimulating aspect of analysis consists first in identifying the principal tonal and metric materials (their nature and dimension) and, second, in following their alteration and variation as the music "grows" through time.

More nearly than anything else this becomes a search for phrase-lengths and "punctuation." Groupings of two and three measures are assembled into "sentences" of fours, fives and sixes: and, gradually, the piece is "paragraphed," so that the composer's thought-processes and intentions become clear. (It is not necessary that the composer be "conscious" of every creative footstep: his musical intuition may pirouette and leap where we have to grope slowly. – But we must "track" his route, and re-trace it.)

That is why the simple numbering of measures can be so meaningful. The numbers represent not only a piling up of materials, but a passing of time. – And, therefore, they lead us into senses of proportion and relationship. Just as each measure may contain a compression or augmentation of metrical impulses, so the groups of two and three measures will relate to other groupings, and we will be conscious of expansion and contraction—matters of energy—but now in ever-enlarging dimensions. – Until, at last, Allah willing, the whole piece becomes a living, breathing soul . . .

R

January 26, 1982

Friends –

Let me see if I can write you a short, but "emergential," note before trying to catch up to the orchestra on tour.

The principal difference between this chorus and others of similar make-up is its unyielding, unstinting (far from tireless) care of musical detail. Articulation—prescribing short (*staccato*) values or long (*sostenuto*) values; inflections and commas; balance—moving voices from part to part and marking preferential sonorities even within a single chord; expressive dynamics—prescribing the precise instant that *crescendo* and *diminuendo* occur, and how far and how fast they range; enunciation—detailing how words are assembled phonetically, and prescribing the precise instant or duration allotted to each of the sounds of speech: – all these—and more—are the irreducible factors of our choral technique, and most of them are marked in the scores which are prepared for you.

If you fail to transfer these editings to your own score, you (1) harm seriously our rehearsal efficiency, (2) deny yourself the principal educational benefit which membership in this chorus has to offer, and (3) rob our performances of their means of escaping glutinous impersonality and wall-to-wall boredom.

It is precisely this kaleidoscopic transforming miracle of detail which allows a massed chorus to escape its mass. These are the elements through which a chorus becomes personalized, which individuate its communication.

Even more importantly, it is precisely these details which allow each of us at every moment to "escape the mass," to find a constant, effervescent and individualizing vitality, even though for the moment caught in a common cause . . .

Think it over.

Robert

WARM-UP, RHYTHM AND TEMPO, PHRASING

Things (the warm-up) should not be: . . . a voice lesson, . . . long . . .

The most sensitive moment of rhythmic execution is the treatment of the upbeat or of up-beat groupings which initiate rhythmic or melodic movement.

Given the fulfillment of certain technical aspects of music-making—good intonation, good sound and good metrics—a very large part of the "personal," "creative" and "artistic" side of music-making lies in "phrasing."

September 16, 1981

Friends:

Thoughts on the rehearsal *Warm-Up* –
Things it *should not* be:

1. It should not be a voice lesson: Voices are as unique as the people they inhabit. What's effective for one person may be a waste of time or possibly even injurious to another. Only the skilled teacher, working privately over a considerable period of time, is in a position to build or aid an effective vocal technique.
2. It should not be long: Too lengthy a warm-up will put the emphasis on the choral sound rather than the repertoire. Choral disciplines (intonation, color, dynamics, rhythm and articulation) are good for something. – But that something is else. They are means and servants, not ends and masters.

Things a Warm-Up *can* be:

1. It can be a quick reminder of all the above disciplines
a. The exquisite refinements of *intonation* available to the human voice.

b. The vast spectrum of *colors* released through the kaleidoscope of language fragments, as filtered through an emotional or dramatic context. (A variety of vowels; recycled consonants.)

c. The extremes of *dynamics* available to massed voices (of which the most exciting probably is *pianississississississimo.*)

d. The dependence of all changes in intonation, color or dynamics upon an absolutely secure *rhythmic pulse.* (– All exercises being done *ben in tempo:* securely in tempo; and *ben misurato:* well-measured.)

e. Coupled with the preceding, shorter or longer reiterative pitches, patterns or scales as exercises in intonation, articulation and agility.

2. A Warm-Up frequently also can excerpt or abstract from a work to be rehearsed a motive, pattern, sequence, or scale of extra complexity, and by isolation and economical repetition prepare the chorus for its subsequent appearance, thus defusing its difficulty.

3. It should also serve to acquaint or remind the chorus of the acoustical nature of the rehearsal room or performance area. (Abrupt releases testing the reverberation time; singing while revolving slowly in place testing reflecting surfaces and ceilings, and contact with other sections of the chorus.)

4. Each Warm-Up should have some familiar "exercises" and some new ones; – and some omissions. Its purpose is to prepare the chorus to get through the rehearsal with a minimum of vocal wear and a maximum of notes learned. The Warm-Up does not build the chorus. *Mrs. Solemnis* does.

– So does a child of our time. How much can you learn about him before Monday?

Affectionately,

R

November 30, 1967

Today's considerations are *rhythm and tempo in choral singing:* Why should they be difficult? What are the real problems? How may they be solved?– For I think we would agree that our single most unifying and communicative force is rhythm—which is also at present our most urgent need.

First, we have to face the fact that while rhythm is a psychological and physical phenomenon that exists innately—this does not mean that each of us is a natural-born expert in its practice. That is just as silly as to suppose that since we all have the same basic physical equipment (toes, legs and arms in even numbers) we all can be one-day wonders at ballet.

There are, after all, basic human differences in rhythmic talent as in every other field. Good rhythm has to be based upon a natural aptitude—but even for the most gifted it is an acquired *skill*. The way we become more expert in the exercise of rhythm and tempo is the way we become better at anything else: namely drill, drill, drill, DRILL!

Two: The human voice is a good deal more difficult to operate rhythmically than any manual instrument. Anyone who has taken typing knows how nimble and precise the fingers can become in a very short time. It's considerably easier to type "beg a caged feed-bag" than it is to sing B-E-G-A-C-A-G-E-D-F-E-E-D-B-A-G. Not only is the voice less agile than the fingers—but, between the sight-recognition of the name of a pitch on a page and the ability to reproduce it in the larynx is an intricate network of neural switches, some of them, for many of us, open ends.

In a similar vein the voice, particularly in the upper registers, requires an enormously complicated system of tensions and relaxations; and when the voice gets "up there" it is not easy to play musical chairs with it. (Think of the difference in physical strain, for instance, between singing a "high C" and playing a piano in the upper octaves.)

Three: (and we've discussed this before) While most of the instruments have fundamentally one method of "attack" of initiating a pitched sound, the voice must master an enormous variety of initial sounds. Any one of the sounds of speech, be it consonant or vowel, is apt to be prescribed. "Spry" obviously will take longer to say than "eye," but so far as rhythmic singing is concerned, these words might conceivably be prescribed on alternating eighth-notes in *prestissimo* tempo.

Four: Very little vocal training or experience really prepares one to sing rhythmically. In the training of the would-be professional solo-voice, attention is centered upon *quality* (quite necessarily), but largely to the exclusion of how a voice is to be used rhythmically. In the solo repertoire (including the popular tune which is the worst offender) the principle target seems to be "personal" communication—no matter how it may stretch, distort or rewrite the original creation.

Five: With the large chorus (and the large orchestra) there simply are "area and distance" difficulties. Compared to the close-up variety, rhythmic ensemble from a distance is a different kettle of fission.

Now, recognition of these difficulties gives us no right to settle for sloppiness. Awareness is even less excuse than ignorance. To enumerate:

With respect to the first danger zone: We will continue to drill, drill, drill.

Two: We will drill also on sight-reading, try to use less piano in rehearsal; when the Bach line gets high, we will use less voice, so it can remain agile.

Three: We simply will put the consonants ahead of the beat, singing vowels on the beat.

Four: It would be productive if we were all more rhythmic in personal vocalises and in solo materials.

Five: One can learn to sing "together with" while a bit "distant from." (Obviously the trombones of the orchestra have to understand the beat differently from the first chairs of strings.) Part of this problem would be solved if you people would occasionally glance at the conductor. Granted that a good deal of our rehearsal technique—or lack of it—is calculated to establish a relationship between yourself and your score rather than between yourself and your conductor, still—'comes a time when only a "visual aid" can bring real cohesion. If some malicious god should suddenly close all the scores at rehearsal half the choir would be nose-less.

R. S.

March 27, 1969

It is the long-established custom of instrumentalists to make a distinction between musicians (in which class they include themselves) and singers—who may be taken seriously in terms of their own career and financial success, or dramatic ability or even physical opulence of sound—but who, in general, in terms of "musicianship" are to be regarded as but little in advance of a trained animal act.

This attitude is not altogether without justification, for certainly the great singers of the past one hundred years are acclaimed not for the impeccable qualities of their musicianship, but for the sheer physical beauty of their voices. Some of them may indeed have been fine musicians—but that is scarcely remembered, or even considered noteworthy. The great voices are infrequent enough to command adulation whenever or wherever they appear.

Now, if we take "musicianship" to mean sight-reading ability and a wide acquaintance with repertoire, on the whole I should think we would have to admit that professional instrumentalists are generally in advance of professional singers; and there probably is a similar status with regard to their amateur counterparts. There are understandable reasons for this. In the first place very few instrumentalists arrive at a professional career who did not begin their study well before ten years of age, frequently at five or six. The finger and eye techniques acquired at this age are almost as naturally learned as those of reading words and adding sums. On the other hand, the singer seldom discovers he has a voice until late in the teens; men frequently are in their twenties before the voice is sufficiently set physically to warrant *beginning* to study. It is scarcely surprising that singers should then be some years behind instrumentalists in sight-reading or repertoire. While one would not recommend the exclusive study of voice, it still is true that the singer is faced with a lot to learn, rather late in life, about vocal technique; and if his attention is fixed almost exclusively upon vocal *sound* rather than upon music theory, it may be regretted, but it is at least understandable.

In the second place, since the voice is not something one can approach with sight and touch, and manipulate to the limits of digital dexterity, it should not be maligned simply because it is not so facile an instrument as the piano, clarinet or violin.

Except for those born with absolute pitch, sight-reading for the singer is a complex business. It is not so simple as putting the next finger down. A good many of us, I suspect, could type sixty words a minute—but we would have a devil of a time sight-singing the comparable ratio of five notes per second. On the other hand, I have known two or three people who could sight-sing, using nonsense syllables, with very nearly this keyboard speed—and who made the most horrible sounds imaginable. It is a terribly difficult thing to sight-read and produce a beautiful sound while so doing.

There are a dozen additional reasons why it is difficult to be a satisfactory vocal "musician." They all have some validity, and we are entitled to find comfort in them equal only to our determination not to be mastered by them. For, whatever the difficulties, the singer who finally masters his musical craft finds a joy in music known only to a few of the very greatest instrumentalists.

I seldom heard Toscanini say anything, in the way of general criticism or exhortation to his orchestra, other than "Sing . . . sing!" and he said it scores of times at each rehearsal.

In the early days of our professional touring company, the first week or two of tour found the instrumentalists keeping their own company, and the singers, theirs. Along about the third week, we'd find the instrumentalists in the wings during a cappella sections of the program, or they'd be turning around on stage during moments they were not playing—shocked and amazed. Within a short time they'd be as interested in the singing as in their own playing, asking questions about breathing, intonation, "How do you get such and such a vowel?" and on into the night and the next county. Time after time, at the end of a tour, instrumentalists have said to me, "I've learned more about tone and phrasing and breathing from listening to this chorus night after night than I learned in years of study."

You people have the unqualified respect of the members of the Atlanta Symphony Orchestra—through such accomplishments as the Handel *Messiah* and Bach *St. John Passion.* I'm sure they think of you as musicians who also happen to sing quite well, and I'd like this conviction to grow stronger as we grow older.

One thought only: rhythmic problems are not primarily problems of reading—for us. We repeat things often enough so that it should be difficult for a sightless person to make more than a few mistakes. The primary problem is that of *feeling.* Now, that is a fairly indeterminate "term," but what I'm trying to say is that the "sense" of rhythm is a mighty complex thing: physical, physiological, psychological, visceral, etceteractual; and our problem as a group is not that of visual identification—two quarter-notes equal one half-note—but that of getting people to *experience* two quarter-notes simultaneously physically, physiologically, psychologically, viscerally and etceteractually. We turn the old grade school apology, "I know what it is, but I can't put it into words," all the way around. We can put rhythm into words—symbols—but we have no idea what it is. There are very few of us who do not have what is known as a "good ear" and a natural "sense of rhythm." (The latter might be better.) These are in line with a large part of folk- and jazz-musicians who have developed their skills and singing and playing "by ear," and some of whom, though unable to "read a note," are enormously skilled musicians. The extensive use of the piano at rehearsal is a determined and ardent attempt to make use of the innate musicality of our fellow singers.

As a matter of fact, far from relying too much upon our "ears" to guide us, I would surmise that *most* of us do not demand enough of our ears. For example, in the Cleveland Orchestra Chorus there were two members of the bass section, who since the time they became members of the Chorus, and in whatever literature, rarely used music after the second or third rehearsal. While the rest of the Chorus was reading week after week the same complexities of pitch or rhythm or text—frequently with recurrent errors as though it were the first time—these gentlemen, through a first and second reading and *listening,* had moved these sight-symbols into a sound-image. After all, isn't this where music begins? Isn't this what was in the composer's mind? Can you imagine with what reluctance and difficulty and compromise he translated his sound image into visual symbols?

There is no doubt in my mind that each of us could demand, and get, a great deal more from his ears, his musical memory and his innate-sense of rhythm:

It is frequently said—though exaggerated, in some respects it was true—that Serge Koussevitsky could not "read a score." Alongside some other technically gifted score-readers he was not so quick. His new scores were played for him by a series of remarkably gifted pianists. – But according to George Szell, Koussevitsky was one of the most gifted musicians of our era and built very probably the greatest orchestra the world ever had heard.

Don't just trust your ear . . . demand more of it.

R. S.

May 14, 1980

To whom it may concern –

The reasons one writes half-note triplets (♩ ♩ ♩) over a *maestoso* ¼ (♩ ♩ ♩ ♩) are three: (1) because he wants an even more majestic arching of his melodic materials; (2) because he wants a broadening of pulse and a disruption of expectability—particularly that of two half-notes; and (3) because he has in mind precisely three melodic notes or harmonics to carry him from the end of the preceding measure to the one following. Usually, of course, the reasons are combined, instinctive and instantaneous.

Given only three melodic/harmonic units to occupy four slow beats the principal possibilities are these:

Plans 1 and 2 obviously represent the reiterative predictability the composer is trying to escape; while Plans 3, 4 and 5 are alike in avoiding that predictability through syncopation, and one similar to Plan 6 in that they move a larger portion of that musical stress which always accompanies duration to the middle of the measure.

– But look, now, what happens if one graphs these various "three-some" plans:

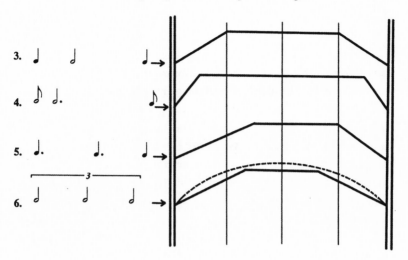

Only Plan 6 really suggests a broad arching and fractures predictability. (Plan 5, which is nearest Plan 6, is linked too severely to predictability precisely by its syncopation.)

Now, the execution of broad triplets against a *maestoso* 4/4 is as simple as one-two-three.

Just prior to the measure in question one postulates a division of triplets on each of the *maestoso* quarter-notes: four beats yielding 3 divisions each, a total of 12 pulses. When the measure arrives, the performer assigns to each of the half-note triplets (♩ ♩ ♩) 4 of these 12 pulses. Thus:

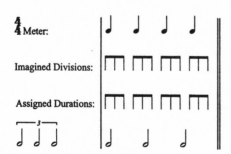

These, then, are the simple mechanics of execution—a lot simpler in face to face demonstration than in writing and reading. – But there they are. Ave atque vale.

R

October 16, 1996

Friends —

Isn't it remarkable what happens to musical understanding and the joys of making music when we finally reach the stage in rehearsal that *tempo*—just and proper—can begin to make its very special contributions?

(Parenthetically, the fulfillment of Barber's *Prayers of Kierkegaard,* Bartók's *Cantata Profana* and Vaughan Williams' *Dona Nobis Pacem*—if, indeed, we manage that within the first seven rehearsals of a new chorus—seems to me an accomplishment quite beyond a scorched-earth victory over any of the established full-evening oratorios.)

— But, back to *tempo.*

One of the early provocations I encountered, which gave *tempo* an intellectual independence and practical significance distinct from its usual associations with rhythm and metric proportions, was in the program notes for one of Igor Stravinsky's own recordings of his *Symphony of Psalms.* (Stravinsky's analysis and extensive introduction to the work appear to be reprinted from *Dialogues and a Diary* by I. S. and Robert Craft, Doubleday and Co., 1963.)

Get this:

"I was much concerned, in setting the Psalm verses, with problems of tempo. To me, the relation of tempo and meaning is a primary question of musical order, *and until I am certain that I have found the right tempo, I cannot compose.*"

Note! Not a key, not an interval or a scale, not a mode. Not a rhythmic motif, not a time-"signature." — Nothing tonal or metric or textual! — Simply such and such a hypothetical, theoretical, as yet silent divisibility of Time's continuum.

Now, note how this lines up with the following extract from Jean-Pierre Marty's *The Tempo Indications of Mozart,* Yale University Press, 1988.

In a letter to his father, dated Augsburg, October 24, 1777, Mozart writes the following about the way the daughter of Stein, the famous piano manufacturer, had played for him the previous night: "She will never achieve the most necessary, the hardest, and the main thing in music, namely Tempo, because from her very youth she made sure not to play in time. Mr. Stein and I have discussed this point a good two hours."

These few words, written in Mozart's own hand, have more significance than a superficial reading would yield.

First of all, let us note that in this letter, written in German, Mozart uses the Italian word, *tempo,* rather than a German equivalent. Actually, it is a word which is used in many languages, but its full significance is difficult to grasp at once. Tempo suggests an idea rather than expresses a clear concept. This vagueness, inherent in the word, is even increased in Mozart's letter by the three superlatives, with which he attempts to pin down the notion: "the most necessary," "the hardest," and finally "the main thing in music." But there is more to it.

Mozart says that because Miss Stein does not play in time, she will never achieve that mysterious element. Obviously he means by this that playing in time is not the same thing as playing in tempo, but that it is a necessary, though by no means sufficient, condition. Playing in time is the first prerequisite to achieve tempo, but playing in time does not automatically guarantee that tempo will be "achieved." A better performer than Miss Stein might very well "achieve" that tempo, which is not only "the most necessary, the hardest, and the main thing" in performing but in music itself.

For the first four weeks, friends, we rehearsed "in time." Just last Monday—for the first time—at several points with each of the words we began to achieve some of the fulfillments and joys of singing in Tempo.

The difference is roughly that of a chicken standing in the dust flapping its wings versus an eagle playing *Mario Andretti and the Red Baron* on his way home to mom and the kids.

Do we need a reminder that next Monday's rehearsal is our last prior to the week of scheduled performances? Ain't that a pity and a shame?

R

October 29, 1969

A bit of review, and one or two new items on phrasing:

Phrasing is a sort of punctuation. We use commas, parentheses, dashes, and assorted devices to group together those words in a sentence which make in passing a sense unto themselves, even though it be subordinate and qualifying to the sense of the whole. Similarly we use periods to terminate the independent ideas which go to make up a paragraph. These punctuations imply varying degrees of pause before proceeding to other, but related ideas.

The successful reading of poetry is the ability to comprehend (and convey) a whole architecture of word groupings—groupings not only of sense but also of rhythm and pitch, color and accent—so that truth and beauty become one. This is more than a little analogous to the successful performance of music.

How do we know what notes are to be grouped together in the musical phrase?

RHYTHM

We have discussed the rhythmic qualifications: how the extended notes in melodies are frequently ports of arrival, and the smaller notes which precede them the route and the labour which makes arrival possible and predictable, and which justifies a degree of repose before proceeding on the new journey.

Similarly, the so-called down-beat (which we are used to calling the "strong-beat") is also a port of arrival, but one which derives its meaning from the energy and thrust of the upbeat. In truer terms the up-beat is marked by the expenditure of energy and the down-beat by repose. (We ought simply to reverse the designations "weak" and "strong.")

TEXT

In some music the words of the text will impose their natural grouping upon musical phrasing though, as we have seen, this is seldom true of an intricate polyphonic work which may take only two or three words and weave them into a musical essay of ten to twelve minutes.

PITCH

In addition, however, to diagnostics of rhythm and text, are there any strictly tonal guideposts which will aid us in the grouping of notes in convincing phrases?

In a previous letter we have remarked that when a melody rises it marks in general an intensification of energy, and when it falls it signifies a relaxation. Therefore we must look for those melodic fragments which bear an upward thrust, and balance them sensitively and minutely with those fragments which signify respite.

Two, progression by scale-wise motion is a vastly different affair from progression by melodic leap. We must look for the succession of notes which are adjacent in pitch, and consider interruption of adjacency to mark a sort of parenthesis or indicate that we're off on a new or qualifying idea.

Three, the repetition of a short melodic pattern in an ascending or descending series we call sequence and imitation. Such imitation (even of fragments) is an "author"-ized guide to what the creator felt as inner or outer boundaries of his phrase.

In reverse summary:

(1) Explore the varieties of sequence and imitation—partial or complete, right side up or upside down, backwards or forwards—and let them be heard.

(2) Grant to adjacent scale-wise motion one sort of articulation and to its interruption another sort.

(3) Convey the inner and hidden dialogue, the ying and yang, the up and down, the question and answer, male and female, boy-girl, tension and relaxation.

(4) Be considerate of the text. It might just coincide with melodic or harmonic accentuation—and this moment is the Pentecost of song.

(5) An up-beat is a spring-board. The higher you have to bound the harder you must hit the board.

(6) Cultivate the forward look. Melody is a vagabond, incorrigibly searching the world for a place "really" to settle down. Even punctuation is not a period of retrospect, but of marshaling strength and scanning the horizon. The last note we sing is the one to which all others lead.

Have you recently considered our situation?

It is entirely possible that out of the whole history of the Western World Bach is the single greatest creative genius. Michelangelo might touch him in painting and sculpture (though I'd have other preferences here). Who would it be in literature?

And it's entirely possible that the *B Minor Mass* is his greatest achievement. (Some people might call for *St. Matthew*—but it's close enough for a fr'instance.)

It is the nature of music, unlike painting and most of literature, that its final creation is not its original creation. Music needs to be sounded, needs to be sung. It needs to be heard. In this sense the composer literally must leave his work to be finished by others. Namely us. Quel im-practique! As Jesus and Barnum have written: greater love hath no man . . . and there's one born every five thousand years.

Can you imagine Michelangelo asking us to come in and help finish the ceiling of the Sistine Chapel?

Us and our dirty little daubers!

R. S.

July, 1987

Guides to Bach-Phrasing

I

Loud mutilates –
Sustained-Loud annihilates.

We can accomplish nothing with regard to Baroque phrasing until we realize that a chorus of our size and general vocal background is precisely and irredeemably the wrong instrument for the performance of Bach's vocal works. The very things which a great symphonic chorus can do natively, uniquely and eloquently are the implacable enemies of Baroque sonority and texture.

– So, while we may study Bach's vocal masterpieces with pleasure, and with rewards to the mind and spirit otherwise unattainable, we do so in the constant danger of killing the thing we love.

The well-disciplined symphony chorus has two notable musical characteristics: it has a remarkable potential for *seamless sound,* and it has an exhilarating capacity for *collective vocal heroism.*

In the first instance, by the skillful overlapping of sectional dominances—or by means as simple as "staggered breathing"—the fluent symphonic chorus is capable of producing phrases that seemingly *never* end. Moreover, while the maximum sonority of the symphony orchestra must be accomplished by the accumulation of new families of instruments—with inevitable alterations in color and texture—the *crescendo* of the symphonic chorus inherently is without seam, mortise or terrace.—And the smoothness of its *diminuendo* can supply a veiled expiration of sound which for most ears in most halls will be all but imperceptible.

In the second instance, given humanity's timeless, instinctual search for community, and today's fashions in vocal style, the urge towards *collective vocal heroism* already may be irreversible.

Today's market features for the masses the mike-to-mouth electronic elephantiasis of hard-to-soft rock, while in the adjoining stall the upper classes ooh-ah-and-drool over vocal tumescence in its natural state, bidding outrageously for a share in the semi-private consumption of voice production by the liquid ton.—And since most of human life—from monasticism to ladies' bowling—appears to be a quest for something or someone to "belong to," the chorus of massed human voices is the primordial muse of "togetherness."

Should it be given, as in a Beethoven's *Ninth Symphony,* a text celebrating the *Freude* of *Bruder*-hood, the prospect of simultaneously hailing human virtue, winning a team-gold in the Vocal Olympics, and whelming a symphonic juggernaut apparently un-hibits the most repressed of larynges, unstints the most reluctant of volunteers and validates delusions of instant and humongous vocal grandeur.

– But it's all bad—for Bach.

Not seamlessness, but articularity,
Not homogeneity, but diversity,
Not universality, but relativity,
Not union, but independence.

Not mass, but motion,
Not size, but function,
Not how much, but how skillful,
Not how soon, but how varied.

Not solidarity, but transparency,
Not with a bang, but a whisper,
Not here and now, but where or when.

II

The assignment in "Bach-phrasing" is to discover and "give a voice" to *melodic function.*

To approach the matter metaphorically, melody is a sort of musical energy; and the long Bach line is a "stream" of musical energy which experiences a variety of subsidiary conditions of motion and repose in its search for a final resting place.

In theory at least (but, I believe also, in potential actual sound) there are only three possible melodic functions:

1. Initiating—or "departing from,"
2. Transmitting—or "passing through,"
3. Concluding—or "arriving at."

Of these three functions the middle one occasionally is missing altogether, so that—under the "microscope"—one frequently may find only "departing from" and "arriving at." On the other hand, one may discover from time to time a multiple of "passing throughs" between a "departing from" and an (however temporary) "arriving at."

One qualification: "initiating," in one significant respect, is a mis-leading term. Obviously there has to be a beginning note to any melody. But, it is seldom in the Bach line, it seems to me, that the melody flows prodigiously *from* the first note—as though it were some sort of generating "spring"—a source which originates, defines and dictates all that which is to follow. Rather, it is more nearly true in a theoretical sense—as it is more productive in a practical sense—that the *final* note is the generative one, the destination *toward which* every other note flows. For me, it is the note of *arrival*—together with the series of interim temporary reposes—which, more truly than the *initiating* note, helps us to discover *function*.

If, then, there are only three forms of melodic *energy* (or *function*) and if, even only occasionally, the middle one of these is absent, it follows that the *long Bach line* is a progressive accumulation of two- and three-note melodic cells or "syllables," at first combining to form four-, five- and six-note "words" and, at last, compounding into "qualifying phrases" and eventual "sentences." Our responsibility, as performers, is to discover and to sound these minutiae of motion.

In an instrument substantially incapable of *crescendo* and *diminuendo*—like the early pipe-organ (devoid of "expression" devices)—the beginnings and endings of melodic "syllables" can be indicated only by *cessation of sound,* however minimal or momentary. Theoretically, if one were responsible only for a single-line melody, even were it composed of a steady stream of staccato eighth-notes, one could increase or decrease tempo at will, and thus make smaller or larger silences between notes to suggest interior "syllabic" groupings.

In point of fact, however, Bach's musical language is primarily a contrapuntal one, involving two to five or even eight lines simultaneously, so that tempo changes which conceivably could make one line clearer or more expressive might at the same moment violate the clarity and expressivity of all other lines.

In performance, therefore, one is obliged to maintain generally a basic and constant pulse, within whose regularity one can suggest syllabic groupings principally by varying what is called articulation: the nearly infinite scale of durations between *sostenuto* and *staccato*. (– Larger durations of non-sound equalling more extended qualities of repose.)

Moreover, one never encounters with Bach a melodic line with unrelieved reiterative pulse division. (– An unending parade, for instance, of sixteenth-notes.) Melodic line of Bach's quality and interest will always have a variety and balance of individual durations—just as it will have variety of pitch and linear direction. (And, as will be noted later, extended duration—even of notes of identical pitch—will imply "arrival at" and momentary repose.)

The first of the ways, then, of shaping melodic "syllables" into "words" into "qualifying phrases" into "sentences" into "paragraphs" is to control the amount of silence between successive notes—even to the minutiae of employing numerous varieties and durations of staccato notes.

Most musical instruments, however, including the human voice, have the capability not only of producing pitches of shorter or longer duration, in quicker or slower tempi, but have also the capacity of varying their *amplitude*—of producing them loudly or quiet. – And a subtle and delicate varying of *dynamics* can also be used to suggest the "syllabic sequence" of a musical line. The terms "subtle" and "delicate" are critical, because we are not concerned with the dramatic explosions of sound (or implosions of silence) characteristic of more homophonic, dramatic or exhibitionistic music. We are suggesting that minuscule and transitory *crescendi* and *diminuendi* can be used along with varieties of articulation, punctuation and silence to create the gathering web of tonal tracery which is Bach's genius and our delight. – And we are cautioning ourselves that these inflections of dynamics must be of such subtlety that were we to add them personally to our vocal parts, we should probably exaggerate them—and others certainly would.

III

Two questions remain:

First, how do we recognize these melodic "molecules," these two-, three-, or four-note syllables that should be grouped according to their *initiating/transmitting/concluding* functions? And second, is it possible to be somewhat more specific as to exactly *how* to "voice" them?

Recognition:

1. *In general*—weak-beat leads to strong-beat, weak part-of-beat leads to strong part-of-beat, and weak part-of-measure leads to strong part-of-measure. – And the note of "arrival" is then punctuated by an appropriate "comma" of silence—or near-silence.

    This is the familiar "cross-bar" or "cross-beat" phrasing; and, while it is not unexceptionable, it is so frequently applicable that it may take the insistence of sequential repetition or persistent text-underlay to contradict it.

2. *In general*—notes of short duration lead to notes of longer duration (after which, again, there is an implied "comma" of appropriate proportion).

3. *In general*—notes of diatonic or chromatic adjacency are to be understood as belonging to a common "syllabic cell," while "leaps" or "skips" more frequently will be found to imply seams or joints *between* cells. The *interruption of tonal adjacency,* therefore, usually will signal the beginning of a new grouping, however minor or auxiliary. (Triads used as melodic cells—as, for instance, the initiating motif of a fugue subject—are obvious exceptions.)

4. *Frequently,* also—*change of melodic direction* will be associated with the beginning of a new auxiliary grouping. It may be worthy of note here that the *seam* between two "syllables" identifiable only by change of direction seldom allows the luxury of a full "comma," unless the pivot point also coincides with a note of longer duration. Particularly in rapid and regular sequential accompaniment patterns, a sensitively placed *staccato* may have to suffice. Or, it is possible that this sort of obscure melodic syllabification can best be indicated only by subtle and transitory changes in dynamics.

To repeat: the four melodic conditions which aid in the recognition and performance of the subsidiary cells of a Bach line are:

1. Cross-bar and cross-beat groupings.
2. Short durations moving towards—and serving—longer durations.
3. Interruption of melodic adjacency.
4. Change of melodic direction.

When more than one voice (or line) is present, however, it is important to recall that—except in the case of final cadences—the "commas" which signal the conclusion of melodic cells *never* can be allowed to slow tempo or delay subsequent pulse. Commas *always* must borrow their time from the cell which precedes them, not from the cell which follows. – Otherwise, a chaotic dislocation and deformation of other voices will ensue.

To recapitulate:

Two of the guides to the cellular components of the Bach line are metric, and two are melodic.

METRICALLY:

1. So-called "weak"-beats (or portions thereof) are really the *active* portions of metrical function; they lead to the so-called "strong"-beats (or portions thereof) which are, in fact, elements of metrical repose.

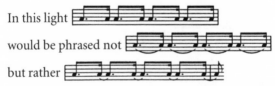

2. Shorter metrical units lead towards larger metrical units more frequently than the reverse.

would be phrased not

but rather

MELODICALLY:

3. Interruption of melodic adjacency frequently will imply a grouping.

Thus,

will seldom be phrased as above, but rather as

4. Change of direction frequently will imply a grouping.

Thus

will seldom be phrased as above, but rather as

It will be noted in both of the *melodic* examples (3 and 4) that more than one principle of grouping is operative. (The "cross-beat/cross-bar" principle is involved in both.) – Such multiplicity will be found to be true in all but a few actual instances. When two or three principles are involved, it not frequently happens that they will suggest different—even contradictory—groupings. One will then have to decide—usually upon the basis of general texture or the movement of more important voices—which principle will "rule."

The remaining question has to be with how these cells/syllables/molecules (– These terms have been used interchangeably.) are to be "voiced." – And most of that question already has been answered indirectly, if not exhaustively.

The method most appropriate to both of the metrical principles is the use of actual *cessation* of sound, or a significant diminution thereof, to suggest what has been termed a "comma."

It also has been noted, particularly in the case of rapidly moving accompanimental sequences, that subtle and evanescent *crescendi* and *diminuendi* can be used to suggest the cellular components of longer lines.

What has to be reiterated at this point is our opening text: "*Loud* mutilates . . . *Sustained-Loud* annihilates." *Everything* is improved by light, pointillistic *non-sostenuto* singing. Each section of the chorus must be absolutely precise as to pitch, time, vowel, timbre and dynamic; and no note—including very long ones—can be sustained in the sense of operatic vocalism. The more voices there are on a part, the less loud each voice can sing, and the more pointillistic (*staccato*) each pitch must be. Inversely, the fewer the number of voices assigned to each part the more "normal" and "soloistic" vocalism may be—so long as one understands "normal" and "soloistic" as the sort of singing which can produce pitches of god-like precision and ineffable beauty at super-sonic speed and at a dynamic which is a declaration of dependence rather than a double-dare.

We should also acknowledge that part of our problem in the performance of Bach's sacred cantatas and oratorios is associated with text. This has no reference to enunciation, but rather to *our* interpretations of the Christian or Judeo-Christian scriptures—personal or inherited. That is to say, if one is thoroughly convinced that "a mighty fortress is our God" should really be sung "a guided missile is the Lord" (" . . . marching as to war"), then he may feel obliged to use his how-great-thou-art Voice. – But if "ein feste Burg" can be considered "an enduring citadel . . . a secure refuge . . . a comforting haven . . . " then one may view with sympathy and even thanks the ruminative, contemplative participation of neighboring voices, weaving strands of mutual comfort and hope.

IV

In conclusion a word should be said concerning rehearsal techniques for the learning of Bach's works. In my experience, unless *all* rehearsal procedures derive from the desire to develop vocal lightness [with] "super-human" precision as regards pitch and articulation, one finds that he is defeated—and defeats also the music—by trying to clamp a diesel locomotive on the gondola of a lighter-than-air-balloon. Buoyant, facile, slightly-staccato singing on nonsense syllables—after a reading or two employing the count-singing devices—will build the necessary disciplines and musical texture—and (in my experience) nothing else will. One adds text only late in the rehearsal process, and only after it has been carefully phonetically disciplined *apart from the music.*

I've just come upon a small s'pose.

S'pose for a moment that we could excise Weight-Lifting from the events of the Vocal Olympics—and substitute Musical Feathers.

S'pose the gold medal were given not for kilograms of decibels, but rather to the team which could keep afloat the greatest number of Musical Feathers. S'pose those feathers could pilot themselves lightly through Time and Tonal Space in the most exacting, elaborate and labyrinthine of contrapuntal maneuvers, never at less than the full speed of sound, and never obstructing, obscuring or deflecting other feathered rights of flight, until they finally floated to common rest in a scarcely audible millisecond of mutual fulfillment.

S'pose what this world really needs is a still small voice?

RS

January 14, 1986

Friends –

In a consideration of the facets of *phrasing* it is helpful, it seems to me, to think of melody as musical *energy*. The child's definition is not utter nonsense: "melody is a note looking for a place to sit down." Melody, as an abstraction, lies in the quality of tension or relaxation passed by each note to its successor (or received from its predecessor) until the musical sentence is complete and the moment of rest occurs.

Obviously, these moments of rest are also of varying duration and energetic quality: "sentences" can be added together to form "paragraphs," and "paragraphs" to form "essays" until the symphony—or mass—is ended (and we all go home).

Given the fulfillment of certain technical aspects of music-making—good intonation, good sound and good metrics—a very large part of the "personal," "creative" and "artistic" side of music-making lies in "phrasing." In a not-too-limited sense, great phrasing *is* great music-making—as well, fortunately, as an accomplishment accessible even to (as they have it in New Haven) "such as we."

One seeks to voice a succession of differing pitches and durations so that:

(1) Each is given a function—satisfying and illuminating, and
(2) One arrives at a resting place with a sense of proportion and completion.

Within the long musical sentence there are, of course, a series of miniature phrases, each also characterized and defined by factors of relative intensification and relaxation. Such miniature groupings ("melodic molecules") may be as short as two or three successive notes, or as long as six or occasionally nine, but even these latter extended groupings will be more instructively perceived as composites of twos and threes.

Abstractions are seldom without a set of contradictory data, but I have found it helpful to theorize that there are but three "postures" (or conditions) of melodic "energy":

(1) "Departing from . . . "

(2) "Passing through . . . " and

(3) "Arriving at . . . "

Or more simply, but less precisely, "beginning, middling and ending."

The means of melodic expression (phrasing) are two:

(1) Variations in *dynamics*.

This can occur over shorter or longer periods of time—from abrupt and temporary stress to various patterns of *crescendo* and *diminuendo*.

(2) Variations in *duration* (always within the prescribed notation).

We know this as "articulation," and we are expected to range from *legatissimo* through *sostenuto* and *marcato* to *staccatissimo* in order to suggest the groupings which add up to good phrasing.

Obviously, one does not have to choose between a variation in dynamics or one in duration, but, depending upon musical style and texture, uses both means simultaneously and in varying proportions.

Now, what was suggested, at last night's rehearsal, was a series of "guides" to Baroque phrasing: ways to recognize the molecular structure of Baroque melody so that the two-, three- and five- to six-note cells can be appropriately voiced.

It is suggested that we look and listen for:

(1) The presence and function of the *anacrusis*—or of cross-beat and cross-bar relationships.

"Anacrusis" is Greek in derivation, and means substantially "up + to strike." (Our "up-beat" is about as close as one can come in meaning.)

For whatever complex of psychological, physiological and neurological reasons, given a repetitive pulse, the human mind appears to desire to group that reiteration into patterns of strong and weak, or heavy and light. (The clock does not say "tick-tick" or "tock-tock.")—And we are advised that the normal, more frequent, and more satisfying grouping is light to strong, or up-beat to down-beat, rather than the reverse. Note that it is not only whole measures which have heavy and light components, but that the beats themselves also have heavier or lighter portions; and these also are more appropriately grouped light to heavy.

(2a) In a succession of notes of differing durations, the preferred grouping most frequently will be short to long, rather than long to short. Regardless of the major metric organization or "signature," small units will want to be treated as "pick-ups" or "up-beats" to a succeeding or larger unit, rather than vice versa. This, of course, is very analogous to the anacrustic relationship, in that the short note is the note of "departure from" and the following long note is the note of "arrival at. . . . "

(2b) Given a melody made up of a succession of rapid notes of the same denomination (a running phrase of sixteenth notes, for instance) an interruption of that regularity will almost always imply a natural grouping—just after the first of the "arrival" notes.

(3a) There are different "energy values," for adjacent (scale-wise, "diatonic") melodic motion and melodic "skips" or "leaps." (– Just as ascending melodic motion is an order of melodic energy which differs from descending motion.) In general, an interruption of melodic adjacency will also imply the presence of a molecular seam or caesura.

(3b) Finally, a part of the composer's craft is working with terse two-to-four-note melodic motives (as well as longer "themes"). Occasionally these motives are persistent and abundant enough to be classed as cliches or stereotypes. Still, one will want to acknowledge their presence and function as molecular units by giving them appropriate dynamic contour and articulation.

We've identified this type of phrasing as "basic Baroque," and it functions supremely well in that literature. – But, since there's no Mozart, Beethoven or Brahms 'thout'n Bach and Handel, and no Hindemith or Stravinsky 'thout'n all the above, it's surprising what riches a sensitivity to the foregoing "guides" can add even to today's music.

Peace—but just enough.

R

QUIET SINGING AND COUNT-SINGING

. . . it (is) such a waste to pour vocal energy into wrong notes.

. . . my first caution is: stay away from text until notes and phrasing are right and ineradicable.

February 16, 1968

Years ago, before touring had taught me differently, I used to wonder how one could keep a performance fresh night after night for seventy or a hundred nights in a row. The answer is, of course, that great music feeds back more than it takes. First performances are the things to dread, not the third or the ninetieth or the one-hundred-and-fiftieth.

Unless one has had this experience, I doubt that it can be understood. Part of the gain, obviously, is simple security. One knows what notes are next; there is no stumbling or surprise. Added to that is the sense of proportion as regards both phrase and the major movements. This means that the singer has found a natural vocal pacing for the work; he doesn't wear his voice to rags in the first ten minutes. – Nor does he have to be terribly conscious of avoiding misuse of his voice. The technique has found its own specific gravity. All the technical detail of playing and singing begins to sound; dynamics cease to be "manufactured"— they become organic, as also do tone-color and tempi.

More and more it seems to me that great performance (maybe, also, great creation in art) is very closely related to the reflective qualities. I am sure that there is a spiritual calm which does not emasculate spiritual urgency. That is to say, one can gallop off in all directions at once, or one can rush iron-willed down a one-way street, or one can find within his deepest and quietest thinking the image of action—and it could be a still-life. What all of us are after in art is the release to things of the spirit. I doubt that that ever can be accomplished without first technical security. – And I also doubt that technical security itself is ever achieved without a sure stillness of the mind and soul. Most choral rehearsals are, quite unnecessarily, a screaming bedlam of tortured throats. Sing, sing, sing! – wrong notes, right notes, but sing.

Until the work becomes clear in the mind, how can anyone sing "full" voice? In recent weeks it has seemed such a waste to pour vocal energy into *wrong* notes. Right notes will demand enough of it. If we consistently begin from the thinking end—rather than the doing end—then we don't trample all over our own big feet.

One hums quietly, as though to himself, and the imagination is free to consider matters of proportion, form and truth in intonation. Bit by bit the dream becomes flesh, and song becomes a "living thing." – And what this last leads us to is the possibility that the reflective qualities are not limited to the products of marathon repetition of performances—but are equally the product of quiet, sensitive, unruffled preparation.

It is also this factor which prompts me to write a few words about one aspect of our musical technique whose eventual mastery I should warmly endorse. Possibly as a result of our few rehearsals together it seems to me at this writing that the element in music which is most productive of poise and naturalness and freedom in musical performance, which somehow bases and relates the other elements, which calls attention to itself only in absence or imperfection, is rhythmic security. It is the element we strive to discover in order that we may forget. It is that which must be mastered so that it can be taken for granted.

Consider for a moment how all of our musical elements and choral techniques depend upon it.

There is no such thing as *good intonation* between voice lines that do not arrive or quit their appointments upon mathematically precise, but effortless schedule.

The principal problem in *enunciation* is not that of acquiring a common vocabulary of phonetic building blocks (that is a necessary and relatively simple acquisition), but of placing these blocks in their precise approved slots in time.

Similarly, *sonority* and *color* are impossible to achieve among 70 voices whose rhythmic progress is casual, erratic and aimless. The matter that breaks bridges is a company of troops marching in strong cadence. That which allows us to sing "over our heads" and beyond our ranges is the support of others near us obedient to a simultaneous instant of attack and an inexorable momentum.

Even *melody* and the sense of phrase (which, by rise and fall of pitch is somehow representative of tension in space—a vertical element counterbalanced by the horizontal tension in time which is rhythm)—even melody depends for its grace and sense of direction upon the steady flow of time beneath it.

All this—and probably more—is why, week after week, we have been struggling to build a sturdiness of rhythmic purpose. Freedom will be its issue—freedom to make the music naturally, humanly and with a full heart. Text will come strongly and clearly. Sonority and color will add to structure—and not at the point of a gun. Harmony can be a language incapable of misunderstanding. Melody will have, no doubt, a more firma *terra* above which to wing and trace in grace its subtler sympathies.

R. S.

October 2, 1991

Friends –

Why is quiet singing so essential to the learning process in choral-singing? Let us "count the ways":

1. It saves voice.

At full voice a three-hour rehearsal on a *Missa Solemnis* at *any* stage of the learning process is cruel and unusual punishment. – But at an early stage in the learning process it can reduce the most secure of vocal techniques to a despairing hoarseness.

Vocal beauty is in large measure a "gift," sometimes a matter of heritage. Vocal stamina is in large measure a matter of learning and technique. The world's most gifted and learned singers simply could not subject their voices to an unremitting stentorian three-hour battle with Mahler's *Veni, Creator Spiritus* or Beethoven's *Et vitam venturi* and expect to make tomorrow evening's recital a thing of beauty. Even more should those of us with lesser gifts guard whatever vocal gold we have.

Now, unremitting quiet singing in the higher ranges also can be tiring to the voice. – But the bass and alto voices seldom—if ever—face this problem; the soprano voice can be relieved by judicious octave transposition; and the tenor voice can switch to a mixture or *falsetto* vocalization to avoid fatigue. (Actually, many voice teachers advise that careful and frequent use of the falsetto or "head" register—as in our few moments of warm-up exercises—will in time extend the operable upward range of the voice and add to its beauty. – My ears tell me that this has happened not only over the years of our working together—but that it happens anew every season.)

2. Quiet singing in rehearsal establishes (and maintains) the proper order of necessities in the learning process. These are:

a. Pitch
b. Rhythm
c. Enunciation
d. Dynamics/Vocal Color

Nothing will wear out a voice or vocal technique quite so rapidly as attempting to sing at full vocal thrust *before* one is absolutely secure as to pitch, rhythm and enunciation. (One can smell the cords burning.) Quiet count-singing, interspersed with nonsense-syllable vocalization—more quickly than any other method I ever have met—offers the quickest and most secure approach to pitch and rhythm. Even here, as we experienced on Monday night, we occasionally have to take some harmonies out of their metric context, and tune them slowly and in isolation.

It is fair to say, I think, that in general the teaching of solo voice does not put primary—or even secondary—emphasis upon intonation. This is not surprising. For one thing, the successful professional solo singer may *never* sing without accompaniment. She—or he—will have, almost without exception, a keyboard instrument or an orchestra to provide tonality and harmony. Moreover, with the exception of music for commercial entertainment—the sequence of fads and styles which are linked umbilically to electronic amplification—the pay-off in the field of "art" music is for vocal size, if at the same time the voice can retain beauty.

On the other hand, even though a chorus may sing with a symphony orchestra—and experience some supports as regards tonality—it still has to satisfy its own inward harmonic relationships. Without such guides as tuned and stable strings and keyed or valved winds it has to be as conscious of intonation as a first-rate orchestra—which is careful indeed. – So, intonation is properly the first concern of group-singing.

The second concern, of a special necessity, must be metrics and rhythm. That special necessity is the inescapable conflict which exists between normal speech rhythms and durations and the abnormal durations which are imposed by musical prescription, invention and development. For example, nobody thinks for a moment that it is peculiar that, while in speech the words "dona nobis pacem" present six syllables of generally equal duration lasting approximately one and one-half seconds (or one-quarter of a second per syllable), beginning at m. 39 of the soprano part in the *Dona nobis pacem* of Bach's *B Minor Mass* the first syllable of "do-na" is allotted approximately one-quarter of a minute (sixty times its normal speech duration) and twenty pitches, while the last syllable is given slightly over one second and one pitch. – And anyone at all familiar with the operas of Gilbert and Sullivan knows how confounding—and hilarious—can be the results of accelerated musical rhetoric.

In my experience, the speediest rehearsal device to achieve metrical accuracy of enunciation is to rehearse text and count-singing simultaneously: one-half of each section on text, the other half singing "by the numbers"—plus its *vice versa*.

Last of all, it seems to me, comes control of dynamics and vocal color. Most of us have heard it said, in deprecation of the choral art, that, as versus the symphony orchestra the chorus is a "mono"-chromatic or even "colorless" instrument. In some aspects there is truth in this: the chorus has not the range of pitch—from contra-bassoon to piccolo, or the range of dynamics—from whispered string diminuendo to brass and percussion fortiss*iss*imo, or the complex of audible hues available to objects bowed, blown or battered.

What the chorus does have, in addition to language's magnificent mélange of meaning, motivation and memory, is the sheer audio-kaleidoscope of speech itself, relieved of meaning and dictionary equivalents. Each line of the choral palette is changing color with each of the tens of thousands of syllables assigned to it. Clarity of enunciation not only clarifies "meaning"; it enhances and enriches choral "color."

– But there are two further enrichments. The first is the ability of the human voice to move from "dark" sound to "bright" sound, from extremes of "hooti-ness" to shrillness and stridor.

The second is even more important to the chorus's ability to communicate. It is the combination of textual clarity with a virtuosic *control of dynamics* which allows a chorus to become convincingly and inescapably communicative. This control of dynamics must operate on two levels. The first is that of large-scale crescendo and diminuendo, and block sections of loudness and quietness. – And the second—and more difficult—is the nuance of syllabic stress: the re-introduction back into a musical line's arching dynamics the urgent but minuscule emphases of speech as *meaning*. Herein, and with great difficulty, the chorus becomes the overwhelming personality and purveyor of the composer and his text.

(On to further rationale for quiet singing at rehearsals:)

3. At dynamic levels of *p* and *pp* everyone is able to hear other parts, other factors in the tonal texture, and find his harmonic function. When one sings loudly one hears only oneself. (Most voice teachers would say that one cannot hear oneself properly at any time anyway.) If one's neighbor sings loudly, one hears only that neighbor. (If he were secure, the neighbor could afford to sing quietly. As frequently as it is his assertion that his and his alone is the only right

pitch, it is a cry for "help!") One simply cannot find function unless everyone sings quietly enough to seek it together.

4. Vocal excess at learning rehearsals (or at performances) always is accompanied by one or more of the following:

a. Disturbances of intonation. Every pitched musical instrument (except a few percussion instruments) can be "forced" out of tune by too much pressure of air, bow or fist. Even the piano will lose intonation during a strenuous rehearsal of a dramatic concerto. – And the pipe organ will respond differently to differing wind pressures. The voice is even more vulnerable to forcing.

b. Distortion of voweling—which will make it impossible to achieve sectional unison.

c. Introduction of wobbles and unacceptable vibrato characteristics, which similarly fracture unison tuning and quality. Surely, some vibrato is as present in beautiful singing as it is in beautiful string playing. – But it should be used as Pablo Casals is reported to have used it: as a variable to both speed and width—depending upon the nature, style and period of the music.

d. Disturbances of vocal color. Just as surely as forcing disturbs intonation, voweling and vibrato, so also it affects color and impedes sectional unison—which is the *sine qua non* of good choral discipline.

5. A quiet, unforced, "reflective" sort of singing at rehearsals not only allows one to hear other voice parts (No. 3 above), but it also allows one to attend to other aspects of one's own responsibilities. Singing is a very complicated and sophisticated process; and if one is not held responsible at every moment of every rehearsal for every factor in the finished choral product (dynamics and color, for instance) one can attend to the niceties of placement of final consonants, or the phonation of foreign-language sounds (as the complications of enunciation begin to be introduced into the learning process.)

6. Quiet singing facilitates the achievement of proper vocal balances. Most choruses, if they are sensitive to structural or harmonic balances at all (and, still, very few are), attempt to achieve it by asking for certain passages or vocal parts to be sung more strenuously than the other vocal parts. This may aid in establishing momentary and appropriate sectional prominence, but it runs the risk of all the above dangers of loud or forced singing.

What always has seemed to me the better plan to achieve structural (polyphonic) balances and harmonic proportion is to move voices to where the dike is leaking; to achieve balance by the *number of voices* on a passage or harmonic factor—along with a careful editing of proportional dynamics—so that no vocal section is faced with the necessity—or probability—of forcing.

7. A last rationale for quiet rehearsing: In general, the individualizing characteristics of different voices are not nearly so prominent at dynamic levels of *pp*

and *p* as they are at levels of *f* and *ff*. When voices sing together quietly with precisely the same consonants, vowels and articulation—as they do in count-singing—not only is each person's performance clarified and sanitized, but a unison sound (pitch and rhythm) occurs as if by magic.

What has to happen from then on is that this unison becomes capable of being increased to appropriate dynamic levels by gradual increments, and transferred to the specified sounds of speech. *At no time in the learning process* can quiet singing on numbers or unanimous nonsense syllables be completely abandoned. It must be used simultaneously with the first ventures into text enunciation and placement. – And in the final mastery of expressive dynamics, count-singing, released from its chains of quietness, is the only secure method by which one can discover precisely where and at what rate of increase or decrease how much of sound is appropriate.

So there. I had in mind to send this letter with an exploration of the human "why?" and "whuh-for" of unison. – But if Nola doesn't get this in the next fifteen minutes you won't get it at all.

Sh . . . !

R

October 7, 1991

Friends –

In last week's letter enumerating the benefits of quiet count-singing as a rehearsal technique, one of the most salutary was omitted. It is this: if one begins with this device, and carries it along as companion to the acquisition of good enunciation and volume controls, it should completely eliminate the trauma of having to *un-learn.*

A chorus the size of a symphony-chorus is a gummy mudder anyway. With scores (or hundreds) of voices bouncing off the walls at *mezzo-forte* to *forte,* boo-boo and blooper, fluff, flub and peccadillo not only have a place to hide, but time to establish permanent residence. If what is desired of the final product is a colossal sang-bang—goody for them!

Our position is a little different. Most of us, I think, would agree that music has meaning beyond sheer auditory entertainment—however mysterious or difficult to verbalize. – But we also realize that these subtle significances are "unlocked" only by those who undertake to fulfill the creator's (composer's) prescriptions. The dove (of mystical revelation) does not descend to a dirty perch.

At this point we begin to touch on that which draws us all together for seventy to ninety nights a year.

In addition to basic physical survival, a very large part of the human experience is a search for two conditions: individuality and community. The thrust of early childhood is away from total dependency to independence: ". . . wanna do it myself!" The teen-ager swivels between home-present and home-future. To prove "independence" of the former he/she may become total slave to a tyranny of fashion-wear, hair-style, video-cult and ghetto-blaster. – And most of the world's religions—certainly *other people's* and *foreign* religions—are evidences of the somewhat more adult endeavor to seek an adequate amount of personal meaning to life's mysteries and sorrows plus, also, a community of ethical behaviour which may reduce some of its pains and injustices.

Animal life—including human-animal-life—desires to herd and flock together; to swarm, school, cluster, huddle and congregate together. Enter: the performing arts. Enter, as queen of them all: the volunteer—the amateur—chorus.

How many human activities are there which can match it for dignity of community product and depth of personal satisfaction? No instrument so direct as the human voice. No art-form so rich as music in indefinabilities. No group-action so free from potential corruptions of professionalism and prostitution. An optimum of common effort with a maximum of self-respect.

The musical means for all this is called *unison*: singleness of sound. "E pluribus unum": out of many, one. As sure as *maters* stand and *Nocturnes* come in threes, singleness of sound begins with the listening, and listening begins with quiet singing.

In the beginning . . . sh . . . !

R

September 20, 1979

Dear People –

At the start of rehearsal #1 I said that our rehearsal techniques were predicated on two principles: first, we want to save voices; and second, we desire to progress in so careful and simple a fashion that nothing need ever be *un*learned.

Nothing could be simpler than "count-singing." It is the single most effective rehearsal technique for the introduction and quick mastery of new or unfamiliar choral materials. It is, of course, the practice of singing each vocal line not upon the text apportioned to it, but upon the appropriate beat-numbers, together with the divisions of pulse on the syllables "and" or "and-uh." Thus:

"one and two"··"and three and-uh one."

Think of how many important things are accomplished thereby.

1. There is absolutely no doubt as to the instant—the beat or its fraction—on which sound is supposed to begin.

2. There can be absolute certainty as to the instant upon which sound is supposed to stop—upon which silence (rest value) is supposed to begin.

3. Because each pitch is articulated for as many pulse divisions as its duration specifies (a whole note will have usually eight 1/8th phonations) the pitch itself is defined 8 times per measure—which is the world's greatest aid to intonation.

4. Since, in two-, four- or more-part writing, pitches may be of varying length in the different voices, count-singing on the pulse divisions aligns all counterpoint in meticulous detail, and allows harmonic changes to be precise and apparent to all.

5. Since problems of crescendo and diminuendo are problems of amount and timing (of "how much" or "how little," "how rapidly" or "where") the sung 1/8th or 1/16th note pulse offers the only convenient time-scale by which to measure increase or decrease of sonority.

6. The alternations of English vowels "uh, ee, oo, oh-uh" (as in "one, two, three, four") give a range of vowel sounds wide enough to avoid tiring the voice (unless done to psychotic excess), and wide enough, more importantly, to stimulate a continuity of tonal core (vocal color, vocal line) through changing pitches and vocal ranges.

All these things "count-singing" does. It forces the common perception of Pitch and Duration; and thus is the principal means to the clarification of counterpoint and harmony. It facilitates the control of Dynamics and Articulation—and, thereby, expressivity. It feeds variety of vowel and successive redefining of pitch into vocal line, and thus reinforces tonal qualities. And—when merged gradually with text qualities and word disciplines—it finally teaches people to sing together the text from which the composer drew his inspiration.

It is the simplest of tools—and the most productive.

– Surely, among the reasons we are not using it well is its relative unfamiliarity to one-third of this year's membership.

Surely, another is the relative unfamiliarity of being required to discipline tone, time, sonority and the elements of speech to such standards of detail and precision.

– But these are not even the principal sources of our slowness in rehearsal. The real source is sloth from Monday at 10 P.M. to the following Monday at 7 P.M. What's being learned the other 165 hours per week? How much personal work is each singer doing at home?

If a first-rate professional orchestra—familiar with the work—is willing to commit four rehearsals to their collective disciplines and the refinements of ensemble, does this tell us anything as to how much time the volunteer singer should spend in *self*-preparation if he has only *five* or *six ensemble* rehearsals with his vocal collaborators prior to meeting with his orchestra?

Not many years ago it would not have been surprising had choral discipline and nuance excelled upon occasion instrumental cohesion and expressivity. Dear People: it's a whole new ball game! – More home work!

R.

October 29, 1991

Since you asked for it –

RUDIMENTS OF CHORAL SINGING: DYNAMICS, ACCENTUATION AND ARTICULATION

Our entire initial rehearsal methods are geared towards learning pitches and rhythms as quickly and as effortlessly as possible. Count-singing and quiet rehearsal are calculated to accomplish these things—but they are not the final product.

That "final product" has two additional elements: first, a convincing over-all profile of dynamic flow and ebbs and, second, a multitude of inner accentuations and shadings—thrust and withdrawal, bump and run, shadow and flicker—each vocal section alive to its particularity and creative responsibility. – And, obviously, I was a flat-out failure at last night's rehearsal insofar as getting our chorus to achieve both the large dynamic contours and the precisions of articulation and accentuation which make for textual clarity and rhythmic propulsion.

After the right notes—there's still all of art.

Unwavering and purposive control of dynamics and accentuation is the means by which a series of notes becomes a musical phrase. – Which means that it is the principal means through which musical "meaning" (whatever that means) is achieved.

Expressive dynamics—the *unceasing* thither and hither of *crescendo* and *diminuendo*—are also the medium through which a choral conglomerate becomes a convincing musical personality. Only under the rarest of circumstances may a musical phrase be left *senza espressione:* without some shaping of dynamics.

It is not enough that we sing *piano* or *forte;* we are obliged to sing *within piano* or *forte.* Merely from *ppp* to *fff* there are no less than eight hierarchies of dynamics: *ppp, pp, pmp, mf, f, ff, fff.* – And within each of these eight categories there can be an infinity of shadings before one arrives at the adjacent level. The choral sound must be constantly on the "wax" or the "wane."

No note or syllable—however short—must be allowed to pass without attention to two factors:

First, its independent profile (its is-ness): a combination of accentuation and enunciative constituents which give it an identity and its "place" in time.

Second, its function in the larger musical phrase—whether it rides a wave which advances or one which recedes.

This is the most complex of the choral singer's disciplines. The myriad sounds of speech (with which no instrumentalist has to deal), all of language's natural rhythms and accentuations make constant war against the tonal and metric prescriptions of music. The choral singer has to subject the linguistic habits of a life-time to the artificial specifications and artistic implications of the composer. – And not until she/he and their collaborators are able to combine discipline and creativity does the chorus become "a living soul."

Consider for a moment the "independent profile" mentioned above. Normal speech patterns have a rise and fall in both pitch and dynamics. When we speak we make certain sounds higher or lower than others, and we make some sounds louder or quieter than others, for clarification or emotional emphasis. Some sounds of speech are also longer or shorter than others—but in no way as extremely disproportionate as some of music's textual demands.

In music's attempt to create a suitable auditory (emotional/psychological/aesthetic) environment for a text, though all sorts of dislocations and distortion of normal speech rhythm and accentuation may occur, the gifted composer still may manage to "personify" or illumine his text.

Such personification and illumination are by *musical* means. With few exceptions this means that the customary rhythms, pitches, durations and accentuations of speech must be replaced by *musical* rhythms, pitches, durations and accentuations. One moves from the "elegance" of the spoken word to the "revelation" of its musical manifestation. (In our time even the spoken word is nearly a lost art, as well as one particularly vulnerable to collective gabble.)

In musical time each note becomes a musical "event"—to be slurred or accentuated, to be increased or decreased, to be lengthened or darkened—or any combination of the above. – But each syllable also bears an additional respon-sibility. It has to provide a discriminating attention to its function as melody or accompaniment in the musical sentence of which it is a part. Each syllable must be crafted with care and precision—and also take its place in a sequence.

This leads to a few over-stated—but basic truisms:

(1) There are no "weak"-beats.

Short notes are no less "vital" than long notes. They simply have a more abrupt accentuation: ($>$ or •) vs (⎯⎯⎯⎯⎯).

(2) One should be able to tell from the manner in which a note is "attacked" how long it will last: (♪ frequently will require $>$ or •) (o will frequently require ⎯⎯⎯⎯).

(3) In *crescendo* one can step up the dynamics by *marcato* ($>$) accents. In *diminuendo* one must "step down" the dynamics by short commas (,) or a series of *poco staccati*.

(4) In general, accompanying materials should be somewhat more pointillistic, less sustained and somewhat quieter than principal melodic materials.

(5) Theoretically, it might be possible to annotate or "edit" a score to within an inch of its life—and that's the problem. Exactly where there are *no* dynamic instructions is where the singer's creativity begins.

The only worthwhile musical collaboration is voluntary, creative and unan-imous. Now is the time for all good persons to come to the aid of their perfor-mance with all the nuances and disciplines the composer didn't have time to—and the editor didn't have the intelligence to—write. Right?

R

September 23, 1981

Dear Chorus,

I thought you might enjoy the excerpt below from a letter Mr. Shaw wrote awhile back to the preparer of the chorus for performances of Bach's *Mass in B Minor*, guest conducted by Mr. Shaw.

Nola

My first caution is: stay away from text until notes and phrasing are right and ineradicable! There is no doubt that Bach was *motivated* by the text; but if we truly seek to contact his own emotional motivation, we have to work "back-wards" through his notes. Phrasing, articulation, intonation, balance and the ebb and flow of dynamics are the means by which we contact Bach's motivation; but if we start with an "interpretation" derived from text translation and our own religious inheritance—however grand, but more frequently feeble—we will miss the possibility of encountering Bach's own penetration of the text or the ritual.

REHEARSAL TECHNIQUES –

1. Counting-Singing

This is simply singing any vocal line *not* with its text or with its own metric organization of long and short notes, but as though it were spelled out in accumulations of its smallest unit.

(a) This, of course, need not be done at performance tempo. Indeed, initially, slow rehearsal will accomplish much more than rapid rehearsal. Rehearsal tempi should be calculated to *prohibit* the singer from making a mistake. Errors should *not be allowed* to happen—or they will accumulate and require *un*-learning.

(b) This should also, initially, never be practiced at performance levels of dynamics, but at the *absolute minimum* of vocal sound—as though one were thinking the pitch rather than singing it. It follows that when the ranges are excessively high, people may sing down an octave (frequent with sopranos; less frequent with tenors—because of the fluency of the male falsetto; almost never necessary with altos or basses).

(c) Sometimes in broad tempi—with a lot of small notes—it will be found practical in 4/4 time to count-sing each measure either as 2 times "1 & 2 & 3 & 4 &" or as a single measure of "1 & 2 & 3 & 4 & 5 & 6 & 7 & 8 &."

(d) This technique accomplishes extraordinary things for intonation because it requires the singer to initiate the pitch of a whole-note, for instance, *eight* times per measure.

But it does even more for rhythms: it makes it impossible for a singer to sing through a rest; and it lines up every measure vertically in terms of the smallest unit.

(e) With respect to articulation, it allows the singer to make each 1/8th or 1/16th note either staccato or sostenuto, either accented or smooth.

(f) When, finally, the appropriate dynamics are added, the singer is forced to consider *where* precisely *how much* of a change in dynamics is to be accomplished *how rapidly.*

Variants of the "Count-Sing"

  1. Neutral, syllable "doo" or "dah"

(a) As successive smallest-denominator pulses (i.e., 1/8th or 1/16th notes).
(b) As staccato pitches on each text-syllable or change of note (singing only the initial fragments of each pitch).

  2. Simple tapping exercises

(a) On each syllable or change of pitch (to isolate rhythmic from pitch problems, and to give the voice a rest).
(b) With a pendulum or metronome maintaining a constant tempo, tapping each syllable or change of pitch, to encounter the difficulty of maintaining a tempo.

SECTIONAL REHEARSALS –

It should be noted that the Count-Sing device is also enormously productive for sectional rehearsals; and that –

The fastest, most productive way for the 4-part chorus to rehearse is for each section to rehearse one to four times separately, and for the conductor to rehearse 4 to 16 times.

VARYING REHEARSAL TECHNIQUES –

By alternating number-singing with text; by altering tempi from too slow to too fast; by arranging choral sections in circles, or by moving them to different locations in the room; by moving from sections to quartets; by having 1/2 the chorus sing numbers while the other half sings text: to throw as many different lights on the music and the learning process as may be possible—will speed, not slow, the learning.

Finally, precisions and rightness are the ultimate convincers and communicators. Anything less than that is musical pornography.

R

ENUNCIATION, LANGUAGE

... I'd like to say a word for enunciation: *"ENUNCIATION SAVES!"*
THE CHORAL ART OF OUR TIME HAS NOT EVEN BEGUN TO UNDERSTAND
AND UTILIZE TEXT AND ENUNCIATION AS THE CONSUMMATE CONJURERS OF
MUSICAL COLOR AND TIMBRE.

May 13, 1987

Friends –

The most frustrating part of any choral rehearsal (for this conductor) is that which has to deal with the disciplines of choral enunciation—and, in particular, those occasions when the language is English.

Recall that our basic principles are only two:

1. Every sound of every syllable must be phonated, and
2. Each sound must be allotted a metric proportion or instant.

Except in extremely rare instances (Gilbert and Sullivan "patter" songs, for example) the tempos and proportions normal to conversation and spoken language simply never appear in a musical setting.

Music imposes its own proportions and rhythms upon language. So far as normal speech is concerned, a musical setting is artificial and arbitrary.

With only occasional exceptions, the customary artifice is a lengthening of the principal vowel sounds of syllables or words—to such an extent that in a Bach aria or chorus a singer may dwell on a particular vowel for a series of twelve to sixty-four pitches over a span of six to eight measures. – And this is not only entirely acceptable, but it bears the sort of aesthetic and emotional significance which is music's reason for being. – But it does make the specific placement of the sounds of speech extraordinarily critical in ensemble singing.

Vowels and pitch-bearing consonants are the only sounds of speech capable of being lengthened. Therefore, all the other sounds of speech—the explosive sounds which are called consonants—occur *instantaneously,* just as they do in normal speech. – And in ensemble singing they must be phonated absolutely simultaneously.

We do this for two reasons:

1. It's the only way the text can be understood, and
2. It establishes that we care about the text, that we care about being understood, and that we care about each other.

Final consonants exploded at individual caprice, indifference or ignorance simply massacre all the above.

Could each of us spend a bit of private time putting his or her text in order?

Thank you,

R

February 22, 1977

Town Meeting –

"Anybody like to say a word for *enunciation?*"

"Yes, I'd like to say a word for *enunciation:* 'ENUNCIATION SAVES!' "

"What does *enunciation* save?"

"Well, what-wise, one thing and another like *time*. But whom-wise, it's a whole new game of ball. The whom it saves may be you.

"For instance, self-destructive-wise, it saves even choral conductors—an already gravely engendered species. But even more important-wise, *enunciation* saves people from receiving letters with Madison-Avenuese in them like 'self-destructive-wise!' "

"I'll drink to that! Hyphen-wise, the beginning of wisdom is the end of understanding."

"Wow! the people that walked in darkness have just unstumbled! Now that I have your attention, and being somewhat redirected as to my drinkin' habits, while you're gettin' loaded I'd like to say a few more words in behalf of *enunciation*."

"Feel freely."

"*Enunciation* is—well—it's just like *life.*"

"Big deal. Who's gonna feed my death-wish? Blest-out are the poor in enunciation, for they shall sing gawd-offal."

"Yuck! (i.e., "eeuhkkh!" FK) I hope you only said that mouthful!"
Parenthesis

Hi-deity or lo-laity:
The eating of words
Ain't whey with curds
Or ever a cause for gaiety.

(I just offer that to prove that where there's spirit swilling the fleshes reek. – Now about *life* and *enunciation* . . .)

Life is like enunciation because:

1. It's *beautiful.*
2. It *communicates.*
3. It's better than the *alternative.*

Number One: Enunciation is Beautiful

In my 25-year-old *Merriam-Webster's Unabridged Dictionary* there are over a half-million entries.

Remove all the puns, sound-alikes, foreign words and phrases, scientific dicta and purposefully un-communicative jargon: – the human voice is still the richest of the sources of musical *sound by hundreds of thousands* of possibilities. We are not considering *semantics*—the meaning of sounds, but simply the sounds of sounds, their all but incomprehensible bounty and variety. (What an incredible pauper the piano *vis-à-vis la voix.*)

Add to the myriad vocabulary of sounds available to the human voice the further richness of permutations in sequence and order, and one encounters a Kaleidoscopic Kornucopia of Kolors to boggle, engulf and dissolve the most adamantine of instrumental preferrers, professors and pretenders.

There are 6 possible orders for only 3 syllables: abc, bac, cab, acb, bca, cba.
There are: 24 possible orders for 4 syllables.
120 possible orders for 5 syllables.
720 possible orders for 6 syllables.
5,040 possible orders for 7 syllables.
40,320 possible orders for 8 syllables.
362,880 possible orders for 9 syllables.
3,628,800 possible orders for 10 syllables.

Were our language limited to only 100 syllables, how many ways could they be arranged? Or given a thousand, and limiting ourselves to groups of five, how many orders? – But there are tens of thousands. – But there are *hundreds* of thousands:

Lo: the miracle of speech: a richness and complexity of color beyond human comprehension—but not beyond *use.*

That's a major part of the miracle: for uncompromising attention to the particulars simply of enunciation will bring intonation, tone and metric proportion into line.

How many times last night did we have to stop for out-of-tune singing, or sectional unanimity of color, or metric definition other than identifying final releases? Almost none. – Yet all three were more nearly right than they had ever been before.

Enunciation is beautiful, and more than skin-deep.

Number Two: Enunciation Communicates

I can feel a chapter coming on that will restate and perhaps reorganize the basic rules of choral enunciation; but suffice it this week to recall that the problems and abstractions of sung-speech arise mainly from one condition only.

Musical forms prescribe relationships in Time, and as they do so they prescribe for the sounds of speech durations which may be foreign or at least "artificial" when compared to normal utterance. When, therefore, a syllable or a word, both of which are almost unexceptionably *complexes* of *several sounds,* are required to be sustained over a span of time longer than their normal period of phonation, it follows that each part of that word or syllable must be identified and placed precisely and proportionately, where it will contribute best to the syllable's recognition and ultimate understanding.

Musical enunciation is an audio-"graph" (a sound-tape?) in a slow-motion but at pitch. (A neat trick.) The problem is to slow the syllable while maintaining and accentuating the features of its identifiability. (A neat trick.)

Remember your high-school chemistry symbol for "will produce" or "yields"? ($\rightarrow$, 'right?) Well,

Enunciation $\rightarrow$ Beauty

and

Phonetics $\rightarrow$ Semantics

– a miracle like unto the first, but even more mysterious.

R

(This is the first of one or more [or less] letters on the perils of speech.)

P.S. I was prepared last night to attempt an answer to the terribly vital question, "How come 'Thomas Lawson?' " But nobody asked. Now we'll probably never know.

R

December 5, 1979

The next morning . . . and the next . . .

Fellow Associates –

Herewith the second essay (meaning mostly "attempt") to examine choral techniques star-lighted by the Christmas Festival repertoire.

Today: Choral Enunciation.

The subject falls quite naturally into two divisions: First, technical aspects— rules, regulations and methods—the hows; second, aspects of motivation and sensation—the existential whys and what-it's-like-when-things-are-right.

The technical theory can be stated very simply. (Problems arise in execution.) Technically only, one is not involved with either words or meaning in the singing of text, but with the succession of sounds ("phonetics") out of which a spoken language is formed.

The composer (in traditional music) has undertaken to supply a musical "setting" for a sequence of syllables, and has allotted to them specified pitches and specified durations. It is the performer's responsibility (1) to assay correctly the precise sequence of phonetic sounds which form each syllable, (2) to evaluate those sounds as to their orders of importance and duration in normal speech rhythm, and their abilities to carry sustained pitch, and (3) to allot to each successive phonetic fragment a precise, proportionate and appropriate instant (or duration) and loudness of utterance.

I suppose the greatest block to good enunciation in singing is the fact that language is learned at such an early age, and therefore used largely on such familiar informal occasions in such abbreviated, slurred, dialecticized, and parochial forms, that almost none of us—unless professionally involved or rapped repeatedly on the head—has any habitual comprehension of what little words indeed are made of. To most of us it comes as a shock in conservatory diction class to discover that a one-syllable word such as "strange" or "strained" can have seven or more phonetic sounds:

s (voiceless sibilant)
+ t (voiceless tongue-point alveolar stop)
+ r (tongue-point trill)
+ e (mid-front-tense vowel: a)

+ x (high-front-lax vowel: i)
+ n (voiced tongue-point alveolar nasal continuant)
+ d (voiced tongue-point alveolar oral stop)
= strained

(Obviously, if a composer in a pugnacious penury of prosody allows us but an eighth-note at a *vivace* tempo to encompass "strained," chorally we are looking at instant linguistic hernia.)

Up to now we've used the word "syllable" without really defining it. I find the *Random House* definition particularly informative: "a segment of speech typically produced with *a single pulse of air pressure* from the lungs, and *consisting of a center of relatively great sonority, with or without* one or more *accompanying sounds of relatively less sonority.*"

Let's recapitulate what already has been said: The composer allots to each syllable of his text a pitch and a duration; the performer must assign to *each of the several* sounds of that syllable an appropriate instant or duration in the music's Time order (– that wonderful complex of Tempo/Meter/Rhythm which is music's everlastingly vanishing canvas). Occasionally, also, the performer must supply a dynamic reinforcement of certain of those sounds—but that is secondary.

In the examination and evaluation process a certain amount of knowledge is expected of the singer. For instance, *Webster's* recognizes a total of 26 English consonantal sounds, 28 vowel sounds, and 6 diphthongs (double vowels). *Random House* assumes that these can be reduced to 24 consonants, 17 vowels, and 6 diphthongs. Without splitting phonetic hairs there surely are 40 to 50 sounds of speech whose individual qualities the singer should be able to recognize and vocalize.

Any standard unabridged dictionary in 1 to 20 pages can give us all the information we ever can use in singer's diction.

Granted, this is a "repertoire" of sounds quite beyond the amateur singer's conscious ken and custom.

– But even these lists can be quickly learned. – And regarding the placement of these sounds in music's temporal designs the rules are few and simple.

Recalling the premise that we must phonate *each and every sound* of *each and every syllable,* the rules are these:

1. The principal vowel sound of each syllable ("the center of relatively great sonority") must be sounded (phonated) precisely on the forward edge of the beat or beat-division assigned by the composer, and it must continue to sound throughout the major portion of the assigned duration.

Corollary (a)—Any consonant or complex of sounds which *precede* this principal vowel must be phonated in the fashion of a phonetic "appoggiatura," *ahead* of the beat (or beat division) assigned to the syllable. (See Footnote 1, below, regarding the pitch of this "phonetic appoggiatura.")

Corollary (b)—Any complex of vowel or consonant sounds which *follow* the principal vowel of a given syllable—especially the vanishing vowel sounds of diphthongs, and voiced nasal consonants capable of sustained pitch—are to be allotted a modest, concluding metric fraction of the total syllable time, bearing in mind the following qualifications:

(1) Since in normal speech these secondary syllable portions are relatively *un*accented, it seems to me that good taste and comprehensibility advise that even their modest, concluding fractions of time should be initiated by an instant of the *principal* vowel sound.

For example, suppose the word "crown" (K + Rrr + ah + oo + N) were to be sung on four slow beats, thus: crown

One would suggest the following assignments of sounds:

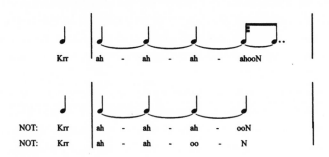

Qualification 2.

Since, between the principal vowel (of "relatively great sonority") and the vanishing vowel or nasal consonant (of "relatively less sonority") there is such a *vast* difference in loudness, the dynamic level of nasal consonants and vanishing vowels (particularly when competing with orchestral sonorities) must be appreciably increased in order to be heard at all. For instance:

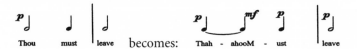

Rule 2, Consonants of "occlusion and release" (those formed by the stoppage and abrupt release of the flow of air from the lungs: principally p, b; t, d; k, g; and occasionally v) *when they conclude a syllable* almost always will have to be "exploded" into the neutral vowel a (phonetic symbol "schwa," sounding like the unaccented final vowel in "fath-er") in order to be heard at all.

Corollary 1.

More importantly, within a continuous musical phrase this release will in fact *add an additional fragmentary syllable* to the preceding and principal syllable; and this additional neutral vowel must be given the smallest possible—*but still perceptible*—metric fraction of its principal's time. For instance:

Corollary 2.

At the end of a musical phrase the dynamic level, duration and pitch characteristic of the release into the neutral vowel will always be subject to factors of tempo, competing sonorities, aesthetics and musical style, and thereby susceptible also to differences of personal opinion. Obviously, it should be loud enough to be unmistakable, and quiet enough not to call attention to itself.

Footnote 1. By declaring that consonants which precede principal vowels in a given syllable should be phonated as an appoggiatura *ahead* of the beat assigned to the syllable, we are faced with the problem—in the case of consonants capable of bearing pitch—of *precisely what pitch to assign to them.*

If the syllable initiates a phrase, there can be no question: they take the *initiating* pitch—but a minute fraction ahead of the beat.

If the syllable occurs in the middle of a phrase—as in many an "A-men"—the answer surely will vary from person to person and time to time, and be responsive also to matters of harmonic change, melodic motion, tempo, musical style, competitive sonorities, aesthetics, tradition and a host of other factors. It is even possible, it seems to me, that a nasal consonant between two vowels which are assigned different pitches might under many circumstances *link* them by being sung on *both* pitches—one as departing from, and the next as approaching toward.

But most serious choral musicians would agree, I think, that, given texts and music of stature and dignity, the fragmentary pitch of consonantal combinations when they precede principal vowels are more satisfyingly and tastefully uttered upon the pitch assigned to that syllable. Therefore, any transfer of a hummed consonant to a previous syllable and harmony must be conscious, exceptional, and listened to very carefully—that it not offend good taste.

To recapitulate:

Technically, our attention must be not upon words or meaning, but upon the succession of phonetic sounds which form syllables—which, in combination with other syllables, in due time will form words and phrases. Syllables have principal sounds and subsidiary sounds which may precede and/or follow the principal sound.

The principal sound must coincide precisely with its assigned beat or fraction thereof, and it must occupy all but the final fragment of the assigned duration.

If a subsidiary sound *precedes* the principal sound, it should also precede as tightly as possible the beat upon which the principal sound begins.

If a subsidiary sound *follows* a principal sound, it should occupy the last perceivable—but unaccented—metric fraction of the total assigned duration.

Neutral vowels are necessary to clarify the releases of final p, b, t, d, k, g, and occasionally v. In the middle of a phrase they must be allowed to add an extra mini-syllable, which also must be metrically proportioned.

So much for theory.

– Now, let's consider the motivational and experiential aspects of enunciation: what happens when—and what has to happen if—all the performer's techniques miraculously are turned into the wine of "communication?"

– Of a sudden—and in this strange context—it strikes me that these are the "existential" aspects of enunciation. Existentialism is the doctrine which proposes that man *is*, in fact, what he *does*. It emphasizes that man is responsible for making his own nature through the exercise of personal decision and personal commitment in an atmosphere of personal freedom—largely home-made.

It seems to me, too, that there are three conditions which have to "exist"—in the performer's commitment and experience—if the miracle of transubstantiation is to occur. They have to exist—and they have to exist in a thoroughly heightened, conscious, self-generating, self-justifying, nearly enraptured form.

To call them "ecstasies" risks the invisibility of over-statement in an ad-man's world—but I think it's a fair call. It suggests intensity, enjoyment and illumination—and that is their nature.

The first of them is the ecstasy of *vocalization*.

One of the psychological fashions of recent years is the technique of group therapy based, in large part, upon "sensory awareness"—touching and feeling. This is an understandable response to the impersonalization and dehumanizing of society which began after World War I, and which has been so cataclysmically accelerated in our own years. Most of us psycho-non-professionals were made aware of these techniques through the publicities surrounding the California Big Sur institute known as "Esalen."

Speech is so familiar to us that we rarely stop to consider its physiology and the complementary physics and physiology of hearing. I am not now referring to the complex chemical/electrical/psychical mysteries of hearing as understanding, but only to the physical disturbances to the infinite membranes of air which emit from one's mouth and fall upon another's ear. Speech is indeed a "touching"—with only the thinnest, most transparent of gloves—and there is a toucher and a touchee.

Acoustically and organically, speech is "breath or voice articulated—formed into speech sounds, transition sounds, syllables and breath groups, with word stress, sense stress, and intonation—by definite configurations and movements of the vocal organs" (*Webster's New International Dictionary,* Second Edition, Unabridged, 1953). These "vocal organs" I take to be the breath support system— lungs and diaphragm, the larynx and throat, and the muscles and adjustable areas, volumes and shapes of the face and mouth.

I suppose all of us have experienced at one time or another—in ourselves or in others—the hypochondriacal preoccupations of the ambitious singer with the health of his vocal organs. Similarly, upon being introduced to an operatic star in the silent corner of a quiet room, some of us have encountered such a vibrant "how-do-you-do!" that we have been tempted to inquire if it would be acceptable to pay at a later date for the voice lesson just administered.

Though amused, we should not be surprised at the intensity or tenacity of a singer's preoccupation with his vocal condition or production: his voice is his nest and his essence, his handle to the universe and his letter to the world.

"Annuntiator Triumphus" *must* be enraptured with the sensations and the sounds of speech: the mouthings and murmurings, the hissing and spitting, the drawing in, the damming back and the letting fly—hullaballoo and balulalow.

That these occasionally are used for *self*-exhibition rather than communication of something *other* does not deny their validity. – For speech is a necessity and an ecstasy—attributes which it shares with the act of procreation. The danger is only that we've used it so indiscriminately, habitually and incessantly we forget its exaltation and transport, and the sheer physical sport of creating sound.

There simply is no vital communication without this urgency and delight.

The second ecstasy is the ecstasy of *speech as color.*

For the past century and today's society the symphony orchestra together with its instrumental soloists would appear to have been assigned the position of pre-eminence among musical institutions, repertoires and patronage. Such an observation might be challenged on behalf of "grand" opera, though that also— even though joined with voice—appears to me in this century to be mainly a "symphonic" form. Similarly, any one of the commercial fads—rock/country/ gospel/disco—could claim from hour to hour a broader, more popular base. (As they say, no kids are trampled to death trying to get into Symphony Hall—some base.) In this instance, however, surely we must grant to maturity and longevity, and the ability to survive fast-fading fads, a dominating eminence.

With the range of color and dynamics available to the symphonic and the symphonic/operatic arts, the solo song and the unaccompanied chorus may be forgiven if occasionally they settle for a "becoming modesty."

(I am prompted to parenthesize that one of the reasons deaf-defying electronic extravagance is so unconvincing musically, intellectually, and humanly is that it's simply *more of the same.*) When Mahler, on the other hand, moves from little lappings to thunderous breakers of sound he does it by increments and inflections of color and instrumentation—and instruments are scaled to people.

Still, in spite of the fact that instruments are frank imitations of the human voice, and that every notable instrumental soloist spends most of his life seeking a "singing" tone and a singer's articulation and phrasing, the human voice—particularly the massed human voice—is considered pale and monochromatic.

What I want to suggest is that this ain't *necessarily* so. – For while the orchestra in its entirety and heterogeneity may indeed be a sonic peacock, each of its components is agonizingly handcuffed and frustrated as regards most of the elements of musical expression—dynamics, vibrato characteristics and varieties of color. Consider for a moment how many unaccompanied tuba recitals you might be able to find successively rewarding.

The fact is that, taken individually, instruments have nowhere nearly the arsenal, inventory or repertoire of sound transformations available to the human voice. Not only does the voice have all the lines, it has also the costumes, lights, scenery and gestures.

Though somewhat restricted as to pitch-range—as compared to a piano (88 instruments) or a 'cello (4 instruments)—the voice has as many ways and timbres of initiating or sustaining its pitches as there are combinations of xty consonants, umpteen vowels and common-law umlauts in sequences *recte et retro* from two to infinity. The color combinations available to the human voice through language literally are infinite.

The choral art of our time has not even begun to understand and utilize text and enunciation as the consummate conjurers of musical color and timbre. Our attention has been centered upon either the "rules" or the "message"—and too frequently these have led to the suffocation of the spirit. We have forgotten that dictionaries offer but silhouetted or graven images of language's meaning. Poetry never quite survives analysis; dissection ends in inquest; and definitions may be most comforting to the deaf.

For those who desire or who can stand the illumination of speaking (and hearing) "in tongues" an ecstasy of color is an existential *sine qua non.*

The third ecstasy is the ecstasy of *language as truth.*

Too frequently, it seems to me, truth is confused with "the message." "The message," of course, is a lot more accessible. It's been seeded, watered, powdered and packaged, pre-tested and digested. "Just close your eyes, grab your nose and swallow!"

In like manner soft rock is more accessible than the *Symphony of Psalms*. (One of the nice things about the *Symphony of Psalms* is that you probably can't get to it at all—ever—by climbing over people.)

Most of the slippage and dodge 'em here is accountable to a lack of intelligence, taste, honesty and industry—in whatever proportion and combination. (It seems appropriate to venture here that the first pair of attributes are directly responsive to the exercise of the latter.)

For the performer it is indeed much easier to throw a traditional institutionalized interpretative role over the knotty, awkward frame of a "sacred" (but still vital) text, than it is to re-think it independently in terms of what the composer may have constructed. – And close kin to this is the sad discovery of a noble text smothered in a syrup of sacred musical confection.

The difficulty in arriving at "the truth" (or enough of it to bet one's art upon) is that great text and great music meet upon a plane so vastly more meaningful than dictionary equivalents or musical analysis that neither can do much more than indicate direction—to that intersection. In reality such truth is a *new* truth. – And, what is even more frightening, it probably is a truth so "existential" that it cannot be experienced *except* in performance. Essence and meaning exist in the doing.

This gives to performance (and rehearsals, too, for they, also, are a doing) a mind-boggling urgency.

There are two things to be said in conclusion. The first is that the ecstasy of the experience of truth is not the only or final urgency, for the whole affair is undertaken because of the desire to communicate. Obviously, we communicate first of all with our collaborators—with one another—but also, and not unimportantly, with those who listen.

Suppose one were born without the ability to make a vocal sound; and suppose, further, that one were capable of realizing that other people did, in fact, communicate through human speech; suppose, finally, a loved one's life in a moment of acute danger depended upon a shouted warning. What might be the urgency to tell the truth—to invent the shout.

For, 'truth to tell, and point number two, though Brahms and the psalmists do point *towards* the truth, for each of us the arrival is from a third direction.

This, of course, is what I have in mind when I urge you not to follow, but to lead, one another. – Or, better yet, simply to do, to be—preferably with everyone.

It literally is true that "none of the important elements of performance are conductible." – But that doesn't mean that they aren't getattable.

What a funny way to teach enunciation!

R

April 1, 1969

I do not wish to bore you with unnecessary repetition of basic choral techniques; but it seems to me appropriate to write a few words concerning such elements as—for instance, this week—choral enunciation.

Let me write first a few introductory paragraphs: what is the general—the *qualitative*—relationship between words and music in choral literature?

One could say that in almost all instances the composer had his text in mind when he began to compose, and that it therefore must be admitted to have had some directing influence. Many composers, of course, have "stolen" from their own work. Bach, for instance, has taken choruses which originally he wrote to secular words, given them new text, and moved them without appreciable alteration into the most sensitive, and even doctrinaire, of religious situations. But, in the main, words certainly guide and influence a composer's musical setting.

There are two elements to the musical setting of text. First there is what is called *prosody:* that is, the manner in which normal word accents and metrics are related to musical accents and metrics, how they match or contravene each other.

For instance, except for the ingenious extension of the opening syllable, observe how delightfully the opening notes of Rodgers and Hammerstein's "Oklahoma!" adhere to the natural-inflection of the title word (even including the exclamation point). Or, think again how closely musical rhythm matches textual rhythm in "Mine eyes have seen the glory of the coming of the Lord."

The other aspect of music's relationship to text is less particular and detailed, but almost certainly more important. It has to do on the one hand with the *meaning* of text, with text as a *value*—its idea content, the whole realm of emotional, aesthetic and spiritual associations which surround and interpenetrate it—and, on the other hand, with the similar significances of the music itself particularly as provided in its larger structure. To illustrate: the opening movement of the *B Minor Mass* is about twelve minutes long. It's text has only two words, and those, out of Greek through Latin. Given five vocal lines and additional orchestral materials, in the twelve minutes there must be literally hundreds of different settings of the words "Kyrie eleison." Obviously, not all of them can offer equally perfect prosody. – And it is therefore in some other direction that we must look to understand the amazing congruity of text and music. The answer is that it is the *entire* musical structure which animates and illuminates the text. Of little matter that a passing accent may be false. Text and music are matched in aspiration and essence.

Once, therefore, we get into the fields of music's larger or more mature architectures the performers treatment of choral text also is qualified.

It seems to me that our responsibilities here are to allow the music, in its total complex of style and structure, to comment upon the text. The opposite attitude would be to force the music to adapt to a preconceived idea of text accentuation and meaning. Though Palestrina, Bach and Beethoven have set the same text, we cannot possibly employ the same rhetorical emphases to styles and understandings so vastly dissimilar. – Or else we indulge in childish, personal disservice to their music, and deny ourselves the possibility of gaining their own particular understanding, in each instance so very much greater than our own.

Thus, when we begin to apply this attitude to our methods of handling text, our first rule must be that the musical language is supreme, and must determine the manner and mechanics of our enunciation.

From a quite different starting point, we are arriving at much the same tactical problem as that discussed in an earlier letter. All of us are aware that music prescribes certain syllables to be sung on certain pitches. We are not nearly so sensitive to the fact that music is an organization in *time*, and also prescribes *when* they are to be sung.

Words are made up of syllables, and syllables may be made up of several sounds—one principal and several subordinate, which may follow or precede it. In all ordinary instances the principal sound is that of a vowel.

– And the basic rule of choral enunciation does double-duty: it is that we are obliged to form every sound in every syllable, and (so that we do not limp, dawdle or stagger) that the principal sound must align with the rhythmic flow of the music, must coincide with pulse.

In the second choral fragment of *The Creation* we have frequently come across the words "springs forth." This is a difficult text to handle. The principal sound of "springs" obviously is the "ee" vowel; but before we can get to it we must form a "ss," a "p!" and an "rrr"; and following it, before we can get to the vowel sound of the word "forth," we must form an "ng," a "zz" and a "f – ." Taking only the first word, by our rule the "ee" vowel must coincide with the pulse of the music, and therefore the "ss-p!-rrr" has to *precede* that pulse as a kind of enunciative grace-note.

R.S.

September 25, 1996

Friends –

Does anyone else have any trouble sleeping Monday nights? I feel sure that water loss is a good thing for over-weight, aging conductors, but when we work as intensely as we have these past few rehearsals, who's going to tell these hyper-kinetic flag-waving notes running around in the brain to "shut up and lie down!"?

I want to qualify by further examination and writing one of the suggestions I made on several occasions Monday night, most specifically with reference to the enunciation of the text of the chorale which concludes the Barber *Prayers of Kierkegaard*. You will recall that I called for more "detached," "almost staccato" singing in order to clarify the positioning of the consonants. (This chorale provides an almost perfect example of enunciative problems, because it places a single syllable on each note, and because almost all the notes are successive quarter-note values.)

Now, no one would deny that a most important part of good vocalism is vocal "line." What we mean by that is unanimity of vocal color through the widest possible range of pitch and dynamics. At its best, "vocal line" issues in a noble legato sound so pleasing and moving that stringed instruments attempt to imitate it by *sliding* with the left hand on the finger-board, rather than by *leaping* with the fingers to successive pitches. (In a sense, of course, the voice is a stringed—or vocally-corded—instrument.) Isn't it an absolute miracle that the brain can direct these vocal chords to leap in an instant from pitch to pitch, rather than glide—however quickly—through all the scale degrees between one prescribed pitch and its follower?

So—good singing calls for good vocal line. – But, expressive and com-municative singing also calls for passionate clarity of enunciation. – And my Monday-post-Midnight suggestion to all of us is that vocal line and enunciation need not diminish and denigrate each other (as sides in a labor dispute) given attention to two conditions:

1. That one attends to every sound in every syllable, giving it a perfectly placed metric position, and
2. That one makes careful and frequent use of the pitched *schwa* neutral vowel to give to those consonants that need it the explosion which they demand.

For an extended conclusion, consider with me the difficulty with which these disciplines of enunciation operate in a symphonic chorus of two-hundred-plus voices. – What degrees of precision and vehemence are necessary to drive a sung text through a screen of symphonic instrumental sound, as versus the percussive (and thereby rapidly decaying) sound of the piano—which is the traditional accompanying instrument for the solo voice?

Assume for the moment that our sections are roughly fifty voices each. Assume, for the moment, that a section is seated not in a block of eight rows, six or seven persons to each row, but all fifty in a line, shoulder to shoulder.

Assume that in the middle of this row—between Singer No. 25 and Singer No. 26—there is a perfect and unvarying metronome.

Assume now that these singers are so perfectly disciplined that they can phonate a pitched syllable within one-hundredth of a second of the phonation of the singer standing directly adjacent.

Now, assume that each of the Singers Nos. 26–50 is successively one one-hundredth of a second behind his or her neighbor to the right and, accumulatively, behind the tempo which was handed down by No. 26: and that Singers Nos. 25–1 are successively one one-hundredth of a second ahead of the neighbor to the left, and accumulatively ahead of the tempo which had been given to No. 25 by the Metronome.

Metronome

No. 1 <-----------------25   26--------------------> No. 50

   <---(getting faster)   (getting slower)--->

This would mean that Singer No. 1, only 1/100th of a second disjunct from his/her neighbor, is actually 50/100ths of a second disjunct from Singer No. 50—who also is only 1/100th of a second apart from *her/his* neighbor. In an *andante* tempo of 60 beats per minute this would mean that Singers Nos. 1 and 50 are a full eighth-note apart. – And in a moderate march tempo of (quarter-note = 120) they would be a full quarter-note apart.

Now, a lot of factors—acoustical, logistical and human—keep this from happening, principal among them the blessed (blasted) human factor that some singers on *each* side of our hypothetical Singing Rockettes are going to be x/100ths *ahead* of the metronome, and some are going to be x/100ths *behind* the metronome. There even might be a few who manage to be *with* the metronome.

At a moderate march tempo (quarter-note = 120) the neutral *schwa* between two explosive consonants on successive quarter-notes would be very near the duration of a 16th-note—or about 1/8th of a second. (If the syllables were "hot dog," the "tuh" of "hot-tuh-dawg" would occupy the final $^{125}/_{1,000}$ths of a second of the first quarter-note. *Simultaneously,* if you please!)

The point is that even diversities of 1/100ths of a second add up; and, while it is enormously productive—and so much easier—to gain strictly musical precisions by count-singing or singing with repetitive nonsense syllables, when one adds the intricacies of enunciation to the fact that we are, for better and for worse, a wannabe sing-le "body" with two-hundred-plus heads and four-hundred-plus vocal cords, it ain't jes' double-dip no-sweat.

'Must close by saying thanks for your home-work. It's making Monday nights a real Ho-ho-sauna.

R

October 10, 1996

Friends –

Here's an addendum to the letter of September 25 detailing the precepts of successful choral enunciation.

There were three:

1. Phonate every sound of every syllable. (Some single syllables may require as much as five or six sounds of speech: i.e., *strain* = s + t' + rr + ay + ee + n'.)
2. Use a pitched neutral vowel ("schwa") following—or between—all "plosives" (explosive consonants).
3. Allot to each of the sounds of speech a precise instant or proportionate duration in the rhythmic flow—at the same time assuring that the principal vowel of the syllable arrives precisely with its prescribed musical notation.

    (This means that the initiating consonants of a syllable must be sung as a "grace note" or "ornament" ahead of the assigned notation. For example, in the phrase "so proudly we hail" the *pr* in "puh-rr-ah-oo-duh-lee" must be phonated before the diphthong *ou,* sufficiently in advance to allow the vowel which carries the principal sonority to carry also the pulse—or beat—of the music.)

In retrospective contemplation of minor miracles of discipline still to be accomplished—as of last Monday night's rehearsal—I'd like to suggest a fourth pylon for the Bridge to Perfection. It has to do with *Accentuation.* At the outset, however, please note herewith a small caveat—a slight disclaimer. While this fourth precept seems to me absolutely essential in the case of the symphony chorus, it need not be so emphatically used with a small unaccompanied chamber chorus, and even somewhat less by the solo singer with piano accompaniment.

I overstate it now in its negative form: "In successful choral enunciation there are *no weak syllables.*"

Rationale –

In language we recognize strong (heavy) syllables and weak (light) syllables.

Similarly, in music there are strong beats and weak beats. Successful prosody (the setting of words to music) almost always—except for intentional dislocation—makes these accentuations coincide.

Music itself has several means of accentuation:

[1] Metric. For whatever combination of psychological and physiological reasons, man groups repeated pulses into groups of two or three: Strong-weak, strong-weak; and strong-weak-weak, strong-weak-weak.

[2] Duration. Length of sound also implies more-stress or less-stress as, for

example: (How love - ly is thy dwell - ing place, O Lord.)

[3] Dynamics. Degrees of loudness can reinforce metric or dynamic stress or, by a composer's instruction, contradict them.

[4] Melodic. In general, probably for psychological or physiological reasons similar to those which influence metric stress, "high" pitches are more stress-ful than "low" pitches.

To repeat, with almost all familiar choral prosody (hymns, carols, folksongs, popular and commercial ballads) the natural stresses of language coincide with, and are reinforced by, the calculated stresses of music—melodic, harmonic, rhythmic and temporal. Try singing

O, say can you see by   the dawn's ear - ly light what   so, proud - ly

In the main, then, the weaker syllables of language, when set to music, are in general assigned not only lesser durations but also the weaker parts of weaker beats.

We also must admit that sheer numbers of voices contribute to enunciative murk. However noble a congregation of believers may sound singing "A Mighty Fortress Is Our God," a top-flight court reporter might well suffer inverse dyslexia trying to transcribe verses five, six and seven without a hymnal. – And even a well-auditioned, talented and well-intentioned chorus of two-hundred-plus voices, by nature of sound and assignment, verges on the gummy, gooey and gloppy.

Even to get through its own choral texture, an extraordinary persistence and incisiveness of accentuation is necessary to deliver syllables twice-weakened by normal language stress and musical notation. – And when a chorus, in addition to its own sonority, has to project a text through or above a symphony orchestra, even the weakest of syllables on the weakest of beat-divisions must become the mite-ee-est of projectiles.

("There are no weak syllables in successful choral enunciation"—for us here/now.)

There is a provocative musical adjunct to this enunciative counsel. It is that while what we call first beats and long notes are considered to be "strong" notes, they are also beats of arrival and rest:

Before each of these long beats is what we call in English an "up"-beat (technical term: *anacrusis,* from the Greek "back—to strike.") Obviously, this has overtones or misty images of "up-thrust," perhaps even "eruption" (as in "volcanic"), but certainly of "energy" and "impact." The last little part of the so-called "weak"-beat, then, is really the beat of *thrust* and explosion.

In competitive diving it would be the strength with which the diver strikes (and depresses) the forward edge of the three-meter board to throw him high enough to give him time enough to complete his death-defying combination of somersaults and twists.

In music it is the *Accentuation* of the up-beat which catapults us into the next instant of arrival, rest and recuperation. Only by persistent and incisive Accentuation do the normally unaccented sounds of speech emerge through musical textures.—Maybe there really are *no weak-beats.*

R

October 1, 1997

Friends –

Some months ago—to demonstrate how essential it was to sing and enunci-ate a split-second simultaneity—I used as an example a symphony chorus situ-ated in several rows of fifty persons each. Let us rather now take as our example our own chorus in concert formation: eight rows of twenty-five each.

Suppose that those singers to the left of center sing successively only one one-hundredth of a second later than the person to their right, and those to the right of center sing successively one one-hundredth of a second *earlier* than their neighbor to their *left.* It would follow that those persons at the outer ends of each row would be twenty-five one-hundredths—or one-fourth—of a second apart (with twenty-three glops in between).

The point is that in the fastest portions of Bartók's *Cantata Profana* and Vaughan Williams' *Dona Nobis Pacem* such dislocation would amount to a disparity of substantially more than an eighth-note. Add to that potential disaster the condition that while front rows may be able to hear (and cohere with) rows in back of them, behinder rows are not only precluded from hearing distinctly the rows in front of them, but they are also farther from the orchestral matrix and its metrics and, therefore, from gearing easily into a common tempo.

Now, move next into the problems created by the fact that choruses are obliged to sing words as well as notes. Singing together rests upon several assumptions:

First: that the purpose of a chorus is to seek and, if possible, establish community on a plane of exalted intellect and emotion. "Togetherness," "fellowship," "brotherhood," "sharing"—all the words disenfranchised by commerciality—are its warp and woof.

Second: that a text selected by a composer is both his inspiration and a part of his "message." He seeks to enhance—to heighten, deepen or dramatize—its meaning by musical means.

Third: that the composer desires—indeed, prescribes—our participation. It is interesting that not all music prescribes or desires an audience; but it always calls for a communion of executants. The monks would sing their services at Solesmes whether or not a few fortunate tourists were in attendance. – But such are the scale and cost of symphonic performing forces that a paying audience or record-buying public, in addition to public and private philanthropy, are today's necessary practice.

Fourth: though instruments may indeed share in the emotional, psychological and physiological excitations induced by music, insofar as *text* is concerned, the symphony orchestra obscures and consumes it. This is particularly true when instruments double vocal lines or when the composer uses outdoor instruments to proclaim heroism, rapture or agony.

Fifth: the symphony chorus (or festival chorus) of 150 to 300 voices is a humongous, glutinous, turgid, inertia-bound instrument. Its articulation—both musical and textual—requires prodigies of skill and will, as also degrees of exaggeration to the point of caricature.

Our usual—and frequent—advices in rehearsal are [1] that in choral enunciation we are responsible *not* for *words,* but for every sound in every syllable; and [2] that good choral enunciation is best signified not as a constant flow of water through a hose, but is better pictured as a necklace of syllabic beads. Last week in rehearsals of a Verdi *Requiem* with a 250-voice symphonic chorus, unable to stem the bleeding of one syllable into the next, I borrowed a metaphor which had hitherto been used to qualify pitches and durations. "Every *syllable* has a beginning, a "passing-through" and an ending. Therefore: finish each syllable before you begin the next." – And it worked wonders.

I want to add something to that advice for our chorus. Vocal "line" is important. It is important to the physiology of singing and to the beauty of music. Though, as a matter of practicality, it is almost impossible to get 200–300 voices to over-articulate, it is a theoretical possibility. – And I want to suggest to us that the best way to avoid *over*-articularity and still be understandable is by a vigilant and frequent use of the *schwa* intervening neutral syllable. It preserves "line" and intonation; and, so long as we unfailingly place the principal vowel of a syllable precisely on its assigned metric particle, no matter what combination of schwa *cum* consonants may precede that vowel, we can work wonders of intelligibility.

While we're on the subject, ain't it an interesting obfuscation of content to entitle a piece *Dona Nobis Pacem* and continue with six additional words in Latin, but seven-hundred-and-sixty-six in English. – Which reminds us that our native language is almost without exception the most difficult language in which to sing: first, because we all have different accents and individual slipshoddities and, second, because music's accents and durations are seldom those of customary speech.

While we're on the subject (No. 2): to counter the occasional criticism that choral sound is so unforgivably mono-chromatic, consider the possibility that finally—even though mystically—communication in language rests not on semantics but upon the krazy kaleidoscopic kolors of speech itself—its musical aspects and energies: pitch, rhythm, duration, fundaments and overtones. What if language were not limited to dictionary equivalents?

What if all the syllables in the prayersofkierkegaardcantataprofanaandwaltwhitman were laid enduhtoenduh?

R?

Appendix: ("Polysyllables" by Leonardo da Bushwah)

October 19, 1994

(Revised/Corrected 10/25/94)

Friends –

Those among you who are long-time associates of the Atlanta Symphony Orchestra Chorus will realize that October is the time for the annual brush-up-and-get-with-it letter concerning choral enunciation techniques.

Prithee, stay with this epistle a moment further—since our enunciative responsibilities are so critical to *Elijah*-in-English and since your correspondent appears to be rapidly moving from the apocalyptic to the apoplectic.

In 1938–39 two choral innovators began dealing seriously with the problems of choral enunciation in English. In the choral anthem repertoire John Finley Williamson, who founded the Westminster Choir College, suggested to choir conductors coast-to-coast that at least a handful of English vowels actually were diphthongs, and that singers in choruses, in order to be understood, had to sing "ay-ee" (for say), "ah-ee" (for sigh), "aw-ee" (for boy), "o-oo" (for so) and "ee-ay" (for yea).

At the same time, in the field of popular music, Fred Waring had coached his "Pennsylvanian" band-members to emphasize by duration and dynamics all the hummed consonants (m, n, ng)—in order to achieve bleNd and MaxiMuM uNderstaNd-iNG.

At about the same time a sweet lady by the name of Madelaine Marshall—who taught "Singers' Diction" at the Juilliard School of Music—published a book on the subject through G. Schirmer, which emphasized the necessity and function of the "neutral vowel." This vowel, called a "schwa" (roughly our "uh") was to follow or separate all explosive consonants, rendering them audible against the stronger flow of the principal vowels—which, of course, are the primary conduits for pitch.

Now, all consonants (excepting sibilants) are to a lesser or greater degree "explosive," as versus vowels. They are not only dramatically quieter than vowels in daily speech, but substantially *inaudible* when sung against the sonic capacities of a symphony orchestra. Through the years, therefore, as the symphonic choral repertoire became the principal venue of my own choral experience, Ms. Marshall's "neutral vowel" loomed larger and larger in importance—for it raised the otherwise inaudible consonant to a dynamic level equal to a principal vowel. It could, of course, never last as long as the principal vowel of a word, but it could be as loud as that vowel and, if given a rhythmic proportion of the time prescribed for its syllable, might even augment metric and rhythmic interest.

Accordingly, let us review the basic tenets of our enunciative technique and rationale. First, *Technique:*

I.   We are obliged to sing (to phonate on pitch wherever possible) not words, but every sound of every word. In a single-syllable word like "smite," that might be as many as seven sounds: (1) "ss," (2) "uh," (3) "m," (4) "ah," (5) "ee," (6) "t," (7) "uh"—"suh-m-ah-ee-tuh."

II. When the final consonant of one syllable is followed by a syllable beginning with a consonant, we are obliged to insert between these consonants the neutral "schwa" syllable. Thus: "and-uh-yet-uh-there-comes-uh-no-power."

III. Since in singing the sounds capable of sustaining pitch are usually greatly lengthened, and since music's time element almost always is rhythmic, measurable and divisible, each of the sounds of speech is to be allotted a precise moment or duration of phonation (however short), with the principal vowel always on the beat and initiating consonants ahead of the beat.

The difficulties we encounter in giving a common voice to these simple rules are three:

1. Our habits of speech are so un-conscious (and so sloppy) in our own language that we are simply unaware of all the sounds which are necessary to make speech itself unmistakably intelligible.
2. Normal speech rhythms—durations and stresses—are almost always contradicted in some regard by music's durations and accentuations.
3. It's just damnably difficult for 200 people to accomplish simultaneity in units of eight one-hundredths of a second (which is the duration of a sixteenth-note in the *Elijah*'s finale).

Our rationale is exciting. First, a glorious musical masterpiece like Mendelssohn's *Elijah* is a "celebration" of its text. It is music which examines and probes, which portrays, comments upon and magnifies a host of personal feelings and convictions, of tribal motivations and religious customs of an historical period and an heroic, prophetic, human figure.

It does this almost exclusively in the most beautiful and powerful language ever written by English-speaking people: the languages of Shakespeare and the King James Bible. It should be considered as great a privilege to sing these words as it is to play a Shakespearean dramatic role—or read his sonnets aloud.

Second, I would want to call your attention to the elements of speech (and therefore of singing) which are beyond simple dictionary definition. There are eloquences in language simply as sound, as there are in music, which remain somehow mystical and un-stateable, but which many of us can sense together— and might even be able to impart to a few good listeners, once our purpose is constant and our techniques are secure.

In the beginning was the Word . . .
– And it keeps on going . . .
– it's still going . . .
– still going . . .

R

PART III

CONDUCTING THE MASTERPIECES

February 9, 1993

Friends –

The economic difficulties of maintaining the traditional American symphony orchestra and its traditional repertoire lead me from time to time to question my tenure as music director as being much too conservative and tradition-bound.

My rationale in the beginning was that if one was intent upon building a symphony orchestra, its disciplines had to be built upon late 18th century and early 19th century classicism and late 19th century "classic" romanticism. Initially, also, since The South historically had a very meager exposure to fine symphonic repertoire—in contrast to its literary heritage—it was clear that a majority diet of 20th century compositions would saddle the orchestra with attendance problems and Box-Office Blues. (As it was, the scheduling of an Ives Cycle was cited by the Executive Committee of the Board when requesting the conductor's resignation in 1972.)

I noted with shame, while conducting the Birmingham (England) Symphony Orchestra earlier this season, that a very substantial—to us, overwhelming—part of its repertoire for the 1992–1993 season was written within my lifetime. Moreover, their ticket counters regularly posted SRO signs—and evidently had done so for more than a century. (Mendelssohn's *Elijah* had its world premiere in Birmingham.)

We attempted, in seasons 1–21, to bridge the gap occasionally between classicism and current "pop," but were really only moderately successful with regard to American jazz—and then usually when blended with some civil rights agenda.

Certainly, many of our country's very finest performing artists were—and are—in the field of jazz; and it has seemed to me that if a music director were really qualified to build a forward looking musical program for a growing American metropolis, he ought to be at least qualified to "sit in" with these jazz artists—as, for instance, friend André Previn does so handsomely.

It will be noted that I have used a jazz word several times. That is altogether conscious. – For I do not believe that the other fads of popular/commercial music are even close to jazz's league of technical mastery, intellectual complexity and taste. The hyped-up stadium- and coliseum-shows of down and dirty roll and rock, in whatever current excessive guise, are more debilitating to the human spirit even than elevator and dentist-chair music.

The point is that my own sense of personal deficiency and guilt leads me sometimes to forget the credit side of commitment to classicism and its preservation. – And there is no reason why you should have to feel guilty along with me.

Every piece of music you folks touch is a plus on the side of human dignity. I was reminded of this as I read an article by Aleksandr Solzhenitsyn in Sunday's *New York Times*. I quote:

"For several decades now, world literature, music, painting and sculpture have exhibited a stubborn tendency to grow not higher but to the side, not toward the highest achievement of craftsmanship and of the human spirit but toward their disintegration into a frank and insidious novelty. . . . If visitors from outer space were to pick up our music over the airwaves, how would they ever guess that earthlings once had a Bach, a Beethoven and a Schubert, now abandoned as out of date and obsolete?

" . . . If we, the creators of art, cease to hold dear the great cultural tradition of the foregoing centuries together with the spiritual foundations from which it grew, we will be contributing to a highly dangerous fall of the human spirit on earth, to a degeneration of mankind into some kind of a lower state, closer to the animal world."

Don't ever forget that what you do on your seventy to ninety nights a year in the Woodruff Arts Center is a big *plus* on Creation's side.

Leave the *minuses* to the hired help.

R

JOHANN SEBASTIAN BACH

Mass in B Minor

Pre-concert Remarks

March 26–28, 1998

It is reasonable, it seems to me, to question the propriety of performing a work of music so specifically and exhaustively theological in text in so secular a setting, before an audience ranging in religious preference from the totally contrary to the totally committed, and ranging philosophically from welcome through indifference to distrust.

Certainly the Masses of Haydn, Mozart and Beethoven, with their four to six movements, are almost symphonic in nature and more appropriate to this hall.

Somehow, however, the fact that extra seats have had to be added for these performances attests to the unique position that Bach's *Mass in B Minor* holds in the minds and hearts of men and women of all faiths—and no faith at all—

except perhaps the oneness of humankind with the universe, and the responsibility of human life to seek beauty and to do good.

It may well be true that Bach's *Mass in B Minor*—assembled, no less than created—has become, some 250 years after he bound its 26 movements together, the most remarkable musical allegory of human existence—its pain, aspiration and promises.

Someone said this week that every time he approaches this work he is conscious of the fact that someone in the audience is hearing it for the first time, and someone is hearing it for the last time.

I assure you that there are those of us on this side of the proscenium who also face these possibilities.

October 15, 1985

Friends –

These notes to myself for *Mass in B Minor* rehearsal last Sunday may be of interest to others of you engaged in Baroque performance responsibilities.

R

BACH'S *MASS IN B MINOR*

Chorus/Concertist Roles – 1985 ASO Performance
(pagination based on Barenreiter edition)
General Aim:
   To reduce the Concertist participation in "Choruses."
Reasoning:
   Differences in sonority. Concertist roles (solo voices) and Chamber Chorus (47 voices) provide too great a contrast for Bach's Baroque lower structure.
   (Bach had 1 to 3 voices per part.)
   Also: Concertist in-and-out deployment calls for changes in numbers of instruments—an option which Bach did not have.
   And: Calls for re-writing of text and occasional notation to fit choral entrances—which Bach did not initiate.
   On the other hand –

1.   Chorus needs some rest (particularly in "Symbolum Nicenum" where it doesn't get it.)

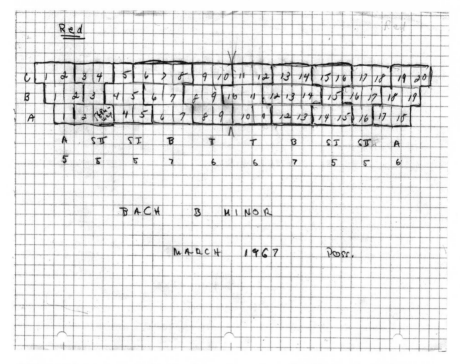

Sketch of chorus stage positioning for performances of Bach's Mass in B Minor

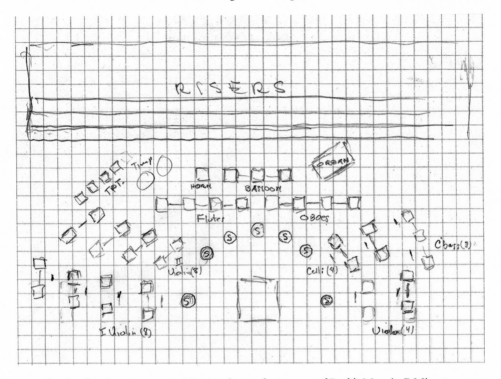

Sketch of orchestra stage positioning for performances of Bach's Mass in B Minor

2. Occasional extended unaccompanied melismatic passages (Bass solo in "Et resurrexit") probably were intended for solo voice.

Missa

1. Kyrie (pages 1–21)
Chorus sings measures 1–4.
Concertists sing progressively measures 30–58, beat 1.
Chorus enters progressively with instruments within Exposition I, and sings to conclusion:

> Bass: measure 45, beat 3;
> Sop II: measure 48;
> Sop I: measure 50, beat 3;
> Tenor: enter with episode #1, measure 58;
> Alto: Enter with episode #1, measure 59.

3. Kyrie (pages 30–35)
> Complete (chorus)

Gloria

4. Gloria in excelsis (pages 36–42)
> Complete (chorus)
5. Et in terra pax (pages 42–53)

> Chorus begins: sings measures 1–13;
> Concertists sing measures 21–38;
> Chorus enters with 6th 8th value, measure 37, and sings to conclusion.
> (Concertists and Chorus overlap for 4 1/2 beats, measures 37–38.)

7. Gratias agimus tibi (pages 61–65)
> Complete (chorus)
9. Qui tollis peccata mundi (pages 75–81)
> Complete (chorus)
12. Cum Sancto Spiritu (pages 94–113)

> Chorus begins; sings measures 1–37 (beat 1);
> Concertists enter progressively; sing measures 37–64;
> Chorus enters again, measure 68; sings to conclusion.

Symbolum Nicenum

1. Credo in unum Deum (pages 114–119)
    Complete (chorus)
2. Patrem omnipotentem (pages 120–125)
    Complete (chorus)
4. Et incarnatus est (pages 144–148)
    Complete (chorus)
5. Crucifixus (pages 149–152)
    Complete (chorus)
6. Et resurrexit (pages 153–168)

> Chorus begins; sings measures 1–66;
> Bass Concertist sings measures 74–86;
> Chorus sings measure 86 (4th 8th value) to conclusion.

January 6, 1981

Dear Friends –

'Enjoyed enormously the rehearsal with you on the *Mass in B Minor*. 'Have spent this morning editing the *Cum Sancto Spiritu* with accentuation, dynamics and phrase groupings, and hope you will find it possible to add these to your scores before the next rehearsal. 'Suggest you check also a few further refinements in *Et resurrexit* and *Pleni sunt coeli*.

We'll begin next rehearsal with those 5-part choruses which we did not touch last night: *Credo in unum*, *Et incarnatus*, *Et resurrexit*, *Confiteor*, (p. 186) *Et exspecto*; and deal seriously with 6-part choruses: *Sanctus* and *Pleni sunt*.

As the women's voices move from 2-part writing to 3- and 4-part writing, there ain't gonna be "no hidin' place down—or up—there." Each person becomes responsible, first, for absolute accuracy of intonation, meter and enunciation; second, for an awesome and unblemished beauty of soloistic sound; and, third, for a common understanding and care for the bevels and nuances of dynamics and accentuation.

– And even within the numerically larger male sections, the more finely drawn and sensitive our phrasing becomes, the easier it is for one careless pitch, vowel or accent to disfigure an exquisite line. (Pornograffiti in a Manhattan subway men's room ain't nearly so visible as a little heat rash on baby's tummy.)

The real joy in working on the *B Minor Mass* is that there is absolutely no end to the refinement which the work inspires and commands. One cannot live long enough—or encounter so frequently conditions appropriate to its performance—that one exhausts it or becomes immune to its marvels. I feel certain that within my experience we now have the finest confluence of forces—instrumental and vocal—which I have encountered.

There are, of course, forces musicologically more certifiable: ancient instruments, fewer participants and boys' voices among them. – But we're beginning now to get a lightness, sweetness and steadiness in our ladies' sound which—pray we amend it e'en further—could end up with equal rights. Moreover, since the initial choice of boys' voices over women's voices was predicted not upon musical grounds, but upon the presumptuous superiority of innocence untested over virtue achieved, the philosophical rationale as regards worship, sacrifice and musical-offerings has taken a distinct and deserved drubbing. Ave! O liberated M(a)sses!

Now—as for next time: Hindemith and Bruckner. Great pieces! – And not a moment too soon! Come early, stay late. – 'Real work party.

'See you Monday.

R

November 27, 1957

I had occasion a few days ago to tabulate the choral portions of Bach's *St. Matthew Passion,* which, as many of you know, is a full three and one-half hours' duration—as opposed to the two-hour performance time of the *B Minor Mass.* I knew beforehand that the *Mass* would show greater choral proportions, but did not realize that there are twice as many measures of choral singing in the *Mass* as in the *Passion.*

Our accomplishment of the *Mass*—loveblindly assuming it be accomplished—is therefore as though we had been able to learn the *Passion* in a five and one-half week rehearsal schedule. – "Oh, who would not sleep with the brave!" (A. E. Housman).

I have been trying to figure ways in which your between-rehearsal study might be most productive, for I realize that, particularly when there is no access to a piano, the vocal lines of the *Mass* are extremely difficult to conceive and to sing. It strikes me that at this stage all of us might profit by going through the fast and difficult choruses, learning perfectly the rhythmic syllabification, which at times is awkward and which is slowing our united rehearsal progress almost more than errors in pitch.

If you will train yourselves to *talk* through the text, or sing it on a monotone, with abolutely secure syllables and rhythm, I think you'll find that the notes will come quickly and cleanly on Monday nights.

In some respects the large amateur chorus is by nature a spongy, imprecise instrument. That two-hundred people will see a gesture in an identical way and respond in a single split-instant, or will feel a tempo and pulse in absolute identity, is more than man has a right to hope. (Timing is trouble enough for two, let alone two-hundred.) Moreover, the "untrained" voice is untrained not only as to timbre but also as to mobility and dexterity. – And Bach's demands on vocal agility are more extreme than almost any we can think of in Western music.

Two things occur to me: first, that Bach demands a scarcely conceivable maximum of *individual* responsibility. It is not as though a chorus or a section of a chorus had x-amount of responsibility, and each person in the chorus one two-hundredth of it. In the main, the jumble rumble jungle of choral imprecision need not exist if each entire person will accept a whole responsibility. Unison is the result not of a timorous collectivism, but of an accountable individualism. When each person sings the right note with the right color with the right loudness at the right time—that's unison. "Leaning of the everlasting arms" may get you into some sort of heaven, but it won't be Bach's.

Secondly, in spite of the practical improbabilities of absolute choral precision, it would be a mistake to undervalue the overwhelming power of Bach's spiritual-musical fervor. The spirit unites, and Bach's spirit unites mightily. It's almost impossible *not* to go along with the *Cum Sancto Spiritu*. You can't fight a fervor that big. You might as well join it.

R. S.

April 9, 1998

Dear ASOCC *(Absolute & Supreme Oracles of Choral Consummitry)* –

When does the next *B Minor Mass* leave?

– And, if these things come along only every 250 years, what do we do for the next 249 and 51/52nds?

Thank you all, and thank we all JSB.

R

St. John Passion

February 18, 1969

It is Bach's phrasing and the value of understanding his architectural energies about which I wish to write. We already have an understanding of Bach's large-scale structure and its energies—what remains for us as musicians is to begin to experience vocally the energetic value of the details. We must break open the long Bach line into its minute and basic phrasings. I think we shall see that these great architectural energies exist also in miniature. – And I think we shall add to the conventional query: "Does Bach's harmony grow out of his melody, or his melody out of his harmony?" – Or a more subtle wonder, "Does his basic motive prescribe his structure, or his structure define his motive?"

The following are notes to guide your own meanings in your own study of the Bach *St. John Passion:*

1. The Bach line is to be understood as *Energy,* and a very directional energy—towards something. (If you want to gain a very practical understanding of that: sing the last note of a phrase; then the last two notes, with the sense of the next to the last leading into the last; then the last three notes leading into the next and into the last; then the last four notes—and so on forever.)

2. Energy is very tight. It is tight melodically—as most of the melodic patterns are diatonic (scale-wise—infrequent leaps). And it is tight metrically: most any running pattern can be broken into small energy units of two, three and four notes. (And while it would be a mistake in the final performance to chop up a beautiful line into these fragments, for purposes of rehearsal it is important that we understand and observe them.)

3. In the main, the Energy is not self-supplied by the "points to which things move," but is supplied by the notes which directly precede these points. It is "pick-up" into the main beat which is the energetic value. It is the 1/8 and 1/16 note which is used almost as a *spring-board* into the larger units. – For rehearsal purposes it should be almost "bouncing" in quality.

4. The recognition of Balance of Energy is the chief clue to proper phrasing. (The awareness that the descending curve is balanced by a thrust from below—or a series of falling values balanced by a series of thrusts; the awareness that the energy of an ascending line sometimes begins to wear thin—and before it does Bach drops below and bounces back up to balance and sustain his impulse.)

5. In all Bach lines (not excepting scale-wise motion) there is an independence due even to the smallest of rhythmic values. It is the "terracelike" quality of

notes which do not glide, but achieve their legato by a masterful sense of direction, not by slurring.

R. S.

April 5, 1962

There is a real musicological and scale-of-forces problem, as most of you know, with our performance next week of Bach's *St. John Passion*. On page *ix* of Arthur Mendel's superb preface to his exceptional edition he writes:

"When a symphony orchestra with sixty or more strings takes part in the performance of such a work, all the proportions are changed, and everything must be reconsidered. My own opinion is that such changes are not for the better, and I am convinced that while Bach might have delighted in the resources of the modern symphony orchestra, the music he would have written for it would have been designed to make the best use of those resources: he would not have welcomed the mere multiplication of having hundreds of performers do what could be done by several dozen. The fresco that covers the wall is not just an enlargement of the tempera painting on the altar panel. Bach's music is as full of eloquent detail as a panel painting, and it is no more improved, to my way of thinking, by performance with multiplied forces than a string quartet played by string orchestra, or a violin and piano sonata played by a dozen fiddlers and pianists. It is a delusion of our time that infinite refinement of detail is not compatible with breadth of conception, and that to be great a thing must be 'great big.' Even in our large concert halls we do not resort to such distortions; and I think even in such surroundings it should be perfectly possible to readjust one's scale of dynamic values so as to be able to listen to Bach's music performed by such forces as he had in mind."

As with our performance two years ago of the *St. Matthew Passion*, we have only two quasi-justifications. The first is that with the amateur choral society the performance exists in some large measure for the enjoyment, instruction and edification of those who perform it. So long as we already-exist as a "symphonic" chorus of two hundred-twenty voices, it would be difficult and not a little unfair to deny 80% of us the opportunity of performing this work.

Still, even this has to be an admitted inconsistency between purpose and organization. Certainly we would all agree in principal that musical societies exist for the optimum performance of music, not that music exists for the optimum self-expression of societies. It follows, does it not, that once one has decided to perform a work of the proportions and textures of the *St. John Passion* one ought to construct and shape his forces to serve the music, not the opposite.

Actually, the only parts of the work which might be "musicolegally" served by our chorus would be the chorales. The opening and closing choruses are grand in design and manner and are not irremedially damaged by a large chorus—though even that should be not so large as ours. – But from there on the musical texture and dramatic situation demand real chamber music forces. Smallest of these forces could be the four soldiers who cast lots for Jesus' clothing in #54; next in order, the Chief Priests of #46 and #50; following these— but still small—the soldiers of #34 or the accusers of Peter in #17; and finally the "crowd" which shouts "Crucify!" "We have a law!" etc. Even these latter choruses—as also the opening and closing choruses—were sung in Bach's time by less than 15 or 16 singers and balanced by an equal number of instruments!

Mendel continues somewhat resignedly:

"Nevertheless, the resources needed for performance of the Bach choral works, with the exacting demands they make on both singers and instrumentalists, are usually hard to find outside our symphony orchestras, and large-scale performances will probably continue to be in the majority for a long time to come. Many musicians and writers have jumped to the conclusion that since the symphony orchestra has five or six times as many strings as Bach had, the woodwinds must be multiplied in proportion (though as far as I know no one has suggested 15 trumpets and 5 pairs of kettledrums for the *B Minor Mass*). The fact is that music and arithmetic are not so simply connected. Sixty strings can play as softly as ten, and five flutes in unison do not sound five times as loud as one."

Here we find a crumb or two of hope. If sixty strings can play as softly as ten, then two hundred voices may be capable of singing as lightly as thirty-three. If, in the few days remaining to us, we really settle only for lightness of tone and clarity of texture, if we occasionally divide our forces to represent the smaller groups of participants, if we save our congregational tone and weight for the chorales, we may get by without burying the work under an eruptive flood of aural lava and ash.

Try, 'come Sunday. First come, first serve,

R. S.

St. Matthew Passion

February 16, 1960

Most of us are aware, I suppose, of the Roman Catholic doctrine of *transubstantiation,* according to which at the consecration of the Eucharist the bread and wine become the actual body and blood of Christ. Well, that may or may not be your faith, but it seems to me that something very like transubstantiation is operative in such master-works as the *St. Matthew Passion*. In the presence of such a creation—whose spirit *must* be very near to that of Jesus himself, "Sense is transfigured quite." We are no longer "play-actors"—and the music itself, I believe, is a Eucharist in which are dissolved the mutually exclusive boundaries of spirit and substance, time and space, the mortal and the immortal.

"Come ye daughters, share my anguish" is not the *picturization* of the spirit of anguish, it *is* the spirit of anguish. We do not engage to portray a mother or a world of mothers crying over the slaughter of their innocent sons. Herein anguish cries only unto anguish—and we *are* anguish.

"Let him be crucified!" is not the simple picturization of the cry of another crowd on another day. By the temper and the stature of this music time is obliterated, and we share that crucifixion. We're participants. We *crucify*. I don't mean figuratively. I don't mean "so to speak." I mean crucify. The scape-goat and the sacrificial slaughter of the Aztec innocents and the crucifixion of Jesus are one and the same. They are the obedience of the human spirit to the knowledge of its own guilt and its own mortality. There was no time when Jesus was not crucified; and his blood assuredly is on us and on our children. I believe the music of Bach says that.

The thing I think I'm trying to say is that we are *not* engaged in the *dramatization* of the death—and triumph—of Jesus. But by the dignity and integrity of this great music, the spirit of which reaches out to touch that of Jesus himself, we are forced to acknowledge our participation in that death and triumph. The *Passion* music is not dramatic in the theatrical sense of acting a part. It is drama in the cosmic sense—of being a part. It is not a series of masques to be put on and manipulated to the maximum "effect." It is—if you are sufficiently mystic—a sort of Eucharist whose physical properties issue in something quite transcending time and place.

It seems to me, therefore, treacherous and abortive to superimpose the imagined excitements of a given crowd on a given day by the devices of accelerando, ritendando and dynamic effect. By the spiritual genius of Bach the greater drama is already built into the musical structure. It is wrong to play the pit; the people must be brought to the music.

I wouldn't say that there is any great danger that it will be otherwise in this instance. But it's nice to keep sights high and feet dry. Anyway, I know now what I meant when I said two weeks ago that rehearsal on the *Passion* should be very nearly a sacrament.

R. S.

(The above was sent to the Collegiate Chorale.)

March 17, 1960

– Just a short word this crowded week to let you know that it is good to be back with you, and that I anticipate, more eagerly than with any other work since coming to Cleveland, the final weeks of rehearsals and performances of the *St. Matthew Passion*.

On this Sunday afternoon, March 20, at 5:30 P.M., I will meet with all of you—sopranos, altos, tenors, basses—whose membership numbers end in odd digits (-1, -3, -5, -7, -9, should there be higher physicists in the crowd). You people form Chorus I, and this is our lone rehearsal. Your attendance is essential.

Have you had occasion during the work on the *Passion* to note the extraordinary range, depth and complexity of roles the chorus plays in the work? There are three major ones. First there are the various groups of participants in the drama—the disciples, priests, crowds, etc., who sing the "action" choruses. Second is the congregation of believers before whom the drama is being played, who respond to the most sensitive moments with their impulsive common chorale. (The first group responds to the act, the second to the retelling of the act. Each of these groups, then, has a time and a place.)

The third role of the chorus is the most complex of all—for it has of itself neither time nor place. Its locale is the universe of ideas, of morality; its time is long before and long after, as well as the instant of the work's creation and the instant of its retelling. The chorus in this role stands apart from both actor and audience, and bears witness to the meaning of the play, its intent and progress.

What is almost beyond understanding is the manner in which these roles are fantastically—almost surrealistically—mixed. For instance, what is the time and place of the opening chorus? Is it an invitation to the play we are about to see? Or is it an invitation to the crucifixion itself? (Note that the congregation in the form of the chorale, which enters at letter A, is responding to the drama before the drama has begun.)

Mark the curious mixture of congregational and priestly functions in No. 26. The chorus this time is an abstract company, somehow a part of, and responding within, the soloist's mind.

What are we to say of the chorus in No. 33? "Loose him! Halt ye! Bind him not!" Who is now singing—the actors, the congregation, or you and I? Who sings, "Have lightning and thunder all vanished? Then open thy fiery abysses, O Hell!" – And what a mixture is No. 35! Congregational chorale—but so developed musically that it stands apart from both actor and audience.

– Perhaps these are the moments in which you and I here and now are most deeply involved.

It is as though there were a theatre on the stage of which a play is being acted—and that is one drama. In the hall of the theatre there is an audience, and this audience interrupts the actors on stage—and that is the second drama. And somewhere above this theatre watching both these dramas stand you and I. – And at incredible moments (Think what craftsmanship this represents on Bach's part)—at incredible moments the actors on the stage are suddenly frozen, their posture or gesture transfixed, the audience in an instant is turned to stone, time holds breath, and you and I become a part of the third great drama—that of the meanings of things and events, of love and hate, of to live and to kill—a drama before and beyond time, before even this particular *Passion,* yet known to us here and now.

There are layers upon layers of art and awareness in the *St. Matthew Passion.*

R. S.

February 27, 1975

Friends –

'Most remarkable minister I ever knew closely was pastor of Shaker Heights Unitarian Church, Cleveland. Robert Killiam's special intellectual interest was the web of moral, ethical and psychological dilemmas of Shakespearean drama; and his sermons were an extraordinary explorative surgery into man's trauma and occasional triumphs.

He had come to music—of a quality to match his reading—rather late in life, and to Bach after the 19th century Romantics. He heard his first *St. Matthew Passion* at age 50-plus, and he was shattered.

He recognized rather early on, I think, the coordinating and contrasting time-frames of Bach's drama: the *then* of the narrative and the "actors," the *now* of the congregational choral responses, and the *ever* of the solo (and occasionally choral) commentary, and he expected, I think, to be moved frequently by Bach's exploration and surgery into the bodies of grief and indignation. – But he hadn't expected to be "had." He had expected to maintain an evaluative and concerned consciousness—just as when he read. – But his sense of place, time and self were fissured, and then refashioned after Bach's "image." I never saw him so baffled and shaken—even dying of cancer much too soon.

"Elijah" is a remarkable, enjoyable and, perhaps, even instructive "entertainment." One delights in the "cast" of characters—even to earthquakes, fires and still small voices.

But in the *St. Matthew Passion* the chief and ever-present character is the mind of man—yours and mine and Everyman's—as it is also antagonist, stage, theatre and audience. We have all the lines.

Lordy, lordy, what a difference that makes.

R

Aus Der Tiefe

Written when he was twenty-one or twenty-two years old, this could well be the *first* of Bach's two-to-three hundred cantatas.

Like the motets the music never quite comes to a complete stop—though there clearly are different and successive sections of slow/fast or solo/tutti.

Jaroslav Pelikan, theologian and historian of Yale Divinity School, recognizes three theological traditions in Bach's music and his choice of texts. There is, of course, confessional orthodoxy and the heritage of the Reformation. There is the influence of Rationalism and the Enlightenment. (Bach was a near contemporary of Voltaire.) And there is the intense subjectivity, moral earnestness, the grievous awareness of inescapable sin which robbed one of personal fellowship with the soul of Jesus and which emerged in Bach's years with the movement called Pietism. Methodism was its logical conclusion.

Can there be a more intense and grievous lamentation than that which opens *Aus der Tiefe?*

And—don't it just beat the dickens out of *The Old Rugged Cross* and *Just as I am without One Plea?*

Spivey Hall Spoken Program Notes
for Concerts by The Robert Shaw Chamber Singers

October 14–15, 1994

Ladies and Gentlemen –

Good evening.

Because the Shaws in recent weeks have had occasion to move their residence and household goods a few hundred feet up the hill, and because that move necessitated the construction of considerable shelf space to accommodate their various libraries, I am in a position to disclose this evening some absolutely gratuitous and inconsequential statistics concerning the life produce of some of music's creative masters.

The last edition of Bach's Complete Works (1851–1899) numbers 45 volumes, totals roughly 13,000 pages and takes about 6 and 1/2 feet of shelf space. Among other things, this means that Bach's creative output was a full 18 inches longer than that (say) of Wolfgang Love-God Mozart.

– And we are told in the *New Grove's Dictionary of Music* of 20 volumes (1980) that since the year Bach's library was divided among his heirs upon his death, roughly two-fifths to one-half of his music has been lost. Did he really total twenty thousand pages of manuscript? – Of that intellectual quality?

Do you recall the Winnie the Pooh story in which Eeyore's house is blown to bits by the wind, and Pooh and Piglet rebuild it in a protected corner of the forest? Eeyore himself takes all the credit—for building, in the first place, an indestructible house: "Do you see, Pooh? Do you see, Piglet? – Brains first, and then hard work. That's the way to build a house!"

Sure, brains first—from the gene pool. – But what about that "hard work?" Who among us, for instance, could copy 20,000 pages of manuscript in a lifetime—let alone, create them?

For anyone who enjoys choral music (and the music of J. S. Bach)—it would be hard to imagine a richer fare than this evening's program.

In the days when there are a professional touring chorus (carefully and consciously misnamed a "Chorale") one had to be extremely careful in building a touring program. The choir and chamber orchestra would be on the road from 10 to 20 weeks at a time; giving 13 concerts every 14 days; in cities and towns, never the same town twice, in concert halls and high-school gymnasia 200 to 500 miles distant from one another—and all before there was an Interstate or two.

Each piece on the program had to have a special and memorable profile—for one had only one shot at any audience. It also had to be music which the *performers* could find both challenging and satisfying night after all day on the bus after night after all day on the bus—for 10 to 20 weeks. Sixty-five *B Minor Masses* in seventy days? Traveling ten to fifteen thousand miles (in a country only 3,000 miles coast to coast)? One hundred thirty Mozart *Requiems* in twenty weeks?

Each of the works we play and sing tonight is a survivor of that rigor. More importantly: each of the works *enabled us to survive*: a musical St. Bernard to the rescue in a potential blizzard of musical monotony.

Historically, the motet began as an unaccompanied choral composition, based on a Latin sacred text, and designed to be performed in a service of Catholic worship. By Bach's time—and with his help—it had grown to encompass three to eleven movements, but with integrating melodies and *without* significant pauses. Usually it was accompanied by organ and bass instruments, and not infrequently had all of its vocal lines doubled by instruments—perhaps for outdoor performance—like funerals.

On the other hand, the cantatas in general were a compendium of several separate movements (one of which might be a motet-like chorus), and with *independent* instrumental accompaniment.

In three respects *Jesu, meine Freude* is unique among Bach's motets:

First: in length. Though not long by symphonic standards, it is two to five times as long as his other motets.
Second: Though one may purposely move quickly from one movement to the next in its performance, there are eleven distinct movements—from one to three minutes in length.
Third: It furnishes a perfect example of Bach's symmetrical musical structure:
Eleven movements –
Numbers 1 and 11 are identical straight-forward settings of the hymn.
Numbers 2 and 10 are similar, nearly identical, choruses.
Numbers 3 and 9 are chorale variations.
Numbers 4 and 8 are choral trios—the first in ladies' voices, the second would be mens'—if one had male altos—which Bach did.
Numbers 5 and 7 are chorale variations.
Number 6 (in the middle) a central fugue.

Very little has come down to us concerning Bach's own performances. He does not always specify which instruments are to play—or how many voices are to be used. With the exception of a motet not on this evening's program, therefore, every performance of a Bach motet is something of a reconstruction: different numbers of performers with different weights of voices, different instrumental doublings. This evening's choir, smaller than our usual Spivey forces, and small by symphonic or classical standards, may still be 3 to 4 times larger than Bach's chorus of men and boys; and our instrumental consort, though small, and seldom more than one on a part, some would think to be denser in texture than was Bach's custom. Against the Festival performance traditions which were the familiarity of my youth, it is, I think, a giant step in the right direction musicologically—while still addressing the presence and function of the Lutheran Chorale—and the size of almost all of today's concert halls—except this one.

It is one "mother" of a piece.

Komm, Jesu, Komm

Our instrumentation for *Komm, Jesu, komm* is directly patterned after the motet for double choir which Bach himself orchestrated, "The Spirit Also Helpeth Us": Choir I to be doubled by solo strings; and Chorus II doubled by double reeds—Oboe, 2 English Horns and Bassoon.

The concluding section, called "Aria," is not an "aria" in our present sense (that is: an extended piece for solo voice with independent and elaborate instrumental accompaniment).

The term derives from the Latin word for "air" or "atmosphere." By the last quarter of the century before Bach it is found in association with the more specific word "canzonetta"—which we might call simply a song. Its text, as you will note from your program, is "rhyming" and "strophic," and, at the turn into Bach's century such strophic verses were set, we are informed, "mostly for three or four voices."

Who among us can match this assurance, elegance, sweetness and near-delight at the prospect of this life's closing.

Christ Lag in Todesbanden

This may actually be Bach's second or third attempt at a cantata. Each of its movements is based upon the chorale melody—known from memory by all good Lutherans.

Each of the six verses is a miracle; but if the eyes do not moisten during Verse Two, either you are dead—or we should be.

Singet Dem Herrn

It sometimes seems to me that the tintinnabulation in *Singet dem Herrn,* so carefully and consciously contrived, is so great that one could as well listen to it simply as sheer noise—as the random but mounting clamor of untuned monstrous bells.

I am aware that religious ecstasy has the power on occasion to move crowds of otherwise nearly-normal human beings into a group pandemonium—Biblically extolled as "speaking in tongues."

I think maybe I mistrust the worthiness of incoherency and confusion when they are exalted as a sign of Deity's presence.

– But I rejoice in the turnabout: Here is Creative Intelligence so secure that it can order frenzy, can risk delirium.

"Sing unto the Lord a *new* song
Make a joyful noise . . ."
a "new" song—267 years old last May 12
and it keeps on going
– and still going –
it's still going.

SAMUEL BARBER

The Lovers

January 30, 1975

Further thoughts on Barber/Neruda's The Lovers *and "Texts Suitable for Group Singing" –*

A couple of rehearsals ago, while suggesting that those of our chorus who found the texts of *The Lovers* personally offensive could (and should) withdraw from these performances without prejudicing their continuing membership in the ASO Choruses, I ventured two further and personal observations.

The first was that, however explicit Neruda's language may be (available to us in this instance only in translation—which leaves our information incomplete), there is no way to equate the candor, fervor and human commitment of this poetry with public comfort-station graffiti. Irretrievably inappropriate would be the snicker, the wick or the mal jest.

Second, it seemed to me then, as it does now, that, human existence being what it is and isn't, it might well prove to be somewhat less than complete should one pass through it without experiencing with another person the fervor, candor and total giving/receiving of which this poet speaks. Subsequently, pursuing the etymology of *porno*graphy, I flushed *connubio*graphy, thereby flying with the greatest of ease (so it seemed) from the salacious to the salubrious.

It has occurred to me since that the question of textual "propriety" hinges not only—perhaps not even most importantly—upon literary excellence and human integrity, but upon the condition whether the "work of art" is intended for *group performance* and *group consumption*.

The current fashion of poetry "readings" notwithstanding (Dylan Thomas was the star in my time—who's yours?), since the invention of printing, poetry probably has become the most "personal" and "private" of the arts; and that which may be uniquely perceptive, "touching," "revealing" and generative in the solitary contemplation of the printed page may prove embarrassing or unredeemably ludicrous in public performance.

The early years of the Collegiate Chorale (1940–1944) were spent in close association with the Fred Waring organization during a time of war. The Chorale's first and most frequent early appearances were at mammoth patriotic rallies—war-bond shows, "I am an American Day," recruitment drives—singing the national anthems and associated "popular" songs: "There'll be blue-birds over the white cliffs of Dover," "When that man is dead and gone," 'cause "Beyond the blue horizon lies a wonderful day"—*ad infinitum victoriam*.

"Begin the Beguine" was the top pop of the time and just before the time, and

I shall not forget the blush of the mind with which I first heard 500 count-em totally sibilized voices ppppping, "Let me whissper to you once again, 'Dahleeng, ah-ee luv eeoo!' "

I formed the theory then, unshaken until now, that the matters large groups of people can sing about—without embarrassment—have to be matters of a fundamental and natural common cause. (This theory puts to one side for the moment—but does not dismiss—the intimate chamber-music delights of mad-rigal singing: "April is in the face of whom?") According to this thinking those texts most suitable for massed voices are those which voice a community of national heritage or current allegiance, and those which confirm a common religious commitment—since both celebrate naturally men's native consan-guinity. By this thinking the *summum bonum* for group singing (word-wise, that is, and one-to-the should be sufficient) would be that text which celebrates some *"Holy War"*—may the Lord send us better judgement.

– To return to *The Lovers,* simply by inventory of physiological equipment involved, it cannot have escaped anyone's attention that sex is a reasonably private affair. The gang-bang is ineluctable hari-kari for the whole-soul. – And it may indeed be that the joys of sex are not increased by singing about it.

(Large parenthesis—one absolutely precious *divertissement:*

Some years ago we issued an album of Robert Russell Bennett arrangements for chorus and orchestra entitled *On Stage*—"All the Things You Are," "Septem-ber Song," "Hallelujah," "Dancing in the Dark"—and many many more.

Some months later I received the following hand-written letter—long, alas, lost—which I can quote almost from memory:

"Dear Mr. Shaw,

"My husband and I want to thank you for your beautiful recording of On Stage. – But why, why, why! did you ever let RCA-Victor put the selections in that order? Couldn't you have put all the fast-loud numbers on one side and all the romantic numbers on the other side:

"When my husband and I feel romantic, we like to turn the lights down low and put on your record. And then just when things are getting *really* romantic (like "Through the Years—I'll take my place beside you—I'll come to you no matter where or when") the chorus and orchestra bust in with "Buckle down, Winsocki!" and one of us has to get up and turn off the phonograph. I could just scream!

"Won't you please see if you can get Victor to change the sequence?

"Sincerely,"

– close parentheses.)

I have one final thought in this matter, and it gives me the hope that our mission is only improbable.

No matter what forces may be assembled for the *performance* of music, *listening* to music—even in a public auditorium—is an almost bafflingly private affair. Even when one goes to a concert with the most intimate of friends or beloveds, listening, and all the associations and imagery which it invokes, is so extraordinarily subjective that no other person really hears the "same" music. (Compare professional critics' reviews to your own participative experiences or recollections.)

The reassuring fact is that just as Neruda's words are personal and solitary, Barber's music is also personal and solitary. He writes from the solitude of his own soul to the solitude of another's soul; and that the event is "inhabited" by many does not qualify the loneliness of the transfer.

The corollary for the performer is that precisely at the point at which—one touches his "deepest," most vulnerable, unsharable selfawareness he touches all other men.

R

P.S. Now, learn your notes.

BARBER'S *PRAYERS OF KIERKEGAARD,* BARTÓK'S *CANTATA PROFANA,* VAUGHAN WILLIAMS'S *DONA NOBIS PACEM*

October 8, 1997

Friends –

Studying again the three remarkable pieces which form our program for November I find myself mulling the differences and similarities in their textual sources and assemblage.

For years it has seemed to me that, since the choral instrument is itself a community of discipline and endeavor, the texts most appropriate to choral composition and performance must be texts which express a community of experience, ideology or hope.—Almost inevitably that leads to literatures— poetic or narrative—of a religious or ethnic/cultural/nationalistic nature. (The popular song of Broadway or Hollywood in the days of Fitzgerald through Hemingway was a one-on-one love-ballad. No matter how skillfully we rehearsed and performed *Begin the Beguine* in the days of radio glee clubs and War-Bond Rallies, there came the dreadful moment when twenty to two-hundred men had to sing in a hushed unison, "Darling, I love you . . ." Talk about over-kill!)

The literary communions invoked by Barber, Bartók and Vaughan Williams are various and fascinating.

Barber's text is unexceptionably religious. Its second prayer, sung by the soprano soloist, is down-right "Christ-y." It's first could almost be the pantheistic meditation of a pre-Colombian American Indian. – And, though they are apparently not drawn from Fear and Trembling, the final two prayers earnestly and violently underline Kierkegaard's horror at the philosophical chasm created by early nineteenth-century scientific "Enlightenment," over which he could leap only by faith.

When Samuel Barber was here for our performances of *The Lovers,* I missed a rare opportunity to ask him how and why he had chosen these Kierkegaard texts. *Prayers* was written more than a decade before his hurt and despair at the critical scorching of *Antony and Cleopatra,* commissioned for the opening of the new "Met" at Lincoln Center; and though we knew each other as "Bob" and "Sam," and met with the natural frequency of Westchester residents and NYC musicians, he never seemed to me a prayer-meetin' Sunday-goin' Promise-Keeper. – But *Prayers of Kierkegaard* is absolutely sincere, and a first-rate work which, though difficult to prepare and perform well, will grow in popular symphonic acceptance through some generations. In time we even may be able to forgive his sexistentialistic "Father in heaven." – Forty-two male deities in pages 40–43 alone! (Do female naval cadets at Annapolis sing "Eternal Mother, strong to save . . ."?)

Bartók's *Cantata Profana,* however, is precisely that: "profana," in the sense of "secular," or "not connected with religious matters." It's text is an ethnic/cultural fable, obscure in origin and meaning.

Is there a "moral?" Are the sons turned into stags because they don't want to work the family farm? – Because they prefer to play in the woods? – And what is the meaning of the mysterious bridge they cross? Must Daddy and Mummy always suffer when kids leave home? Finally, what happened? Did Daddy just give up and go home? – Apparently the boys/stags are still out there somewhere. Dodgin' bullets?

– But isn't it a fabulous piece? – meaning "fabled." And fabulously colored—both instrumentally and chorally? Like many folk-tales, myths, legends and epics, truth lies somewhere in the middle. – Because there is no ending? As Kurt Vonnegut has it: " . . . and so it goes . . ."

R. Vaughan Williams, however, stands astride both religion and cultural/nationalistic secularity. – Yet the texts—sacred and secular—so it seems to me, integrate handsomely and reinforce one another . . . to even the most intimate of details. Not only does Walt Whitman, in the words of the baritone soloist, "draw near, bend down and touch lightly with my lips the white face in the coffin," but the Hebrew psalmist sings in the finale that "righteousness and peace have kissed each other." (More recent Biblical translations have it in a future tense: "justice and peace will meet . . . and kiss.")

The millennial prayers of the psalmists and prophets find resonance and reverberation in Whitman's poetry of the American Civil War. (Will that one ever be over? – Though economic and political positions may by now be reconciled, ethical fallout still hovers.) Whitman, by the composer's selection and by proximity to ancient Hebraic scripture, loses his frequent verbosity and pomp. – And I find nothing in these scriptural texts, excerpted from a pastoral religious culture thousands of years old, which does not also make good and necessary sense for a cybernetic civilization.

The concert hall, I think, has no right to become a mourner's bench. To each his or her own bumper-sticker and dash-board ornament. (Barber may indeed sail almost too close to the shoals of inadvertent conversion—a condition which he would deplore and deny.)

We are accustomed to calling music a "universal" language. Is it possible that music's "universality" is of such power that it can rub even the rough and doctrinaire edges off the stones in Kierkegaard's Kiddleys? (I said Kiddley, diddle I?)

Certainly Bach's *Passions* and *B Minor Mass,* Beethoven's *Missa Solemnis,* Mozart's *Requiem,* Bloch's *Sacred Service,* Stravinsky's *Symphony of Psalms* and Britten's *War Requiem* appear to be able to create sanctuary, to propose a human contract well beyond their sectarian confines.

Isn't it nice that composers gave us beautiful words to sing? Don't you wish we could?

Pax,

R

BÉLA BARTÓK

Cantata Profana

September 12, 1996

Friends –

The first order of business is to clarify the variety of individual vocal assignments in Bartók's *Cantata Profana*.

The confusion (some of which, unfortunately and inadvertently, has been carried over even to our present editing) has two sources:

First, there is Bartók's own carelessness or thoughtlessness about the circumstances of performance. (There is some evidence that he considered the *Cantata* of such difficulty that it would be many years before it would be performed.) – No doubt, for its time it was difficult. – Actually, written in 1930, it was first performed in London in 1934 and, so far as I can ascertain, its first performance in the United States was by an augmented (42-voice) RSChorale on January 2, 1952.

Bartók's choral writing asks for 3 different systemizations of the choral forces:

1.   The conventional four-part SATB chorus.
2.   The Double-Chorus: Two equal four-part SATB choruses used antiphonally.
3.   A "Double" Chorus which is, in fact, a single 8-part (S1 S2 A1 A2 T1 T2 B1 B2) chorus used not antiphonally, but as the normal four-part chorus with each part divided.

Digress for a moment: In the small chorus of professional voices, given equally skilled musicianship, there are real advantages in a performing schematic which places the singers in quartets. (Number One), they feel freer to use their optimum vocal abilities; and (Number Two), hearing easily the other vocal parts around them gives them a richer experience in ensemble singing.

Note, however, the difficulties involved: Number One, it takes an enormous amount of skill and will to maintain a sectional identity and purity of sound when surrounded by three or seven different parts, and voices of individual timbre.

Number Two: from the conductor's point of view—since there is no way he can urge one section to sing louder or more quietly, the music must be meticulously edited both as to relative dynamics and to the number of voices assigned to each note or series of notes.

Number Three: The audience is substantially limited to a nonaural experience: the sound comes only from one central source; there is no Soprano/Stage Right and Bass/Stage Left, (Violins/Stage Right, Celli and Contrabasses/Stage Left). – Some would say that this diminishes a listener's enjoyment—as monovisual (one-eyed) sight would diminish information received and enjoyment.

The symphonic chorus is, of course, a different vocal animal. In our century its membership must be large enough to match the sonority of today's symphony orchestra, and to deliver a composer's text above that sonority. In the United States, and, probably, most of the world that programs Western symphonic music, symphonic choruses almost without exception are "volunteer," or 90%–95% volunteer.

Though associated for years with the development and performance of professional choruses in the U.S., I happen to be one who believes very, very strongly in the importance of amateur music-making.

Amateurism may have to stay after school to meet today's symphonic performance standards—but it also is our greatest gift to our civilization (uncivilization?) as well as our own great personal joy and accomplishment.

Mostly because of its size, the symphonic chorus has unique problems when it comes to performance logistics. All of us understand that our membership encompasses a vast range of talents, both vocal and musical. We have from time to time super sight-readers (mostly instrumentalists) whose *fortissimo* at a distance of 12 inches would not twich the ears of an insomniac Doberman Pinscher; and we've auditioned a King-Kong-Sing-Song or two capable of blowing Levine to the Third-Tier at the Met, who thought that sight-singing was "singing with your eyes open."

For a number of reasons, therefore, the "symphony" chorus seems to work most efficiently in *sections*.

1. Some of us, fortunately, are (relatively) "leaders," and some of us, less fortunately, are (relatively) "followers"—and sectional singing allows the followers to sing more comfortably and more productively.
2. The vocal sections basically line up with their orchestral string counterparts: S/A voices and instruments to Stage-Right and T/B voices and instruments to Stage-Left.
3. This offers to the audience a natural binaural listening experience.

All this, my friends, is prologue to the work of the week, which is Bartók's *Cantata Profana*. Get your pencils and mark your scores:

I. Bartók's Double Choruses: those which are clearly antiphonal in nature, or which have conflicting tonalities, and would therefore gain from the following performance schematic:

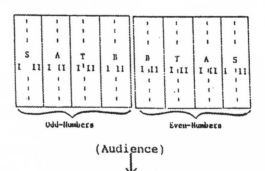

This Odd-Even division of parts holds for the following pages: (Mark each page!)

1. p. 2 thru p. 10 (ms. 17 thru 53)
2. p. 16 thru p. 18 (ms. 126 thru 139, Mvt. II)
3. p. 28 thru p. 31 (ms. 21 thru 37, Mvt. II)
4. p. 42 (ms. 188 thru 192)

II. Bartók's "Double Choruses" which have an antiphonal function, and which are best served by the conventional 8-part divisi, with Chorus #1 formed by S1, A1, T1 and B1, and Chorus #2 formed by S2, A2, T2 and B2. (Mark these pages carefully!)

1. p. 24 and p. 25 (ms. 180 thru 189)
2. p. 45 thru p. 49 (ms. 1 thru 34)
3. p. 52 thru p. 54 (ms. 65 thru 93)

III. Bartók's Choruses which call for a united single chorus (not "Double"), usually calling for 4 parts only (SATB), but also expanding to 6-voice and 7-voice writing. Note well the following:

1. p. 11 thru p. 15 (ms. 74 thru 119)
2. p. 19 thru p. 23 (ms. 140 thru 179)
3. p. 32 (ms. 38 thru 41)
4. p. 35 (ms. 98 thru 102)
5. pp. 36, 37 (ms. 108 thru 114)
6. p. 40 (ms. 163 thru 166)
7. pp. 50, 51 (ms. 35 thru 64)

Most of these assignments already are clearly marked in your scores.

IV. Now, please note two changes in your printed score, which I discovered after Monday night's rehearsal, while examining a facsimile of Bartók's hand-script score which I found in my analytical and performance notes of 1952.

A. I found that on our pages 26 and 27 (Mvt. II) Bartók had intended for Chorus #1 only (our Odd-numbered/Stage-Right) to begin this fugato. Therefore, mark ms. 9, 13 and 17 Chorus #1 only. Chorus #2 enters on p. 28 at m. 21.

   The odd-numbered treatment also applies to pages 15–16, m. 120 through the first beat of m. 126.
B. Turn to pages 16 and 17, ms. 126 thru 131.

I find that Bartók expected these measures to be identical in both choruses. That is, each chorus had three women's voices and two men's voices. Perhaps for reasons of printing (or for some unprintable reason) the engravers allotted the top female voice to the Sopranos of Chorus #1, and the middle voice to the Sopranos of Chorus #2, leaving the low voice identical in both choirs. This would result in imbalance. Therefore, ladies: please add the Chorus #1 Soprano voice to Chorus #2, and add the Soprano voice of Chorus #2 to Chorus #1, and use our customary 3-part female *divisi*.

C.   Movement I, m. 139.

The editors made a similar error here, making it impossible to arrive at an intelligent *divisi* at m. 140.

1.   Change m. 139 in the Alto parts of both choruses to read:

The A-flat on beat 2 will be a continuation of the middle voice, which in the previous measure was printed in the Soprano staff.

2.   Similarly, change the Bass parts of Chorus #1 and Chorus #2, m. 139, to read:

Now, it's taken a lot longer to write this than it will be for you to read it and write 'em in. In spite of the fact that Rev. Hallmark has made a mint of money out of it, "togetherness" really is one of September's precious fewnesses, and we shouldn't have to stop the onward march of 220-plus eager *Cantata* sanctifiers next Monday for a handful of *Cantata* Profaners.

R

October 24, 1996

Friends –

There never has been any doubt in my mind that Bartók's *Cantata Profana* was the most difficult of the three twentieth-century works scheduled for next week's program. – But that we should have spent the major portion of our rehearsal time on it, and still be well below our usual standards of performance, is both frustrating and perplexing.

Think of it. There are fewer than ten minutes of choral singing in the

Cantata (vs. eleven-plus in Barber's *Prayers,* and approximately twenty-five in Vaughan Williams' *Dona Nobis Pacem*), but the latter two are on the cusp of performance temperament and vitality, while *Profana* still has dreck to shed and speed to learn.

There are three factors in our *status-quo* to be examined. (– Defined by some home-spun filosofer as "the mess we's in.") First is the nature of the instrument—the volunteer symphony chorus. Second is the nature of the music itself—its harmonic/metric/melodic languages and the scoring thereof. Third is the nature of the teaching/learning process—including methods and time allotted.

1. The volunteer symphony chorus has both credits and debits, merits and demerits. Principal among its credits is that it allows the general citizenry to participate in the study and reproduction of "Works of Art" at the very highest level of human aspiration and accomplishment. That this benefits the general community (church/school/social structure) as well as its participants has been proved time and again.

The debits of the volunteer symphony chorus relate to its size and to the diversity of the individual attainments of its members.

As regards size, most of us recognize now that it simply is not appropriate to expect aesthetic satisfaction or spiritual "revelation" from a performance of Bach's *Mass in B Minor* by two-to-three-hundred voices—whatever gratifications it may offer to some of its executants.

Two-hundred-plus voices—even singing quietly—simply create too thick a vocal texture to allow clarity and alacrity.

Moreover, all of us realize that we are—without denigrating anyone's contributions—a "Motley Crew." Our membership ranges from extremes of "superior vocal gifts tied to modest technical musicianship" to "modest vocal gifts tied to superior musicianship."

– And, together, size plus the diversity of individual proficiencies provide us with an instrument extremely susceptible to musical phlegm, flatulence and inertia.

2. Now, for a moment, consider the demands of Bartók's *Cantata Profana.* As regards the harmonic language it is highly personal, frequently switching tonalities and scales within tenths of seconds. In terms of vocal density it ranges from unison to twelve-part writing, and from a single chorus to two types of double-choirs. While, with very few exceptions, the vocal ranges for S, A, T and B are quite customary, in terms of sonority and tempo the work's demands are exceptional. The major fugue and climax (I: ms. 74–163) severely tax both vocal athleticism and musicianship. The *Cantata* ranges from calls for *a cappella*

sensitivities to demands for vocal superiority over the most bombastic of brass and percussion sonorities.

I have very nearly—but reluctantly—concluded that the *Cantata Profana*, like Bach's double-chorus motets, might better be served by smaller forces of equally-but-exceptionally skilled singers—say, two choirs of 48 voices each. Given singers like those who used to form our touring and studio choruses of 40–50 years ago, a wonderful recording could be made—but one still would have to edit (and balance) the orchestral materials very carefully indeed to insure a satisfying live performance. – Both live performance and recording had been my dream of our "volunteer symphony chorus."

3. The third of our appraisals was identified as the teaching/learning process. This is obviously my responsibility and/or failure, but other than adding a rehearsal, I do not know how our rehearsals could have been better organized or paced. – And I congratulate you earnestly on how quickly you dealt with the Barber and Vaughan Williams works. They are in better shape in shorter time than ever I remember.

In a perfect world, next Monday night's rehearsal would be devoted to acclimatizing a 1996–97 model symphony-chorus to the acoustics and logistics of Symphony Hall stage plus, hopefully, the flow and glow of landfall.

Given the present phlegm, fuzz and viscosity attending Mr. Bartók's *Cantata*, we need to deal first and above all on clean, firm pitches, distinguished (and distinguishable) elements of speech, tonal variety and splendour, profile of principal melodic materials, and speeds appropriate to take-off.

At this writing I have no idea whether or not circumstances will allow us to perform and record these remarkable works as scheduled. That does not concern me nearly so much as the possibility that, given the opportunity, we would not prove equal (hell! – superior) to it.

In the past our chorus has been disciplined to a point that it frequently has been mistaken for a smaller, completely "professional" unit. Actually, our "disciplines" are a lot more refined and wider-ranging than those of the professional choruses of a generation ago.

The question is whether or not on next Monday night we can reach or extend our own standards. Can any nine and one-half minutes of music defeat the determined onslaught of two-hundred-fifteen hear and knowers?

R

LUDWIG VAN BEETHOVEN

Missa Solemnis

January 13, 1987

Friends –

During the month remaining before the performances and recording of the *Missa Solemnis* I hope that I will be able to find the time—and the in-sight—to find the out-words for those aspects of the work which, for me at least, make it one of the extraordinary vessels of man's aesthetic and religious thinking.

Since its composition the question has been repeatedly asked, and variously answered, as to Beethoven's own "religion." Was he, in fact, a "Catholic"—since the mass is a Catholic text? Was he even a "Christian"—since his treatment of the text is so "personal," as opposed to "liturgical," and since his humanitarian, humanistic (and "heroistic") leanings seem to be so clearly documented. (Historically, of course, "humanism" is the clear descendant of Christian thought as to the values and potentials of human life itself. It does seem to me that the contemporary paranoia concerning the dangers of humanism and its categorical conflict with Christianity betray an intellectual and ethical sensibility equal to the McCarthy witch-hunts of the early post–World War II years.)

Although he did receive the last rites of the Church and taught his nephew Karl to pray, Beethoven apparently did not attend church regularly, and "for the most part kept his religion to himself." In one of his notebooks of the period he cautions himself, "In order to write true church music—look through all the monastic church chorales and also the verses in the correct translations and perfect prosody in all Christian-Catholic psalms and hymns generally." – And he is reported to have told Bettina von Arnim (one of his few fair-sexed enthusiasts—and -asms), "Well I know that God is nearer to me than to other artists. I associate with Him without fear; I have always recognized and understood Him, and have no fear for my music."

It strikes me that it is about as pertinent—and sensitive—to ask if Beethoven was "religious" as to ask if Jesus was "Christian." The answer to both questions is substantially the same—and a further question: *whose* religion, *whose* Christianity?—How comfortable were either of them with orthodoxy and Pharisaism? – Or how would they have viewed the Crusades, the Spanish Inquisition or the Salem Witch-Hunts?

Moreover, should we grant—which seems fair—that the general thrust of Beethoven's creativity and personality shows urgently and repeatedly his quest for the nature and fulfillment of human life, is there not foremost among those humanistic concerns—simply by logic or definition—the concern for mankind's (and womankind's) spiritual perceptivities, commitments and ultimate "destiny"—including their relationship to the Unknown?

I am very quickly reminded of Robert Bridges' observation concerning "man being made in God's image" and "God being made in the image of man," that "both these truths are one, . . . – for surely as mind in man groweth/so with his manhood groweth his idea of God,/wider even and worthier, until it may contain/and reconcile in reason all wisdom passion and love."

Obviously, the *Missa Solemnis* is its own greatest argument as to Beethoven's "religion." It is its own testimony—and his testament. That it uses an ancient Latin Christian text should bring only comfort—and healthy, occasional self-examination—to those who denominate themselves "Christians"—by inheritance or wrestling. But beyond that, Beethoven somehow manages to address himself to a uniquely ecumenical "congregation," undivided by sect-ual preference or previous condition of servitude. (Do you suppose it could take a lost shepherd to gather in the lost sheep?)

In the understanding of the general character of the *Missa Solemnis*, singers have the advantage over instrumentalists in that they are working with the text (with which, of course, Beethoven began). While we are not yet into all the psychological subtleties of textual illumination, we are by now far enough into rehearsal to realize what an extraordinarily *illustrative* work it is. Some of it is almost primitively—even childishly—pictorial: the heavenly high register of *in excelsis* contrasted with earth's lowly *et in terra pax* (ms. 29–38 and 43–78) of the *Gloria;* the downward and upward leaps of "descendit de coelis" (ms. 112–118), and the whirlwind ascent of "et ascendit in coelis" (ms. 194–202) in the *Credo;* and of course, the trumpets and drums of warfare (ms. 164–185) in the *Agnus Dei*. – And we discussed briefly last night the possible psycho-philosophical inferences to be gleaned from the fracture of the word "kyrie" into discrete and contrasting *forte* and *piano* fragments.

Two things remain to be said *in general* concerning Beethoven's setting of the text of the Mass (before we begin our movement by movement and section by section analysis). The first is that though page after page of the music does offer examples of such textual representation as these cited above, *by far* the greatest revelations have to do with the human animal/mind/spirit itself as he/she/it faces (and is faced by) the text—and by inference and extension the Great Unknowns which the text is attempting to fathom. They have even more to say about the Seeker than about the Sought.

The second, and equally noteworthy, aspect of the representational nature of the *Missa Solemnis* is that its illuminations are not limited to musical motives of modest duration and textual explicitness, economy and propriety, but that these are but elements of a larger force and form—which, indeed, provides the grander illumination.

The *Missa Solemnis* is not painting by the numbers, but a symphonic dramaturgy on a scale of gigantic to infinite, whose meanings inhere to and are released by architecture and structural proportions even more than particularities, however trenchant.

– As witness the opening *Kyrie*, which sets but three words—"Kyrie," "Christe" and "eleison"—but issues in a trinary form of approximately ten minutes' duration, while the *Credo*, which has one hundred sixty-six words encompassed in eight sections, lasts less than twice that long. They are equal triumphs of a musical mind over verbal matter.

See you Monday.

R

December 5, 1963

I wonder if there is anything in the choral-symphonic repertoire which can prepare the singer for the ordeal of the *Missa Solemnis*. Certainly it must be true that those who have endured for some weeks the physical and intellectual agony of "getting it into the voice" are uniquely prepared for its deeper understandings.

The *Missa Solemnis* is symphonic in scope and detail. Instrumentalists are not only more familiar with its style and technical demands; their instruments also render them more capable of coping with them.

For the singer, however, the work is a frightening and frustrating experience. He is asked to perform feats absolutely unequalled in vocal literature—still unique after almost a century and a half.

The ranges are excruciating: all voices are asked to encompass an octave plus a major sixth, and the bass voices cover over two octaves. Sopranos face seemingly endless high A's and B-flats. Basses have vocal leaps of an octave and a fifth.

Still, extended range of itself would not offer insurmountable difficulties if it were not coupled with two other technical demands. The first of these is the cataclysmic abruptness and profusion of dynamic markings. Within the first six measures that the sopranos of the chorus sing they are given three high A's on the syllables of the word "Kyrie"; and, in a moderately fast tempo, it is specified that the first two syllables are to be sung *fortissimo*, and the third, *piano*. Almost any "A" can be difficult, but successive *forte* and *piano* A's are an enormous physical-vocal problem. It is roughly analogous to asking a ball carrier to change direction while both feet are off the ground. In another instance in the *Credo*, within just eleven measures (which count thirty-two syllables ranging nearly two octaves) there are thirteen different dynamic markings: *f, p, sf, sf, sf, f, sf, sf, sf, sempre piu, f, ff.* (The voice is scarcely a natural "*sf*-ing" instrument.)

The second factor which compounds with extremity of range to present extraordinary problems is that of tempo. The concluding fugues "et vitam venturi" in the *Credo* presuppose a vocal agility—a break-neck speed of syncopation—not to be believed. They rush, spent and breathless, into a *grave* which prescribes some seven *sf*'s on top of *fortissimo* at the extreme upper limits of the voice at the broadest possible tempo.

The point of course is not that Beethoven did not know how to write for the voice. He knew precisely what he wanted to say. He exhausted, exploited and ennobled the voice. He gave it things to say which never had been imagined. In this sense the *Missa Solemnis* is a terrifyingly *avant-garde* piece of music.

Finally, of course, what all the agony stems from and comes to is the explosion which he has proposed to the aesthetic, emotional and religious nature. None of the religious—or anti-religious—traditions of Western civilization can prepare us for this.

We may not be able to verbalize this experience. ("Music exists to convey that which cannot be otherwise conveyed.") But those of us who have bet our voices against his notes, who have suffered through the long hours of rehearsal and performance, may have a closer sense of what Beethoven may have suffered in the writing.

R. S.

December 31, 1975

> Lines from a condominium—
> or it could have been verse:
>
> 'Twas the day before New Year's,
> And all through Atlanta
> Not a noodnik was stirring
> Except Nola and Santa.
>
> The carols were filed
> All according to plan,
> On surmise that the *Missa*
> Would soon hit the fan.

Mama in her kitchen
And father the freak
Had been with their loved ones
For almost a week.

    (The children were ready
    To call it a day
    In the hopes that their parents
    Would go out and play.)

"Fear greatly!" said Frinkly,
"What's wripe to be wrought.
This Missals a Mothah!
I tidings you not!

"Though it's Missa Impossible –
To psing it or psyche it –
Should the bahstahd be mahstahd
There's nothing quite like it!"

So pledge resolutely
Your blood, tears and sweat.
What Beethoven asked for
He's going to get!

RS-anta

February 5, 1987
(Updated January 1992 for Carnegie Hall Workshop)

Friends –

Every time I sit myself down to add to our *Missa Solemnis* commentaries, I am faced by vast areas of uncharted ignorance—like the history of the liturgical mass from early Christian times, and the musical settings of Beethoven's direct predecessors and contemporaries—and I end up with a lot more information than I can digest and the answers to a lot of questions none of you has asked.

The principal texts of the Mass—those set by Beethoven—apparently evolved between the 7th and 11th centuries, and they are known as the Ordinary. They do not change from day to day or service to service; and custom, including musical custom, has codified them into a "cycle" of five: the *Kyrie, Gloria, Credo, Sanctus* (including the *Benedictus*) and *Agnus Dei* (including the *Dona Nobis*).

In any actual religious service, these texts are imbedded in what is collectively called the Proper: a series of prayers, lessons and chants which do change from day to day, according to season, "feasts," and possibly even locality.

Theoretically, with the "proper" accompanying features, Beethoven's *Missa Solemnis* could be a part—or the main frame—of a religious service even now. (Denis Arnold, in *The New Grove Dictionary,* writes that "the *Missa Solemnis* in no sense can be considered unliturgical by the light of its own time.") – But it surely would take exemplary forces, an exalted setting and a transcendent occasion to match its musical magnitude.

The last six masses of Haydn, written one each year to 1802, in the view of today's writers, also are considered among "the greatest settings ever made"—and we undoubtedly should have our noses rubbed in them more frequently. Together with the early Masses of Mozart, the later Schubert Masses, and both of Beethoven's Masses, they show the influence of late eighteenth century *sonata form* and *symphonic style.*

The noteworthy exception to the emerging symphonic style is Mozart's extraordinary, mature but unfinished, *"Great" Mass in C Minor,* KV 427 (417a)—which we are scheduled to perform and record next season. Its *Gloria* sections and the famous *Et incarnatus est* qualify it as a "cantata mass," after the style familiar to us from Bach's *Mass in B Minor,* with separate movements for fragments of the Mass text, according to the composer's thought and "inspiration." The following table is of interest:

Bach	Mozart
Kyrie	Kyrie
1. Kyrie eleison	1. Kyrie / Christe / Kyrie
2. Christe eleison	
3. Kyrie eleison	
Gloria	Gloria
1. Gloria in excelsis	1. Gloria / Et in terra pax
2. Et in terra pax	2. Laudamus te
3. Laudamus te	3. Gratias agimus tibi
4. Gratias agimus tibi	4. Domine Deus
5. Domine Deus	5. Qui tollis / Qui sedes
6. Qui tollis peccata	6. Quoniam tu solus sanctus
7. Qui sedes ad dexteram	7. Jesu Christe / Cum Sancto Spiritu

8. Quoniam tu solus sanctus /
   Jesu Christe
9. Cum Sancto Spiritu

Credo	Credo
1. Credo in unum	1. Credo in unum / Patrem / Et in
2. Patrem omnipotentem	unun
3. Et in unum	2. Et incarnatus (Incomplete)
4. Et incarnatus	
5. Crucifixus	
6. Et resurrexit	
7. Et in Spiritum	
8. Confiteor	
9. Et expecto	

Sanctus/Pleni sunt coeli	Sanctus/Pleni sunt coeli
1. Osanna	– Osanna
2. Benedictus	Benedictus
3. Osanna (Repeat)	
4. Agnus Dei	
5. Dona nobis pacem	
	– Osanna (Repeat) (Incomplete)

In Mozart's case, it would be fair to assume, I suppose, that particularly in its organization of the *Gloria*, he may also have been influenced by *operatic* procedures, in which separate and distinct musical numbers followed one another—arias, duets, choruses, etc.—each carrying a minimum of text and occasioning at least some textual repetition. – But even in the case of his *C Minor Mass*, simply by looking at the above chart, one could infer that Mozart's opening *Kyrie* and the first part of his *Credo* might show symphonic influences; and that is correct.

Today's musicologists are not happy with the term "sonata form," first, because it leaves out whole centuries and nationalities of compositions which their composers called "sonatas" and, second, because almost from the moment theorists codified sonata form in systematic detail (around 1870), their textbook model appears to have been as frequently honored in the breach as dishonored in the observance.

It is good for us, at this moment, to separate sonata *cycle* from sonata *form*. Roughly a sonata cycle is a group of pieces, called "movements," at least one of which (usually the first) is in sonata *form*. The early sequence of a sonata cycle was simply "fast-slow-fast." Czerny, in the 1879 English translation of his *School of Practical Composition*, describes a somewhat grander sonata as a *four*-movement cycle: "Allegro, Adagio or Andante, scherzo or minuet, and rondo or other finale." (By these tempo indications it becomes clear that a "movement"—as one should be able to theorize—is a composition characterized initially by a certain speed and quality of *motion*.)

It should be observed, also, that the terms "symphony" and "sonata" are roughly interchangeable as regards *form*—if one understands that "sonata" refers almost exclusively to a cycle of pieces to be performed by a single instrumentalist (or a very few soloists), and "symphony" to a cycle of pieces to be performed by large, numerous and concerted forces—even including, since Beethoven's *Ninth Symphony*, vocal soloists and a chorus.

As regards "sonata form" (the usual form of the first movement of a sonata or a symphony), while the most knowledgeable historians seem loath to pin themselves down to any definition that isn't identified with a certain piece of a certain composer on a certain date, the textbook definition still has some referential validity. It refers to an intellectual and psychological organization of musical materials, rather than one primarily calculated to accommodate or adapt to physical patterns of movement, such as dancing or marching.

In textbook theory, sonata form has three components: 1. An *Exposition,* in which the principal materials are introduced (in theory, also, there are two main contrasting ideas, each capable of containing subordinate materials or motives); 2. A *Development* section, during which the themes may be fractured, varied or related, and led through a parade of associated tonalities; and 3. a *Recapitulation,* during which the themes return in near-native garb, but in keys which lead "home" to the beginning tonality.

It seems to me important for us to note, then, that the "symphonic" influences upon Beethoven's *Missa Solemnis* operate on two levels. The first of these is as a *cycle* of forms. The five movements of the *Missa* (Op. 123) are only one beyond Czerny's school-book cycle of four, and—what is more important—actually two *fewer* than those of Beethoven's *String Quartet No. 14* (Op. 131), a seven-movement "sonata-cycle" which followed the *Missa* by only three years. By these references only, it is not at all inappropriate to view the *Missa* as a huge sacred symphony (*sinfonia sacra*) for voices and instruments based on the traditional 5-cycle text of the Catholic Mass.

The second level of sonata/symphonic influences deals with the musical-textual details and structure to be found *within* each movement. Obviously, we should expect to find reminiscences of the ternary scholastic Exposition-Development-Recapitulation order. – But *each* of the traditional symphonic/

sonata movements also had its formal characteristics; and, in the following paragraph reprinted from *The New Grove Dictionary,* all of us will recognize formal devices and fragments encapsulated in several of the *Missa* movements— as also in the finale of the *Ninth Symphony.* (Arnold, Denis. *The New Grove Dictionary of Music and Musicians.* 1980.)

"The first quick movement is most often the one showing textbook sonata form. The slowest movement, often only a suave moderate Andante or Grazioso rather than the introspective Grave or Adagio in some of the greatest works, may also approximate to sonata form, though usually with less development, more regular phrase (structure), faster harmonic rhythm and only a short coda; other common forms include simple, homophonic ABA or AB designs, rondos, variations and free fantasias. Among the forms used for inner and final movements are the scherzo (the minuet's chief and more intense replacement), the rondo, variations, other dances—like the siciliano (and wild, passionate fugatos) and various types of (combinations)."

To sum up: what we have in the *Missa Solemnis,* then, is not so much a sacred cantata (like Mendelssohn's *Elijah* or even his *Lobgesang*) as it is a gigantic sacred symphony, wherein the symphonic influences are to be found not only in its arching entirety, but within each of the movements themselves. (We even may find that one or two of the movements—the *Gloria* and the *Credo,* for instance— are very nearly small-scale, but complete, sacred symphonies in themselves.) – And it will surprise none of us, I am sure, to find that these musical movements and fragments of movements are linked indissolubly and dramatically to Beethoven's serious exploration and illumination of the Mass text.

I

Kyrie

> A 1–85 Kyrie #1 2/2 *assai sostenuto* (D Major) 85 measures
> (Introduction = 1–20)
> B 86–127 Christe 3/2 *andante assai* (b minor) 42 measures
> A 128–223 Kyrie #2 2/2 *Tempo I* (D Major) 96 measures (Introduction: 128–139)
> (Coda: 216–223 or 206–223)

I suppose that the most striking first impression of the *Missa Solemnis* is that of unqualified seriousness, solemnity and majesty. One has no way of knowing, in the opening seconds, how long this heavy, slow pace will—or can—continue. (The custom of a slow and somber introduction to a vivacious first movement is a familiar and convincing one.) When, however, the chorus enters with three fortissimo (and altissimo) cries so dramatically and inhumanly stifled, it surely must be inescapable to the serious listener that there will be no easy questions and no glib answers . . . Beethoven's sacred symphony is going to begin not with a slow introduction, but with a 10-minute slow movement. It is marked *Assai sostenuto* (very sustained), and its ABA form is both appropriate to symphonic slow movements, and liturgically sound (Kyrie/Christe/Kyrie).

Its numerical and temporal proportions are interesting. Out of a total of 223 measures, 85 are devoted to the first *Kyrie* (A), 42 to the *Christe* (B), and 96 (including a Coda of 8—or 16—measures) to the final *Kyrie* (A). Beethoven purposely obscures the beginning of the Coda by an ingenious overlapping of materials and motives; but, particularly if one allows, say, a dozen measures for general conclusion, it is clear that the two *Kyrie* pillars are almost exactly twice as long as his *Christe*.

These proportions are further heightened when one considers the comparative *tempi* of the sections. Most performers have agreed that the half-note of the 2/2 *Assai sostenuto* should be assigned a metronome marking somewhere in the high 40's or low 50's, and that the half-note of the 3/2 Andante *assai* (very flowing) should lie somewhere in the high 60's or low 70's. For all practical purposes this means that *two* beats of the *Kyrie* tempo will equal *three* beats of the *Christe* tempo; and thus the proportions of two-fifths (*Kyrie*) plus one-fifth (*Christe*) plus two-fifths (*Kyrie*) (plus Coda) represent not merely an amusement for the eye, but genuine proportions in living time (including anyone's life-time).

For me, at least, this sort of proportion need not be conscious in the mind of the composer or the "eye" of the listener to convey its structural message of solidarity, weight, sobriety, balance and completeness.

As singers, the structural relationship which most concerns us, of course, is the relationship between the *text* and the *music*. In this particular movement the text is so minimal that the musical materials—motives and melodies, metric patterns, harmonic check-points and dynamic contours—have a function much broader and deeper than that of simple word-setting. There are, after all, only four words for more than ten minutes of music—and even one of those words is a repetition.

Concerning the mighty explosion with which the piece opens and whose mighty cry the chorus echoes, two things need to be said. The first is that there really is no way of knowing the metric significance of its duration until it has been sung two or three times by the chorus, and one has had a chance to savor and evaluate additional melodic and harmonic information, in particular the two-bar motives (i.e., ms. 6–11 and 23–24) which answers the explosion. There is no way of knowing from the first sound alone that the explosion begins a half-measure before what is always numbered as Measure No. 1—but which is really the second measure of the *Kyrie,* as is finally proved by ms. 21, 25 and 29, all of which introduce four-measure phrases. The point is that Beethoven begins his work with silence. He deliberately obscures the metric function of the very first explosion—as though to add to its elemental chaos and mystery, and to our doubts and confusion. Further, by using a full-measure diminuendo in Measure No. 2 (really m. 3), which the voices never imitate, the natural sequence of 2-bar phrases in ms. 6–11 is in danger of being "tilted" and "off-balance" until somehow righted by the three-measure phrase before letter A.

In the second place, some rational answer has to be found for the mind-blowing gag tossed down the throat of the opening choral "Kyrie!" (The perfect metaphor for this delectation is not easy to find—but I'm getting closer: The scene is an old-fashioned Western hanging. You're standing there with the noose around your neck, and an extra six feet of rope. Some idiot with a badge springs the trap, and as you fall you shout "KY-RI—!" – The "eh" comes when you run out of rope.)

The most obvious "interpretation" is possibly the correct one. The *Kyrie eleison* ("Lord, have mercy upon us") has existed since pagan antiquity, and its polarity is the awesome power of the Almighty Whatever as against the frail and whimpering little me. In Beethoven's setting this "interpretation" may well be reinforced by the fact that the Almighty Whatever is sounded by the orchestral and choral *tutti* in extreme ranges and forte/fortissimo; and precisely at the sudden *piano* the lonely solo voice enters (without separate dynamic instruction) over a quiet, questing, descending figure.

Though I can find no musical representation to support further philosophical speculation, it is interesting to me to consider that "Lord-ship" itself has aspects potentially portrayable by a sudden reversal of dynamics. In one instance, "Lord-ship" or "God-hood" theoretically would have the capacity to *remove* itself from daily human traffic—representable by an abrupt withdrawal of sound. (According to Genesis 32, this happened to Jacob after he wrestled with God.) – And in the second place, it is felt by some Christian philosophers that "God-hood" does not exist as Omnipotence only and Assured Everlasting Victory, but must prove itself by its own suffering and heroism in the face of adversity. (They cite the Crucifixion as proof and argument.) By this thinking the sudden piano could represent the inescapable shudder and anguish of "Lord-ship" itself. – All this is speculation.

What is *not* speculative is that we have, in the "A" sections of the *Kyrie,* cataclysmic explosions and up-thrustings of sound on the word "Kyrie," which are abruptly—even rudely—hushed, to be followed by a series of pliant and twining motives, most of which are associated with the word "eleison."

We also continue to have surges and recessions of sonority, as well as abrupt *fortes* and sudden *pianos,* which frequently operate independent of—indeed, almost "in spite of"—customary vocal ranges and conventional phrasing. Thus, these specifications as regards dynamics—loudness and quietness—become an equal partner with melody, harmony and rhythm in both structure and expressivity.

This must have been for its time a disturbing originality. It certainly was not a part of Baroque practice. – And, other than a few measures in the "Representation of Chaos" (the introduction to Haydn's *Creation*), I cannot recall its practice among Beethoven's near-contemporaries.

In almost all musical matters, the *Christe* operates in a less "awesome" manner. The tempo flows more graciously. 3/2 meter is less "square"—has more curves—than 2/2. Dynamics are less violent in their changes, and do not reach the extremes of the *Kyrie.* All this could be held to suggest that "Christ-hood" is a little less frightening and incomprehensible than "God-hood." – That God has taken a human form, is more approachable, sympathetic, understanding and understandable.

Two additional things could be said. The first is that we still have a duality of motives: the first, a 2-note invocation and address to the "Christe," and the second, an arching melodic pleading on the word "eleison." It must be noted that the "Christe" motive is a direct descendant of the tenor soloist's opening phrase in ms. 23–25, and the "eleison" motive is a simple contraction of the principal melody of ms. 3–6. (Casual economy—or symbolism?) These pass through a cycle of imitative solos and duets in both the quartet and the chorus and finally subside into a distant, mysterious murmuring just before the return of the *Kyrie* "A" section.

– This subsiding is the second noteworthy event: Letter G (m. 122) for the chorus is marked *pianissimo;* and a part of that quietness could be understood as Beethoven's desire that the chorus should get out of the way of the soloists. But the surprise for me, this week, was to discover that the *pianississimo* markings of measures 126–127 provide the *only triple piano in the entire work.* – You'll think of a dozen mysterious and hushed places—as did I—but you'll find them all marked only *pp.* I suppose it's possible that, since the entire *Missa* was written over a period of years, the composer could forget that in one spot he'd actually asked for triple *piano.* – But that this particular moment should be the single quietest moment in the entire performance—isn't that provocative?

I'd like to call your attention to three aspects of the return of the *Kyrie.* The first is the abruptness with which the chorus is thrown into what was measure No. 12 of the Introduction. Measures 1–11 are repeated note for note in ms. 129–

139; but ms. 12–20 are omitted, and at m. 140 the chorus explodes with what was originally its entrance at m. 21—except that it is now a fourth higher (in G Major) and therefore not only half-again as loud, but also twice-too-soon. (This is roughly similar to standing on the rim of Mt. St. Helens with all the instruments necessary to forecast the probability of its eruptibility—and having Mt. St. Helens take off right now.)

The second reminder is that the timid, whispering, unadorned *Kyries*, first heard in m. 51, but now reiterated in ms. 166–170 and coda-measures 209 – 212—always in the quietest of circumstances—are really *diminutions* of the monstrous out-cries of ms. 21–30 and 140–149. – Even as regards the syncopation: an inexhaustible, unspeakable urgency even as it fades away.

The third item of particular interest is how subtly and deceptively Beethoven slips into the coda of the *Kyrie* movement. Judging by the orchestral bass only—or principally—the coda begins when the bass reaches the low D in ms. 216. – But 10 measures prior to that, in m. 26, a low D of considerable finality is reached by the orchestra—only to be subverted by the chorus which is in the process of arriving at an entirely different conclusion.

This item is of extra interest, for it mirrors what has been a most remarkable structural premise of the entire composition: avoided conclusions. Time after time one arrives at an ending—only to find that it's really a beginning. – And he recalls that the only real beginning began out of no time and nowhere.

II
GLORIA

	a		Gloria in excelsis (Allegro vivace) (D major)	1– 42	} 65
	b		Et in terra pax	43– 65	
A	a	(+b' fragment)	Laudamus (+ Adoramus) (D)	66– 83	
	c	(+a' ext's. + b' frag.)	Glorificamus (+ Adoramus)	84–103	} 65
	c	(+a' ext's. + b' frag.)	Glorificamus (D to G/C)	104–130	
I					
B	(d)		Gratias agimus tibi (Meno Allegro) (F/Bb to Eb)	131–173	43
	a"		Domine Deus, rex coelestis (Tempo I) (Eb)	174–195	
A	e(d'–ish)		Domine fili (g minor)	196–209	} 56
	a"		Domine Deus, Agnus Dei (F)	210–229	
				Total 229	

	a + a'		Qui tollis (Orch + Quartet) (Larghetto)(F/d)	230–241	
A	b		Miserere nobis (Answer)	242–246	
	a + a'		Qui tollis (Quartet + Chorus)(D to F)	247–256	} 39
	c + c'		Suscipe (Answer:257–262, 263–266)	257–268	
II					
	d		Qui sedes (Bb)	269–273	
B	e		Miserere nobis (Answer)	274–281	
	d'		Qui sedes (D)	282–283	} 41
	f–f'		Miserere nobis (2 Answers) (D to f#)	284–309	
				Total 80	

Finale

	Recitative & Fanfare (Introduction)(A/C/D)	310–359	50
III	Fugato I (D)	360–458	} 165
	Fugato II (Variation)	459–524	
	CODA: Presto (Variation of "I–A")	525–569	45
		Total 260	

February 10, 1987

There probably is more information in the above chart than most of us find useful. – But the left margin should interest all of us. If valid, it shows that the *Gloria* movement of Beethoven's Sacred Symphony is itself a *mini sinfonia sacra:* (I) an *Allegro vivace* ABA, with overlapping congruities and inner miniature developments; (II) a *Larghetto* AB, with a host of repetitions, modulations and extensions; and (III) a four-on-the-floor Finale, complete with a *Recitativo* Introduction, two irrepressible *Fugatos* which flaunt augmentations, inversions, strettos and codettas, and a true Coda which harkens all the way back to measure #1.

The performance timings and proportions are not unlike those of an early classical symphony:

I	4:45	(fast)
II	5:30	(slow)
III	5:15	(fast)
CODA	0:45	(outta sight)

The energy levels of Beethoven's symphonic finales are a special source of amazement. – But I wonder if, even in the *Ninth Symphony,* he ever achieved the rocket-like thrust of this Finale. Beginning with the *Quoniam* choral fanfares (m. 310), it continues to gather energy through Fugue I with strettos and augmentations (ms. 428, 440, 447), leaps forward again at the *alla breve* Second Fugue (m. 459), receiving additional thrust from its syncopated codettas (ms. 502, 514), and finally blasts completely out of earthly orbit with the true Coda (m. 525).

Given a secular context, and placed at the end of the entire work, this acceleration and accumulation of psychic, musical and vocal energies would have listeners leaping and screaming in the aisles over the chorus' final "Gloria!" That the thrust has been so successfully prepared by the proportions and motive powers of the preceding two mini-movements only adds to the creative miracle. Whenever the *Gloria* comes close to being adequately performed, it's a wonder that the performance can continue—or needs to.

Now, to textual-musical relationships of particular pertinence to singers:
Measures 1–42

The theme itself ("Gloria in excelsis . . ." Glory in the highest . . .) is a child-like charge (in the brightest of keys) to the upper reaches of instrumental and vocal sonority. The "heavens" are reached severally but, at this tempo, quickly: by the orchestra in ms. 3–4, by the tenors at m. 9, by the basses at m. 13, by the sopranos at m. 31 and by all voices at m. 37—the entire stampede of the "wings of song" taking no more than forty seconds.

Note, in the introduction, how close the orchestral flutter is to the edge of articulative clarity and perceptibility. At this tempo the strings are playing more than ten notes per second. (These, of course, are supposed to be played precisely together—and be heard as such.)

Note, also, how rapidly the theme ascends once it has begun to move; a half-note grip on the syllable "Glo-," but the next five syllables are jammed into ascending eighth-notes at the rate of five per second (the fact that "cel-" is held beyond its initial one-eighth of phonation doesn't mean it doesn't have to begin as an eighth)—only to freeze at the glassy summit 'til St. Bernard arrives with the brandy. – Five different syllables—ten distinct sounds of speech (rr, ee/a/ee, n/eh, k, s/ch, eh)—to be sung at the top of the vocal range and at the maximum sonority—in less than one second. – Small wonder that the simplest of major scales can be so difficult to sing!

Note, in addition, that the sequence of note-values *without* their prescribed

bar-line grouping $\left[\text{♩ ♫♫♩♩. ♪} \right]$ more nearly represents one

glo - ri - a in ex-cel - sis

3/2 measure than two 3/4 measures. This means that the "natural" rhythm of the main theme is constantly at war with the prescribed meter, and skirmishes with the harmonic rhythm. – Surely, exultation and ecstasy ride the border-line of hysteria.

How about a brace of metaphors?

1. *Loolilooing:* to shout joyously, to welcome with cries of joy; – from the cries among some African peoples made by hitting the mouth with the hand. (*Webster's Dict.*)

2. *St. Vitus Dance:* irregular and involuntary movements of muscle groups, the name deriving from the hysterical dancing mania of the late Middle Ages: persons in the grip of the mania attended the chapels of St. Vitus, who was believed to have curative powers. (*Encycl. Brit.*)

3. *Glossolalia:* Greek *glossa*, "tongue," plus *lalia*, "talking"; *tongues, gift of;* utterances approximating words and speech, usually associated with intense religious excitement. The speaker is considered to be possessed by a super-natural spirit . . . or the channel of a divine proclamation . . . the speech is presumed to contain a message despite unintelligibility of the sounds. . . . At Pentecost (*Acts ii*), the gift appeared as a sign of the indwelling of Holy Spirit. . . . The Apostle Paul referred to it as *charisma* (!!) and claimed that he possessed exceptional ability. . . . In the Old Testament there are references to ecstatic speech (*Num. xi*, 26–30). . ∴. The utterances of the Pythian priestess of Apollo at Delphi may be considered examples of it. (*Encycl. Brit.*)

    (Glossolalia in excelsis Deo!)

Measures 43–65 ("et in terra pax . . . ")

– Another child-like musical illustration: From the Soprano A-natural in "the highest" it is a drop of three octaves to the Bass A on *terra* (earth) below; if one uses the extremities available to the orchestra, it is a *five*-octave drop from the First Violin's A to "Ground"-bass A. Moreover, to suggest the serenity and repose in *pax in terra*, dynamics drop from *sf* on top to *fortissimo* to a cradling *piano,* and the frequency of instrumental impulses from twelve per measure to two or three.

Measures 66–126 ("laudamus te . . . ")

As the ecstasy returns we are in a developmental area, complete with short-ened and overlapping principal motives, exultant shouts hushed by awe-stricken murmurs, and a pair of *fugato* episodes which add the chaotic tensions of polyphony to what up to now has been an excitement mainly of speed, rhetoric, sonority and predictable phrase lengths.

Measures 127 (or 131)–173 ("gratias agimus tibi . . . ")

– A gracious moment of respite in the tumult. A melody reminiscent of the *et in terra pax* episode enters in a more reflective tempo, and in the gentler sonority of solo voices, to enjoy a short but fulfilled development. – A sweet exercise of "good manners," as though, in the excitement, one just barely re-members to say "Thank you"—for earth's bounty and God's mercy.

Measures 174–227 ("Domine Deus . . . ")

– The third and final seizure for mini-movement I: – an ecstatic, slashing roll-call of all the names and attributes of the dual Christian Deity. Note how the voices erupt through the orchestra's *Gloria* theme as though *by chance*. (— Aleatoric "design" prefigured by nearly a century and a half.)

I find interest, also, in two additional things: – First, at m. 196 is the sudden subsidence of tumult as the text moves from aspects of the Fattier Almighty to the "only begotten" (just-born?) Son. (This is reflective, also, of the change in the *Kyrie* from the monumental shouts associated with God-hood to the tender petitions addressed to "Christe.")

Second, on the syncopated third beat of m. 185, take a good look at the triple *forte* on "omnipotens." Recall, for a moment, the loudest moments we've re-hearsed: the fractured shouts of "Amen!" in the *Credo* (m. 463), the despairing "Agnus Dei!" (m. 332 of the *Agnus Dei*), the final "Gloria!" (m. 569 of the *Gloria*). There is no doubt that we raise these events in our minds and voices to a *tutta forza*—and possibly justly so; but Beethoven's only *fortissimo* in the entire *Missa* comes precisely with the first entrance of the Trombones on the third beat of m. 185, and with the chorus' "all-powerful." In his mind—just as the "Christe" of p. 6 is the most secret murmur—this is the ultimate ecstatic sonority.

Measures 228–309 ("Qui tollis peccata mundi . . . ")

The slow movement of the *Gloria sinfonia-sacra* is a longish AB song-form in which the vocal quartet plays the principal role. The chorus has wonderful dramatic responses (ms. 245, 261 and 273), participates structurally and melodi-cally at ms. 253 and 288, and actually initiates the two "B" sections at ms. 269 and 282. In the responses of the "A" sections the dramatic function of the chorus is simply to suggest that, indeed, it is *all* of mankind—and not just a few soloists—in need of "mercy." – And in the later *forte* entrances which tell of the "seat of power at the right hand of the Father" manifestly we are called upon to represent that power with appropriate vocal and instrumental sonority.

On to the Finale—

Measures 310–359 ("Quoniam tu solus sanctus . . . ")

I've called this a "fan-fare," and it seems to be reasonable designation, though there's not as much brass in evidence as there might have been had Beethoven had today's valve instruments. That Beethoven saw this also as an "Introduction" to the fugues is evidenced by the fact that all the text of the fugues is already contained—and repeated (ms. 354–359) in the fanfare. My favorite moments are two: First, the sudden hush (m. 319) at the mention of "holiness" (*sanctus*: the "unspeakable" mystery). This opening acclamation of the tenors ("Only Thou art holy") is the premise from which all the subsequent glory streams. The second moment is the sequence of progressive textual impacts in ms. 345–348: one syllable in the first measure, two in the second, three in the third, and four in the fourth—which surely had to be conscious.

Measures 360–458 ("in gloria Dei patris, amen")

– It is a fugue subject of enormous energy. The long hold on the first note (and syllable) seems to dam back fathomless melodic forces, so that when the dam breaks, the forward rush is not only irresistible but—one fears—inexhaustible. The subject also has extraordinary manipulative capacities tonally. Though it begins on a tonic pedal, the scale-wise motion of its second and third measures suggests, in reality, that that *tonic* is a *dominant*. Moreover, Beethoven does not provide us with a text-book "follower" subject to return us to home tonalities but, after the first four reasonably predictable entrances, with the flick of an accidental (C *natural*, Bass voices m. 381; as the bumper sticker says: Accidentals Happen) leads us—dazed and severally scathed—through a mine-field of unsuspected tonalities and modulations to a temporary haven marked F-sharp minor (ms. 426–427)—only to open the door on D Major and two fabulous strettos (ms. 428 and 440).

The *alla breve fugato* is given to the solo quartet, with the chorus plotting in the crypt below to blow up the Mothuh Church—if there's any time left. – And there is—barely. (The roof begins to come off at m. 488.)

By the time the Coda has been reached (m. 525)—though the tune is the same—the tempo simply is too fast for strings to play the sixteenth notes which opened the *Gloria*. The tempo is limited not by how fast the instruments can play, but by how fast human voices can sing at maximum power. We've been rehearsing at a metronome marking of approximately 72–76 *measures* per minute. That is probably a little faster than it needs to move. (My mark through the years has been ♩. = 69–72.) – But even the slower marking means that our voices are called upon to shout syllables and pitches at the rate of *seven* per second, instead of the initial five. (– Perhaps even that wouldn't be so bad if we could speak *in* tongues, rather than *with* them.)

The vision of the past several minutes has been one of tumultuous and endless "Glory." – Or rather a succession of tumultuous, endless "Glories," each more tumultuous than its predecessor. (Do you suppose there will be any time just to "lay down?")

Thanks,

R

III
CREDO

	(Modulation)	1- 2	
a	Credo in unum Deum (Bb to d)	3- 30	⟩33
	(Addendum: et invisibilium)	31- 33	
	(Modulation)	34	
a'	Credo in unum Dominum (Bb to G)	35- 55	⟩30
	(Addendum: ante omnia saecula)	56- 60	
b₁	Deum de Deo (G to F)	61- 69	⟩29
b₂	Con substantialem Patri (Bb to Db)	70- 89	
c	Qui propter nos homines (Db)	90- 97	
	(Addendum: descendit de coelis)	98-101	
c'	Qui propter nos homines (Rpt. Bb)	102-111	⟩34
	(Addendum: descendit de coelis)	112-118	
	Codetta (overlapping at 118 & 124)	118-123	(c. 4:15)

Five Textual Fantasias

Et incarnatus	(Adagio: d min.)	124-143	
Et homo factus	(Andante: D Maj.)	144-155	
Et crucifixus	(Adagio espr. d min.)	156-187	140
Et resurrexit	(Allegro: G Maj.)	188-193	
Et ascendit	(Allegro molto C/F Maj.)	194-263	(c. 7:10)

A a"	Credo in Spiritum Sanctam (F Maj.) Developmental	264-305	(c. 1:30)
	Recap. (Linking; could be considered climax of Scherzo)		
Two Fugues			
	Et vitam venturi #1 (Allegretto: Bb to D)	306-372	⟩133
	Et vitam venturi #2 (Allegro c. moto: D to Bb)	373-438	
			(c. 4:30)
Coda			
	Amen (Grave: g/Bb)	439-472	34
			(c. 2:15)

Left margin labels: I; II Slow Mvm'nt; III Scherzo; IV Finale

February 11, 1987

Generally and formally:

The *Credo* is much the wordiest of the five *Mass* texts and, therefore, in some respects its musical structure is the least "symphonic." – Which is only a half-truth, since neither a single one of the major sections, nor any of the "textual fantasias" which, in the graph, constitute the "II" section, ever is allowed to reach a conclusion. The listener waits in vain for a resolution to F-minor at m. 187, has no clue as to the ultimate tonal function at the B-major climax of m. 193, finds himself tugged urgently across a bridging figure (m. 155) or thrown precipitously into a totally unexpected tonality (ms. 127 and 264).

The return of the opening martial theme at m. 266 is suggestive—for the moment—of both ABA and Rondo forms. – But it has been nearly ten minutes since we heard the *Credo* "call," and we soon realize that Beethoven is using the motive as a frame upon which to hang additional yards of text and—even more seriously—as an arching declamatory introduction to two breath-defying fugues and an extended cadenza for solo quartet. It is a shock to realize that in the final six and one-half minutes of the *Credo* (approximately one-third of its *total* duration) Beethoven introduces absolutely *no new text*. The text is completed by m. 303.

What is perhaps more significant to those of us who are interested in the text-music relationship is that the music for "Credo in unum Deum" (ms. 3–12) is repeated literally during the first ten measures of "Credo in unum Dominum" (ms. 35–77)—lest anyone doubt that the "one God" and the "one Lord" are really of the same substance.

Moreover, this means that the return of the same music on the text, "Credo in Spiritum Sanctum" (m. 267), becomes not a mere musical formalism, but a theological affirmation that the "Holy Spirit"—if one holds to doctrine—in fact "doth proceed from the Son and the Father." – All this from the Beethoven who was a reluctant church-goer, who harbored mottoes and who was perceived as that current horror of horrors, a "humanist."

If one judges only by Beethoven's tempo indications, his positioning of the *Credo* theme, and the durations of the various segments, one could conclude that there are three main sections. His opening section clearly is ended abruptly at the harmonically deceptive *Adagio* of "Et incarnatus" (m. 124). The five "Ets" of Section II are brought to an abrupt close with the harmonically deceptive return of the "Credo" theme (m. 264)—a reprise which enters at such a peak of speed and sonority that the sense of "Recapitulation" is all but impossible to avoid. But, with "instant" Resurrection accomplished in fewer seconds than the Baritone recitative of the *Ninth Symphony,* and the whirlwind of "et ascendit" recalling Elijah's fiery chariot, it is all but impossible not to file what follows under "Run" rather than "Ruminate"; we probably are better off thinking "scherzo," even though our cyclonic triple meters are well behind—or still to come.

– A strange Recapitulation it is! By a head-long rush of hammered text within the *Credo* motives, and by the rocket thrust of the unison chorus whose ecstasy at the expectation of resurrection knows no vocal limits, we are lifted to a vision of "the life of the world to come"—wherein we're privileged to dwell for nearly six and one-half minutes. (Obviously, Beethoven is so excited at the prospect that he can't wait to tell us about it—and since it is a new world it must be new music.)

This means—I think—that the *Credo* fanfare motives (together with their short sections) are somehow invocatory and introductory. – And, therefore, one might be justified in thinking of the entire *Credo* in two *large* blocks rather than three:

A	1 – 123	4:15 >c.11:25	fast
B	124 – 263	7:10	slow/fast
and			
A	264 – 305	1:30 >c.8:15	fast
C	306 – 472	6:45	moderate/fast/slow

There is, of course, no reason why it has to be one thing or the other; both could be true.

I suspect the uncertainties as to over-all structure arise from the inherent imbalance of the *Credo* text. Fourteen words are used to delineate the belief in "One God," while one hundred and one words are used to characterize "the Christ." Of these, 48 describe the relationship with the "Father" (ms. 1 –123) and 53, earth's events and the ascension (ms. 124–263).

Beethoven crowds the final 49 words into the *Credo* recapitulation, the first 26 of which deal with the "Holy Spirit." – And he very nearly *hides* his belief in the "holy apostolic church" (ms. 281–284) under a canopy of soaring soprano "Credos." (The reluctant church-goer?) Some idea of the density of text can be gathered from the fact that the Recapitulation arch sets 49 words (116 syllables) in something under 90 seconds, while the final six and one-half minutes of the *Credo* are devoted to only five words totalling 11 syllables. Now, to *details* and *specifics* of the text-music relationship:

Measures 1–68

The very beginning has fascinating things to tell us.

(1) Lest the heavens still be ringing (and reeling) with the ecstasy of the D major "Gloria!" (with F-sharp on top), the very first notes of the orchestra lift us up a half-step to E-flat major (with G on top), sustain it for a long, long time, then drop us severely down through the most basic of harmonic means (IV, V, 1) to B-flat major. That is to say: the first two measures are partly modulation—a setting up of tonal ground rules—and partly an awesome "Hear ye!"(– After the manner of the farmer who hits his mule on the head with a hoe-handle: "Now that I've got your attention—!")

(2) The *Credo* then begins with measure #3, which means that the entrance of the Basses is a response, not a beginning. We can't be sure of this until the Sopranos in measures 9 and 10 echo the Tenors of measures 5 and 6, yielding two perfectly imitative four-measure phrases—which we have every right to expect in a march.

(3) – For it is a march. The orchestral bass line (m. 4), the ascending bass scales (ms. 7 and 8) and the syncopation of upper orchestral voices (m. 10) leave no doubt. It is not a "quick-step." (*Allegro*—"but not too much") – nor is it a majestic, ponderous and ceremonial march. – But it certainly is a "*Forward, march!*" and an "Onward, . . . soldiers of the Cross" sort of march. Its sense is that of generations and centuries of true believers—what theologians call the "body of Christ"—in absolute and ineluctable, measured motion forward.

Because it's really impossible for you to hear the complete march-tune when you're singing, let me point out to you where it lies. It's an almost-square 32 measures in length (ms. 3–34):

> 1st 8 (3–10) – 2 ms. each: Orch., Bass, Ten., Sop.
> 2nd 10 (11–20) – 4 + 6: Sop. principal voice
> 3rd 8 (21–28) – 4 + 4: Princ. voice in Flutes & Vns. I (R.H. piano accomp.
> but significant counterpoint in Bass followed by Sop.)
> 4th 6 (29–34) – 3 2's: Princ. voice in Sop., which overlaps with "Hear ye!"
> of Orch. (m. 34). (Phrase #4 shortened by 2 ms. to balance Phr. #2
> extended by 2 ms.)

(4) Consider, finally, the four-note *Credo* motive. It is a perfectly serviceable four-note tune as first played by the woodwinds and trombones, but it is of such simplicity and predictability (college football rooting sections have heard it as a unison dirge: "Poor old Nay-vee!") that lesser composers might have stayed away from it.

The interesting thing about its textual and motivational inferences, however, is that, though it is only a four-note motive, it twice declaims a single two-syllable word. Once the chorus has picked up the "tune" in m. 5, we hear substantially nothing in the next six measures but six "Credos!" – And since "Credo" is a verb and, equally important, a verb in the first person singular, this throws a pulpit-thumping importance upon the *believer* at the momentary expense, at least, of what is *believed*. (Think, for instance, of the modest beginning of the *Credo* of Bach's *Mass in B Minor,* a Gregorian chant woven into Baroque textures; Bach's following *Patrem omnipotentem* uses a reiterative "Credo" as an accompanying figure, not as an announcement from which all else must flow. – Janáček's *Msa glagolskaja* also begins with a double asseveration.)

To be sure, ninety percent of that which follows is going to be concerned with *what is believed*—rather than with the believer. The "I believes!" of ms. 37–42 are going to have to last for the next ten minutes. But, consider again the prominence accorded the three "Credo, credo!" announcements (ms. 5–10, 37–42 and 267–286). One would be justified, at least, in raising the question as to whether Beethoven was not proposing, "I believe, – therefore . . . *You* are!"

One could argue that such vehemence is a proof of insecurity (and that the quiet serenity of Gregorian chant is the model of assurance.) – But wouldn't that be carrying musico-textual "exegesis" too far? Liturgical chant is not Beethoven's language (though he could write a magical Gregorian substitute on the men's unison "et incarnatus est") and he should not be accused of blasphemy—or even of irreverence—if his "faith" be "writ" in his own words.

– Perhaps he simply figures that a very long dog is entitled to at least one very loud bark.

Measures 34–89

Though textually and by musical repetition proclaiming the identity of the Son with the Father, this is the first of the developmental sections in the *Credo;* and the "Deum de Deo" shouts are like the roll-call of the names of Deity in the *Gloria* at m. 176: streaks of lightning through the orchestral tempest.

The short fugato on "consubstantialem patri" brings to mind the perfect psychological essence of fugal writing: many voices—from many places (entering on different pitches)—at many times (entering at different measures)—*all* saying *one* thing. – Absolute unanimity within diversity. It is an eerily appropriate text: "Of one substance with the Father, by whom all things were made."

Measures 90–118

This is a beautiful short tune, like that of the "gratias agimus" in the *Gloria,* and it serves a similar function: that of relief from the persistent forward motion and pulse of its matrix. In this instance, without any change of tempo, the accompaniment figures and the half-speed harmonic rhythm allow us to phrase as though the metric structure were *alla breve* rather than pulsed by quarter notes. It offers momentary respite before the dramatic and precipitous descent (ms. 111–119) as "the Son" plunges from the heavens.

This entrance of the men's voices certainly is one of the most transcendent and "un-earthly" moments in the entire *Missa*. (I have not been able to trace the origin of the allotment of these lines to the tenor soloist. In the Breitkopf full score they are clearly allotted to the entire section. Our use of *all* the men allows the lines to be sung even more quietly than if sung by fewer voices.) For generations before Beethoven the hovering of the flute had been associated with the presence of the "Holy Spirit." (Bach uses it in the "Benedictus" of the *B Minor Mass* to personify the blessedness of "him who cometh in the name of the Lord.") Beethoven now gives it an improvisatory fluttering over the solo quartet and an octet of strings (the only specified diminution of orchestral forces in the entire *Missa*), and the chorus closes with a very *non*-Gregorian, pulsing chant. (Some musicologists have held that, in consonance with medieval painting, the dove is more appropriate to the "Annunciation" than to the "Incarnation" and that, in any event, Beethoven's flute solo sounds less like a dove than a blackbird.)

Measures 144–155 ("et homo factus est")

In an almost Schubertian song-like melody, the tenor soloist announces— and the chorus confirms—that the "Son of God" did in truth become "Man." The sudden hush of the verb "is" cannot be laid to the fact that the tenor soloist enters over the choir's exit, but must be accounted to Beethoven's sense of indescribable mystery of life itself. – The mystery is in the "is-ness."

Measures 156–187 ("et crucifixus . . . ")

By a very great deal the longest of the "Ets," the "Crucifixus" begins with the most literal of Beethoven's musical illustrations. With a 32nd note syncopation before m. 157 and, similarly, before this measure's second beat, the orchestra begins a series of *sfpp* strokes—which can be nothing but the hammering of nails through flesh into wood. They are repeated two and four measures later as the tenor, the alto and, finally, the soprano and bass duet take up the principal theme. The chorus echoes their "for us" as though in awe-struck, voiceless disbelief, and leaps immediately into an anguished forte as with a *fore*-knowledge of death. Then begins a tragic, laboured, sequential melody in the bassoon and violins as life's blood slowly drips away. The chorus at last rouses from an accompaniment role to swell the sadness of the passing—only to choke. It is unable to continue. Twice it tries—each time it is forced to stop. It cannot say the words. . . . At long last, in near silence, it lays the body in the tomb.

Measures 188–193 ("et resurrexit . . . ")

The expectable "depth of the grave" is F minor. That is to say, though the "Crucifixus" has been in D minor, and though there are momentary D major and G major cadences in ms. 182 and 183, the final descent of the chorus and orchestra ends on a low C with antecedents, however muted, which lead us to expect F minor. – But this is not to be.

One would have "fallen" into an F minor tonality. Beethoven selects a tonality two dominants *above* the F minor (which also assures him of an absolutely fresh B natural). He begins and ends his "Resurrection" in G major—four naturals and one sharp above all expectation—and it's over in ten seconds. (I suppose that Bach's little "Resurrection Symphony" in the *B Minor Mass* is the longest of the standard concert "resurrexits." It takes about four and one-quarter minutes. Mahler's "Resurrection Symphony" takes eighty-four and one-quarter minutes.) Beethoven prescribes only two extended ad libitum silences in the entire work: just here (m. 193), and later between the "Pleni sunt" and the "Osanna" in the Sanctus.

Interestingly, Schubert in his masses, though he never omitted Jesus' resurrection, for some reason did not set the resurrection text which occurs in the last sentence of the *Credo,* just before "et vitam venturi." Beethoven's setting, ms. 290–295, just as that following the Crucifixion, takes also no more than ten seconds. – But it certainly takes an earth-quaking vocal sonority to make these ten seconds wipe away all the tears of the Crucifixion.

Measures 194–263 ("et ascendit . . . ")

When we are at last able to continue, after the shock of resurrection, we drop first to C major to begin a "pride" of ascending scales to an F major *alla breve* "rejouissance" (rejoicing) in m. 202.

Ascension is a whirlwind of orchestral tones and accompaniments through which the chorus' recitative barely emerges except for a few middle measures wherein the trombones announce the judgement of the LOUD/LIVING and the silent/dead. This is a magical moment for, if one stops to isolate the initiating and highest dotted half-notes of ms. 221, 223, 225 and 227, one finds that he has just sounded the four-note "Credo, credo!" motive—in "ascendit-ing" order.

When the orchestral "chariot to heaven" swings around the second time (in D major, m. 240) the chorus climbs on board section by section with a tune derived from the *Credo* motive (Basses, ms. 251–252), and ends with rapturous shouts of No! No! No! on the proposition to "end the Kingdom" (ms. 262–264).

Measures 264 – 305 ("Credo in Spiritum Sanctum . . . ")

We've already spoken of the four elements important here. They were:

(1) –The explosive shock administered to the D natural of the Chorus, which thought it was going to conclude as the tonic of a D minor tonality, but finds itself in the third of a B-flat chord about to migrate to G major.

(2) –The persistent hammering of the chanting voices as they fill the larger frame of the *Credo* themes with unrestrainable reiterative vitality.

(3) –The irresistible upward swing of the unison voices on "et expecto resurrectionem" rising to the absolute limits of human vocal range (ms. 290–295).

(4) –The fact that the "et vitam venturi saeculi amen" text is delivered *in toto* and in supreme rhetorical splendour before the fugues even begin, so that the finale can be its very own thing—can have a life of its very own.

Measures 306–438 ("et vitam venturi . . . ")

The great gift of the *Credo* recapitulation and its climactic upward sweep is that it allows the "life-to-come" to emerge out of quietness and mystery. The first four measures of the *Allegretto ma non troppo*—before the chorus begins— are not even yet in the proper tonality. Except for a four-measure climax (m. 329) to a short crescendo which began with the last voice to join in the fugue (Bass, m. 322), and a final climax of 16 measures, fully two-thirds of the fugue is marked to be sung *piano*. – Now, this is not easy to do. – And, consequently, it seldom has been done.

– But if it *is* done—so it seems to me—it allows the first of the fugues to have a completely different identity from the abandoned "dance of life" which is to follow. Beginning out of contemplative stillness—*and staying there*—"the life that is to be" comes into being as a tentative, almost timid questing, as though it were too great a miracle to be conceived—let alone grasped. The first crescendo (ms. 322–332)—the first hint of fulfillment, which is, in fact, delayed until the last of the contrapuntal voices has entered—proves to be so much too soon that the music must fall back into its murmuring quest – And when, at last, assurance begins to arrive (at the final crescendo: ms. 350's and 360's) it is as though awakening life had fueled a faith—rather than that a faith had ensured a life.

– So it seems to me.

Whatever—there is no doubting the abandoned and passionate embrace of "new life" in the fugue and the peroration which follow. In all of music these pages are unique. The total resources of voices and instruments—as fast and as high as music can fly, as quickly as it can reverse its field, as loudly as it can roar, as abruptly as it can command silence—all are thrown into the vision of the "life to be."

The immovable object into which we run at m. 432 is probably the only way of stopping this irresistible force. – And one asks again the question which was asked at the end of the Gloria: is there ever going to be any time just to "lay down?"

Measures 439–472 ("Amen . . . ")

The answer is "yes."

Beginning on the dominant of the relative minor, and accompanied by chorus murmurs, the solo quartet unhurriedly moves back to B-flat, where it begins to weave a wonderful tapestry of ascending B-flat and E-flat major scales—all on the word "Amen."

We are accustomed to hearing Beethoven criticized for his "un-vocal" writing. When these "Amens" are sung by great voices, no vocal texture yet written can surpass their sound.

The orchestra joins the tapestry of ascending scales and, at the moment of matchless serenity and quietest solemnity, the chorus bursts forth with two shocking, explosive, *fortissimo* "Amens!" – After which the simple scale moves from the lowest to the highest capabilities of the orchestra, the quartet and the chorus join in a final "Amen," and a solo trombone echoes distantly "et-vi-tam-ven-tu-ri."

What does it mean (in ms. 463 and 464) to fracture such tranquility and solemnity?

We may have heard just in this moment from one of Life's biggest "Yea-Sayers."

R

February 11, 1987

IV
SANCTUS

I	a	2/4 Adagio: Sanctus Dominus	(b minor/D major)	1– 83	
	b	4/4 Allegro pesante: Pleni sunt coeli	(D)	34– 52	
	c	3/4 Presto: Osanna in excelsis	(D)	53– 78	110
	d	3/4 Sostenuto ma non troppo	(D–G)	79–110 (+1)	

II	12/8 Andante molto cantabile Benedictus	(G)	111–235	
	Intro + Solo Violin	112–133	(22 ms.)	
	Block I Quartet + V'ln	134–175	(42 ms.)	125
	Block II Quartet + V'ln	176–213	(38 ms.)	
	Osanna Chorus + V'ln	214–234	(21 ms.)	

The *Sanctus* is a large two-part form with the quartet of vocal soloists—later joined by a solo violin—having by far the greater part of the musical and textual responsibilities. Though the measure totals do not reflect it, almost two-thirds of the musical time is devoted to the *Benedictus,* which places the series of "I" sections in the position of being somewhat "introductory."

The "Sanctus" and Praeludium (*Sostenuto ma non troppo*) sections form so much the larger parts of the first group that the short bursts of the chorus on

"Pleni sunt" and "Osanna" punctuate for a moment—but scarcely modify—the sense of an endless sustained flow of musical serenity.

Measures 1–33 ("Sanctus dominus Deus Sabaoth")

B minor is said to be a very rare and dark tonality for Beethoven. Though he is clearly in D major by m. 9, the exclusive use of low instruments, the solemn presence of the trombones, the use of the Solo Quartet's lowest registers and the *messo voce* admonition to the soloists yield a texture of obscurity and mystery. Contrast this with the splendour and swinging rhythms of Bach's *Sanctus* (*B Minor Mass*)—and nearly every other setting you can recall. (Mozart's in the *Requiem* and *C Minor Mass* begin with brilliance—though the latter falls back shortly into a ghostly shudder. The late Haydn *Sancti* most frequently begin *piano,* but principally to dramatize a *crescendo* to *forte* before the *Pleni sunt coeli.*) Already Beethoven in his early *C Major Mass* had written a *Sanctus* which was entirely piano. – But this later one, in his rarest of tonalities, is a mastery of mystery.

Measures 34–52 ("Pleni sunt coeli . . . ")

The emphasis of this *Allegro pesante*—so it seems to me—must be upon the adjective *pesante:* enough heaviness of tempo and tone to suggest the majesty of heavenly glory—as distinct from the frenzied delights of the earlier "glorias!" The vitality of the ending is much enhanced by a *piu forte* at the final five syllables and a "tua" which approaches a shout.

Measures 53–78 ("Osanna in excelsis")

The Osanna moves swiftly at one beat per ($\downarrow$.), which is only a little slower than the previous quarter-note perhaps four-fifths ($\downarrow$ = 84 to 88 vs. $\downarrow$. = 69) of the "Pleni sunt." Much in the manner of the ecstasy of the *Credo*'s "et vitam venturi" (m. 432), it comes to an abrupt halt at m. 77—in order to ponder the solemn but sweet moments of the *Praeludium* which usher in the *Benedictus.*

Measures 79–110 (*Sostenuto ma non troppo*)

The most somber of low string colors blend with flutes to prepare the way of "him who cometh . . . in blessedness." – You must write you own "program" for this. These are immensely moving measures. Though only a few moments in length they seem (happily) endless. After two brief melodic archings they fall deeper and deeper into tonal and psychic mysteries—so that the faint light, when it appears, comes from very, very high indeed.

Measures 111–234 ("Benedictus qui venit . . . ")

Together with its *Praeludium,* this is one of the most beautiful of Beethoven slow movements, as well as a solo for violin which matches his Concerto, Op. 61. Until the *Osanna* the chorus performs largely responsive or accompanimental roles: its measures 159–175, though particularly expressive—even rhetorically so—must be adjusted in dynamics and weight to allow the violin to portray the principal voice of "him who cometh" and the source of "blessedness." (Note the similarity of the 3-note motif in ms. 160–161 to the beginning of the *Sanctus*.)

The stately "Osanna" (m. 214) has nothing to do with the vibrant animation of the earlier setting. At its highest point (m. 222) the violin re-enters as the "still small voice" of blessing. All is secure, majestic and, in the end, a sweet endlessness.

The *Benedictus* is the vast, timeless repose towards which the *Gloria* and the *Credo* have been rushing. One hopes that it will go on forever, and is grateful that Beethoven had the sense of proportion to make it as long as was necessary.

– More to come,

R

V

AGNUS DEI

Part I

| 4/4 Adagio "Agnus Dei..." | | m. 1-95 |
| | | |

	a	Introduction & Bass Solo	m. 1-26
	a'	Introduction & Alto/Tenor Duet	m. 27-52
	a"	Introduction, Soprano Solo and Quartet	m. 53-81
		Codetta & Transition	m. 82-95

Part II

Group I: Allegretto vivace "Dona nobis pacem"			m. 96-163
	Intro:	Triadic descent; sequential stirrings	m. 96
	a	Children's game-song	m. 107
	b	Chorale	m. 123
	c	Imitative Motive #1	m. 127
	d	Broad diatonic descent	m. 131
	e	Imitative Motive #2	m. 139 (overlapping with-)
	f	Homophonic shouts	m. 150

| Sounds of War #1: Allegro assai | | m. 164-189 |
| | Trumpets & anguished cries | |

Group II: Tempo I			m. 190-265
	a'	Development of introductory	
		triads and sequences	m. 190
	b	Chorale phrase	m. 212
	c	Development of Imitative Motive #1	m. 216
	d	Broad slow descent	m. 241
	e	Development of Imitative Motive #2	m. 249 (overlapping with-)
	f	Homophonic shouts (Despair or Triumph?)	m. 260

Sounds of War #2: Presto		m. 266-353
	a. Revelry/Chaos/Dissension, etc.	m. 206
	b. Trumpets & anguished cries	m. 326

Group III: Tempo I, Fragmentation			m. 354-418
	Intro:	Descending triads & sequences	m. 354
	a	Children's game-song	m. 374
	f	Shouts	m. 378
	a	Children's game-song	m. 380
	f	Extended shouts	m. 384
	a	Children's game-song	m. 394
	b	Chorale	m. 402
		Sounds of War	m. 406
	b	Chorale remnant	m. 410
		Sounds of War	m. 412
	b	Chorale remnant	m. 416

Coda		m. 419-434
	Scales in contrary motion	m. 419
	Chorale, complete + echoes	m. 425
	Concluding contrary scales	m. 431

February 11, 1987

PART I

4/4 *Adagio* "Agnus Dei . . . " m. 1–95

    a Introduction & Bass Solo m. 1–26
    a' Introduction & Alto/Tenor Duet m. 27–52
    a" Introduction, Soprano Solo and Quartet m. 53–81
    Codetta & Transition m. 82–95

PART II

Group *Allegretto vivace* "Dona nobis pacem" m. 96–163

    Intro: Triadic descent; sequential stirring m. 96
    a   Children's game-song m. 107
    b   Chorale m. 123
    c   Imitative Motive #1 m. 127
    d   Broad diatonic descent m. 131
    e   Imitative Motive #2 m. 139 (overlapping with –)
    f   Homophonic shouts m. 150

Sounds of War #1: *Allegro assai* m. 164–189

    Trumpets & anguished cries

Group II: *Tempo I* m. 190–265

    a   Development of introductory triads and sequences m. 190
    b   Chorale phrase m. 212
    c   Development of Imitative Motive #1 m. 216
    d   Broad slow descent m. 241
    e   Development of Imitative Motive #2 m. 249 (overlapping with –)
    f   Homophonic shouts (Despair or Triumph?) m. 260

Sounds of War #2: *Presto* m. 266–353

    a.   Revelry/Chaos/Dissension, etc. m. 206
    b.   Trumpets & anguished cries m. 326

Group III: *Tempo I,* Fragmentation m. 354–418

    Intro: Descending triads & sequences m. 354
    a   Children's game-song m. 374

 f Shouts m. 378

 a Children's game-song m. 380

 f Extended shouts m. 384

 a Children's game-song m. 394

 b Chorale m. 402

 Sounds of War m. 406

 b Chorale remnant m. 410

 Sounds of War m. 412

 b Chorale remnant m. 416

Coda m. 419–434

 Scales in contrary motion m. 419

 Chorale, complete + echoes m. 425

 Concluding contrary scales m. 431

Except that Part I (or "A") of the *Agnus Dei* is a twice-repeated *arioso* (plus a *codetta*), while Part I of the *Sanctus* sets forth four distinct musical entities, the larger forms of the *Agnus Dei* and *Sanctus* have a good deal in common. In both instances the earlier portions form a sort of prelude to the substantial musical "message" which follows.

In terms of musical time there is a slight difference in that the "Benedictus" of the *Sanctus* is considerably longer than its four preliminaries combined, while the two large sections of the *Agnus Dei* are substantially of the same duration. – But each begins in B minor, and moves at an Adagio four beats per measure which stresses, of course, their congruities.

Measures 1 – 95 ("Agnus Dei . . . ")

The threefold invocation to the "Lamb of God" is liturgically correct, though the third petition normally ends only with "grant us peace" rather than a third "have mercy" before the prayer for peace. Though it admits the violins to participate in the accompaniment, it keeps their lower register and gives the principal voices to bassoons, 'celli and basses. The responses of the chorus to the vocal soloists begin also with its lowest register and rise only as the alto, tenor and soprano soloists are involved and move up in their ranges. The tonality is dark, the tempo burdened and the atmosphere anguished and suppliant—appropriate to the text. For most of the third statement of the *arioso* and the *codetta* there is a questing, meandering line in the violins, whose almost unvarying eighth-note motion demands a very sensitive treatment by the chorus of its quarter- and half-note accompaniments. An all-but-whispered "Agnus Dei" from the chorus on the dominant of D major (ms. 93–94) prepares the entrance of the first of the several "Dona nobis pacem" motives and the Finale to the entire *Missa*.

Measures 96–434 ("Dona nobis pacem")

The above chart tells most of that which can be told about Beethoven's pleas for peace. The music alternates a series of supplications—of varying urgencies and descriptive qualities—with the sounds—the anguish, chaos, terrors and rumbles—of war. Progressively the sounds of war become more insistent and more pervasive, and they continue to be heard so shortly before the final cadence that Beethoven has been criticized time after time for not giving a work of this size an appropriate ending. (More of this in a moment.)

Consider now the character of the supplications for peace. I don't want to cartoon these for you, for they surely mean more separately and in combination than words can convey. But –

What I've called an "introduction" is as much an independent motive as any other. It is a simple triadic descent through the dominant and tonic to set up a series of accompaniment figures and sequential ascending thirds which prepare us for the pastoral qualities which are to follow. To me they inevitably recall the "quality of mercy" which "droppeth as the gentle rain from heaven." Their sound is sweet, unforced, simple and quietly assured.

Measure 107: "a," for me, is a happy, carefree children's game-song. It has elements both of folksong and of dance. If the superior voice (Soprano in the first setting) is slightly more sustained, while the accompanying voice (Bass) is a bit quieter and bouncier, the music will have a cleaner profile.

Measure 123: "b" is the "world's shortest hymn," and its principal voice (Soprano) is going to become a *fugato* subject, but it is long enough and homophonic enough to suggest the solidarity of congregational singing—and, thus, the congregation of mankind, womankind, childkind and earthkind. These are the same voices which we will hear again in m. 150, except that now (in m. 123) they are united in prayer, rather than despair.

Measure 127: "c" is a *fugato* on the chorale motive. The piling of voice, in stretto fashion, compounds earnestness into urgency—in a momentous maelstrom of private and individual yearnings.

Measure 131: "d" is the slow, broad descent of blessing (not unlike the introductory triads), in response to the tentative questing scale-wise ascending petitionings.

Measure 139: "e" yields a longer and developed *stretto* involving solo quartet as well as chords—on a new motive which is (at least in melodic directions) an inversion of the first *fugato* motive.

Measure 150: "f" brings the first real shouts of urgency and the first intimations of fear and despair.

Of the three "War" sections, the first (ms. 164–189) introduces war's "alarums" (trumpets, timpani, fanfares) and human fears, individual and shared.

The second (m. 266 – 353) always has been for me out-and-out holocaust, total disruption, disintegration and terror. Recently, I came across a musicologist who was absolutely sure that the choral shouts of ms. 260–265 were shouts of victory—in which event ms. 266–325 became a sort of ticker-tape celebration. A slightly more subtle assessment divines them as a sort of thoughtless busy-ness—an occupation with myriads of material and meaningless minutiae—which could only lead to another experience of man's anguish (ms. 326–352). The third of War's presences (ms. 406–415) is as memory and menace. As noted above, when placed so very near the end of the piece there is no way to deny its final portent.

For Beethoven it would appear that he might be able to find peace in the world around him. – But largely in the pastoral qualities of nature: in growing things and, perhaps, even in growing people—so long as they remained simple, child-like and gentle. – Or that he might be able to create it in his music—but only at the cost of his own inner suffering.

His answers to the problems of human inhumanity are as complete as his honesty will allow. The menace is with us. – And some of the answers may be children's songs, an occasional hymn, kindness and years of grass to cover what's left—of things or people—if any.

R

January 28, 1987

To All MISSA*naries—Solemn and Risible:*

For some years I've had a sort of *bench-mark* for volunteer symphonic choruses: it is that the carefully-auditioned and well-disciplined symphony chorus, using the most efficient rehearsal techniques, should be able to master a *Missa Solemnis* in four rehearsals.

As a matter of practical experience—fifty years ago no one would have dreamed that possible; but during the past thirty years, with both the Cleveland and the Atlanta symphony choruses, four rehearsals (prior to orchestral collaboration) have proved to be roughly effective—depending, as one could foresee, upon how recently the work has been performed, and how great a turnover there has been in chorus membership.

We've just finished our fourth rehearsal, and while the notes are, in fact, pretty well lined up, there are three areas wherein a lot of work still remains. These are *Text, Dynamics* and *Sonority.*

As regards text we have first of all to discipline ourselves as to the correct pronunciation of Latin. Though there are other—and defensible—ways of pronouncing Latin, ours has been geared towards that "according to Roman usage." All of you have received the guidelines in this regard; and everyone (our newer members more than veterans) needs to review and practice the text at home—so that we do not dissipate our common psychic and vocal energies on thoughtless personal minutiae.

Beyond punctiliousness and sheer accuracy, the more important step is to see that our text is illuminated—even "transfigured"—by a commitment to language simply as *colour*. This will be no news to some of you, but: the fabulous distinction that vocal sound has from instrumental sound is the aural kaleidoscope of the myriad sounds of speech. I'm not talking about text as meaning, or even, yet, as mood. Both of these things, of course, text can generate. What I'm trying to recall to your attention is the communicative miracle in the Babel of human speech simply as sound: consonants explosive, sibilant and sustained; vowels closed, open or triphthonged. "Christe," for instance, has two syllables— and usually, for the instruments, issues in a two-note motif—but we singers are responsible for the communication of *six* successive sounds of speech, differing vastly as to inherent loudness and duration (K-Rrr-Ee-S-T-Eh); and none of them is disposable.

The second concern of our remaining rehearsals must be that of *Dynamics*. I am not now dealing with general vocal sonority ('more about that in a moment), but with the *structural* and *expressive* drama of Beethoven's use of quietness and loudness.

We are accustomed to consider harmony, melody and metrics as the main divisions of musical form and analysis. – But so frequently in the *Missa Solemnis* does Beethoven ask for a seemingly "inhuman" vocal volcanism and acrobacy (how about *that*!) that dynamic change, contrast and proportion are elevated to an eminence and near-separate structural category.

These vocal cataclysms are so clearly text-motivated that the question finally becomes not whether we can physically perform the prescribed triple somersault with a full twist, but whether or not we're able—or willing—to credit Beethoven's vision of the philosophical dynamite hidden in a routine liturgy.

The third concern for the days ahead must be what was referred to as "general vocal *Sonority*." The Beethoven "sound" is not easily achieved by voices which are in the main classifiable as "volunteer" and "amateur." (This is not cause for shame, but it has to be cause for concern.) We may have the musical intelligence and, equally important, the *desire* to discipline our singing into a unified musical product; but there is no denying the fact that our native vocal endowment and training make it a lot easier for us to perform suitably a Fauré or Duruflé *Requiem* than a Beethoven *Missa*.

The Beethoven "sound" is an "heroic" sound. (Think for a moment of what you would like to hear from soloists in *Fidelio*—or the *Missa Solemnis*.) – And most of us have found things to do with our lives other than an all-consuming pursuit of vocal "heroism."—Now, with note-learning largely behind us, we are freer to seek and to exercise a nobler, goldener (and occasionally deeper) throat.

Surely all of us are convinced that the *Missa Solemnis* has some big things to say—things that undoubtedly would be a lot more convincing if said by big people.

Don't you think?

R

Tuesday and Wednesday,
May 3 and 4, 1994

Erstwhilees—

After last night's rehearsal I found myself wondering if the most awesome thing about the *Missa Solemnis*—(Is it true also of *every*thing he wrote?)—is its inexhaustible, unforgiving, relentless *energy*.

Metaphors which came to mind were mostly in the field of athletics: a Wimbledon consisting only of match-points played in a hurricane on cactus-grass barefoot; a marathon up Mt. Everest in skivvies and ankle-Reeboks with free oxygen courtesy of R. J. Reynolds; an English Channel freestyle swim in mid-February as the first leg of a twenty-four hour Triathlon; or an Indy-500 with all the odd-numbered cars racing clock-wise.

How many slumberous, reflective moments are there in the *Missa?* – And what of duration? Well—except for the *Benedictus*—very, very few, and measurable in seconds rather than minutes. Most of the quiet passages are a hush of heart-pounding, urgent gravity.

Where, one asks, is the nearest recovery room? The answer, of course, is that—mostly—there ain't.

That factor is the one that so frightened me the rehearsal before last.

In the main Beethoven demands a vocalism of unremitting "heroism." Even the quietness is the quietness of vast reservoirs of strength. – And the loudness is the fully steady lyric roar which sounds as though there were "double that" if needed.

Most of us simply are not equipped physically to play in Beethoven's league. *However*—by group disciplines based on absolute security as to pitch, time, tone and text we can come close. Indeed, we can come closer even than those choruses which may engage singers of greater individual vocal gifts—but lazier disciplines.

One need feel no shame in being vocally inferior to the *Missa Solemnis*. The whole world is inferior to it. Woman-kind and Mankind may *never* catch up to it. That's *His* problem.

Ours is to link and match our disciplines of pitch, time, tone and text so perfectly with those of our fellow-inferiors that the walls of Jericho do indeed "come tumblin' down."

Last Monday just every once in a while I thought I detected a few cracks in that wall.

Go for it.

R

Mass in C

Tuesday, September 19, 1989

Friends –

I want to add a foot-note to the few words I said in rehearsal last night about the metric measure-groupings of the Beethoven *Mass in C* and the frequent recurrence of overlapping and linking phrases.

All "time-signatures" and "bar-lines" are a recognition of psychological rhythmic groupings which somehow seem to be inherent in the human animal. In all probability, in their most primitive forms, they derive from the fact that *homo sapiens* has two feet and two hands. The natural walking or marching rhythm—left-right, left-right—issues in music (or the cadenced doggerel of military marching) that is 2/4 or 4/4 or, occasionally, 6/8 (when it is fast enough to be felt as two beats per measure).

Triple meter on the other hand, of which the most basic form is the waltz, is a recognition of *im*balance, of eccentricity—waiting for a second 3/4 measure to balance the first.—So, phrases of successive 3/4 measures most frequently contain an *even* number of measures, so that the "questions" asked by measures 1, 3, 5 and 7 can be "answered" by measures 2, 4, 6 and 8. By contrast, particularly in slow musical motion, consecutive phrases of 4/4 or 4/2 meter can quite comfortably be 3, 5, 7 or 9 measures in length, possibly because the final "odd" measure itself carries an inner resolving balance between its halves.

Speech also, of course, reflects the innate nature of the human animal to group auditory sequences—into units of "*heavy*/light, *heavy*/light" (twos or fours) and "*heavy*/light/light, *heavy*/light/light" (threes or sixes).

In the case of *fives* the psycho-metrical grouping almost always is a complex of two plus three or three plus two.—Which is intriguing, because the oppositional structure of the human hand would lead us to expect four (fingers) against one (thumb).

Thus, for whatever combination of physical and mental factors (probably including the fact that the human brain has two hemispheres, and *homo sapiens* walks upright on two legs), we group auditory sensations *through time* into molecular units of heavy and light, or strong and weak, and we are more comfortable with regularity, repetition and expectability than we are with their absence.

What Stravinsky did so effectively in his *Rite of Spring*—and what so angered his premiere audience—was to eradicate the "tyranny" of the bar-line. He completely scrambled his listeners' predilection for expectability.

Now, if it is "human" and "natural" to group the beats of a single measure into strong beats and weak beats, it certainly comes as no surprise to discover that musical phrases of several measures' duration have strong measures and weak measures. Just as the beats within a measure are grouped in twos and threes, so measures within the phrase may be grouped in twos and threes. (The designations which I find a bit more meaningful than "strong" and "weak" are "initiating" and "answering.")

It follows that if one wishes to escape the "tyranny"—and the tedium—of unrelenting expectability, he could take an "answering" or passive measure at the end of one phrase and use it to *initiate* the immediately subsequent phrase. An ending becomes a new beginning.

The terms for this event are *overlapping* or *linking*. These terms are somewhat more phlegmatic than their theological equivalent of *resurrection;* but their effect can be similarly invigorating.

Recently I spoke of Beethoven's *Mass in C* as using a musical language substantially more in the direct line from Haydn and Mozart than his language of the *Missa Solemnis*. "New wine in old bottles"—it was suggested.

The *symphonies* of Haydn and Mozart do, indeed, utilize the "overlapping" and "linking" construction whereby concluding measures serve also as new beginnings. (In particular, Mozart appears to have been so creative that it was easier for him to invent a new melody than to finish the old one.)

– But *text* has its own punctuations: beginnings and endings, commas and semi-colons and periods: and when the *Mass* is set to music it obviously implies punctuations and conclusions.

In the liturgical settings of Haydn and Mozart I do not recall any wherein a Phoenix (initiator) so phrequently rises from the ashes of the answerer.

With the *Mass in C* this undoubtedly has a generative and invigorative impact on the text itself, giving it urgency and coherence. – Contributing, no doubt, to the piquancy, depth and headiness of the "new wine."

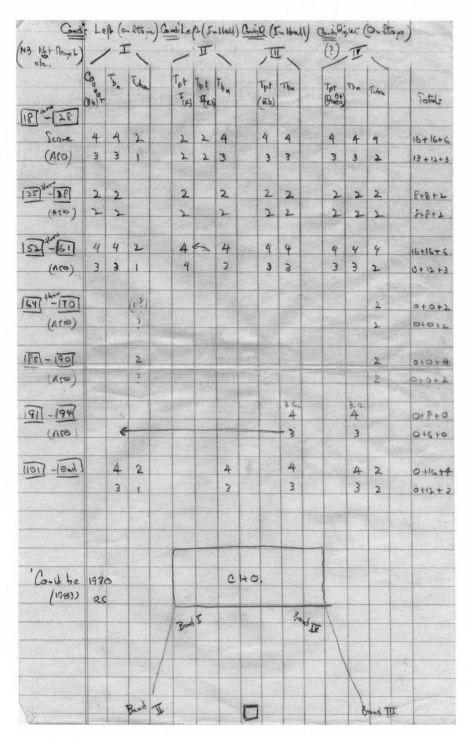

Sketch of band and chorus stage positioning with general score notes for performances of the Berlioz Requiem

HECTOR BERLIOZ
Requiem

May 5, 1970

Berlioz is never easy, either to understand, feel or perform. He himself was not a "natural musician." He played no instrument except the guitar; did not sing. His knowledge of what is graceful or easy for voices or instruments was entirely theoretical, and so his passages for instruments seldom "lie under the fingers." Likewise, his songs and vocal works are apt to have difficult *tessituras*, with a melodic curve that places the most important tones of a melody in the most awkward part of the voice. But he had the greatest ear before Wagner—his imagination was the most vivid and original in the domain of sheer sound that music has known—his mind was strong enough to shape his musical passion into convincing forms. Because of these qualities, Berlioz remains the greatest French composer of the 19th century, and his works are enjoying today a worldwide revival. Always it is the "sound" that finally convinces and then overwhelms in a work of Berlioz—this is true whether you think of a brilliant virtuoso piece for orchestra like the *Overture to the "Roman Carnival,"* or the simple and tender "Shepherds' Chorus" from *L'Enfance du Christ.*

For there is always the great danger with Berlioz of forgetting that not everything is *fortissisissimo grandioso*. He was also a master of the subtle and gentle; and upon reflection, it is obvious that his stunning effects of mass are effective just because they are contrasted with passages of calm serenity. As Jacques Barzun reminds us about the *Requiem,*

"Throughout we find premeditation, balance, unity, and minute care as to the smallest details of composition. The four brass choirs must not hypnotize us—out of possibly 1,400 measures in the whole score they play in about 80. Out of 10 numbers, only one whole and a half of two others bear any character that can be called genuinely violent. The *Requiem* possesses in fact what Baudelaire thought the supreme form of grace—energy. And this energy is not merely let loose; it speaks to us intelligibly; listening to the Mass we find ourselves feeling as though an entire people were come in a rapt and lofty mood to offer sacrifices, to pacify the living, to celebrate with fitting rites the unnumbered multitudes of the heroic dead."

When the first ASO Chamber Chorus met in 1967 at Georgia State University, each member received a booklet entitled *The Correct Pronunciation of Latin According to Roman Usage*. That booklet is now out of print, and we are, therefore, enclosing excerpts from that booklet dealing with the most important aspects of Latin pronunciation. We hope you will find it useful in your "at home" preparation before our next meeting.

R. S.

September 14, 1976

Friends –

'Ever take an audition? 'Ever try to make a living with your voice? 'Ever hear of Berlioz the Big Chorus-Singer?

Read on! Charlie Brown Berlioz wins through to hunger and obscurity!

Time: 1825 or '6. Hector, age 22, has convinced his father to allow him to return to Paris and continue his musical studies on condition that if it becomes apparent he can't make a success he'll resume his studies in medicine.

Mother, meanwhile, being the kind of woman preceded only but always by the adjective "good," views artists and poets as children of the Evil One, and, finding the young man impervious both to argument and entreaty, gives him her formal curse and throws him off forever. (Msry loving her own company.)

Paris; funds at low ebb, our poor but recently anointed sob tries to get a position as flutist with several orchestras. In vain. At long and dreadful last he applies for the position of chorus-singer at the Theatre of Novelties. (*Mère* knew *mieux* all the time.) Here is his account:

"The examination of candidates was to take place in the Free Mason's Hall in the rue de Grenelle-Saint-Honoré. I went there. Five or six poor devils like myself were already awaiting their judges in anxious silence. I found among them a weaver, a blacksmith, an actor who had been turned away from a small theatre on the boulevard; and a singer from the church of Saint-Eustache. The examination was to be for basses; my voice could only pass for a fair baritone; but I thought that our examiner might perhaps not be too particular.

"It was the stage-manager himself. He appeared, followed by a musician of the name of Michel, who now plays in the orchestra of the Vaudeville. They had neither piano-forte nor pianist. Michel's violin was to accompany us.

"The trial begins. My rivals sing in turn after their own fashion several airs which they had carefully studied. When my turn comes, our enormous stage-manager, whose name was, oddly enough, Saint-Leger, asks me what I have brought.

" 'I? Nothing.'

" 'How nothing? What will you sing then?'

" 'Faith, what you like. Isn't there some score here, some *solfeggi,* or a book of *vocalises*? . . . '

" 'We haven't got anything of the sort. Besides,' continues the manager in sufficiently contemptuous tone, 'you don't sing at sight I suppose? . . . '

" 'I beg your pardon, I will sing at sight anything you show me.'

" 'Ah! that alters the case. But as we haven't any music, don't you know some familiar piece by heart?'

" 'Yes, I know by heart *Les Danaïdes, Stratonice, La Vestale, Cortez, Oedipe,* both the *Iphigénies, Orphée, Armide* . . . '

" 'Stop! Stop! The devil! what a memory! Let us see, since you are so learned, sing us the air from Sacchini's *Oedipe: Elle m'a prodigue.'*

" 'Certainly.'

" 'Can you accompany it, Michel?'

" 'Of course I can; only I have forgotten what key it is in.'

" 'In E-flat. Shall I sing the recitative?'

" 'Yes, let's have the recitative.'

"The accompanist gives me the chord of E-flat, and I begin:

" '*Antigone me reste, Antigone est ma fille,*' etc.

"The other candidates looked piteously at each other as I sang the noble melody, and saw well that compared with me, who am yet neither a Pischek nor a Lablache, they had sung, not like shepherds, but like sheep. And in fact, I saw by a little look of the manager that they were, in stage language, knocked into the third row underground. Next day I received my official nomination; I had beaten the weaver, the blacksmith, the actor, and even the singer from Saint-Eustache. My service began immediately, and I had fifty francs a month.

"So here you see me, while waiting for the time when I can become an accursed dramatic composer, a chorus-singer in a second-rate theatre, outcast and excommunicated to the very marrow of my bones."

(Hector Berlioz, by William F. Apthorp, Henry Holt and Company, 1879.)

I am much encouraged by the rehearsal of last night. The schedule in my mind had been something like this:

Rehearsal #1: Reading of the entire work, but detailed attention to Movement I to re-acquaint ourselves with standards and disciplines.
Rehearsal #2: One basic and exhaustive notes-and-metrics survey.
Rehearsal #3: Text emphasis: primarily technical-enunciation exactitudes plus definitions of phrase lengths and limits; but also the beginning of changes in colour and dynamics.
Rehearsal #4: Go for vocal flow: Sonority, stamina and fluency. "Semi-

final" balances (where alto voices sing tenor parts, where mezzo-soprano, etc.).

Rehearsal #5: Quartets? – This is a great way to do this piece. 'Extraordinary what singing in quartets can add to intonation, sonority and expression.

Your responsibility: Spend some time with the text and translation (handed out last Monday) so that the Latin words winging by call up an occasional emotellectual crunch which is the music's due and could be your delight.

Peace—but not too much,

R

January 12–17, 1993

Notes to myself on the Structural and Affective Aspects of the Berlioz *Requiem* Assembled for Carnegie Hall Workshop

Foreword

Our structural study, together with any affective inferences therefrom, begins with the numbering of musical measures, and their assembly into groups of twos, threes and combinations or multiples thereof, based upon melodic/harmonic metrical function.

Possibly because the human form has two feet and two hands, early dances and marches—together with the tunes which arose to accompany them—were in duple time. (Left-right, L-R, L-R, etc.) (Had man been given three legs, our marches would be waltzes.)

The idea of three-ness is something of a psychic adventure since it countenances the possibility of imbalance (Left-Right-Right, L-R-R, L-R-R) and not infrequently the psychological distress which accompanies it. (In music one frequently finds distress expressed in triple-metered *tarantellas* or "dances of death"; while, on the pleasurable side, one may enjoy the swinging sensation of grand waltzes with their air-borne *tenuto* on the second beat.) – All this in spite of the fact that the three-legged milking stool is the lone seating arrangement devised by man which remains stable on uneven ground.

At any rate, for whatever combination of physiological and psychological reasons, man would seem to group successive units of time (pulses, beats or their divisions) into groups of twos and threes—and their multiples and combinations—and to feel these groupings as STRONG-Light or STRONG-Light-Light, etc.

Man does not feel this way because composers write this way. Composers write this way because man feels this way. Some composers (Brahms, for instance) took delight in contradicting the psychologically expectable groupings. (Hemiolas: taking advantage of the fact that ♩ ♩ ♩ plus ♩ ♩ ♩ equals ♩ ♩ ♩.)

Just as streams of pulses (beats) are grouped by composers into metric "molecules" called "measures," so measures are assembled by melodic, harmonic or metric means into structural units called "phrases," "periods," "blocks," "groups"—or nothing at all. But, again, these groups of measures usually are identifiable in units of twos and threes—or their combinations. – And now the measures themselves will begin to assume the functions of "strong" or "light," "prime" or "subsidiary," "initiating" or "responding," "animating" or "resting," and of breathing "in" or breathing "out."

Awareness of this is a major help in memorization for performance, of course; but more important are its contributions to matters of articulation, balance, expressive dynamics and qualifications of tempo: the scaling of crescendo and diminuendo, the profile of major materials over accompaniments, the identification of when to push forward and when to rest.

So—these countings and their gatherings together are not the numbering of inanimates. With music we are dealing with living tissue and living bone. Our "analysis" is an attempt to understand the materials and the functions of music's "arm"—how it works—to enable it to throw whatsoever understandings however far to hit whatever marks.

A second thing needs to be said concerning large-scale concerted music and its relationship to text.

In the "pop"-ular song one expects and accepts a very close relationship between word-accent and musical accent (usually heightened pitch or lengthened duration). Even in folk songs of fine quality, *first* verses may well have this coincidence of musical and textual senses. (It also is found, though not so frequently, in the finest of songs for solo voice.)

In concerted vocal music, however, which may accommodate as many as eight musical lines plus accompanying materials (a Bach motet, for instance), though there may be a satisfying coincidence of textual and musical emphases in an opening statement of thematic material, the emotional and intellectual import (the "meaning") of the music may not be linked primarily to that initial coincidence, but rather to how the musical development and the entire musical structure *in musical terms* may match—or enlarge—the aspiration, inspiration and worth of the text in *its* terms. (For instance, in his *Mass in B Minor*, Bach takes twenty minutes to ponder musically the import of three words: "Kyrie," "Christe" and "eleison.")

We must grant, I think, that while music's meaning may be inspired by text, it is not limited by text. – And it is in music's structural elements—tonal and temporal—that "revelation" lies.

I. REQUIEM AND KYRIE (INTROIT)

> *Requiem aeternam dona eis, Domine,*
> *et lux perpetua luceat eis.*
> Rest eternal grant them, Lord,
> and may perpetual light shine on them.

> *Te decet hymnus, Deus, in Sion,*
> *et tibi reddetur votum in Jerusalem.*
> *Exaudi orationem meam;*
> *ad te omnis caro veniet.*
> To you praise is meet, God, in Zion,
> and to you vows are made in Jerusalem.
> Listen to my prayer;
> unto you all flesh shall come.

> *Requiem aeternam*
> *dona defunctis,* Domine,*
> *et lux perpetua luceat eis.*
> Rest eternal
> grant to the dead, Lord,
> and may perpetual light shine on them.

> *Kyrie eleison;*
> *Christe eleison;*
> *Kyrie eleison.*
> Lord, have mercy on us.
> Christ, have mercy on us.
> Lord, have mercy on us.

> (*defunctis added by Berlioz.)

LARGE BLOCKS

1–25 Introduction
26–77 Group I (Themes I)
    26–54 (15 + 14) 1A + IB
    55–77 (9 + 8 + 6) IA + New responses

78–109 Group II 5 + (8 + 11) + 8 (Themes II)

110–170 Group III (Quasi Recapitulation)

    110–127 IIIa

    128–145 IIIb

    146–170 IIIc

171–209 Coda

CLOSER LOOK

1–25 Introductio 2: (4 + 2) + (4 +3) + 3:2

    1–19 2: (4 + 2) + (4 + 3)

Motif "a": – An ascending G-minor scale, with chromaticism between C-natural and D which intensifies the line. Beginning four times (ms. 1, 7 and 13/15) out of silence and mystery, and rising further in pitch, loudness and chromaticism with each succeeding entry, each ends in an exhausted monotonic rhythmic fragment ♩　　　♪.　♪|♪ which will become the pattern of the chorus's "Requiem" entrance.

    20–25 3:2

Introductory motif "b": – Three times the succinct fanfare of a falling fourth—a natural answer to the ascending gathering of energy and expectancy created by the initiating three phrases, and the source of the accompaniment motives of ms. 25 and 41.

Emotionally, we are assured that "something is about to begin."

26–77 Group I

    26–54 IA and IB

    26–40 Ia (3:4) + 3

That "something" is theme IA beginning in the Bass voice *piano* and *mezza voce* (hushed with awe or grief) and descending by falling thirds—in answer to an introductory theme which ascended step-by-step and half-step by half-step.

It is moving to me to note that the theme hesitates (the tie and dot) on the first note, and that even its fall is interrupted by a silence (the rest in m. 27) as though, with the emotional heaviness, it were necessary to breathe between each word.

Note, also, that the principal accompanying line in the Tenor voice finds it necessary to breathe even between *syllables*. After four of these shattering petitions comes immediately –

41–54 (2:4) + (3:2)

A more lyric and seamless petition of the Tenor voices. IB1. Note the new and *major* tonality of B-flat, relative to G minor and proposing for a moment the possibility of comfort. These are simple arching phrases of parallel thirds—the least disturbing of intervals, garlanded by Soprano triadic melodies, themselves saved from sounding too cheerful only by the weight of the tempo.

Ms. 49–54 bring us still a third quality of petition. The Soprano phrase is an inversion of the Introduction's rising scale (ms. 7–10) as well as its contraction in time. It also manages to sound like a hurried imitation of the Tenor counterpoint at m. 28 (or Soprano at m. 36). But note, also, how the speed of its fall together with its prescribed diminuendo suggest the collapse of breath and the return of despair. Should that correlation be missed, the composer has also prescribed an echoing fall in ms. 51–52—the faintest of murmurs.

55–77 1 A2 (3:3) + (2:4) + (3:2)

M. 55 begins a restatement of Theme IA in the new and Major tonality of B-flat—but at a dynamic level which would suggest the presence of an "emergency." Its principal counterpoint this time is a reiterative, concise metric fragment which begins in the V'celli in m. 57, but is picked up by the Bass voices in m. 59 on the text "dona eis."

It batters on the triple bar-line with duple hammer strokes, and it ascends as urgently as its reverse role-model (the tenor line) plaintively did in ms. 28–30.

We have also, at this "exposition" of the principal theme, the announcement of a second counterpoint—which is to loom larger and larger as the piece unfolds. It has grown out of the tenor counterpoint at m. 28, but it emerges now in the orchestra only, and in an uninterrupted form, in the violins at ms. 57–59. So determined is the orchestra to declare its despair that no matter what pitch the chorus may choose as the initial note of Theme IA, and no matter what harmonies may be implied by the theme's descending thirds, the wail of the orchestra is a never-altering B-flat, A, A-flat, G, F-sharp, G. So much for comfort and assurance!

78–109 Group II (3 + 2) + [(2:4) + (7 + 3 + 4)] + (2 + 4)

At m. 78 we get an ending in G minor and an interlude ("bridge") of 5 measures, which serves to return us to the relative major tonality: B-flat. The tonality, as well as the beginning, in the Tenor voices is sure to recall the short comfort-station which began at m. 41, and one might wonder at this moment if he were not in some rondo-esque stroll through the viewing-rooms of grief. – But the length and repetitious quality of the transition suggest a more extended contrasting section, and that is what follows: the "B" part of Song-form, or the Theme II of Sonata-form.

32 measures, though longer than the 14 measures of ms. 41–54, is not very long for a "B" section in a 209-measure work, but with its strong reminiscences of the Tenor duet heard only two minutes earlier, it could prove soporific to pursue the matter further, so the composer, critic now as well as creator, in four fast measures (106–109) borrowed from his introduction, throws us into a major section which manages to be both developmental and recapitulative.

110–171 Group III

110–127 IIIa (3:2) + (2:2) + (4:2)

The entrances of Theme Ia in ms. 26–40 followed each other at 4-measure intervals, and those in ms. 55–65 at 3-measure intervals. Those at m. 110 now follow at intervals of 2 measures. It doesn't take a genius to note that this is a tightening of musical structure, but it is in what follows this conclusion that shock lies. With a prescribed silence (m. 116) of less than half a second (for a cathedral with a 4- to 5-second reverberation decay!), he prescribes *pianissimo* to follow *fortissimo* and homophony to succeed polyphony. – Instantaneous transformation of musical style: extreme polarities of dynamics, complete reversal of textual treatment! That which seemed about to become a reconsideration of the familiar shudders to a halt in an unexpected stutter and stammer. Nothing is allowed to qualify this breathless but brutal simultaneity.

128–145 (4:3) + (3:2)

– And what of this second "recapitulation?" Note that though the Sopranos begin their re-incantation at m. 129, the true recapitulation is a series of 3-measure phrases which begin with the chromatic and wordless cry of the orchestra in m. 128. The text has become the counterpoint. Has grief become too great for words?

146–171

Note, now, the beautiful consequence of the second "recapitulation." At m. 146 the music seems to halt and hover for a few moments in another of G minor's relative majors—E-flat—only to explode in a sun-burst of musical light (m. 160) on the verb "to shine" (not upon a static noun), and seems at last to conclude in the consolation of G major (m. 165), followed by a sweet codetta and an affirmative ending at m. 171.

171–209 Coda 1 + [2: (2 + 3) + (3:2)] + [(3 + 3) + (2 + 2) + (2 + 5 + 3)]

What, then, of ms. 172–209? – Surely, one of the most remarkable codas in the symphonic-choral repertoire.

Consider first what has been the most "persistent" and "generative"—

the most "fertile" of our musical materials. Even more than what we called "Theme I" (Basses: ms. 26–28), has it not been the descending lament which we first met in ms. 28–29 in the Tenor voices? We heard it also in ms. 32–34 from the Basses, and in ms. 36–38 from the Ladies' voices; we felt its contraction in ms. 49–50—though somewhat expanded tonally; it dominated the orchestral writing in ms. 57–67 and the entire musical structure of ms. 128–143; its inversion was the springboard into the recapitulation (ms. 105–109); and the last half of it was the thread which bound together the concluding measures of 146–165.

Second, consider what has been the most "dramatic" and "evocative" of the text settings. Has it not been the abrupt, shuddering, terse and unanimous chanting of ms. 116–128? There were hints first in the fragmented Tenor whimpers of ms. 28–31. The Basses and others added miniaturized and almost violent repetitive emphases in ms. 57–67. And chanting, too, interrupted and concluded both attempts at a Recap-by-the-Rules (m. 116 and m. 148).

Therefore—as we reach those most ancient and mysterious of words, "Kyrie eleison" (older than all the Latin text)—what better means to sum up all the trembling and the fear? He takes the most primitive of musical means: the unison, monotonic, rhythmic chant—almost certainly the earliest concerted expression of earliest man. – Intoning three times (one of the occult numbers), each time down an octave, we are led deeper and deeper into the abysses (graves?) of mystery.

We might have to guess whether 37 years were sufficient time for a Berlioz "Tuba mirum" to suggest something to Verdi about off-stage brass. But, surely 93 years was enough for Berlioz's "defunctis Domine" to have reached the consciousness of a nice young "French" composer like Igor Stravinsky, whose "Laudate Dominum" (movement III of the *Symphony of Psalms*) in 1930 honored not only the Boston Symphony Orchestra, but also Hector Berlioz's *Requiem*.

II. DIES IRAE

1–140 Part I "Cantus" + Counterpoints and Variations

    1–67 Group 1 A minor (12 + 12) + (12 + 16 + 11) + 4
    68–103 Group 2 B-flat minor (12 + 8 + 12) + 4
    104–140 Group 3 D minor 2 + (12 + 8 + 11) + 4

141–251 Part II "Tuba mirum" Fanfares, Recit.s, and Coda

    141–201 Group 1 E-flat major
    202–239 Group 2 B-flat/E-flat major
    240–251 Coda E-flat major

Part I

1–67 Group 1 "Cantus firmus" and accumulation of Counter-melodies and Variations (A minor)

> *Dies irae, dies illa*
> *Solvet saeclum in favilla . . .*
> *[Teste David cum Sybilla.* (OMITTED)]
> Day of wrath, that day
> Will dissolve the world in ashes . . .
> [As witness David and the Sybil.]

1–24

    1–12 (4 + 5 + 3)

Initial statement of Theme A: unison Vc. and Cb. Solemn, stately, severe, moderate in tempo (4/4: ♩ =88–92), but with the solemnity of 2/2. – Most expressive moment: *subito p* at m. 10.

    13–24 (4 + 4 + 4) Counterpoint No. 1 *No* "cantus")

Unison high woodwinds with Soprano-I voices—as of children singing, vibratoless, suppliant, innocent, *pianissimo.*

Note that, though conceived to be played and sung eventually against the main theme, it has a different phrase structure (4 + 4 + 4, rather than 4 + 5 + 3).

    25–63

– Further introduction of Counterpoints (Tenors, m. 25) and of "B" section of cantus (m. 37). M. 25 begins the first *full* statement of the Cantus—forcing the first 24 measures into a nearly "introductory" function.

    25–36 (4 + 5 + 3)

Bass voices and instruments voice the Cantus against a new Counter-melody (No. 2) sung by the Tenors, again in a contradictory 4 + 4 + 4 grouping.

    37–52 "B" sections of Cantus (4 x 4 ms.)

> *Quantus tremor est futures,*
> *Quando judex est ventures.*
> [*Cuncta stricte discussurus.* (OMITTED)]
> What trembling there will be,
> When the judge shall come.
> [All shall thoroughly be shattered.]

    37–40 First statement of "B" phrase in D (Dorian) modality.

    41–44 B's Counterpoint No. 1, with no Cantus voice placed against it. (Exactly as ms. 13–24 introduced Theme A's first Counterpoint.)

45–48 Third "B" group with Counterpoint B3 added in unison Tenors—mirroring ms. 25–36 construction of "A" Counterpoints.

49–52 Fourth "B" group, with Counterpoint B4 added in Soprano voices, *anticipating* what is going to happen to Theme "A" in ms. 53–63.

53–63 Final A minor statement of Cantus "A" with addition of Soprano Counterpoint No. 1 (as in ms. 13– 24) and Tenor Counterpoint No. 2 (as in ms. 25–36), (4 + 5 + 2) + 4.

The principal intriguing formal aspects of this Group 1 (ms. 1–67) are (1) the omission of the third line in each of the first and second verses of the "Dies irae" (as also in each of the "A" and "B" sections of the "Sanctus"); (2) the metric and melodic frictions which are invited at ms. 9 and 10 of every Cantus unit due to the 4 + 5 + 3 organization of the Cantus versus the 4 + 4 + 4 organization of all counterpoints; (3) the exacting parallel between "A" and "B" elements of the Cantus as they accumulate their counter-melodies—even though "A" is 12 measures in duration, while "B" is 4 measures only.

In performance, this suggests to me that each element as it is introduced should be allowed some reflective and unhurried care, not exaggerating its unique expressiveness—but also not yet as hurrying to some more important destination.

64–67 A scurrying string chromaticism modulating to B-flat minor.

68–103 Group 2 B-flat minor (12 + 8 + 12)

– The "Dies irae" Cantus is now assembled into its final symmetry: A + B + A = 12 + 8 + 12, with, however, the addition of two new Counterpoints (Nos. A3 and A4).

68–79 Cantus "A" (4 + 5 + 3)

– Accumulating Soprano/Mezzo Counterpoint No. A3 at ms. 69, 73 and 77 in patterns of 4 + 4 + 4 but in the *second* bar of every 4-bar grouping; and accumulating the Tenor Counterpoint No. A4 at m. 72 and subsequent 4-measure units.

80–87 Cantus "B" (2x4) E-flat Dorian

Note that this is now only half the duration of "B" in Group 1 (ms. 37–52)

88–99 Cantus "A" (4 + 5 + 3 and 4 + 4 + 4 simultaneously)

– Similar to the initiating 12 measures (68 – 79), with Counterpoints 3 and 4 gaining in sonority.

In performance the compression and solidifying of the Cantus "A" and "B" portions suggest to me that we are now headed "somewhere." There is also the *un poco piu animato* which urged the orchestra forward at the modulation bridge (ms. 64–67). (I always had suggested a similar *animato* at the orchestral bridge which leads to Group 3 [ms. 100–103], and we now find this supported by the new Bärenreiter orchestral score.)

Note also that Line 3 of Verse 2 is now incorporated into the Cantus of the Bass voices and that Line 3 of Verse 1 is incorporated into the Soprano and Tenor Counterpoints, and that the attempt to force Line 3 into the Bass Cantus leads to very awkward text settings in ms. 74–79 and 94–99.

Tenor voices throughout this entire "variation" should be allowed almost to "shout" the short 2-syllable phrases. (A lyric singing will not give them enough presence; and it has been my experience that a more controlled singing is more vocally demanding than "shouting," and leaves the Tenors exhausted for the difficult ms. 104–138 still to come.)

Also, the lower notes of the women's three-part expostulations may be given numerical reinforcement in a 5-4-3 (or, even, 4-3-2) ratio of Alto to Mezzo to Soprano.

100–103 Orchestral bridge and modulation.

104–140 Group 3 (D minor) $[(2 + 12) + (8 + 11)] + 4$

(No new text)

– Final statement of the complete Cantus, with a new Tenor Counterpoint No. A5 and a Soprano series of unison fanfares in quasi-monotonic phrases which are reminiscent of their role in Group 2, but posing 3-measure phrases against the Cantus' $4 + 5 + 3$. The Tenor line is almost a free diatonic improvisation of running eighth-notes, nearly always coinciding with the slower Cantus' harmonies (now intoned by the Basses and Tenors in parallel thirds) but occasionally acting as suspensory notes.

Note also that the Tenor Counterpoint initiates this whole Group 3, beginning 2 measures before the Cantus of the Basses. It apparently does this not to set up its own metric group structure, but somehow to give itself a few seconds of prominence—to guide the ear to itself—before it becomes hidden in the Cantus' parallel thirds and the Soprano's ascending textual fanfares.

As in Group 1, this "variation" ends with a final overlapping measure, which also serves as the beginning measure of the orchestral 4-measure bridge-modulation:

137–140 Bridge-modulation to Part II.

PART II

> *Tuba mirum spargeris sonum*
> *Per sepulchra regionum,*
> *Coget omnes ante thronum.*

The wondrous trumpet, spreading its sound
Throughout the tombs of all regions,
Will gather all before the throne.

Mors stupebit et natura
Cum resurget creatura
Judicanti responsura.
Death will be stupefied, also nature,
When all creation arises
To answer to the judge.

Enter: four Brass Bands: North, East, South and West in Cathedral setting, with Symphony Orchestra at the center of the transept and the Chorus banked up either side of the chancel—or "Choir";—but in most concert halls easier to keep together and in synchronization with proscenium or "stage" forces when placed on Downstage-Right (Band I) and Downstage-Left (Band IV), and Front-Edge Hall-Balcony-Right (Band II) and Hall-Balcony-Left (Band III). The cohesion between the Brass Choirs and the Timpani/Percussion forces is also aided if the "Battery" can be gathered together in an orchestral "pit" or "improvised pit" at the front edge of the stage between the orchestral-choral forces and the audience, at what would normally be the conductor's back. (At very critical junctures the conductor may then turn to the Percussion, Brass Bands [and audience] to insure and control "traffic flow.") An orchestral pit, of course, allows the Percussion to be somewhat below audience level, and also gives the front rows of the audience a better chance to hear what may be happening on-stage.

In concert situations where the Timpani must all be placed at the rear of the

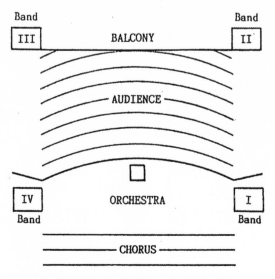

Band III · BALCONY · Band II

AUDIENCE

ORCHESTRA

Band IV · Band I

CHORUS

orchestra—with the Chorus behind them—it is substantially impossible for the voices of the Chorus to surmount the din of the Timpani (or to hear themselves sing at all); and to quiet the Timpani sufficiently to give textual profile to the choral voices robs these grand moments of their grand-ness.

141–201 Group 1 E-flat major, 4/4 Piu largo

141–162 2 + (5:4)

After 2 measures of fortissimo E-flat major from the four Brass Choirs, surrounding and enveloping the listeners/performers and/or worshippers, comes a series of five 4-measure phrases in common time, assembled from all sides and mounting to an E-flat fermata even grander than its opening sound.

163–201 "Tuba mirum" text (Verses 3 and 4 of "Dies irae" with brass accompaniment and interjections)

163–178 (4:4)

Beginning and ending in E-flat, a setting of Verse 3 in men's unsion recitative, forte-fortissimo.

178–201 (4:2) + 4 + (4:2) + 3

Verse 4—and the fearful, shuddering, scarcely voiced fears in four-part harmonization (ms. 184–186).

202–239

202–223 2 + (5:4)

Except for ms. 202–206 (beginning in B-flat instead of E-flat), this is a repeat of ms. 141–162 with men's unison voices added with Verse 5.

Liber scriptus proferetur
In quo totum continetur,
Unde mundus judicetur.
A written book will be brought forth,
In which everything is contained,
By which the world will be judged.

224–239 Verse 6 Repeat of ms. 163–178 (4:4)—but in canon with women's voices.

Judex ergo, cum sedebit
Quidquid latet, apparebit;
Nil inultum remanebit.
When the judge is seated,
Whatever is concealed will be exposed;
Nothing will remain unavenged.

240–251 (2:3) + (3:2) + 1

A wonderful, contrasting coda, using lines 2 and 1 from Verse 4 of the "Dies irae." – Extraordinarily difficult to achieve the vibratoless Renaissance vocal textures after the extravagant, extroverted excesses of the previous "Calls to Judgement." – But worth every effort.

REHEARSAL SUGGESTIONS

1. Use all male voices (rather than Basses only) for ms. 163–178 and 203–222.
2. Brass Choirs and Timpani:

   A. For even the largest of regular indoor concert areas, Brass Choirs of exactly half the personnel Berlioz requests will (1) cover all the notes, (2) make a satisfying (even terrifying) sonority, and (3) fit into acoustically desirable locations which would not accommodate larger forces. (For stadium or arena performances with a chorus of 500–1000, "the more the scarier.")

   Thus:

   I NORTH: Downstage-Right (behind Violins I)

   2 Cornets in B-flat
   2 Trombones
   1 Tuba

   II EAST: From the Balcony (or Rear-Hall) Stage-Right (Violins side of Orchestra)

   1 Trumpet in F
   1 Trumpet in E-flat
   2 Trombones

   III SOUTH: From the Balcony (or Rear-Hall) Stage-Left (V'celli side of Orchestra)

   2 Trumpets in E-flat
   2 Trombones (including 1 Bass Trombone)

   IV WEST: Downstage-Left (behind V'celli)

   2 Trumpets in B-flat
   2 Trombones (including 1 Bass Trombone)
   2 Tubas

   B. If the "first reading" of the Brass can take place in a small enclosed area, rehearsal time will be saved when they finally are placed in concert positions—at dis-concerting distances.

C. IV WEST Tuba can play the "Osanna" cues beginning at m. 146 in the "Sanctus," and I NORTH Cornets can play the Cornet cues beginning at m. 195 (eliminating the necessity of hiring three players for these few measures only).

D. If Brass and Timpani are called for one hour before the full orchestra readings, they will be able to (1) rehearse their sections without wasting the full orchestra's time, and (2) depart one hour ahead of the full orchestra so that the several movements which do not involve them can be rehearsed—saving time, money and nerves. A normal 2½-hour rehearsal schedule would read:

1:00–3:30 P.M. Brass and Percussion
2:00–4:30 P.M. Rest of Orchestra

E. Cloyd Duff, distinguished "Timpanist emeritus" of the Cleveland Orchestra and noted teacher during George Szell's years, made a "reduction" of the 8 Timpani parts to 4 parts only, playable by I (4 timpani), II (3 timpani), III (2 timpani) and IV (2 timpani). His students are in major orchestras throughout the U.S. and, if approached kindly, frequently will share this remarkable legacy. (Other major Timpani teachers also have crafted the parts into "affordable" packages.)

Caution: Let us make much of the "Thunder and Lightning" elements of the *Requiem,* but let us not forget that the quiet, introspective, meditative portions are the larger share, and the dearer.

III. QUID SUM MISER

1–24 Part I 4 + (4:2) + (7 + 5) G-sharp minor 4 / 4

Quid sum, miser! tunc dicturus?
Quem patronum rogaturus,
Cum vix justus sit securus?
What am I, miserable one!, then to say?
What patron shall I request,
When the righteous are scarcely secure?

1–4 Introduction
– Repeat of ms. 1–4 of "Dies irae" (Movement II) with Counterpoint No. 1. Bassoon and English Horn duet.

5–12 (4:2) Ms. 1–4 fragmented and alternated:
Ms. 1–2 Cantus (Vc—CB)
Ms. 1–2 Counterpoint No. 1 (Tenor)
Ms. 3–4 Cantus (Vc—CB)
Ms. 3–4 Counterpoint No. 1 (Tenor)

13–24 (1 + 6) + (2 + 3) Vc. and Cb. fragment and alternate with Tenor voices using ms. 5–12 of "Dies irae" Cantus theme. While Tenor voice becomes freer (less imitative of "Dies irae" Counterpoint No. 1), Violoncelli and CB remain true to Cantus, even repeating ms. 10–11 into whole close at m. 24.

25–49 Part II (4:2) + (2 + 2:2) + (7 + 4)

Recordare, pie Jesu, (Jesu pie)
Quod sum causa tuae viae;
Ne me perdas illa die.
Remember, merciful Jesus,
that I am the cause of your voyage;
do not lose me on that day.

Oro supplex et acclinis,
Cor contritum quasi cinis:
Gere curam mei finis.
I pray, bowed and kneeling,
my heart contrite as ashes;
take care of me at the last.

25–32 (4:2)
Cantus "B" phrase fragmented and alternated with Tenors on a phrase derived from "Dies irae" Counterpoint No. 1 (Sopranos, ms. 17–18 of "Dies irae"). Note that the Cantus "B" phrase (Bassoon, m. 25) is not tonally identical, but begins on the fifth of the G-sharp minor tonality, rather than the fourth—as it originally was in A minor (m. 37 Dies irae).

33–38 2 + (2:2)
– Becomes freer, beginning with sequential imitation of ms. 3–4 of original "B" ("Dies irae": ms. 39–40) and moving into B-major.

39–49 (3 + 2:2) + (2:2)
Initiated by Vc. CB Cantus playing ms. 5–6 of Cantus theme—and repeating m. 6 three times (the last in augmentation)—the chorus substantially "bumps" into a concluding augmented phrase at m. 46 and a lovely ending in G-sharp minor at m. 49 (difficult to tune instrumentally).

PERFORMANCE SUGGESTIONS

A. Tenors singing *quasi-mixto* or even falsetto are easier to blend into the composer's "humility and awe" requirement.

B. Most professional instrumentalists will prefer to play the Bassoon and English Horn parts as solos—rather than unisons—for reasons of intonation. If the Tenors sing with sufficient "humility and awe" this seldom offers balance problems, except perhaps occasionally for ms. 42–46. Obviously, at least two Bassoons are necessary for the final chord.

C. Though the least complex or difficult of the *Requiem*'s ten movements, this piece can become uniquely affecting with tender, loving care.

IV. REX TREMENDAE

LARGE BLOCKS

1–29 Group I

> 1–10 I A1
> 11–16 I A2
> 17–24 I B1
> 25–29 I B2

30–75 Group II

> 30–40 II A
> 41–63 II B
> 64–75 II C

76–110 Group III

> 76–85 Recapitulation of B1
> 86–110 Recapitulation of B2, A1, A2

CLOSER LOOK

1–29 Group I E-major 4/4 *Moderato maestoso*

> *Rex tremendae majestatis!*
> *Qui salvandos salvas gratis,*
> *Salva me fons pietatis.*
> King of dreadful majesty!
> Who freely saves the redeemed,
> Save me, fount of mercy.

1–16 (6 + 4) + 6

1–10 (A1) Initiating massive, sonorous fermatas in root position.

11–16 (A2) Imitative vocal fanfares ending in E major.

17–29 (4:2) + (2 + 3)

17–24 (4:2) Dolce-piano imitative lyricism leading to diminshed vii of B major.

25–29 Importunate mounting cries for "salva"-tion and animando No. 1.

30–75 Group II [(6:2) + 1] + (4 + 3) + (8 + 2) + 6

Verse 8 (Rex tremendae) + Verse 9:

Recordare, Jesu pie,
Quod sum causa tuae viae;
Ne me perdas illa die.
Remember, merciful Jesus,
That I am the cause of your voyage;
Do not lose me on that day.

30–41 Sequential imitative phrases mounting step-wise from B7 to F-sharp 7 and finally V to E-major.—Overlap at m. 41.

41–57 (4 + 3) + (8 + 2)

Confutatis maledictis, Jesu,
Flammis acribus addictis,
Voca me! [*cum benedictis.* (OMITTED)]
Silencing the accursed, Jesus,
To acrid flames consigning them,
Call me! [with the blessed.]

41–47 Rhetorical dramatic phrases; a sort of sequential choral recitative leading to:

48–57 (8 + 2) and further imitative shorter sequences, culminating in a despairing shout at m. 56.

58–63 (3:2)

Et—de profundo lacu.
And—from the deep pit.

– A violent interruption—of silence.

– followed by a sotto voce chanting of the fragment of text from the "Offertorium."

64–75 Group II C 6 + 6

A further mounting imitative sequence on text borrowed from the "Offertorium," halted abruptly and again quietly at m. 75 (another overlapping measure).

> *Libera me de ore leonis,*
> *Ne cadant in obscurum,*
> *Ne absorbeat me Tartarus.*
> Deliver them from the lion's mouth
> Lest they fall into darkness
> Lest Hell swallow them.

76–110 Group III

76–85 (5:2)

B (V) pedal section with recapitulation of "B1" material (at ms. 17 – 24) resolving to E major.

86–110 6 + 4 + 6 + (2:4)

Further short recapitulation, all introduced by a unison whimper from varying choral sections, and utilizing fragments of A1, A2, B2—all fading away into *ppp* E major (as Dominant V to Movement No. 5, "Quaerens me").

PERFORMANCE SUGGESTIONS

A. The most critical ensemble problem is the animando which begins at m. 25 and issues in a tempo at m. 42 which is asked to be "twice as fast as the beginning." Once the notes themselves are secure (at comfortable tempi and, if necessary, in lower octaves) the chorus will respond to the animando more easily if all notes are sung absolutely staccato (NOTHING SUSTAINED) so that all voices can experience the inner compound metrics. I have found the following tempi comfortable for the choruses: $\bullet$ = 66–68 at m. 17; c. 80 – 84 at m. 25; c. 96 at m. 30; c. 112 at m. 37; and c. 128–132 at m. 42. (The learning process is also speeded by "Count-singing" and by using nonsense syllables before graduating to text.)

B. At m. 58 the music seems to me to phrase more expressively if ms. 58–63 are conducted in two at, however, the same tempo as ms. 42–57 $\bullet$ = 132; $\bullet$ = 66) – Returning to 4/4 at m. 64.

V. QUAERENS ME

TEXTS: VERSES 10, 11, 12, 13, 14, 15 OF THE "DIES IRAE"

Quaerens me, sedisti lassus;
Redemisti crucem passus.
Tantus labor non sit cassus.
Seeking me, you remained exhausted;
You redeemed me by suffering the cross.
Such great labor should not be in vain.

Juste judex ultionis,
Donum fac remissionis
Ante diem rationis.
Just judge of vengeance,
Make the gift of remission
Before the day of accounting.

Ingemisco, tanquam reus . . .
Supplicanti parce Deus.
I sigh as one accused . . .
Spare the supplicant, God.

Preces meae non sunt digne,
Sed tu bonus fac benigne,
Ne perenni cremer igne.
My prayers are not worthy,
But you, good one, be merciful,
Lest I remain in burning flames.

Qui Mariam absolvisti,
Et latronum exaudisti,
Mihi quoque spem dedisti.
You who absolved Mary [Magdalene]
And listened to the thief
Have given me hope also.

Inter oves locum praesta,
Et ab heaths me sequestra,
Statuens in parte dextra.
Among the sheep grant me a place,
And from the goats separate me,
Setting me in the portion on the right.

This is Berlioz's gesture towards a Renaissance motet, and demands the sort of vocalism (minimum or no vibrato), timbre, tuning and control of dynamics appropriate to an "O vos omnes" of Vittoria.

The shortened version, totalling seventy-four measures and omitting ms. 40–79 of the earlier editions (with slight changes in the Bass-I part, ms. 38, 39 and new #40), would seem to be the preferred one these days.

Structurally, the piece is straightforward.

1–30 Group I A-major 4/4

> 1–16 I A
> Voices entering on I, IV, I, and vi, ending B minor.
> 17–30 I B
> Voices on vi, V, IV and IV (Soprano m. 27), with ending in E major.

31–41 Group II

Pyramiding stretto entrances of a second subject modulating to C major at m. 39, and diminishing in a Bass I chromaticism to A major at m. 42.

42–74 Group III Recapitulation and Coda

> 42–57
> Repeat of 1–16 with interchange of voices, and with addition of a reiterative percussive ("shuddering") pedal phrase in Bass and Tenor voices—for heightened tensions (?).
> 58–69
> Begins as repeat of 17–30 (58–63 = 17–22) but at m. 64, with the entrance of a Bass subject in B-minor, crescendos to an abrupt subdominant pause followed by:
> 70–74 (2 + 3)
> Endings in A major.

REHEARSAL SUGGESTIONS

Despite its polyphonic intentions, the "Quaerens me" motet has significant homophonic aspects—which add, it seems to me, to the difficulties of performance, particularly as regards intonation:

1. It moves from strict three-part writing to four, five, and even six parts at cadences.

2. Its reiterative pedal motives are more comfortably "intoned" by instruments than voices.

3. It demands wide ranges of pitch and dynamics (Altos: octave plus a seventh; Basses: two octaves; All *ppp* to *f*), constantly urging towards varying (even competing) styles of vocalism.

In addition to the customary cautions ("sing small intervals descending and large intervals ascending" and "redefine, even 'sharp' all repeated notes"), we have found it valuable:

1. to rehearse the entire motet against a constant A-natural 440 audible to everyone in the room;

2. to rehearse in succession—without help from a keyboard—the principal cadences: ms. 15–16, 29–30, 38–39, 56–57, 69 (Soprano I: octave lower) and 70–74; and

3. to rehearse the motet with all voices in unison singing the principal entrances at ms. 1, 4, 8, 12 (Tenor), 17, 20, 23, 31, 32, 33, 34, 42, 45, 49, 53 (Tenor), 58, 61, and 64—in each instance staying with the principal voice until the next voice enters.

VI. LACRYMOSA

Lacrymosa dies illa!
Qua resurget ex favilla
That tearful day!
When from the embers rises

Judicandus homo reus.
[Huic ergo parce Deus. (OMITTED)]
Guilty man, to be judged.
[Therefore, spare him, God.]

Pie Jesu Domine,
Dona eis requiem. [Amen. (OMITTED)]
Merciful Lord Jesus,
grant them rest. [Amen.]

This grand conclusion to the "Die irae" Sequence—and, vocally, the most exhausting of the Requiem movements—is a giant AB:ABA chorus on the last six lines of the Sequence text—now two-line stanzas, rather than the flood of triple rhymes which had preceded them.

LARGE BLOCKS

Part I (Roughly)

    1–42 A
    43–90 B

Part II (Roughly)

    91–124 A
    125–163 B
    164–201 A

CLOSER LOOK

Part I A 1–42 2 + (3:11) + 1

1–2 Introduction

Short motives in lower Strings and Woodwind and slashing syncopated accentuations in upper Strings.

3–35 I A1

3–13 Tenor statement of principal theme A in A minor:

A ranging, exhausting melody in triple/triple meter which departs from maximum vocal sonority at both upper and lower vocal ranges.

(Even with professional voices, it seems to me wise to support the melody by Alto voices in upper ranges and by Baritones in lower ranges. Since it is a soli unison line against skeletal [though strenuous] orchestral accompaniment this is possible—though never quite comfortable. [Ends down a fourth in E minor.])

14–24 Women's subject in E-minor with Tenor Counterpoint.—Generally a more comfortable and sonorous range (a "natural" Mezzo-soprano range), and ending down another fourth in B minor.

15–35 Bass soli line begins on B-natural—reasonably comfortable and sonorous—but harmonized as was the woman's entry in E-minor. At m. 30 the subject drops a step so that it may finish in A-minor (a fifth below its beginning tonality rather than a fourth). Basses have been accompanied by both Tenor and female voices in new patterns, though the instrumental materials have remained constant.

36–42 A2

An interesting, stretto'd climax to this section very nearly quoting the first four notes of the principal theme. Though the Bass voices have the stronger of the three lines, and though the pattern descends a third with each mea-sure's repetition, the Bass-Tenor-Soprano order of entrances forms a three-note ascending sequence which preserves energy until the ending is reached in C-major.

Part I B 43–90

43–74 I B1 (8 + 8) + (6 + 10) C major
43–58 2 + (2:4) + (4 + 3)

– A severely contrasting theme, even though built with melodic materials which are very close to Themes A1 and A2. A plaintive, pathetic Soprano/Tenor quote of motive A2 is answered by a Bass hesitating, nervous near-quote of the second measure of A1 before Theme B begins to assume a more complete form in its fifth to eighth measures (ms. 48–51).

59–74 (2:3) + (2:4) + 2 (including overlap)

Fractioning, variation and imitation of B materials to C ending at m. 74.

75–90 1 B2 (2 x 4) + (2:4)

– A lovely consoling Tenor melody (4 x 4 measures, with varying tonalities) which serves as the sole setting of the two-line prayer which concludes the "Dies irae." Particularly affecting are the First Violins' descant which begins in m. 77 and the Soprano imitations which aid the ending in E major (third inversion V2 of A minor).

Part II A1 91 – 124 (3:11) + 1

– A literal repeat of ms. 3–35—*with the addition* of the Brass Bands.

N.B.: A2 is now omitted—which leads to an interesting conflict of Major/Minor tonalities on the first beat of m. 124. The A major accompaniment pulse begins in the strings on the second eighth note of m. 124—while the sound of the Brass endings in A minor are still sounding in any concert hall—and would be echoing in St. Louis des Invalides (for which it was written) for several seconds.

Part II B 125–163 (8 + 8) + (6 + 8) + (3:3)

125–140 II B1 2 + (2:4) + (4 + 3)

Repeat of 42–58 in A major with the addition of a new Tenor Counterpoint. (Previously the Tenor sang with the women in unison.)

141–154 II B2 Repeat 59–72 down a minor third with new Tenor imitation added.
155–163 New rhetorical extensions gathering dramatic energy, and reiterating a flat second (F-natural) to the Dominant (E) of A minor.

Part II A 164–201 (5 + 6) + (4 + 5) + (5 + 5) + (2 + 4 + 2)

164–174 Repeat of A 1 substantially as it was in the Bass soli section, ms. 25–35, but tutu unison – or harmonized.
175–193 (4 + 5) + (5 + 5)
– Massive blocks of sound with both rhetorical and motivic repetitions ending in A major.

194–201 (2 + 4 + 2) Cadence A major

CHARACTERISTICS AND PERFORMANCE SUGGESTIONS

The "Lacrymosa" gets its great "swing," impetus and urgency from its triplet subdivisions within a triple meter. Dependent upon the acoustics of the performing space and the size of the performing forces the specific tempo (quarter-note = 60) seems to me a sound one in general, though I would suggest that the "A" sections be three to four points faster than MM. = 60, and the "B" sections be two to three points slower than MM. = 60. These differences should not be strongly marked, but they must be present. (Mahler has a marking which may be appropriate: "imperceptibly faster" and "imperceptibly slower.")

These are slow tempi, and it is not easy to keep them both "weighted" and "alive." Years ago, in early performances I found that I was pushing the tempo of the "A" sections in order to achieve "life" (and, possibly, to take some of the strain off these voices carrying the main theme). A wiser course would have been to see that the accompanying materials, both instrumental and vocal, were inflected and articulated to the most minute detail. Similarly, cross-accenting the textual hemiolas, as in ms. 179–181, will add significantly to the interest of repeated harmonies.

A second major difficulty lies in keeping the quiet sections really quiet. Given even the best of intentions, the "B" sections (ms. 42–90 and ms. 124–154) will get louder and louder unless rigorously controlled. With all the striving for "expressiveness" and textual emphasis one neglects the diminuendo which should follow each stress, however momentary—and all are caught in completely unintentional crescendo.

If one has significant choral forces, cutting the number of female and Tenor executants at ms. 43 and 125 (in line with the composer's instructions) would add to the intimacy of those sections. (Though I have never done so, it seems to me now that a smaller body of strings might be useful here, and a lesser doubling of English Horn and Bassoon parts.)

The next-to-final measure of the movement is marked with a fermata. So that the orchestra and the chorus may scale their diminuendo properly I have found it practical to beat the last two measures as though in 9/8 (each eighth-note equal to the previous dotted quarter). There are thus eleven beats within the diminuendo—with beats #10 and #11 initiating the final measure and silence beginning as though on beat #12. This makes approximately an eleven-second diminuendo—which seems to me an appropriate duration—and one easy for everyone to coordinate.

So far as the psychological and emotional qualities of the piece are concerned, I find myself moved and "enspirited" by its unswervable "three-ness." Two-ness and four-ness are balance; but three-ness is a "tilt," an off-balance, a psychic edginess and uncertainty. It is the medium and metric of tarantellas (tarantulas) and dances of death. – And that the language is triply tripled adds for me to its psychic convulsion. Realizing intellectually that the clarity, profile and expressivity of the interior, inferior voices are what will bring "life" to this rather slow, stubborn and extended tempo, I still want the movement to fly, flash, slash and swing. In general, lines played by multiple instruments in unison or sung by many voices may gain in mass, but lose in accentuation. – And even the largest of the "Lacrymosa's" lines (with the exception of ms. 75–90), it seems to me, should have the elasticity, curl and crack of a cattleman's (or a lion-tamer's) whip. – Or the heel-stamp of Spanish dances. These demand a common awareness to those unprescribable or uneditable accents—some of which might be textual and some musical—but must be in everyone's desires and hopes for this piece.

What a gift to the chorus to follow the strenuousness of Nos. IV, V and VI with the vocal relief of No. VII! It can, and should, be sung seated—in the most intimate and introverted of murmurs.

VII. OFFERTORIUM

[Bracketed text omitted by Berlioz; and some text re-ordered.]
Domine Jesu Christe! Rex gloriae!
Libera animas omnium fidelium
defunctorum de poenis.
Lord Jesus Christ! Glorious king!
Free the souls of all the faithful
dead from punishment.

Domine, libera eas
de poenis inferni
et de profundo lacu!
Lord, free them
from punishment in the inferno
and from the deep lake!

Libera eas [de ore leonis,
ne absorbeat tartarus,
ne cadant in obscurum: Sed signifer]
et sanctus Michael signifer
repraesentet eas in lucem sanctam;
quam olim Abrahae et semini ejus
promisisti, Domine Jesu Christe.
Amen.
Free them, [from the lion's mouth,
lest the abyss swallow them up,
lest they fall into darkness: May the standard-bearer]
and may St. Michael the standard-bearer
present them in holy light,
as once to Abraham and his seed
you promised, Lord Jesus Christ.
Amen.

– A marvelous mixture of forms—Theme and Variations, Fugue, Aria, Motet—and, in some respects, the most personal and mystical of all the Requiem movements. Until the final few measures the chorus murmurs only one- or two-word phrases on a monotone unison A-natural (with a B-flat suspended a half-step above it as the slowest of measured trills) at moments seemingly unrelated to the musical design, or related by nothing more than chance or caprice. An orchestral piece of some length which began as a fugato becomes, from time to time, an aria almost operatic in its expressivity, while the chorus murmurs itself into an almost Eastern-religious trance, and bows out with an inverted pyramidic conclusion and Coda.

1–59 Group I—Fugato and Transition.

1–13 (3:4) + 1
    Theme A beginning in D-minor in Violin I and moving to A-minor.

14–26 (3:4) + 1

Theme A beginning in D-minor as Violas with Counterpoint #1 in Violin I, and moving back to D-minor (by leaping downward a minor sixth—instead of an augmented) before the last measure.

27–39 (3:4) + 1

Theme A in D-minor in Violoncelli and Contrabasses with Counterpoint #2 in Violas, and Counterpoint #2 (Variation) in Violas, ending in A-minor.

40–52 + 1

Theme A in Violin II with Counterpoint #3 in Violin I, and other accompaniments in Violas and Violoncelli/CB responding to Counterpoint #3 as well as Theme A. Ending D-minor.

53–59 (1 + 3:2)

Ascending sequence in V'celli/CB related to opening motive Theme A, and moving to relative-major tonality: F-major.

60–111 Group II Introduction of B and Development.

60–66 (4 + 3)

"B" Aria fragment in F major—a full-throated, rhetorical melody in Woodwinds and Strings which forms a climax for the "Exposition" of Theme A but yields immediately, as though back to a second exposition.

67–77 (2:4) + 3

Theme A in F-major in Viola/V'celli with cascading unison Woodwinds, and broad Violin I descant.

78–84 (4 + 3)

"B" Aria fragment in B-flat major but leading this time to a reflective developmental section at:

85–97 (5 + 8)

– which quotes from both "A" and "B" sources, and returns at:

98–105 (4 + 4)

– quoting "A" directly in A minor and D minor—reaching a climax at:

106–111

– which ends with the last three measures of "B" in F major.

112–154 Group III Quasi Recapitulation/Conclusion

A fragmented and modulating traversal of "A" motifs.

112–130 (4 + 6) + (6 + 3)

Orchestral fragmentation ending in a half-close at m. 131.

131–136 (3 + 3)

Extended chanted A pedal.

137–146 (3 + 4 + 3)

Descending "pyramid" on D major triads and whole close in D major.

147–154 (3 + 3) + 2

Coda.

REHEARSAL SUGGESTIONS

The difficulties lie in trying to achieve—and maintain—the atmosphere of motionless silence. Ideally, except for a few moments of climax, the chorus should sound as though it were in another room—engaged in "silent prayer."

An inescapable crescendo is built into the orchestra, as section after section is added to the fugato texture and as the Woodwinds abandon their pedal or short expostulations for more lyric involvement—but even those sonorities should range from pianissimo to piano. The "B" lyricisms are extended intensifications for which one can be grateful—but they make it even more difficult to return to "motionless silence." The triplet Woodwind accompaniment beginning at m. 112 even with solo instruments is too loud *on paper*—let alone with the doublings specified at the beginning of the movement.

One wishes it were possible to achieve this miracle of trance—but one never quite does.

VIII. HOSTIAS

[Bracketed portions omitted.]
Hostias et preces tibi, [Domine]
laudis offerimus.
[tu] Suscipe pro animabus illis,
quarum hodie memoriam facimus . . .
[fac eas, Domine,
de morte transire ad vitam.
Quam olim Abrahae promisisti
et semini ejus.]
Sacrifices and prayers to you, [Lord]
we offer with praise.

Receive them for the souls of those
whom today we commemorate . . .
[Make them, O Lord,
to pass from death to life
as once you promised to Abraham
and his seed.]

– A slow solemn homophonic chanting by the male voices of the first half of the "Hostias" text punctuated at rhetorical intervals appropriate to the text by fermata harmonies voiced by "pedal" Trombones and Flute triads distanced by four octaves and as much as forty to fifty meters of physical space.

Given a stone cathedral acoustic with five to six seconds of reverberation decay, this piece can be a miracle of mystical sonority.

The movement is in two severely parallel blocks:

ms. 1–19 (plus 20–21 fermata) C major to B-flat major.
ms. 22–40 (plus short coda) E-flat major to B-flat minor.

The vocal difficulties arise from surprising enharmonic changes—so that tempered (keyboard) tuning is absolutely necessary—and from occasional unnecessarily awkward voice leading (–which can be countered by sensitive divisi voicings.)

The instrumental difficulties arise from the extreme instrumental ranges and the difficulty of hearing across the distances between the orchestra (Flutes) and the Brass Choir (placed at the extremes of hall or cathedral). A *musical* "last resort" solution for this *in concert halls* is to have the Trombone pedal notes played by the Brass Choir at Stage Right and Stage Left (or by those closest to the stage). This selection, though, does deprive one of the possible dramatic and mystical experience of tonal space and spatial tone.

From most seat locations in the acoustical environment for which the piece was written, one could not tell where the men stopped singing and the instruments began their sound—or whence came their sounds. *All* of our concert halls are simply too "dry" for a full experience of this piece. Cautions:

(1) Mark the Flute and Trombone parts well as to which beat the *sf* climax of the crescendo-diminuendo is to be sounded.

(2) Note the changes in dynamics for the men's voices, the result of new scholarship in the most recent editions.

Question:
Why did Berlioz not set the last half of the "Hostias" text? Did he not believe in the Christian "here-after?"

Half-Answer:

Schubert, too, had a little problem with "expecto resurrectionem." You pays yo' money and you finds out later . . . too later.

IX. SANCTUS

> *Sanctus, sanctus, sanctus*
> *[Dominus] Deus Sabaoth.*
> *Pleni sunt coeli et terra gloria tua.*
> Holy, holy, holy
> [Lord] God of Sabaoth.
> Heaven and earth are filled with your glory.
>
> *Hosanna in excelsis.*
> Hosanna in the highest.

LARGE BLOCKS

Group I

   1–45 I A Sanctus
   46–91 I B Hosanna

Group II

   92–138 II A Sanctus
   139–203 II B Hosanna

CLOSER LOOK

Group I A 1–45

A dialogue: a Tenor soloist, with echoing responses from Treble voices. Four solo Violins in high ranges supported by tremolando Violas in four parts, together with a hovering solo Flute, supply an almost motionless and scarcely audible gauze of harmony through which the voices are heard.

1–5 (2:2) + 1
   Introduction based on solo phrase #1 (D-flat major).

6–15 (2:5)
   Phrase #1; repeated by Treble voices, harmonized in D-flat major.

16–25 (2:5)

Phrase #2; echoed by Treble voices down a diminished fourth; but beginning in D major, ending B-flat major.

26–35 (2:2) + (2:3) Phrases #3 and #4

26–29 Tenor B-flat major; Treble echo A-flat to a diminished 7th.

30–35 Tenor D-flat major; Treble echo D-flat major.

36–45 (4 + 2 + 4)

Tenor concludes over broad harmonies with D-flat major whole close.

Group I B 46–91 "Hosanna" Fugato I

"Hosanna" fugato in three voices with doubling Strings, and with the following entrances:

Exposition No. 1 (4:7)

m. 46 Treble voices and Violins II on A-flat in D-flat major.

m. 53 Bass voices and Contrabasses on D-flat as though in A-flat.

m. 60 Tenor voices and Violoncelli on A-flat momentarily in A-flat.

m. 67 Episode No. 1—with Treble-Bass imitation.

Exposition No. 2 (2:7) + 4

m. 74 Bass voices and Contrabasses on D-flat in D-flat major.

m. 81 Treble and Tenor voices in stretto at distance of one-half measure.

m. 88 Conclusion with Tenor-Treble imitation and ending with fermata on V of D-flat.

Group II A 92–138 1 + (2 x 5) + (2:5) + (4 + 6) + (4 + 2 + 4) + (2 + 4)

92 Fermata D-flat

93–132 (2 x 5) + (2:5) + (4 + 6) + (4 + 2 + 4)

– Literal vocal repeat of ms. 6 – 45

– Literal instrumental repeat—but with significant addition of Bass Drum, Cymbals and a Violoncello bass line which enriches the harmonic texture.

133–138 (2 + 4)

The Treble voices echo and harmonize the final six measures of the Tenor ten-measure concluding phrase.

Group II B 139–203 "Hosanna" Fugato II

139–166 Exposition I (4:7)
Literal repeat of 46–73—with addition of Woodwinds and Ophicleides.

167–194 Exposition II
167–173 (4 + 3) Bass entrance: Literal repeat of m. 74.
174–182 (4 + 3 + 2) Trebles and Tenors in stretto: Literal repeat of ms. 81–89.
183–194 (4 + 4 + 4)

– A series of stretto entrances of the Head-motif only—frequently *non*-coincidental with the customary text, and occasionally even with false textual accentuation. Note the following:

m. 183 Tenor
m. 184 Bass: beat two
m. 185 Treble
m. 187 Tenor: "cel-sis hosanna"
m. 189 Tenor: "in ex-cel-sis"
m. 191 Bass: "san-na, ho-sanna"
m. 193 Bass: "cel-sis, ho-san-na"

– For many, many listeners this movement is more memorable—even than the Brass Choirs of the "Dies irae" and the "Lacrymosa." Much of this, it seems to me, is enhanced by taking spatial advantage of the composer's antiphony in the "Sanctus" sections. Since the Treble voices are usually placed behind the Violins on Stage Right, it has been our custom to place the Tenor soloist at the Left Rear of the hall, if possible in a hallway or elevated position, so that the Treble voices' response is spatial and directional as well as musical.

Because the tempo is so slow and the harmony so static one seldom encounters any problems of coordination or, since echoing phrases come frequently, any problems of intonation. The listeners are thus surrounded by the sound, and the sweet "holy-ness" (otherworldliness) of the Tenor solo is enhanced by being unseen.

A very special voice is demanded for the Tenor solo role. Voices appropriate to either German or Italian opera almost certainly would be inappropriate here. A light very high, lyric voice—one fluent, comfortable and sensitive to Bach's Evangelist requirements should find this "soupe de canard."

Question:

Note the absence of the "Benedictus." Any reason? None that I can find—other than thinking of a "concert" occasion rather than a liturgical one.

X. AGNUS DEI

> *Agnus Dei!*
> *qui tollis peccata mundi,*
> *dona eis requiem . . . sempiternam.*
> Lamb of God!
> who removes the sins of the world,
> grant them rest everlasting.
>
> *Te decet hymnus, Deus, in Sion,*
> *et tibi reddetur votum in Jerusalem.*
> *Exaudi orationem meam;*
> *ad te omnis caro veniet.*
> To you praise is meet, God, in Zion.
> and to you vows are made in Jerusalem.
> Listen to my prayer;
> unto you all flesh shall come.
>
> *Requiem aeternam*
> *dona defunctis, Domine,*
> *et lux perpetua luceat eis,*
> *cum sanctis tuis in aeternum, Domine,*
> *quia pius es.*
> *Amen.*
> Rest eternal
> grant to the dead, Lord,
> and may perpetual light shine on them
> with your saints in eternity, Lord,
> because you are merciful.
> Amen.

(Fragmenting texts of the "Requiem aeternam" [No. I] and the "Lux aeterna" [No. X, "Communion"] and mixing them rather personally.)

LARGE BLOCKS

10–81 Group I "Agnus Dei" A-major to B-flat major.

– A two-section male chorus chant patterned after the "Hostias" movement.

82–171 Group II "Te decet hymnus" B-flat major to G-major.

– A recapitulation of ms. 81 – 170 of Movement I.

172–200 Group III "cum sanctis tuis."

– A concluding section [(7 + 7) + (7:2) + 1] with "Amen" coda.

Closer Look

1–81 Group I

– Slow, solemn chanting by the male voices punctuated at rhetorical intervals appropriate to the text by pedal Trombones and Flute four-part triads distanced by four octaves and forty to fifty meters of physical space (see notes for No. VIII, "Hostias").

1–39 Block I
    1–12 (6:2)
– Six austere root-position chords in Woodwinds, each with an echo and reverberation decay scored for four-part Violas (divisi), modulating from A major to V of G major.
    13–39 (9 + 6 + 4 + 8)
– Four slow textual fragments with Flute, Trombone fermatas—moving enharmonically from E to B-flat minor.

40 – 81 Block II
    40–51
– Six austere root-position chords in Woodwind with echoing Violas—moving from A-major to E-flat major.
    51–73 (9 + 6 + 4 + 4)
– Structures similar to ms. 13 – 38, but moving from E-flat major to B-flat major.
    74–81 (4:2)
– F-pedal in Flutes with chromatic descent in Trombones to A-natural and implied V (first inversion) to B-flat and recapitulation of Movement I ("Requiem" and "Kyrie").

82–171 Group II (Literal repeat of ms. 81–130 of Movement I.)

(See notes for "Requiem" and "Kyrie.")

172–200 Group III

172–178 (2 + 2 + 3)

New textual conclusion "Cum sanctis tuis . . . "—punctuated by Timpani triads, choral pedal G-naturals falling where "Kyries" occurred in Movement I.

179–185 (2 x 2) + 3

Sweetly expressive short melodic conclusion—which seems so "expectable," "familiar" and "right" (note phrase proportions identical to the preceding seven measures)—because it is a direct quote from the concluding measures of the "Rex tremendae," transposed from E major to G major.

186–200 (6:2) + 3

Six final "Amens" accompanied by Trombones and punctuated by Timpani triads: C-G; B-G; A-G; E♭-G; A-flat-G; D-G. – Ending with pianissimo pizzicato Strings and Timpani.

PERFORMANCE SUGGESTIONS

The things said about the acoustical marvels inherent in the sonorities and dynamics of the "Hostias" apply with doubled intensity in the "Agnus Dei"; for, in addition to the Flute and Trombone punctuations, we have the Viola echoes of the Woodwind sonorities in ms. 1–12 and 40–51. In a dry hall (and all halls are dry compared to a Renaissance ecclesiastical acoustic) the attack of the Violas should be so quiet that it is not heard (being covered by the tied eighth-note of the Woodwinds), and the Viola chord should be held long enough so that it can be "discerned" by the audience—even at *ppp*.

Though it would be folly to talk of the "greatest" or the "noblest" of the *Requiems* which share its text, that by Berlioz must be counted among the most "dramatic," "original" and "influential." The influence on Verdi, and through Verdi on Britten, is inescapable. Each of its movements is a musical "event," something that "doesn't happen any place else." The coherence is not the coherence of liturgy, and not, I should think, of conventional Christian faith; but, rather, the coherence of an active, sophisticated mind that has the musical genius to probe at a remarkable centuries-old liturgically enriched text, and bring it into an era of historical, scientific, intellectual and psychological inquiry, experiment and enlightenment. In this respect it could be that it does for the text of the *Requiem* what Beethoven accomplished for the text of the *Mass*.

(Translations of the *Requiem* text by Nick Jones, 1984, Woodruff Arts Center, Atlanta, Georgia. Used by permission.)

April 16, 1980

BERLIOZ

>One rarely knows—with Berlioz—
>From how he starts just where he goes.
>
>It's like—before you're really seated.
>From toes to ears you're over-heated.
>
>His tunes and chords are nicely tended,
>But where they'll end he just invented.
>
>His texts are neat, no cloud appears,
>When oops! You're up to here in tears.
>
>It's strange to think that this sensation,
>Alive, should lack appreciation.
>
>'Tis true . . . he's not the straightest arrow,
>—But Frenchmen dote on snails and marrow.
>
>Our times must be just so abstemious
>We need some other-lovin' genius.
>
>What Hector has
>is quel pizz-azz.

INTROIT

>Berlioz, Verdi and Brahms
>Were a trio of psingers of psalms.
>What Berlioz wanted he never quite got,
>And Verdi went "oom-pah" as often as not,
>While, as for Brahms' love-life, it wasn't so hot.
>But nothing impaired the musical chahms
>of Berlioz, Verdi—
>of Berlioz, Verdi—
>of Berlioz, Verdi and Brahms!

BALLADE

> Hector's love for his music
>   —And make no mistakes here—
> Was short of his passion
>   For W. Shakespeare.
>
> He offered to France
>   *Benvenuto Cellini,*
> But all Paris wanted
>   Was works by Rossini.
>
> Held by those in his time
>   Less sublime than deplorable,
> The balance still wavers:
>   Banal to adorable.
>
> Like the ghost in Macbeth
>   —A sorrowing spectre—
> He hovers and haunts
>   The theatrical sector.
>
> He challenged the heavens;
>   —And half his frustration
> Is being renowned
>   For his "fine orchestration."

R.

JOHANNES BRAHMS

German Requiem

1997

That the world celebrates this year the 100th anniversary of the death of Johannes Brahms with uncountable performances of his *German Requiem* is testimony not only to the esteem in which his music is held by a large part of the Western World, but also to the very special affection in which his *Requiem* itself is held.

Though it was his longest work, and acknowledged as very pivotal to his growing renown, he himself was not really satisfied with the title of *German Requiem,* saying that it referred solely to the language in which it was written. He would now prefer, he said, a "human" Requiem, for he was writing in exploration of a universal human experience.

It should be reported also, that he appeared to find very little comfort in the ritual or dogma of his day. He deliberately abstained from the Latin tradition of centuries in favor of a text which he himself assembled from the Hebraic/Christian Scriptures in Martin Luther's translation.

Certain things are abundantly clear: first, that he knew these scriptures very well indeed: the text which he gathered to form the seven movements of his *Requiem* has some sixteen widely separate sources among the thousands of pages of the *Old* and *New Testaments* and the *Apocrypha*.

In the second place, it is clear that he was more concerned with comforting the hearts of those left to mourn, rather than with escorting the departed through the medieval horrors of Wrath and Judgement.

The latter half of the nineteenth century was a period of historical, scientific and intellectual enrichment of the Hebraic/Christian tradition. Though the Latin rites for the dead are deeply embedded in the religious history of Western Civilization, there can be little doubt that Brahms uses his text to welcome the consideration of death as a relevant and illuminating aspect of life itself.

"Lord, help me to understand that my life on earth must have an end, that I must depart. Blessed are they that mourn, for they shall have comfort. Yea, I will comfort you as one whom his own mother comforts."

And finally, of course, the text with which he chose to conclude,

"Blessed are they who die in the Lord, for their works do follow after them."

March 11, 1997

Friends –

The understanding generally assigned to Brahms' choice of text for his "German" *Requiem* is that, rather than setting the traditional prayers for the safe journey of the souls of the departed to their theologically correct heavenly rest, he chose to be concerned with bringing some degree of comfort to the sorrowing who remain.

I am not sure I ever have "heard" Brahms' *Requiem*—strictly as a member of an audience. At this moment I can recall only performances in which I was a participant—the first, of course, as a singer.

My point is that, however varied and personal its comfort-bearing qualities may be to the listener, there can be no doubt about its exhilarative effects upon those who perform it. Is there any piece in our symphonic choral repertoire which is so enlivening to sing?

Time after time singers and instrumentalists have come to me following a performance, saying, "My (mother, grandmother, aunt, father, uncle, sister, brother . . .) passed away last month, and this was 'especially meaningful' to me." These comforts do exist, and they undoubtedly vary from person to person in proportion to how completely a listener or performer is comfortable also with traditional Christian doctrine as to resurrection and an after-life.

My attention at the moment is to these extraordinary "life-fulfilling" joys that singing the Brahms *Requiem* affords its participants apart from doctrinal reinforcement. 'Strange, isn't it, to contemplate the joys (perhaps even "pleasures?") of singing a Requiem? But, there they are.

R

February 17, 1972

Someone asked this week why I had occasionally advised a phrasing (or an implied phrasing) in the middle of a syllable—"Does this not interrupt the meaning of the words?"

There are two answers to this question, and many of you have heard them before. The first is practical: Most frequently this advice has been given with reference to subsidiary or accompanying materials. The composer, of course, begins with his text, and his principal concern is to create a musical statement which will fit and enhance the given elements of speech, and which will, in addition, enrich and deepen the meaning of the text. If he is a composer of song-forms (as is Brahms) then his principal melody will bear close relationship to the line of text. But as he creates other voice lines which accompany and comment, his text is liable to be fragmented, extended or turned around to make it more usable. In these instances one frequently recommends phrasings which go with the music rather than with text—for the composer's attention here would seem to have been primarily musical rather than textual.

The second answer is a bit more in the field of general ideas and purposes. The truth is that only the most primitive sort of song has a kind of "one-to-one" relationship between tune and text: ("All alone by the telephone"). All great melody, however, assumes a great deal more independence for itself. For instance, all of us can think of melodies where we may have as many as five to twenty notes to sing on a single vowel: ("Ich hoffe," p. 37, *Requiem*).

While great melody does manage to "fit" (in varying degrees) the *mechanics* of speech, the thing that really makes it great is its ability to illuminate the *spirit* of the text—even occasionally by employing little inner musical groupings which imply textual interruptions.

This is not to say that music is independent of the text or that the composer is not "inspired" by it. Rather, it is to say that music is also a language: it has its own laws and methods of structure and expressivity. The great composer does not merely "highlight" or "under-line" text; he creates a musical fabric in tone and time which matches or transcends or illumines the text, but is also law unto itself and its own reason for being.

As artists—and as human beings—our concern is not with how we feel about death or the textual imagery of the *German Requiem,* but how Brahms felt about these things. And the way we learn about his feelings is by learning to "speak" his language—as perfectly and as trustingly as we can.

We have to believe that Brahms has something to say. We have to recognize that for the next few weeks and in this place we are his voice. We have to realize that he speaks in terms of intonation and tone "colors" and rhythms, and that these are privileged to be truly the sound of his mind.

When one obeys traffic laws he may reasonably expect fewer traffic tickets and an increased chance of survival. – Not much, but something. – But when one lovingly and earnestly obeys the laws of great music there is always the chance that the flesh will be made word and dwell among us.

R.S.

April 22, 1980

LIEBESLIED

> Brahms' morning-star was slow to rise
> – Vienna had its slights:
> His little wick of flame was dimmed
> By Wagner's acolytes.

He won his first esteem as a
    Piano virtuoso;
But soon his songs—as well as hands—
    Were known, and maybe more so.

Some say he had affairs of heart
    – If not, he'd not be human.
(One hopes he helped to dry the tears
    Of Mrs. Robert Schumann.)

He must have viewed his times askew:
    Among his legacies
Are triplets over bars in two
    And duplets over threes.

Forever probing after Form,
    By nature and upbringing
His large designs all sheltered first
    The song and then the singing.

And so Vienna grew to love
    His walks and habitats;
And even folk across the street
    Would nod, and tip their hats.

And we who love his *Requiem*
    Confess it and concede here:
The final Brahmsian pilgrimage
    Still takes us to his Lieder.

Odes

February 25, 1988

Friends –

We send the translations of Brahms' choruses as the first (and lasting) installments of required reading towards the degree of Doctor of Melancholia. (– Small wonder that a minor messianic Judean sect offering "salvation" made such a startling impact on the Greco-Roman world.)

The four texts together offer an almost overwhelming and despairing assessment of the "human condition." (Whether that despair was totally and appropriately a response to Greco-Roman mythology/ontology/theology—or whether it in large part represents German Romanticism of the early nineteenth century is a good question.)

Cecil Gray in his *Survey of Contemporary Music* (1924, Oxford University Press) writes,

"The art history of every civilization viewed collectively is the progress from classic to romantic values. All romantic art is a swan-song, the final expression of a civilization, the rich autumn tints of decay, the writing on the wall, the flaming comet heralding the approach of anarchy and dissolution, known to Plato and called by him the 'rebellious principle.'"

In his view the Greco-Roman world, whose arts we always have called "classical," was, in fact, closer to the autumnal aspects of Romanticism precisely because of its positioning of humankind subject to divine whim and indifference.

At any rate, Brahms chose these texts evidently over a span of a dozen years, and they are remarkably similar.

They offer substantially none of the occasional hope-inspiring assurances of his *German Requiem*. (Even in the *Requiem,* however, these assurances do not occupy a dominant amount of the total time, and the pervading atmosphere is that of attempting to comfort and console in the abiding presence of grief.)

Lest anyone give up and take to a monastery, let me propose that the mulch of tragedy, impermanence, frailty and—possibly—even decay are the only ground upon which human heroism can grow. (As others have noted, even a Christian God had to prove his God-hood by assuming human suffering.)

All of us, I would guess, have come to love the *German Requiem* as the richest lode of Brahms' musical ore, but I wonder now if these four autumnal odes of despair have not prompted Brahms' most heroic compositional talents.

If so, the works themselves offer the chief rebuttal to their texts.

R

SCHICKSALSLIED (SONG OF DESTINY), OP. 54

You wander in the light
On gentle ground, blessed spirits;
Luminous heavenly breezes
Touch you gently,
As the fingers of musicians
(Touch) sacred harp-strings.

Without destiny, like the sleeping
Infant, breathe the divine;

Kept pure in encasing bud,
Forever bloom their souls,
And their blessed eyes
Gaze in still, eternal clarity.

But to us is given no place to rest;
We wither, we fall, suffering mankind,
Blindly from one hour to another,
Like water from rock to rock thrown,
Year by year in uncertainty below.

NANIE (ELEGY), OP. 82

Even Beauty must perish:
   Though mortals and gods vanquishing,
It cannot move the steel-hardened heart
   of the Stygian Zeus.
Only once, at the pleading of Eros,
   the Ruler of Shades relented,
And ruthless even then, he recalled
   from the threshold of freedom his boon.

No balm could Aphrodite bring
   to the fair boy, sore wounded,
There where his tender flesh fiercely
   the wild boar had torn.
Nor the immortal mother give life
   to her godlike hero,
When at the Scaean gates falling,
   his fate he fulfilled.

But she doth rise from the sea
   with all the daughters of Nereus,
And lifting her voice in lament, mourns
   for her glorified son.
See how they weep, the Immortals;
   all the goddesses are weeping,
That beauty must fade,
   that the perfect must die.

To be even a song of lament on the lips
   of the beloved is glory,

For 'tis the common lot to go unsung
  down to Hades.

GESANG DER PARZEN (SONG OF THE FATES), OP. 89

The gods are to be feared by mankind!
They hold their mastery
In everlasting hands
And can employ it as it pleases them.
He should fear them doubly, whom they exalt!
Upon crags and clouds
Are chairs set at golden tables.

If there arises a quarrel, the guests
Are thrown down, insulted and reviled,
into night-black depths and wait in vain,
In darkness bound, for equitable judgement.

They, however, they remain
For eternal feasting at golden tables.
They stride from mountain
Across to mountain:

From abysses of the deep steams up to them
The breath of suffocating Titans,
Like offering fragrances,
A gathering of fleecy clouds.

The masters turn away their beneficent eyes
From entire generations
And avoid seeing in the grandchildren
The formerly beloved, softly expressive
Features of the forefathers.

So sang the Fates;
The banished one hears in dismal caves;
The old one [hears] the songs,
Thinks of children and grandchildren
And shakes his head!

RHAPSODY, OP. 53

But who is that, alone?
In the bushes he loses his path,
Behind him the shrubs spring together,
The grass stands up again,
The wilderness swallows him.

Ah, who can heal the sorrows
Of him, for whom balm turns to poison?
Who drank hatred of men
From the fullness of love?

Once rejected, now a rejecter,
He secretly feeds on his own worth
In unsatisfying self-absorption.

If there is on thy psalter, Father of Love,
One tone that can reach his ear,
then refresh his heart:
Open his clouded sight
Upon the thousand springs
Near to him who thirsts in the desert.

BENJAMIN BRITTEN

War Requiem

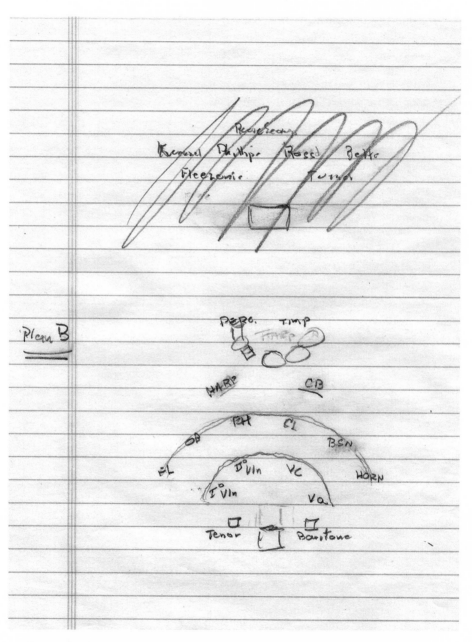

Sketch of orchestra and soloist stage positioning for performances of Britten's *War Requiem*

November 10, 1993

Address re: "The Texts of the *War Requiem*"

The originality and genius of Benjamin Britten's *War Requiem* lie in his infusion of Wilfred Owen's World War I poetry into the history-laden Latin *Mass for the Dead*.

The *Requiem Mass*, quite apart from its religious significance, is a remarkable poetic and dramatic accomplishment. Its central poem is the *Dies Irae*, attributed to Thomas of Celano in the thirteenth century, describing with extravagant imagery but terse poetic severity, the "Final Judgement" of Christian tradition.

And the poetry of Wilfred Owen, while tragically limited in total output, is vast in its human concern, and almost certainly without an equal among the English/American "war poets" of this century for invention and individuality.

However, given these two great texts, it still is Britten's own literary sensibilities and dramatic vision which inspire and structure the *War Requiem*. No composer of our time has been so sensitive to the values of words. Certainly no English composer has set so many distinguished English texts, lyric or narrative, and ranging over six or more centuries.

Wilfred Owen was killed in action just seven days before the armistice in November of 1918—upon his return to the front-line trenches *after* being wounded and hospitalized. And Britten dedicated his score to the memory of four of his own friends killed in action in the Second World War a quarter of a century later.

But they shared a passionate conviction: that war in their time was an intolerable outrage, and a violation not only of human goodness, but of Christianity itself.

Britten's plan was simple, but remarkably effective. He gave to an adult mixed chorus and soprano soloist, accompanied by a full symphony orchestra, the complete and traditional Latin text of the *Requiem Mass*. At four points in the *Mass* these adult voices are joined by the voices of boys, singing from a distance (or another area) Latin texts peculiarly appropriate to the innocence of children.

But at nine eloquent moments—philosophically appropriate and profoundly disturbing—Britten interrupts the sequence of the *Mass* to let Owen's poetry shine through, in its native, living English, as commentary—or even contradiction. These words are given to a tenor and a baritone, accompanied by a chamber orchestra—and by the end of the work we realize that they also represent an English and a German soldier, and that both are dead.

1. Early in the *Requiem* the choir sings: "Unto thee all flesh shall come." – And the English soldier interrupts: "What bells for these who die as cattle?"

2. At the beginning of the *Dies Irae* the brasses announce the "Day of Judgement." – And the German soldier responds wistfully, "Bugles sang . . . but only bugles answered. . . . Voices of boys were by the riverside," . . . but "Sleep mothered them."

3. With the *Rex Tremendae* the choir laments its fear of standing at last before the "King of awful majesty." – But the soldiers brag and boast together—with patently false bravado: "Out there, we've walked quite friendly up to Death."

4. With the *Recordare* and the *Confutatis* the chorus pleads, as sheep, not to be numbered among the damned—while Owen's poetry addresses the awesome cannon of World War I: " . . . May God damn you, and cut you from our soul!"

5. At the *Lacrymosa* the Latin prayer asks that on the day of resurrection, "This newly departed soul arise with the saved." – And the English soldier sings haltingly of his comrade, just now killed: "Move him into the sun . . . if anything can rouse him . . . the kind old sun will know."

6. With the *Offertorium* the choir recalls the glorious promises of Jehovah to Abraham that the "souls of the faithful" . . . will be led "into the holy light." – And the soldiers join in a bitter, satirical revision of Abraham's sacrifice of Isaac, in which Abraham ignores Jehovah's command, "and slays his son, and half the seed of Europe one by one."

7. With the *Sanctus* the orchestra and chorus join in flourishes and shouts of "Hosanna in the highest!" – And at this holiest of moments the composer and poet resign themselves to an inconsolable denial of the Christian theological assurances of immortality. "Shall life renew these bodies?—When I do ask white Age he saith not so."

8. At the *Agnus Dei* the choir chants softly its litany: "O Lamb of God . . . grant us peace," and the tenor interjects, recalling a roadside crucifix beside a French farm road, in which the Lamb of God has a leg shot off—victim of the scribes and priests of the State and the Church who condone wars.

9. And, finally, in the *Libera Me,* as the choir for the last and most terrifying time pictures the Judgement Day and falls back trembling and silent, the two soldiers meet. Symbolically the place of meeting is a trench, a tunnel, a dugout. The reality is the grave (—or Hell): "I am the enemy you killed, my friend. Let us sleep now . . . "

William Plomer, in the liner notes to Britten's own recording, writes: "There seems to be general agreement that the *War Requiem* is the profoundest work Britten produced. It has been received as a work of vast scope, in which the composer, by giving it all the technical resources and emotional power at his command, so transcends the personal that he seems to gather together the sufferings, and to probe the potential goodness, of all humankind."

[Of] the major works of music created since World War II, it is doubtful if any has made so profound, immediate and universal an impression. Audiences have wept, critics in most instances have surrendered to its impact, and the work has been found on the news and editorial pages as well as among the musical reviews.

It has not found universal favor however among avant-garde composers or like-minded critics. It has been accused of being "eclectic"—a paste job of past composers' creativity; of being "contrived" and "formalized"—both as to musical content and calculated effect.

To a certain extent such evaluation is understandable. A great deal of the choral writing shows enormously the influence of the Verdi *Requiem*. Except for the *Lux Aeterna*, which Britten saves for a giant coda, the *War Requiem* borrows Verdi's basic textual and formal groupings for its six main movements. In some instances his writing amounts almost to a personal paraphrase.

For example –

The opening *Requiem aeternam* begins with the *pianissimo* unison chanting of the chorus.

The *Dies Irae* has the fanfares which Verdi shared with, or derived from, Berlioz, and almost identical splashes of choral/brass rhetoric in a disturbing and animated tempo.

The *Lacrymosa* recalls inevitably, by tempo and by texture, the slow, plaintive lyricism of Verdi's *Lacrymosa*.

The formal similarities continue with—

The *Quam Olim Abrahae:* a brisk *fugato*.

The *Agnus Dei:* a slow, hymn-like unison tune.

And the *Libera Me,* polyphonic and dramatic, recalling the fanfares of the *Dies Irae* and enclosing a soaring soprano solo.

But Britten never felt obliged—so far as I know—to invent an absolutely novel and solitary musical language. If the Cages and Stockhausens are true prophets of a new musical order, then Britten may be hopelessly lapped and doomed to be forgotten.

It is worth noting in passing, however, that Bach did not invent a new and personal language—nor Haydn, nor Mozart—nor, indeed, almost anyone until the strange psycho-social compulsions of our century: of which Stravinsky writes in his *Poetics of Music:*

"It just so happens that our contemporary epoch offers us the example of a musical culture that is day by day losing the sense of continuity and the taste for a common language.

"Individual caprice and intellectual anarchy, which tend to control the world in which we live, isolate the artist from his fellow-artists and condemn him to appear as a monster in the eyes of the public; a monster of originality, inventor of his own language, of his own vocabulary, and of the apparatus of his art. The use of already employed materials and of established forms is usually forbidden him. So he comes to the point of speaking an idiom without relation to the world that listens to him. His art becomes truly unique, in the sense that it is incommunicable and shut off on every side.

"Times have changed since the day when Bach, Handel and Vivaldi quite evidently spoke the same language which their disciples repeated after them, each one unwittingly transforming this language according to his own personality. The day when Haydn, Mozart and Cimarosa echoed each other in works that served their successors as models, successors such as Rossini, who was fond of repeating in so touching a way that Mozart had been the delight of his youth, the desperation of his maturity and the consolation of his old age."

I asked Morton Gould some years ago about avant-garde concert life in New York: pianists immobile before a keyboard for 6 minutes of composed silence, cellists hanging from balconies in mini-bikinis, 100 metronomes set at different speeds and simultaneously released—the last to run down determining the length of the composition: "Robert," he said, "a lot of it goes a little ways." Elizabeth Sprague Coolidge—asked why she had put on the series of avant-garde concerts in Washington's Art Galleries—replied, "Young man, I may be deaf, but I'm not blind!"

So the *War Requiem* lies somewhere between Palestrina and Stravinsky, and not far from Bartók in musical language—but within only two decades, it is less and less difficult for us to perform, and—more importantly—for both performer and listener it packs an enormous emotional wallop. It communicates.

It was written for the consecration of the rebuilt Cathedral of St. Michael in Coventry in the Spring of 1962.

This, roughly, is its thirty-first anniversary and for Owen's text, the seventy-fifth anniversary, and, of course, the eightieth anniversary of the birth of Benjamin Britten, in what begins to emerge as nearly an entire century of uninterrupted war.

The Mass, of course, is a social as well as a religious phenomenon.

The company of believers gathers together to consider and to celebrate the fact of death—which is also to say "the facts of life."

For these are the ultimate questions. In a sense, there are no others.

Anyone who has held the hand of a dying friend—has been lost in the No Man's Land of IS and IS NOT.

And Birth is its own mystery: and a biological/religious/sociological/political/legal conundrum and controversy as well. At what moment does the embryo—or incipient animal—become "a living soul?"

Therefore—

Behind the elaborate and codified petition for the preservation—for the "salvation of the human soul," the Mass is a somewhat grim—though mostly unspoken—celebration of survival: we the "present company" (those worshipping—for the moment) are "excepted."

William Plomer, also a British poet and librettist-collaborator with Britten, writes: "Owen was only 25, but his poems were profound, and are profoundly disturbing. They made no appeal to the accepted opinions of his time about poetry or war. They were not about what soldiers gloriously did, but what they had unforgivably been made to do to others, and to suffer themselves. Owen did not accept what he called 'the old Lie' that it was necessarily glorious—or even fitting—to die for one's own or any other country, or that a country was necessarily or perhaps ever justified in making the kind of war he knew. As he saw and experienced it, war appeared as a hellish outrage on a huge scale against humanity, and a violation of Christianity. He shared the destiny of millions on both sides, but he had the sensibility to see what war now really meant, and the power to explain it.

"I am not concerned with poetry! My subject is War," Owen wrote, "and the pity of War. The Poetry is in the pity."

Into his poetry went the pity, not of a detached outsider or a sentimentalist, nor simply that of a humane officer for his men whose lives he cannot save and to whom he cannot hold out hope, but the pity of an imaginative man for fellow-sufferers unable to speak for themselves to later generations.

"I suppose I can endure cold and fatigue and face-to-face death as well as another," he wrote to Siegfried Sassoon, his friend and inspiration; "but extra for me there is the universal pervasion of Ugliness. Hideous landscapes, vile noises, foul language, and nothing but foul, even from one's own mouth (for all are devil-ridden)—everything unnatural, broken, blasted; the distortion of the dead, whose unburiable bodies sit outside the dugouts all day, all night, the most execrable sights on earth. In poetry we call them the most glorious. But to sit with them all day, all night—and a week later to come back and find them still sitting there in motionless groups, THAT is what saps the 'soldierly spirit.'

"Your letter reached me at the exact moment it was most needed—when we had come far enought out of the line to feel the misery of Rest and Recreation; and I had been seized with writer's cramp after making out my casualty reports . . . I cannot say I suffered anything, having let my brain grow dull. That is to say, my nerves are in perfect order.

"It is a strange truth: that your 'Counter-Attack' frightened me much more than the real one: though the boy by my side, shot through the head, lay on top of me, soaking my shoulder, for half an hour.

"Catalogue? Photograph? Can you photograph the crimson-hot iron as it cools from the smelting? That is what Jones' blood looked like, and felt like. My senses are charred.

"I shall feel again as soon as I dare, but now I must not. I don't even take the cigarette out of my mouth when I write 'Deceased' over their letters."

Plomer continues:

"War has been the central horror of European history in this century; and Owen, mourning young lives tormented and treated as expendable, was to speak as directly to mourners in 1945 as to those of 1918; furthermore, since the fear of war is now universal, his elegies speak to us directly. They are a warning.

"To nobody grieving for the deaths of friends in the War which broke out again more than twenty years after his death did Owen speak more directly than to Britten. And since there is no motif more predominant and recurrent to Britten's works than that of innocence outraged and ruined, what could be more natural than that Britten, deeply moved by Owen's poetry, should be no less moved by the fate of the man who wrote it, his youth, his promise, his passionate tenderness, his rare talent cut off by the senseless violence of war? Being so moved, Britten's impulse was to set Owen's most memorable poems for singing. It was a sure instinct that prevented him from setting them separately, or as a sequence. Certainly they have a kind of monumental nobility that enables them to stand alone; but he saw, as nobody else could have seen, that they could stand beside the sacred liturgy of the *Mass for the Dead,* and, musically, be combined with it."

Let us now turn to Britten's libretto, and examine that combination.

I am going to suggest that all of us read together—in a quiet, collaborative, undemonstrative murmur—the traditional Latin verses . . . with an occasional glance at the parallel translation.

Then, if I may, I will call your attention to those lines which triggered Britten's selection of Owen's verses. I shall read them aloud . . . with your silent complicity, and then, simply add those things which occur to me concerning the conjunction and values therein.

I. REQUIEM AETERNAM

Chorus

> *Requiem aeternam dona eis Domine*
> *et lux perpetua luceat eis.*
> Grant them eternal rest, O Lord,
> and let everlasting light shine on them.

(Note the poetic value in having the noun and verb share the same linguistic root—"lux . . . luceat" vs. "light shine.") (Latin & romance vs. English German.)

Boys' Choir

Te decet hymnus, Deus in Sion;
et tibi reddetur votum in Jerusalem;
exaudi orationem meam, ad te omnis caro veniet.
To Thee, O God, praise is meet in Sion,
and unto Thee shall the vow be performed in Jerusalem.
Hearken unto my prayer: unto Thee shall all flesh come.

(Note that the undisturbed purity of Boys allows them to sing this Hymn.)

Tenor Solo

What passing bells for these who die as cattle?
Only the monstrous anger of the guns.
Only the stuttering rifles' rapid rattle
Can patter out their hasty orisons.
No mockeries for them from prayers or bells,
Nor any voice of mourning save the choirs, –
The shrill, demented choirs of wailing shells;
And bugles calling for them from sad shires.

What candles may be held to speed them all?
Not in the hands of boys, but in their eyes
Shall shine the holy glimmers of good-byes.
The pallor of girls' brows shall be their pall;
Their flowers the tenderness of silent minds,
And each slow dusk a drawing-down of blinds.
" . . . Hearken unto my prayer: unto thee *shall all flesh come.*"
"What passing bells for those *who die as cattle?*"

In addition to the myriad disturbing fragmentary associations that surround this juxtaposition—cattlebells, man-made flesh, man-made meat, butcher-boys, boys butchered—in addition to these connotations, here within the first few minutes of this extended work, is squarely placed its rather total argument, titled (by Owen) "Anthem for doomed youth."

Let me call your attention to the verbal elements of assonance, alliteration and the like—those matters of speech which exalt meaning with mystery and music.

Lines three and four bring us not only the alliteration of "*rifles' rapid rattle*" but, even more importantly, the inner onomatopoeic alliteration of "stu*tt*ering, ra*tt*le, pa*tt*er."

Lines five and six set forth "no mockeries for them" or "voice of mourning." Obviously, we have the "m" alliterations, though they are reversed. Perhaps more significantly we have a "v" sound poised against a voiced "th" sound. Both of these are voiced consonants and both made at the forward wall of the mouth and teeth. The effect in consonants is similar to Emily Dickinson's "half-rhymes." Repeat a few times, "mockeries for them . . . voices of mourning." Concentrate upon the alliteration, the half- or false-alliteration, and the reverse orders. These seem to me moments wherein music and mystery enter.

Line twelve brings us a beautiful play upon robbing "pallor" to provide a "pall."

Consider the last few words in each of lines thirteen and fourteen: "tenderness of silent minds . . . drawing down of blinds." Note the parallelism of "n" sounds (7 "n" sounds in 8 words). These certainly contribute enormously to the poem's wistful, saddened diminuendo.

CHORUS

> *Kyrie eleison,*
> *Christe eleison,*
> *Kyrie eleison,*
> Lord, have mercy upon us,
> Christ, have mercy upon us,
> Lord, have mercy upon us.

II. DIES IRAE

CHORUS

> 1. *Dies irae, dies illa,*
> *Solvet saeclum in favilla,*
> *Teste David cum Sibylla.*
> The Day of Wrath, that day
> shall dissolve the world in ashes,
> as witnesseth David and the Sibyl.

2. *Quantus tremor est futurus,*
Quando judex est venturus,
Cuncta stricte discussurus!
What trembling shall there be
when the Judge shall come
who shall thresh out all thoroughly!

3. *Tuba mirum spargens sonum*
Per sepulchra regionum
Coget omnes ante thronum.
The trumpet, scattering a wondrous sound
through the tombs of all lands,
shall drive all unto the Throne.

4. *Mors stupebit et natura,*
Cum resurget creatura,
Judicanti responsura.
Death and Nature shall be astounded
when the creature shall rise
to answer to the Judge.

BARITONE SOLO

Bugles sang, saddening the evening air,
And bugles answered, sorrowful to hear.

Voices of boys were by the river-side.
Sleep mothered them; and left the twilight sad.
The shadow of the morrow weighed on men.

Voices of old despondency resigned,
Bowed by the shadow of the morrow, slept.

"BUGLES SANG . . ."

It is of course a "natural" to couple the *Tuba Mirum*, the "wondrous trumpet," with "Bugles sang." But by the extraordinary collaboration of Britten and Owen in one moment we have the "Tuba Mirum" calling, even "driving" *all* unto the Throne; and immediately following bugles are calling, are "singing," but *only bugles answer,* "sorrowful to hear." The voices of boys who used to be by the riverside can never again respond.

During the first several readings I found this poem a bit obscure. I could not place the boys "by the riverside" in their time. *When* were they by the riverside . . . and what time is now?

The poem is incomplete, probably about half of its intended duration; and some of the subsequent lines, even though incomplete, dispel some of the obscurity. Lines nine and ten read:

"(Blank) the dying tone
Of receding voices that will not return."

Almost certainly the poet is recalling the voices of his and others' youth, voices of friends now "mothered" by the sleep of death—"receding voices that will not return." The "voices of old despondency" are those which remain, "bowed by the shadow of the morrow," who are able to *sleep* only the sleep of fatigue and resignation, knowing that sooner rather than later the more final sleep will also "mother" them (including Owen himself . . .).

Again, note the beautiful rhymes, "air . . . hear, side . . . sad." Recall, also, the sensitive contrast between the "wondrous trumpet" of the *Dies Irae* which wakes the dead and this sad song, answered only by further sorrow.

SOPRANO SOLO AND CHORUS

5. *Liber scriptus proferetur,*
In quo totum continetur,
Unde mundus judicetur.
A written book shall be brought forth
in which shall be contained all for which
the world shall be judged.

6. *Judex ergo cum sedebit,*
Quidquid latet, apparebit;
Nil inultum remanebit.
And therefore when the Judge shall sit,
whatsoever is hidden shall be manifest;
and naught shall remain unavenged.

7. *Quid sum miser tunc dicturus?*
Quem patronum rogaturus,
Cum vix justus sit securus?
What shall I say in my misery?
Whom shall I ask to be my advocate,
when scarcely the righteous may be without fear?

8. *Rex tremendae majestatis*
Qui salvandos salvas gratis,
Salva me, fons pietatis.
King of awful majesty,
who freely savest the redeemed;
save me, O fount of mercy.

TENOR AND BARITONE SOLOS

Out there, we've walked quite friendly up to Death;
Sat down and eaten with him, cool and bland, –
Pardoned his spilling mess-tins in our hand.
We've sniffed the green thick odour of his breath, –
Our eyes wept, but our courage didn't writhe.
He's spat at us with bullets and he's coughed
Shrapnel. We chorussed when he sang aloft;
We whistled while he shaved us with his scythe.

Oh, Death was never enemy of ours!
We laughed at him, we leagued with him, old chum.
No soldier's paid to kick against his powers.
We laughed, knowing that better men would come.
And greater wars; when each proud fighter brags
He wars on Death—for Life; not men—for flags.

The essence of this poem and its placement obviously is its *bravado*—satirical, cynical and, finally, sorrowful. In a Hallmark world, cynicism is not highly rated. But we may need to be reminded that it is not the *lack* of sensitivity which makes a cynic, but a strong sense of vulnerability.

Lin Yutang wrote in 1935 in *My Country and My People:*

"To learn tolerance, one needs a little sorrow and a little cynicism of the Taoist type. True cynics are often the kindest of people, for they see the hollowness of life, and from the realization of that hollowness is generated a kind of cosmic pity.

"Pacifism, too, is a matter of high human understanding. If man could learn to be a little more cynical, he would also be less inclined toward warfare. That is perhaps why all intelligent men are cowards. The Chinese are the world's worst fighters because they are an intelligent race, backed and nurtured by Taoist cynicism and the Confucian emphasis on harmony as an ideal of life. . . . An average Chinese child knows that by fighting one gets killed or maimed, whether it be an individual or nation."

It is entirely possible, of course, that the West by now has sufficiently "oriented" the East in the virtues and devices of killing to provide its own destruction.

– Back to Hail fellow, well-met—Hell-fellow, wail-met. Note in lines four, five and six the terms borrowed from the first-hand experience with poison gas: "the thick green odour of his breath . . . sniffed . . . wept . . . spat . . . coughed."

Compare, for example, the latter half of his poem entitled "Dulce et Decorum Est."

> Gas! Gas! Quick, boys!—An ecstasy of fumbling,
> Fitting the clumsy helmets just in time,
> But someone still was yelling out and stumbling
> And floundering like a man in fire or lime. –
> As under a green sea, I saw him drowning.
>
> If, in some smothering dreams, you too could pace
> Behind the wagon that we flung him in,
> And watch the white eyes writhing in his face,
> His hanging face, like a devil's sick of sin;
> If you could hear, at every jolt, the blood
> Come gargling from the froth-corrupted lungs,
> Bitter as the cud
> Of vile, incurable sores on innocent tongues,
> – My friend, you would not tell with such high zest
> To children ardent for some desperate glory,
> The old Lie: Dulce et decorum est
> Pro patria mori.

I. Anglicize

> . . .
>
> My friend, you would not tell in such high mood
> To youth, susceptible to your effrontery,
> The old Lie: sweet it is and very good
> To die for country.

The most pathetic of all in "Out there . . . " it seems to me, is the line "but our courage didn't writhe;" paralysis, choking and spasm omnipresent, except in our will . . . or so we brag.

"We whistled while he shaved us with his scythe"—a bitter turn of metaphor, and certainly intended pun. ("Close-shave" courtesy of the "Grim Reaper.")

"We laughed at him, we leagued with him"—a nice parallelism between "laughed" and "leagued," but the line reads more richly if you can point up the disparate "at" and "with" without losing forward motion.

"No soldier's paid to kick against his powers"—of course not, soldiers are paid to greet him "old chum"; soldiers are paid to die.

> The last three lines are a bit obscured, I feel, by punctuation:
> "We laughed, knowing that better men would come,
> And greater wars, when each proud fighter (then will) brag
> He wars on Death—for Life, not men—for flags." (Repeat poem)?

CHORUS

> 9. *Recordare Jesu pie,*
> *Quod sum causa tuae viae:*
> *Ne me perdas illa die.*
> Remember, merciful Jesu,
> that I am the cause of Thy journey,
> lest Thou lose me in that day.
>
> 10. *Quaerens me: sedisti lassus:*
> *Redemisti crucem passus:*
> *Tantus labor non sit cassus.*
> Seeking me didst Thou sit weary:
> Thou didst redeem me, suffering the cross:
> let not such labor be frustrated.
>
> 11. (Verse omitted)
>
> 12. *Ingemisco, tanquam reus:*
> *Culpa rubet vultus meus:*
> *Supplicanti parce Deus.*
> I groan as one guilty;
> my face flushes at my sin.
> Spare, O God, me, Thy supplicant.
>
> 13. *Qui Mariam absolvisti,*
> *Et latronem exaudisti,*
> *Mihi quoque spem dedisti.*
> Thou who didst absolve Mary,
> and didst hear the thief's prayer,
> hast given hope to me also.

14. *Inter oves locum praesta,*
Et ab haedis me sequestra,
Statuens in parte dextra.
Give me place among Thy sheep
and put me apart from the goats,
setting me on the right hand.

15. *Confutatis maledictis,*
Flammis acribus addictis,
Voca me cum benedictis.
When the damned are confounded
and devoted to sharp flames,
call Thou me with the blessed.

16. *Oro supplex et acclinis,*
Cor contritum quasi cinis
Gere curam mei finis.
I pray, kneeling in supplication,
a heart contrite as ashes,
take Thou mine end into thy care.

BARITONE SOLO

1*   Be slowly lifted up, thou long black arm,
2*   Great gun towering toward Heaven, about to curse;
3   Sway steep against them, and for years rehearse
4   Huge imprecations like a blasting charm!
5*   Reach at that arrogance which needs thy harm,
6*   And beat it down before its sins grow worse;

7   Spend our resentment, cannon, yea, disburse
8   Our gold in shapes of flame, our breaths in storm.
9   Yet, for men's sakes, whom thy vast malison
10   Must wither innocent of enmity,
11   Be not withdrawn, dark arm, thy spoilure done,
12   Safe to the bosom of our prosperity.
13*   But when thy spell be cast complete and whole,
14*   May God curse thee, and cut thee from our soul!
(*B.B.: lines 1, 2, 5, 6, 13, 14)

The chief relationship between the Latin and Owen here is Britten's sensibility to the imagery of "cursing." Obviously, it is the center of Owen's poem:

"Great gun . . . about to curse!" However for the moment you appear necessary, once your malignancy is accomplished, "*May God damn you! and cut you from our soul!*"

The association with the Latin is made clearer by a better translation of "Confutatis maledictis." "Male-diction," ill to speak; to curse. Therefore, "When the ac*cursed* are confounded and adjudged to sharp flames. . . . "

Notice, also, the parallel imagery between the Latin "flammis acribus"—sharp flames—and Owen's "shapes of flame" in line eight.

I find lines nine and ten provocative for two reasons: first, the use of the word "malison." We are well acquainted with the word "benison," from the Latin "bene"—well (bene-diction: to say well); therefore, a blessing. The suffix "son" is both Middle English and Old French in different spellings. It might well come from roots which give us words like *sound* and *sonar*. If so, then as "benison" is a blessing, "malison" is a cursing.

The second interest for me in these lines is that this "blasting, storming, flaming, cursing" must ultimately "wither" (burn) the enmity out of all men, spoiler as well as spoiled.

This is [the] only one of Owen's poems—to my knowledge—which implies a partisan "right or wrong" to that war. In the main his subject, as he states over and over again, is "war and the pity of war, the pity war distills." It is *all* wrong. There is *no* right.

But in this poem, in lines five and six, he says to the "great gun . . . about to curse," "Reach at that arrogance which sorely needs thy harm, and beat it down before its sins grow worse. . . . " Taken in its entire context, one can only assume, I think, that the "arrogance" which he had in mind, for the moment, at least, was Prussian. It could be a partisan line.

I'm not really *sure* of this. Lines seven and eight are so utterly cynical, and lines thirteen and fourteen so impassioned, that it's possible that he may have been totally satirical throughout; that is, he feeds us a crumb of political expediency, leads us to the brink of a justification for war, only so that it may crumble beneath the weight of our own arrogance.

For Britten—and this is the stinger—gives the entire poem to the baritone soloist who, in the great final "Strange Meeting," turns out to be the *German* soldier!

Soprano Solo and Chorus (Returns and concludes the *Dies Irae*)

17. *Dies irae, dies illa,*
   Solvet saeclum in favilla,
   Teste David cum Sibylla.

The Day of Wrath, that day
shall dissolve the world in ashes,
as witnesseth David and the Sibyl.

18. *Quantus tremor est futurus,*
Quando judex est venturus,
Cuncta stricte discussurus!
What trembling shall there be
when the Judge shall come
who shall thresh out all thoroughly!

19. *Lacrimosa dies illa,*
Qua resurget ex favilla,
Judicandus homo reus,
Huic ergo parce Deus.
Lamentable is that day
on which guilty man shall arise
from the ashes to be judged.
Spare then this one, O God.

TENOR SOLO

Move him into the sun –
Gently its touch awoke him once,
At home, whispering of fields unsown.
Always it woke him, even in France,
Until this morning and this snow.
If anything might rouse him now
The kind old sun will know.

Think how it wakes the seeds, –
Woke, once, the clays of a cold star.
Are limbs, so dear-achieved, are sides,
Full-nerved—still warm—too hard to stir?
War it for this the clay grew tall?
—O what made fatuous sunbeams toil
To break earth's sleep at all?

"Move him into the sun . . . " surely is one of the most beautiful and touching of Owen's lyrics.

Its linking with the *Missa de Profunctis* is at two points. Immediately preceding the poem are the final couplets of the *Dies Irae* (notable also because the entire *Dies Irae* with the exception of these concluding four lines has been in three-line verses; the two couplets bring a severity and finality to the whole poem). "Lacrimosa dies illa . . . "—"lamentable is the day on which *guilty man shall rise* from the ashes. . . . Spare then *this one,* O God."

The first point is that resurrection, a reawakening, is the common theme. On the one hand "man shall *rise* . . . "; on the other, "If anything might *rouse* him now, the kind old sun will know . . . was it for this the clay grew tall . . . broke the earth's sleep?"

The second point is that the Latin speaks very specifically, "Spare then *this* one . . . "; and, similarly, the poet also takes as his point of departure a very specific occurrence, this here-now boy, just-now dead.

Note the poet's equation of sunlight with life. – And how succinctly documented by evolutionary recall in the second stanza. (I'm trying for the moment to remember my "beginnings of life" lessons. Was it that the "star" finally cooled enough to support life, or was it that the sun "woke, once, the clays of a cold star?") Whatever the evolutionary sequence, it was certainly not for a moment such as this that the "clay grew tall," that mud became man.

> "O what made fatuous sunbeams toil
> To break earth's sleep at all?"

Note the wonderful rhymes:

> Sun, sown, once, France
> snow, now, know
> Seeds, sides, star, stir
> tall, toil, all

We conclude together:

Chorus

> *Pie Jesu Domine,*
> *Dona eis requiem. Amen.*
> Merciful Lord Jesu:
> give them peace. Amen.

III. OFFERTORIUM

Boys' Choir

> *Domine Jesu Christe, Rex gloriae,*
> *libera animas omnium fidelium*

defunctorum de poenis inferni,
et de profundo lacu:
libera eas de ore leonis,
ne absorbeat eas tartarus,
ne cadant in obscurum.
O Lord Jesus Christ, King of Glory,
deliver the souls of all the faithful departed
from the pains of hell
and from the depths of the pit:
deliver them from the lion's mouth,
that hell devour them not,
that they fall not into darkness.

CHORUS

Sed signifer sanctus Michael
repraesentet eas in lucem sanctam:
quam olim Abrahae promisisti,
et semini ejus.
But let the standard-bearer Saint Michael
bring them into the holy light:
which, of old, Thou didst promise unto Abraham
and his seed.

BARITONE AND TENOR SOLOS

So Abram rose, and clave the wood, and went,
And took the fire with him, and a knife.
And so they sojourned both of them together,
Isaac the first-born spake and said, My father,
Behold the preparations, fire and iron,
But where the lamb for this burnt offering?
Then Abram bound the youth with belts and straps,
And builded parapets and trenches there,
And stretched forth the knife to slay his son.
When lo! an angel called him out of heaven,
Saying, Lay not thy hand upon the lad,
Neither do anything to him. Behold,
A ram, caught in a thicket by its horns;
Offer the Ram of Pride instead of him.

(– WAIT –)
But the old man would not so, and slew his son, –
And half the seed of Europe, one by one.

And then it goes on:

BOYS' CHOIR

> *Hostias et preces tibi*
> *Domine laudis offerimus:*
> *tu suscipe pro animabus illis,*
> *quarum hodie memoriam facimus:*
> *fac eas, Domine,* make them, O Lord,
> *de morte transire ad vitam.*
> We offer unto Thee, O Lord,
> sacrifices of prayer and praise:
> do Thou receive them for the souls of those
> whose memory we this day recall:
> to pass from death unto life.

CHORUS

> *Quam olim Abrahae promisisti,*
> *et semini ejus.*
> Which of old Thou didst promise unto Abraham
> and his seed.

This, of course, is the most "natural" of all the linkings: "As once thou promised to Abraham and to his seed" to "So Abram rose . . ." and disposed of his own as well as "half the seed of Europe, one by one." – But even this is not the entire linking; for it is immediately followed by "Hostias et preces tibi . . . ," *we offer* unto Thee *sacrifices* with *prayer*. Note that these sacrifices are also "animal"—*human* animal, humanimal.

The obvious linking is a natural verbal and narrative association, contrived between liturgy and poet by the composer: the story of Abraham and Isaac. The deeper linking somehow includes all of us as participants in that "sacrifice." What began as a parable, with the *Hostias* now infuses the liturgical service with "offerings, sacrifices and prayers"; and however "concert" versus "worship" our participation may be, we are present at the shedding of today's blood.

Britten makes it doubly sure that we understand. After the parable of "the old men and the young" (Owen's title) and after the *Hostias* (sung in our behalf by more *innocent* voices)—after the parable has been completely turned upside down from its original Biblical telling—we are once again allotted the music for "Quam olim Abrahae" (note well!) completely upside down, melody inverted, dynamics reversed!

Involvement and responsibility are the price of understanding. It's easier to seek an addiction which obliterates, booze or main-line. Owen carries us even one step beyond Britten's involvement with Abram. Line eight has those who understand building their own "parapets and trenches"; for narrative purposes—to catch Isaac's blood; but for Owen's purposes—whole dugouts full. Pick a war from I to X.

IV. *SANCTUS*

SOPRANO SOLO AND CHORUS

> *Sanctus, sanctus, sanctus*
> *Dominus Deus Sabaoth.*
> *Pleni sunt coeli et terra gloria tua*
> *Hosanna in excelsis.*
> Holy, holy, holy
> Lord God of Sabaoth.
> Heaven and earth are full of Thy glory.
> Hosanna in the highest.
>
> *Benedictus qui venit in nomine Domini.*
> *Hosanna in excelsis.*
> Blessed is he that cometh in the name of the Lord.
> Hosanna in the highest.

BARITONE SOLO

> After the blast of lightning from the East.
> The flourish of loud clouds, the Chariot Throne;
> After the drums of Time have rolled and ceased,
> And by the bronze west long retreat is blown,
>
> Shall life renew these bodies? Of a truth
> All death will He annul, all tears assuage? –
> Fill the void veins of Life again with youth,
> And wash, with an immortal water, Age?

When I do ask white Age he saith not so:
"My head hangs weighed with snow."
And when I hearken to the Earth, she saith:
"My fiery heart shrinks, aching. It is death.
Mine ancient scars shall not be glorified,
Nor my titanic tears, the sea, be dried.

This is the most dense and grave of the poems in the *War Requiem*. Alongside the lyric fluency of "Move him into the sun," it is lumpy and knotted. Alongside "Out there we've walked quite friendly up to Death . . . " and "So Abram rose . . . " it has not even the laughter of cynicism or satire. After its matted, unrubbed honesty, "One ever hangs . . . " comes like Lenten doggerel.

Its apparent link is the visual ecstacy of "Sanctus, sanctus, sanctus"—the sublime eruption of heavenly light—with "the blast of lightning from the East." I say *apparent* because, though Britten has taken the *Sanctus* and *Benedictus* very seriously musically, and developed them at some length with flashes of brilliance and shadows of tenderness, what has happened textually is that he has linked the *Sanctus* imagery to the first line of Owen's poem in order to introduce a most uncompromising, unpalatable (to Christian traditionalism) and hope-forsaken sermon on Life and Death.

This is a brave despair to raise in the holiest moment of Christian liturgy. And the lines betray this weight. The poem rather lurches along. Neither in word nor rhythm is it fluent. Almost all the lines are loaded with thick nouns and gigantic verbs. Out of one-hundred-fourteen words, ninety-four are words of one syllable. This in itself need not yield gnarled density if the poet were content to *waste* a few of them (as in "One ever hangs . . . ").

Certainly in terms of theological argument this poem would find its proper environment at a point of denial of one of the "resurrection" references. That in the *Dies Irae,* however, was beautifully handled by "Move him gently. . . . " Moreover, it was too early for this *summation*. And, once one has begun the "In paradisum . . . " it is *much* too late. Were one to consider putting this poem as epilogue—one could not have written the mass at all. Actually, the *Hostias* offers the most direct confrontation: "Make them, Lord, to change from death into life" with "It is death! Mine ancient scars shall not be glorified." And Britten has Owen say it just as soon after that as he can.

It had to be said, if Owen was to be a part of the *War Requiem*; and "I am the enemy you killed, my friend . . . " had to be saved to the last. Perhaps there is some significance in saying, "It is death," at this holiest and most mystical moment. Certainly there is no equivocation. Neither Age nor Earth, "snow" nor "fiery heart" credits immortality. "Some say the world will end with fire . . . some with ice . . . " For Owen, too, "either would suffice."

V. *AGNUS DEI*

Tenor Solo

> One ever hangs where shelled roads part.
> In this war He too lost a limb,
> But His disciples hide apart;
> And now the soldiers bear with Him.

Chorus

> *Agnus Dei, qui tollis peccata mundi,*
> *dona eis requiem.*
> Lamb of God, who takest away the sins of the world,
> grant them rest.

> Near Golgotha strolls many a priest,
> And in their faces there is pride
> That they were flesh-marked by the Beast
> By whom the gentle Christ's denied.

Chorus

> *Agnus Dei, qui tollis peccata mundi,*
> *dona eis requiem.*
> Lamb of God, who takest away the sins of the world,
> grant them rest.

> The scribes on all the people shove
> And bawl allegiance to the state,
> But they who love the greater love
> Lay down their life; they do not hate.

Chorus

> *Agnus Dei, qui tollis peccata mundi,*
> *dona eis requiem sempiternam.*
> *Dona nobis pacem.*

Lamb of God, who takest away the sins of the world,
grant them rest eternal.
Grant us peace.

This is a logical, "occasional" choice for linkage with the *Agnus Dei*. It appears to have been written for an actual roadside crucifix near Ancre ("At a calvary near Ancre" is the title in his book of published poems). Undoubtedly the Jesus figure on the cross had lost a leg in action.

The metaphor sounds as though the poem came quickly; the priests and the scribes, church and state—ever enemies of the Lamb of God; peace, to be found only in self-sacrifice.

One of Owen's letters from the hospital on the Somme (before his convalescence in England and final return to the Front) can be quoted at this point:

"Already I have comprehended a light which never will filter into the dogma of any national church; namely, that one of Christ's essential commands was: Passivity at any price! Suffer dishonor and disgrace, but never resort to arms. Be killed; but do not kill. It may be a chimerical and ignominious principle, but there it is. It can only be ignored; and I think pulpit professionals are ignoring it very skillfully and successfully indeed. . . . Am I not myself a conscientious objector with a very seared conscience? (In War himself.)

" . . . Christ is literally in 'no man's land.' There men often hear his voice: 'Greater love hath no man than this, that a man lay down his life for a friend.' Is it spoken in English only and French? I do not believe so. Thus you see how pure Christianity will not fit in with pure patriotism."

I find this more concentrated, intense and moving than the verses which Britten selected; but the others make their point, and a natural three-part form as well—and perhaps the most tear-provoking moment in the entire work.

VI. *LIBERA ME* (FINAL MOVEMENT)

SOPRANO SOLO AND CHORUS

Libera me, Domine, de morte aeterna
in die illa tremenda:
Quando coeli movendi sunt et terra:
Dum veneris judicare
saeculum per ignem.
Tremens factus sum ego, et timeo,
dum discussio venerit,
atque ventura ira.
Quando coeli movendi sunt et terra.

Deliver me, O Lord, from death eternal
in that fearful day:
When the heavens and the earth shall be shaken:
When Thou shalt come to judge
the world by fire.
I am in fear and trembling
till the sifting be upon us,
and the wrath to come.
When the heavens and the earth shall be shaken.

Dies illa, dies irae,
calamitatis et miseriae,
dies magna et amara valde.
Libera me, Domine.
O that day, that day of wrath,
of calamity and misery,
a great day and exceeding bitter.
Deliver me, O Lord

TENOR SOLO

1   It seemed that out of battle I escaped
2   Down some profound dull tunnel, long since scooped
3   Through granites which titanic wars had groined.
4   Yet also there encumbered sleepers groaned,
5   Too fast in thought (or death) to be bestirred.
6   Then, as I probed them, one sprang up, and stared
7   With piteous recognition in fixed eyes,
8   Lifting distressful hands as if to bless.
9   And no guns thumped, or down the flues made moan.
10   "Strange friend," I said, "here is no cause to mourn."

BARITONE SOLO

11   "None," said the other, "save the undone years,
12   The hopelessness. Whatever hope is yours,
13   Was my life also; I went hunting wild
14   After the wildest beauty in the world.
15   For by my glee might many men have laughed,
16   And of my weeping something had been left,

17 Which must die now. I meant the truth untold,
18 The pity of war, the pity war distilled.
19 Now men will go content with what we spoiled.
20 Or, discontent, boil bloody, and be spilled.
21 They will be swift with swiftness of the tigress,
22 None will break ranks, though nations trek from progress.
23 Miss we the march of this retreating world.
24 Into vain citadels that are not walled.
25 Then, when much blood had clogged their chariot-wheels
26 I would go up and wash them from sweet wells,
27 Even from the wells we sunk too deep for war,
28 Even the sweetest wells that ever were.
29 I am the enemy you killed, my friend.
30 I knew you in this dark; for so you frowned
31 Yesterday through me as you jabbed and killed.
32 I parried; but my hands were loath and cold."

BOTH

33 "Let us sleep now."

BOYS' CHOIR, CHORUS AND SOPRANO SOLO

In paradisum deducant te Angeli:
in tuo adventu
suscipiant te Martyres,
et perducant te
in civitatem sanctam Jerusalem.
Chorus Angelorum te suscipiat,
et cum Lazaro quondam paupere
aeternam habeas requiem.
Requiem aeternam dona eis, Domine;
et lux perpetua luceat eis.
Requiescant in pace. Amen.
In paradise may the angels lead thee;
at thy coming
may the martyrs receive thee,
and bring thee
into the holy city Jerusalem.
May the choir of angels receive thee,

and with Lazarus, once poor,
mayest thou have eternal rest.
Rest eternal grant unto them, O Lord;
and let light eternal shine upon them.
May they rest in peace. Amen.

"Strange meeting" is Owen's title for this poem. Unfinished, it is the most haunted and haunting of his war-poetry. It is undated, but it is surmised to have been written in the last few months of his life. The editor of his poems, Edmund Blunden, reports that it was written in ink with corrections in pencil.

First—I would call your attention (for a last time) to the uniquely sensitive rhymes. They almost make a poem themselves:

" 'scaped . . . scooped
groined . . . groaned
'stirred . . . stared
eyes . . . blessed
'moaned . . . mourn
years . . . yours
wild . . . world
laughed . . . left
told . . . 'tilled
spoiled . . . spilled
tigress . . . progress
world . . . walled
wheels . . . wells
war . . . were
'friend . . . frowned
killed . . . cold"

Second, it is interesting to note that Britten has edited the poem in one significant passage. (Eleven lines are omitted in Britten's setting—two or three of them, I feel, of real value; and two lines are added from a series of couplets which closely parallel this poem and may have been sketches towards its final form.) – But, as regards the "significant" omission: Between lines eight and nine of the *War Requiem* text, Owen had written –

"And by his smile, I knew that sullen hall,
By his dead smile I knew we stood in Hell.
With a thousand pains that vision's face was grained;
Yet no blood reached there from the upper ground."

Now, certainly the last of these lines joins nicely to "And no guns thumped, or down the flues made moan"; but the presence of the first two of them would do gross injury to the final great moments of the *War Requiem* (as, I think also, they harm Owen's poem). The necessary dramatic point is to maintain the obscurity, mystery and place of this "strange meeting" until the final "I am the enemy you killed, my friend." One must not know until this moment that both are dead. Or if one surmises it, he must not be told.

Here is Britten's great sense of poetry and drama helping the poet to complete his "unfinished" work, with an eraser.

Bernard Rogers—in a class at Juilliard—when asked "How do you compose?" responded, "Start with a blank piece of paper and an eraser—when I've erased everything unnecessary . . . I have a piece of music."

Of interest to me are the following discarded readings:

Line 1: "It seemed to me that from My dugout I escaped"
(for: "out of battle." How greatly that sheds light on lines two, three, four and five: so much more based now in experience, than imagination.)
Line 12: "The unachieved" (for: hopelessness)
Line 18: "The pity of war, the one thing war distilled."
(for: "the pity of war, the pity war distilled.")
Line 29: "I was a German conscript, and your friend." Or: "I am the German whom you killed, my friend."
(for: "I am the enemy you killed, my friend.")

Compare a few parallel lines from the groups of couplets:

Lines 19–22:
21: "Be we not swift with swiftness of the tigress."
22: "Let us break ranks, and we will trek from progress. Let us forgo men's minds that are brutes' natures. Let us not sup the blood which some say nurtures."
Lines 27–28: (for: "Even the sweetest wells that ever were." –
these are not in "Strange Meeting"; Britten added them from the couplets. They might have been followed or preceded by:)
"For now we sink from men as pitchers falling,
But men shall raise us up to be their filling."

"Finally," remarks Blunden, "widely as the setting and substance of 'Strange Meeting' are felt and apprehended, it is peculiarly a poem of the Western Front of 1918; it is a dream only a stage further on than the actuality of the tunnelled dug-outs with their muffled security, their smoky dimness, their rows of soldiers painfully sleeping, their officers and sergeants and corporals attempting to awaken those for duty, and the sense presently of "going up" the ugly stairway to do someone (in the uglier mud above) a good turn. Out of these and similar materials Owen's transforming spirit has readily created his wonderful phantasma."

What is the final poetic and dramatic result of Britten's "fabrication?" Certainly, in the first place, we have an enormous humanizing and contemporizing of an ancient and remote liturgy of remembrance. The wars of this century are our wars; Owen's death, his pity at the death of others are remote neither from our memories nor our premonitions. – And so the ancient words are fused with the immediacy—of tomorrow.

Second, and conversely, Owen's words gain a catholicity, a dignity of historical association. His "pity" becomes somewhat grander by the setting of his parable of Abram and Isaac in a centuries-old matrix. All of his poetry gains stature.

But what of the final philosophic confrontation:

"Shall life renew these bodies? Of a truth
All death will He annul, all tears assuage?"

I suppose most of us will call it as we've learned it. Certainly for Owen, Age and Earth answered a resounding "No!"

It is interesting to note, it seems to me, that in terms of text alone (setting aside, for the moment, the accretions of tradition) the *Missa* is entirely a *petition:* "Make them, Lord, to change from death to life. . . . Deliver me, Lord, from death eternal. . . . In paradise may the angels lead you. . . . May eternal light shine on them. . . . May they rest in peace." Some, undoubtedly, could recite this in full confidence that it already had been achieved. With others, even of similar religious tradition, it might be murmured "bowed and kneeling" with "heart contrite as ashes." – And uncertain—insecure.

For still others it might suffice that after all, there is still in our being—and our un-being—a mystery into which none of the statistical forms of man's intelligence can carry him. That it involves a life beyond the present most men have hoped and few gainsaid.

For me, it is wonder enough that Owen's words and Britten's vision are a part of the life-force in the man-thing. Whether any one of us "make it" in a hereafter I find somehow less important than the presence of humanity such as this.

November 24, 1982

My Thanksgiving
By Bobby Shaw
(Grade A – Raw)
> I want to thank you for making the *War Requiem*
> such a distressing, heart-breaking, debilitating,
> ghastly, unnerving, inconsolable, depressing,
> grievous, harrowing and tragic experience.
> The days since then have been just unbearable.
> Wishing you a joyful turn of events.
> Your pal,

R

Hymns

Oct. 15–16, 1993

Spoken Program Notes for Britten concerts at Spivey Hall

Ladies and gentlemen –

Good evening.

Very nearly the entire world of serious music will take some recognition this season of the 80th birthday of Benjamin Britten—born in the sea-side village of Lowestoft, England, on November 22—on St. Cecilia's Day—the Matron Saint of Music.

In 1964 he was invited to the United States (it was only one of several trips) to accept the first Aspen Award for his outstanding contribution to "the advancement of the humanities."

No composer in our century (it seems to me)—perhaps no artist in any medium—has placed such boundless virtuosity in the service of such specific philosophic and humanistic concerns.

He was a pianist of prodigious talent: solo artists, vocal and instrumental—Vishnevskaya and Rostropovich among them—thought him without equal as a collaborator. Orchestras—those which he formed and those for whom he was a guest—found his untutored technique sufficient to convey rare and unprecedented revelations of his musical understanding. Unlike Stravinsky he composed *away* from the piano and under deadlines—since he wrote, as he said, seemingly always for specific occasions and for particular performers, places and times—his creative flow was so fast that multiple copyists and those responsible for piano reductions of his operas simply could not keep up with him.

His humanistic concern had at its core an outrage at the violation of innocence—particularly of children, and a companion concern for the rights of the individual versus institutions—political and ecclesiastical. So convincing was his pacifism to his country's armed services, for instance, that, unlike many of his friends and fellow declared pacifists, he was deferred from even quasi-civilian assignments in World War II.

His *Hymn to the Virgin* was written at an age when—in our system—he would have been a sophomore in high school. Among the earliest of his compositions allowed to reach the public eye, it was also that which served as his funeral anthem.

Compare that affectionate, intimate adoration of the symbols, saints and myths of Christianity with the irony and bitter humor of *The Lift Boy*. Against the sanctimonious, unforgiving doctrines of main-line ecclesiasticism, it raises what Arthur Hope called "one-half of a V-for-Victory sign." Britten, like the "Lift Boy," has had enough of a gospel of hate. So, "damn us all! every damned one!"

He has one other inside joke. In his Aspen speech of acceptance he lamented the existence of the loud-speaker which gave to anyone and everyone the ability to listen to music without an appropriate commitment of time, energy, money or travel.

"Can a phonograph lie?" he asks—or even begin to tell the truth. Isn't this a major sense of humor—and irony—for a very young man?

O DEUS, EGO AMO TE

Here's a young man's "Hymn to Jesus."

What kind of a church service would it take to accommodate this ecstasy in its Sunday service?

Textually it is a confessional chant: its syllables and sentences fall absolutely unanimously, and its harmonies are made of conventional triads—all in fundamental positions.

But, in rhythm and dynamics it is flammable and explosive.

Here is a violence equal to that of the *Lift Boy*—but on *behalf* of faith—not targeted at its institution.

HYMN TO ST. CECILIA

Principal among Britten's early intellectual and philosophical influences was the poet W. H. Auden. Britten had emerged into manhood (at that time between Europe's major wars) perplexed—and ashamed—by his own sexuality. He and his life-long companion, Peter Pears, detested the word "gay," as also our more recent society's designation of its "life-style," institutions, politicking and exhibitionism.

W. H. Auden, in private conversation, personal correspondence and even published poetry, voluntarily undertook the task of freeing Britten from what appeared to be his natural inhibitions, of accepting without shame the physical and psychological conditions which had been handed to him—to "get on with life"—which for Britten meant accepting also the obligations of his unique and tremendous talent.

Later events would show that the "freedom"—not to say "license"—which Auden himself enjoyed was considerably more than Britten desired for himself. – But there can be little doubt that the happiness and the comfort which Britten experienced as he found a loving alliance, and founded a home which lasted a life-time, ushered in a period of happy productivity which yielded some of his most delightful works.

Fortunately for us, several of these works were choral, among them the three major compositions which are the substance of the first half of tonight's program.

The *Hymn to St. Cecilia*, simply as poetry, was specifically addressed by Auden to Britten. Its text is certainly more than occasionally obscure, but it is clear that it mixes erotic imagery (Blonde Aphrodite) with artistic and even religious symbolism.

For me there is little doubt that in the beginning of Part II ("I cannot grow, I have no shadow to run away from . . . ") Auden is urging Britten to begin to have "a past"—a "shadow" from which he *can* grow.

Certainly, his concluding line could not be less ambiguous, "O wear your tribulation like a rose."

What a happy, sweet, comforted piece of music it is—a new and delightful, delicious voice—all in the midst of the Battle of Britten.

REJOICE IN THE LAMB

"Rejoice in the Lamb" may well be every choral-lovers favorite Britten. He had an extraordinary gift for the discovery and selection of great texts. His numerous song-cycles—in several languages—bring literary riches equal to their musical wealth.

Here is Britten's celebration of the innocence of children—and fools. Chris Smart's whimsical fantasy—the words of a certified lunatic—are a bit off-balance by the strictest of grammarian standards. – But "right on," if it is the function of the "artist inimitable" together with "all creatures of his God and king" to sing "Alleluia."

CEREMONY OF CAROLS

It is doubtful that there is a person in this room who has not heard some performance of Britten's *Ceremony of Carols*. Striving, as we were in building this program, to organize a bit of a "retrospective gallery" of Britten's work, we could not find time for the entire twelve movements.

We programmed what I always have assumed to be the first half of the *Ceremony.* I also have assumed for years that though there is no such specification in the published score, Britten intended the work for boys' voices. There is no doubt that Britten treasured the sound of boys' unchanged voices. He used them increasingly thereafter in his operas and his oratorios—and to heart-clutching effect in his *War Requiem.*

Imagine my undiluted joy when I discovered last week in the new Britten biography that the original version—never published—of the *Ceremony of Carols* contained only the carols which we perform tonight; and further, that they were originally written for female voices.

Our pleasure in tonight's performance is doubled by having as our harp soloist the sister of William Preucil—who, for so many years, was the loved and respected concertmaster of the Atlanta Symphony Orchchestra—Anne Preucil Lewellen.

THE BALLAD OF LITTLE MUSGRAVE AND LADY BARNARD

The Ballad of Little Musgrave and Lady Barnard was written at the request of the brother of an acquaintance of Peter Pears who sang in the BBC Singers. Richard Weed was a prisoner of war in Eichstadt, Germany, where he had organized a choir of fellow prisoners.

It is a masterpiece of 3-part writing for male voices with piano accompaniment. Britten occasionally will obscure the text—not only to suggest narrative conditions of confusion or haste, but also to give out-and-out direct vocal enjoyment to the singers.

And what about that choice of text?

Is it not precisely the sort of narrative that would bring smiles into the lives of men who had been prisoners of war for month after month after month. I sometimes have wondered—studying the piece—if I were not watching a fluttery old-fashioned silent cinema serial, in which it was absolutely obligatory to hiss the villain and shriek in falsetto at suspenseful moments.

CHORALE (ON AN OLD FRENCH CAROL)

Britten's *Chorale* sets Auden at his intellectual and philosophical best. It is for Britten a chance to experiment with dense choral sonorities which usually are identified with Eastern European or Russian traditions.

—But his *Shepherd's Carol* is a bit of a conundrum:

It has the world's sweetest refrain. But its verses are totally anarchic and satirical. If it is intended to suggest, as Bottom says in Shakespeare's *Midsummer Night's Dream,* that "man is but a fool"—somewhere over the mountains—as over a rainbow—there is a land of sweet by and by.

GLORIANA

Benjamin Britten was made Lord Britten just a few months before his death—the first and only musician ever to be so honoured. His relations with royalty, and particularly the Queen Mother, were characterized by mutual respect and suitable affection. These varied and lovely choral dances from the opera-entertainment written to honor the coronation of QE II are just that: not instrumental dances, but real dances to be accompanied by voices.

SACRED AND PROFANE

Sacred and Profane are settings of medieval lyrics written under the shadow and prescience of imminent death.

It seems to me that they bear a remarkable summary title—for they are in their attitudes so like the three very earliest of pieces which began our program, and which had been written a life-time earlier—possessing almost identical adorations and ironies.

The first is a more complex, strenuous, and perhaps, more desperate *Hymn to the Virgin.*

The second may suggest that the lot of the birds and fishes and flowers is substantially easier that the lot of man—whose very intelligence enables him to realize that he is capable also of madness—that he can "waxe wod."

The third directly parallels "O God, I love Thee," but adds, in a most touching fashion over a relatively simple congregational reflection on the crucifixion of Jesus, the long, soaring and seering, discordant despair of the solitary everywoman or everyman, naked and alone, in weakness.

And the fourth just could be a backward glance at a life-time—at "seven nights full and a day."

What was the food?

What was the drink?

What was the home bower?

– Flowers, fresh well-springs and the red-rose and the lily,

– Some dear friends, some honors, some work

– And not altogether bad.

CHRISTMAS CAROLS

December 11, 1972

Everyone knows what a carol is. At least in this highly stimulated, more than slightly terrifying season of giving and getting (without forgetting) one should certainly be able to recognize a Christmas carol if he heard one.

Well—I'm not so sure. At least I find it very difficult to write a satisfactory definition of a carol. The closer I come to it, the more it appears that most of the churchly tunes with which we in our Sunday School voices ruffled the silent, holy night were not really carols at all—but a species of hymns, in many instances less vital in tune and text than those which I have since come to know as true carols.

In a delightful article in the *Oxford Companion to Music*, Percy Scholes allows that "most of what we call by the name 'carol' would be included in 'a religious seasonal song, joyful in character, in the vernacular and sung by the common people.' "

He suggests that there would be an element of *dance*, "for the early carols were danced as well as sung" (perhaps even *before* they were sung, for the word in its medieval French derivation means *round dance*). There would also be an association with the *open air*. (To "go caroling" in my youth meant a Christmas Eve caravan to the cottages of the elderly or ill—obviously those, it occurs to me now, who would benefit more from rest than a shivaree. We would stand outside the bedroom window, on what was usually a clear Southern California night, harmonize tentatively two or three of the familiar Christmas hymns, shout a loud "Merry Christmas," and noisily push off to the next unsuspecting shut-in. We never did accept what they might have wanted to tender, which Mr. Scholes so nicely designates as "hush money.") Carols also would be characterized by *simplicity*, perhaps even *crudity*; and finally by *age*, for the "best carols have served generations of men."

I find myself in sympathy with most of this, except that, in my experience, I find this simplicity more often sensitive than crude. And in instance after instance, both in tune and text, I find a bitter-sweet mingling of the tragic with the joyful: haunting minor melodies, and verses which juxtapose birth and crucifixion.

So it seems to me that there should be a way of stating the *essence* of the carol. How does it differ, for instance, from "Adeste Fidelis" (a magnificent hymn), or "O Little Town of Bethlehem" (by any standards other than auld acquaintance, rather dullish)?

In the first place, the carol is in the direct line of folk music. It *is* "aged"; it *is* "in the vernacular and sung by the common people"; but this is so precisely because the common people wrote it—a long time ago. Borderline cases exist, but in the main carols were written by no-one and by everyone. In the upper corners of the page where credits are inscribed to author and composer, one writes "Traditional . . . Anonymous . . . Unknown."

In the second place (and herein I would guess lies their deep attraction) their origin, anonymous and truly "popular," has wrought a strange amalgam of secular experience and religious story, of Christian and pagan symbolism, of the other-worldly and this-worldly—and all is told in terms naive and profound, simple and surrealistic.

It is not surprising that the Christmas story should inspire this extraordinary mingling. The birth of a child in poverty and oppression, common shepherds granted the first supernatural pronouncement, the royal magnificence of a caravan of kings kneeling in a stable: these are affairs and symbols intuitive to the hearts of men. Here the secular and the sacred do meet and mingle, or, perhaps more truly, speak as though never separate.

A few years ago we recorded a second album of Christmas carols (the first had included the traditional hymns) and the selection of materials was an illuminating experience.

In England, surrounded by seas, one sings unperturbedly of "three ships, sailing in" to a geographically land-locked Bethlehem, "bearing our Savior Christ and His Laydee." In the "Cherry Tree Carol," Joseph bitterly—and so humanly—remonstrates with Mary, "Let the father of thy baby gather cherries for thee!" The "Holly and the Ivy," ancient Roman symbols of fertility, bear a "blood-red berry" and "prickly thorn" in tender imagery of Mary's birthing and poignant presentiment of Jesus' death.

In the Spanish carol "Fum, Fum, Fum!" one honors the birth of Christ by listing those cakes and candies available on the anniversary thereof. In "Hacia belen," a little donkey arrives in Bethlehem laden with chocolate, gypsies and a young man wearing a sombrero. "Maria, Maria, come quickly!" says the refrain, because "the chocolate is almost gone, the gypsies are stealing the swaddling clothes, and the donkey is eating the sombrero!"

A German love-song extolling the faithful evergreen as a symbol of human love has no trouble shifting its analogy to divine love in "O Tannenbaum."

With the exception of the Negro spiritual, America has developed few native Christmas carols, possibly because "the Pilgrim Fathers held the Puritan view as to the observance of the Church's seasons." But there is one affecting carol which John Jacob Miles relates he discovered on the Sunday afternoon of July 10, 1933, in Murphy, North Carolina, during the last meeting of a band of traveling evangelists. "Anne Morgan stood up," Miles recalled, "and, without benefit of any accompaniment, sang 'I wonder as I wander out under the sky,' " continuing (I would add) after the ancient and knowing tradition of the unknown folk-singers, "how Jesus the Savior did come for to die/for poor o'nery people like you and like I," not until the second verse touching at all the events of His birth.

Thus the carol grows, out of anonymous centuries of day-to-day longings and delights, clothed with a melodic grace approachable by only the most gifted of composers, and bearing imagery which but a few poets could achieve.

> "If Jesus had wanted for any wee thing,
> A star in the sky or a bird on the wing,
> Or all of God's angels in heav'n for to sing,
> He surely could have had it,
> 'cause His pappy was King."

R. .S.

Undated

More than any other program which we perform, the Christmas Festival—because of the largely homophonic and strophic nature of the carol/folk-song/hymn literature—brings us face to face with two areas of choral technique that are not quite so critical in more polyphonic forms. They are (1) enunciation and (2) problems of tempo elasticity and flexibility associated—for us in this instance—with text emphasis and expressivity.

Because we never formally have undertaken this latter matter, let's attend to it first.

Almost all of the Christmas repertoire is basically "strophic"—has several verses, and "homophonic"—is "chordal" with simultaneous text in all voices. The Parker arrangements, in particular, offer polyphonic interest and imitation, but even these usually begin or close with hymn-like textual identity.

This means, of course, that the same melody—and frequently the same harmony (as in "Lo, How a Rose," "Lully, Lullay" or Berlioz's "Shepherds' Farewell")—is used to express what may be substantially different ideas, word emphases, speech rhythms, and poetic groupings.

We are so accustomed to this musical form that we are not greatly disturbed by it. Church hymns are so much a part of the musical experience of most of us that we scarcely note that verses two through six don't really fit the tune as neatly as verse number one. And, indeed, the really important part of congregational hymn singing is not that it be a distinguished artful accomplishment, but that it be a common, "all-one-body-we" act of worship.

On the other hand, a strophic song—either folk or composed *lied* in the care of a sensitive solo artist—is so subtly altered from verse to verse according to the poetic or expressive requirements of the text that we seldom become consciously bored by the seven-to-seventeen-fold repetition of the melody.

The transfer of this soloistic expressivity to two hundred voices is both desirable and difficult. (Even congregational hymn singing is improved when, given the proper stimulus and guidance, congregations begin to treat the various verses of their hymns with a little interpretative individuality—such things, for instance, as changes in dynamics or organ registration, a switching from unison to four-part singing, or the addition of descants.)

The more obvious and easiest of verse characterizations are those accomplished by comprehensive changes in dynamics. The forte of Verse No. 2 in "Lully, Lullay": "Herod the king in his raging . . . " and the pianissimo of Verse No. 3 in the "Shepherds' Farewell" are familiar cases in point.

But what of the exactly parallel phrases in the first verse of "Lo, How a Rose?" "Lo, how a Rose e'er blooming / From tender stem hath sprung! Of Jesse's lineage coming / As men of old have sung." The first of these is handsomely served by a slight accentuation and tenuto (a "holding") on the word "rose," (also marked by a fortuitous "rise" in the melody) but the second line—cast in the exact mold of line No. 1 harmonically as well as melodically—has to cope with the word "lineage"; and if the same melodic emphasis is observed, the word "lineage" is in danger of being stretched until it breaks, fracturing understanding with it.

In addition, therefore, to the dynamic alteration of entire verses, and available to the chorus as well as to the soloist, is the underlining of certain syllables or words of particular import by one or both of two means: (1) dynamic stress and (2) a "holding"—a stress of duration. It is this latter stress which needs examination.

It seems to me that our "a priori" assumption ought to be that the composer's time values were as carefully selected as his pitches, and ought to be abandoned only infrequently, consciously, and with extreme reluctance and good reason. Rafael Druian, concert violinist and former concertmaster in Minneapolis, Cleveland and New York, has said, "I always ask myself: 'How would the composer have written it if he had wanted it to sound the way I'm playing it?'"

—But it also seems to me that we probably are generally agreed that the strains occasioned by fitting multiple texts to a single tune do indeed offer, however reluctantly, "good reason" for elasticity. The problem, then, is how to make the alterations in tempo—the elasticities and flexibilities—large enough to characterize new text emphases, yet small enough to preserve the balance and grace of the original melody—to remain substantially "imperceptible."

Let's say, first of all, that this requires an extraordinary acuity and subtlety— psychological as well as musical—from each one of us. Dictatorship/followship is far too heavy-handed a condition to produce much of value here. To achieve the kind of nuance which allows text and music to flower and flow together, we have to be guided by a common set of principles and understandings, improvising on the instant the stretch or the hastening of tempo.

Those principles, it seems to me, are the following:

1. The principle of the *Balance of Motion*.

If we should find it expressive—and tasteful—to stretch tempo for textual emphasis, that "dragging" (Italian: *trattenuto*) must be balanced as quickly and subtly as may be possible by a surge of forward motion. For every holding back there must be a hastening, for every heaviness (*pesante*) a leavening lightness (*leggiero*), for every slowing "down" a quickening "up."

This balance may be sought—and expressed—over a span of phrases or within the limitations of only two syllables. (Such is the case, it seems to me, with the words, "rose, e'er," in the phrase, "Lo, how a rose e'er blooming . . . " in which the tenuto on the word "rose" is immediately balanced by the shortening of the word "e'er," so that the following "blooming" comes almost in tempo.)

2. The principle of *Proportionate Rates* of Tempo Change.

This is a little more difficult to state; and the above designation is not really self-explanatory, though the proper terms are there.

Its concern is with the *rate* with which change in tempo occurs; and its premise is that occasionally even considerable changes in tempo are allowable— or, at least, more palatable—if their beginnings and endings are nicely proportioned. A *fermata*, a suspension of forward motion (through time), must be prepared. It has to be "led up to." It should not simulate a speeding car crashing into a concrete abutment. However slightly, one should *de*celerate into a fermata, and *ac*celerate out of it. – And both deceleration and acceleration must be qualified by *proportion* and *rate*.

This, perhaps, can best be shown by the principle which governs—and keeps vital—*ritardando* and *accelerando* wherever they occur. It exists in the paradox that every successful ritard is a stepping up (a quickening) of pulse and every successful animando is a stepping down (a slowing) of pulse. This is somewhat easier to illustrate in person than by letter; but if you will undertake to put a nonsense syllable to each of the notes in the following 6-measure ritardando from m.m. ♩ = 120, to m.m. ♩ = 30, you will readily realize that while forward motion (and the quarter-note with it) is slowing down, the inner pulse is quickening in step-wise fashion measure by measure:

The converse, *accelerando,* would look like this:

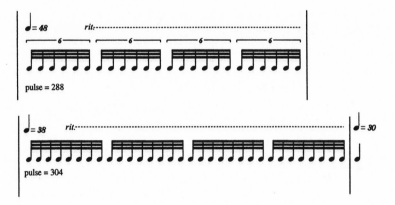

Though the tempo has increased over four-fold, (from m.m. 60 to m.m. 262), the inner pulse—as indicated by the diminishing number of notes per measure—has decreased measure by measure from m.m. 120 to m.m. 66.

Now, this inner pulse may not indeed always be represented by a diminishing number of notes per measure precisely as illustrated above; but if it exists in the performer's mind, it will be sufficient to give the accelerando a logic, scale, proportion and a rate—all of which mean pretty much the same thing. Scale and proportion also insure the vitality of both *accelerando* and *ritardando* and offer an expectability upon which 200 singers (and 100 instrumentalists) can unite.

The point is that elasticity and flexibility in tempo have no business being willful, arbitrary, abrupt or dictatorial. Changes in tempo must be balanced and proportioned, logically introduced and gracefully ended—and totally conscious.

Music is the organization of tone and timbre in Time. Its concern is to organize Time, to give it beauty and meaning. – And it may well be that its most telling expressivity is to be discovered in the balanced and proportioned elasticities of Time.

R

P.S. This may be more than any of you wish to know about anything—ever—again.

ANTONÍN DVOŘÁK

Stabat Mater

October 13, 1998

Friends –

Reflections following our first rehearsal (your 5th) of the Dvořák *Stabat Mater,* which almost certainly also will prove to be a first performance for 90% of us—including the conductor—in two weeks.

1. Deepest thanks to all those involved in the audition process. There can be little doubt that this year's edition of the ASOC, while leaner, is clearly cleaner than those of the "good old days."

2. Now thank we also our Super-NorMan—from whom all lessons flow.

3. – As to the piece: Those of us for whom singing the choral/orchestral repertoire is one of the principal joys of existence are accustomed to eating awfully high on the hog. We get the best dishes out of every chef's kitchen. Baroque? – *B Minor Mass, St. Matthew Passion* and *Messiah.* Classical? – Mozart *Requiem* and Beethoven *Missa Solemnis.* Nineteenth Century? – *Requiems* by Brahms and Verdi. Twentieth Century? – *Symphony of Psalms* and a *War Requiem.*

That these and a few other "master"-pieces became richer and richer through repetition through the years carries with its satisfactions also the danger of blinding us to other repertoire or under-valuing it.

My guess is that Dvořák's *Stabat Mater* is going to become the more precious the better we know it. Here was one for whom music was the air he breathed, the water he drank and food he ate. His musical roots were as deep in the people's (popular? folk?) music of his time as they were in the international languages of the classical masters. Over the period of a few years he had to bury three of his children in infancy or youth, the last two within weeks of one another. Who among us would care to look at the members of his own family and contemplate that agony?

Under these conditions he undertook the setting of this litany of bloody grief.

– And then you die.

R

October 20, 1998

Friends –

I was about to suggest that it would be good for us before next week's rehearsals to become re-acquainted with the text of the *Stabat Mater* by referring to Nick Jones's translation given to you some weeks ago. (I had almost finished pasting into my full score the word-for-word, non-grammatical translation— which is the absolute and minimum requirement, it seems for me, for singing text in a foreign language.)

Repeat: "I was about to . . . "—when I re-read the text in its entire, English, grammatical, unambiguous form. – What a grim, bloody, despairing sorry-go-round it is!

Folk medicine has it that a dose of castor oil, a hair shirt, and a knee-walking pilgrimage up Stone Mountain in a hail-storm is a sure cure for the giggles. Here, in the *Stabat Mater,* we have our own antidote to unprovoked joy, our own com-de-pression chamber.

Dvořák's setting has come under some criticism for being "expanded . . . to the proportions of an oratorio by rather tiresome repetition of both words and music and the use of unremittingly slow tempos" (*The New Grove Dictionary of Music and Musicians*).

What a spoil-sport! Some people like slow music. – Particularly those who sing it. – It lasts longer. What a relief it is from Disney-Land! – And stand-up comics!

Like the *Dies Irae,* its near-contemporary and probable superior in literary stature, for nearly eight centuries the *Stabat Mater* text has inspired composers, not inhibited them.

It was beautiful last night. – And there's still more grieving to be done. Aren't we lucky?

R

P.S.

Gentlemen –

Enclosed is the Gregorian setting of *Stabat Mater*. We will use Verses 1, 3 and 5 as a pianissimo prelude to Movement I of Dvořák's setting. Please become acquainted with it before Monday.

R

November 3, 1998

> Stabat pater fortunatus
> Happy as a hippopatus
> Up to here in muck and mire.
>
> Hearing sounds beyond believing,
> Angel voices Halloweaving,
> Quel orchestrand WHAT A CHOIR!

R

GEORGE FRIDERIC HANDEL

Messiah

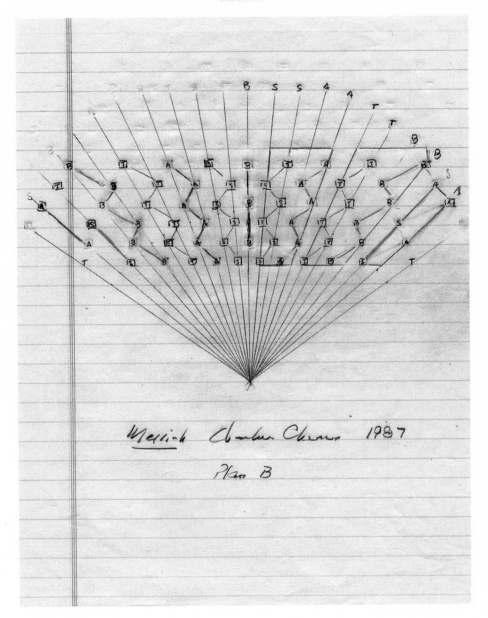

Sketch of chamber chorus stage positioning for performances of Handel's *Messiah*

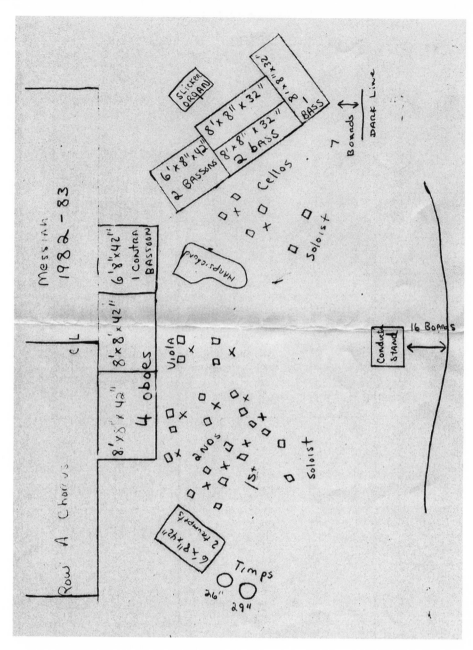

Sketch of orchestra stage positioning for performances of Handel's *Messiah*

December 2, 1965

One of the most stimulating musical adventures of recent years has been the study and preparation of these performances of *Messiah*.

During even the last decade earnest, distinguished scholarship has resulted in the publication of two new performance scores predicated directly upon Handel's own performance practices (which varied impressively, especially as regards solo assignments). These new scores are the works of an Englishman, Watkins Shaw, and an American, Alfred Mann of Rutgers University. Slightly preceding these performance editions are two significant books, *Handel, A Documentary Biography* by Otto Erich Deutsch (A&C Black, London, 1955) and *Handel's Messiah* by Jens Peter Larsen of the University of Copenhagen (W. W. Norton, New York, 1957). This week's performances are based upon those which Handel himself conducted as appraised in these studies and the new scores. We actually are using Watkins Shaw's orchestral and vocal parts (Mr. Mann's are not yet ready for publication), but have relied heavily upon Mr. Mann's score, his personal advice and his "realization" of the organ and harpsichord parts.

One of the very few points of difference between the Shaw and Mann scores regards the parts allotted to the oboes. (The Baroque "sound" is in a large part the result of two practices: first—according to symphonic standards—the greatly reduced number of players and second, the larger proportion of winds—particularly flute, oboe and bassoon—to string players.)

Watkins Shaw hypothesizes that Handel's four oboes probably were allotted two and two to doubling the soprano and alto voices and/or first and second violins. (This would have been Bach's practice.) Mann feels it likely that all four of Handel's *Messiah* oboes would have been assigned to doubling the soprano part (and/or first violin), since it was sung only by boys' voices while the alto was more aggressively sung by adult male altos.

However, given a proficient contemporary choral balance, Mann readily responded that it might indeed be reasonable to have all choral voices doubled by a reed instrument—as they are doubled frequently by strings. I have constructed, therefore, a special "optional" bassoon part for this performance, which, in the main, doubles the tenor voice (leaving, meanwhile, two bassoons and a contra-bassoon to support the bass voices) since it was the only vocal line uncolored by double-reed plangency.

As to which "system" will be used in performance I cannot say at this point. Perhaps we will change from concert to concert. The heavy double-reed doubling of only the soprano and bass parts would call attention to the "two-voice" attributes of this music—and that is thoroughly justifiable. The more comprehensive doubling, enhancing the inner voices, could yield a greater polyphonic interplay—without a sacrifice (given this choir and this orchestra) of the outer sonorities. Rehearsal will tell.

I believe uncompromisingly that we cannot expect to discover Handel's "spirit" without recreating insofar as possible the number, nature and disposition of his musical forces. This is precisely the opposite of basing a performance on the proposal of "what he might have written had he had today's grand symphonic and vocal forces." A composer's meaning is not to be separated from the sound he "heard" in his inner ear and prescribed.

At the same time, when we have done everything possible to recreate that musical scenario, there still are problems and possibilities through which only our "ears" and instincts can guide us.

If our labor is valid—the result should be that *Messiah* sheds its ponderous, sanctimonious, morbid, musical and religious pomposity, and becomes again what Handel certainly intended it to be, a light, bright, chamber-oratorio, celebrating with a secular deftness a remote but responsive religious mystery. This is scarcely the place for an intellectual face-off between the sacred and the secular, but the point is not to be avoided, that *Messiah* was drugged, smothered and finally buried by nearly two humorless centuries of the civilization which bore his name.

I should like to report, on behalf of the chorus, soloists and myself, writing prior to this week of orchestral rehearsals, that once we had divested ourselves of old associations—the heavinesses of sonority, tempo and accent, once we had achieved a chamber music clarity and lightness—the spiritual aspects of the piece were extraordinarily enhanced. All that had been daubed, stuccoed and garmented for public display now became simple, genuine, human and convincing.

That grandest of "Hallelujahs" (which—horrors: I once conducted with five thousand voices in one of our country's leading live-stock arenas) "is become" a joyous, iridescent madrigal of men and angels. (If anyone stands up during its performance at these concerts out of deference to the tradition instituted by a remote monarch who mistook it for the national anthem, or who did not realize that an intermission followed directly, he can have his head back.)

R. S.

PAUL HINDEMITH

When Lilacs Last in the Dooryard Bloom'd: A Requiem "For Those We Love"

January 9, 1963

When Lilacs Last in the Dooryard Bloom'd: A Requiem "For Those We Love" is a setting of the complete text of Walt Whitman's poem in memory of Abraham

Lincoln. It was commissioned by The Collegiate Chorale in the winter of 1945 and completed April 20, 1946. It is Hindemith's first major choral work since "Das unaufhörliche" (1931).

The twenty sections of Whitman's text (Edition McKay: 1900) have been compressed by the composer into eleven musical numbers, which again have been apportioned among four major movements. The setting thus provides a reciprocal commentary—the poet upon the musician, and the musician upon the poet.

I

Whitman's first stanza is a prologue introducing the trinity of the symbols which are the motivating images of his elegy—lilac, star and bird. In the three subsequent stanzas he qualifies them, assigning to each its own particular atmosphere:

"Star" . . . fallen star . . . tearful night . . . harsh surrounding cloud;

"Lilac" – with the perfume strong I love . . . in the dooryard, old farmhouse . . . and "Bird" – thought of him I love . . . song of the bleeding throat . . . Death's outlet song of life.

Before he approaches the text, the composer has provided a musical prologue in the form of a short orchestral prelude. It is based on a continuous pedal C-sharp upon whose minor tonality the entire work is founded. Its initial theme (A-C-F-E) already suggests associated tonalities, and out of this theme grow lines of increasing and decreasing harmonic tension, embracing in their arch the temper and spiritual qualities of all that is to follow.

The composer then binds the poet's first three stanzas into one musical structure beginning with a baritone narration-song (C-sharp minor), "When lilacs last in the dooryard bloom'd"; moving through a choral section, contrasting in mood (F minor) but preserving the thematic material, "O powerful, western fallen star!"; and concluding with a return to the opening song, "In the dooryard . . . stands the lilac bush." (It is significant for Hindemith's larger forms that each section is complete in itself, but at the same time integrated into an organism of the whole, which respect they have in common with Bach's choral works and Mozart's operas.)

Thus, the composer moves to the poet's fourth stanza (his own No. 2); he builds an alto arioso, rounded in itself, but preserving the tonality and musical materials of the beginning. " . . . A shy arid hidden bird . . . warbling a song."

The poet up to this point has set a stage—has painted an atmospheric landscape. He now (in Stanzas 5 through 7) moves to a second general section and pictures a coffin passing through an earthly landscape.

In a larger line, the composer makes these stanzas the concluding part of his first great movement, awakening in us the thought of the identity of the two landscapes. This No. 3 is a slow and solemn choral March, "Over the breast of the Spring," whose theme is a variation in the original tonality of the baritone narration-song. Stanza 6 becomes simply a middle-part, a sort of Fugato-Trio, "Coffin that passes through lanes and streets," culminating in a three-part canon in Stretto-form inspired by the "Tolling bells' perpetual clang." The last two lines of Stanz 6 serve as a modulation back to C-sharp minor, and the theme of the March returns, this time sung by the baritone and concluding with the Stretto-Canon between solo and orchestra. The first movement begins and ends in C-sharp minor.

II

With Whitman's Stanzas 8 through 11, the poet becomes an actor in his own drama. The involvement is at the stage of receiving knowledge, the first understanding: "O western orb . . . Now I know what you must have meant" (Stanza 8); "O singer bashful and tender! I hear . . . I understand you" (Stanza 9). There follows immediately the poet's reaction—questioning: "O how shall I warble myself? . . . O what shall I hang on the chamber walls?" And self-answering: "Pictures of growing spring, and farms, and homes," and climaxing in a triumphant carol of life, "Lo! body and soul! this land!"

This unity is reaffirmed by the composer in his second large movement (Nos. 4 through 7). Just as the first movement had a unifying tonality (C-sharp minor), so the second movement is based mainly on the tonality of A minor, ending with a fugue in the key of the dominant (E-minor-major).

No. 4 "O Western Orb" is given to the baritone solo with an echoing chorus at the beginning and the end.

Restless and almost-fevered melodic phrases appear over a wind-like orchestral accompaniment, driven up in a step-wise progression by blocked interjections, and finally disappearing, falling back into an open tonal space. The ending tone B-flat is best understood as a leading tone back to the prevailing A tonality.

The second bird-arioso (No. 5, alto solo) brings the word-image of the bird to the near-concreteness of a sound-image, drawn by instrumental color, persistent rhythm and the motive of falling thirds.

The question and answer involvement is brought first into a song form, a dialogue between baritone and chorus, so rounded that it allows a literal repetition (Straophenlied).

As the flood of answers continues, the composer leads the melodic line through a mounting choral recitative, culminating [in] a double fugue (E minor), "Lo! body and soul! this land!" The first subject is worked out in the form of a simple fugue ending in A minor, in which key the second subject, "Lo: the most excellent sun" is introduced, and similarly treated. The double fugue, combining subjects one and two (again E minor), begins significantly on the words " . . . enveloping man and land." A broad coda, "Lo! this land!" begins on a C minor chord and ends in a brilliant E major climax.

III

The poet now deepens the color. He moves from the state of receiving knowledge, with its shock and its ecstasy of tribute, to the state of possessing knowledge. "With the knowledge of death . . . and the thought of death . . . and I in the middle . . . as holding the hands of companions." And he rises from the occasion of Lincoln's death to the consideration of death itself. The Death Carol is his song of welcome.

The composer begins his third movement with a three-part form in C minor (alto solo, baritone recitative, and duet; No. 8).

In the alto solo, once more associated with the symbol of the bird, the ear will be struck by a short but intensive series of pure triads, infrequent in this musical language. "O liquid and free . . . O wondrous singer! you only I hear. . . . " We note that these pure harmonies occur at points of particular poignancy and expressiveness in the text (for example: "song of the bleeding throat," No. 2). (May this not be compared with the pure colors of Mathias Grunewald's "Isenheimer Altar" which inspired "Mathias der Maler?")

The middle section, a baritone recitative, centers in the hymn "For those we love." The form of the chorale is chosen at the moment when the poet speaks of the "knowledge and thought of death." On the fermatas of the orchestral chorale the baritone interjects his melodic phrases.

The duet is a return of the alto arioso, to which is added a baritone counterpoint continuing the text. Surely it is true that over the music of the Death Control (No. 9) hovers a sense of anxiety. There appears to be little in the actual lines to support this feeling unless it be the over-vehemence and ecstasy of the welcome, proposing even "glad serenades . . . dances . . . adornments . . . feastings . . . to thee, O Death." The composer finds considerable uncertainty and disquiet in the phrases "Dark Mother, always gliding near . . . the night in silence"; and the "glad serenades," become a masque.

The second part of the Death Carol, "Approach strong Deliveress," is a passacaglia over a five-measure repeated bass, a motive already suggested in the first part on the words "Praise! Praise! Praise! for the sure-enwinding arms. . . . "

The tonality of the Death Carol is F minor, and it may be worthwhile to note that we have had the following order of main tonalities: C-sharp, A, C, F, which are also the opening tones of the Prelude. The next important tonality has been E (if not in this order), which would then round out the opening theme.

IV

Whitman's sections 17 and 18 complete the panorama of death. He envisions "armies—myriads of battle-corpses . . . white skeletons of young men." Then (his final two stanzas), "passing the visions," passing also lilac, star and bird, "unloosing the hands of his comrades," as if the intense knowledge of death and the over-reality of the symbols were given only in moments—he keeps forever their memory.

Of Stanza 17 the composer forms a recitative in F-flat minor, whose musical material reappears in a visionary march (Whitman's Stanza 18) ending in a B-flat major off-stage bugle call. There is an orchestral ritournel in F-sharp minor colored by a D tonality which at the end is used as a leading-tone back to C-sharp minor.

The Finale, "Passing the Visions," moves in a slow dotted rhythm, touching again some of the associated tonalities, and comes to rest on a C-sharp minor chord. A Coda echoes the memory of "lilacs and star and bird . . . twined with the chant of my soul."

– *Julius Herford and Robert Shaw*

March 13, 1986

Dear People (– that should be safe enough),

There are two technical virtuosities in Hindemith's *Lilacs* which, after forty years' familiarity, continue to astonish me. I wonder if ever in the history of music so vast a text has been set in such a concise musical time.

In the first twenty minutes of music, six short movements which follow the short instrumental prelude—in which secco recitative figures not at all, and accompanied recitative only fragmentarily—Hindemith manages to set something like *nine hundred words*. – And these are words not lightly tossed into the composition heap. They are Walt Whitman words, burdened with emotional ponderosity and ponderability.

By contrast, the first twenty minutes of Bach's *Mass in B Minor* present only four words, or—if one wanted to be persnickety—just three: *Kyrie, Christe,* and *eleison.* In the first twenty minutes of the *St. Matthew Passion,* which alternates narrative with contemplative processes, Bach manages to set approximately 450 words (or one-half Hindemith's quota), but nearly one-half of these are accountable to the Evangelist's recitative which occupies only three of the twenty minutes.

Hindemith's mastery is a double triumph, for Whitman's poem has scarcely any narrative aspects at all; at no point does it allow the natural and near-speech tempos of story-telling. It is lyric and reflective, expansive and rhetorical—though certainly not as extravagant as some Whitman texts—and it calls for music which "contemplates" and "amplifies," rather than rushing forward to a tale's dire ending.

I would guess that those elements in music which allow and invoke "reflection" probably depend in one way or another upon aspects of repetition and recall, either of principal melodies or accompaniment motives. That is to say, it is somehow the recurrence of musical materials, and their accumulative gestative familiarity, which induce the psychological state (or illusion) of contemplation.

Enter Hindemith's double jeopardy: for now he is obliged to invent melodic materials which can be adapted to a variety and succession of texts. All of us, of course, are familiar with the process in the singing of hymns; but we also realize that singing verses one through five is an expression of congregational solidarity, not of textual revelation.

An eloquent theatrical reading of the complete text of *Lilacs* by a sensitive actor probably would take nearly twenty minutes. To get twenty minutes of expressive spoken text into fewer than sixty minutes of expressive musical time is an absolutely staggering accomplishment.

The second technical virtuosity of *Lilacs* which continues to amaze me is the variety, order and inventive richness of vocal forms. Historically, the principal forms of music for solo voice and orchestra have been aria, arioso and recitative (or some modification thereof). At one end of the scale stands the *aria,* with a minimum of text and a maximum of musical exploration and elaboration. At the other end stands *recitative* with a maximum of text and a minimum of metric and melodic accentuation. – And in between the two stands *arioso,* attempting to be true to both loves.

And precisely here, it seems to me, is Hindemith's most extraordinary, and sensitive, creativity. Though only two of the ten musical movements are entitled *arioso,* all of the solos and duets lean heavily upon its resources. (The *arioso* elements in No. 1 occur at measures 24 and 36, in No. 3 at measure 118; No. 4 and No. 6 are arioso/aria hybrids, with the presence of the chorus in No. 6

attempting a tri-brid; even in the gigantic double fugue of No. 7, the episodes at ms. 43, 86, 107 and the climax at m. 164 have *arioso* qualities; the hymn in No. 8 enfolds an *arioso;* No. 9 begins with an *arioso* for chorus, as does No. 10 for baritone; and No. 11 is an *arioso* from start to finish.)

But, note also the richness of other forms. There are two substantial marches (No. 3 and No. 10) complete with trios. Normally an instrumental form, these now are given almost completely to voices: in the first instance to the chorus, and in the second instance, though not so extensively, to the baritone. – And that most congregational and strophic of all musical forms, the *chorale* (hymn), in No. 8 is given only to instruments, though on repetition it is punctuated by the declarative phrases of a solo male voice. The *Death Carol* is a kaleidoscope of musical schematics, including arioso, recitative, motet, aria, passacaglia and fanfare. – And the prelude is all but compulsively devoted to the reiteration of a four-note *ostinato.*

These, of course, are formal elements of Hindemith's great familiarity. One finds them throughout his major works, symphonic or operatic; but it is rare to find historic vessels of such durable beauty so handsomely filled with potable twentieth-century wine.

– So much for pure science. What about the heart?

It seems to me we have to begin—as did Hindemith—with the poetry. Whitman may be the most frequently "set" of American poets. – And for me there are two aspects to his poetry which composers of choral music—both symphonic and unaccompanied—appear to find irresistible. The first is its sense of Community. Whitman's posture, and perhaps his capacity, is somehow that of speaking—of proclaiming—for all of us. – Particularly, for all us Umurricuns. His is an ecstatic but undeniable passion for the breadth of this land and its formative dream of "brotherhood." In the gangrenous wards of Civil War tent hospitals he was his brother's keeper, and every man was his brother. Whitman loved his fellow man—singular, plural, living, dying or assassinated.

And "fellow-ship" and "brother-hood," a century before they became sexist and chauvinist words, were the natural habitat and ambience of the choral art.

In the second place Whitman's language and posture is expansive and ex-alted. (For some it may seem also extravagant, exaggerated and exhibitionistic; some might even prefer that "shy and hidden bird" Emily Dickinson.) – But Whitman's passionate declamation appears to cry for musical collaboration (while Dickinson's would appear to defy it). The sense of emotional intensity—even emotional excess—behind Whitman's words is an invitation to the composer to add the "unspeakable" to the already spoken.

It ought to be said that *Lilacs* is not one of Whitman's most expostulative elocutions. Its prospect is large (a verbal cyclorama) and occasionally rhetorical

("Lo! Body and soul! this land!). But, in the main, it is sensitive, thoughtful, rich in imagery—and the major accomplishment of a major poet.

– At least, that is the way it comes out in Hindemith's setting Hindemith's grief is thoughtful and private—as, perhaps, grief ought to be. Hindemith avoids every opportunity for excess. Except for a short early choral heart-burst at the thought of the fallen star, the only forte passages in the work are those which voice the breadth of the landscape (No. 7); the hymn, "For those we love," as it is interrupted by the cries which acknowledge death's universal companionship; the few fervid moments in death's praise (No. 9); and the raucous irony of tragedy of death on the field of battle (No. 10). Even these are transitory, and move quickly back to the pervasive and quiet grief of life's final darkness.

It is as clear as anything can be that in 1945 Hindemith used the death of Lincoln as a metaphor for all the heroic and wasted lives consumed in the holocaust of World War II. Consider that he was at that time one of the world's leading artists, intellectuals, humanitarians and citizen activists. (He was one of Hitler's most implacable foes.) Moreover, he must have known personally—on both sides of the conflict—as many distinguished artists, intellectuals, human-itarians and accomplished citizens of whatever activity as any man of his time. In Europe there could have been scarcely a family untouched by death. By 1945 the world of Hindemith's closest companions must have been all but gone.

The whole of *Lilacs* is a hymn for those he loved. It has nothing to do with proclamations of national mourning, the public beating of breasts, but with quiet private grief and a lonely broken heart.

R

April 18, 1996

Remarks on Hindemith's *When Lilacs Last in the Dooryard Bloom'd*
Yale University, New Haven, Connecticut

Ladies and Gentlemen: Good Evening.

It is probable that no foreign-born composer has made such a direct and healthy contribution to American music as Paul Hindemith—with his 14 years of teaching at Yale, and the books and scores of his mature years written during his North American exile for composing music which lacked the proper Nazi philo-sophical outlook: operas, for instance, wherein peasants rise against authority, and artists forsake their art to become activists in the struggle against tyranny.

As a musician, Hindemith knew more about the nature and capacities of musical instruments, and had a greater acquaintance with historical musical styles, forms and literature than any composer of his century—and perhaps, because there was now so much which could be known, more than any other composer in the history of music.

As a man, he was a thorny, cantankerous, but life-loving humanist. "All my life," he responded to a reporter in Chicago who had asked him if he were now giving up composing to spend more time conducting, "All my life I've struggled to be an honest musician, and now you want me to become a bloody, damn conductor!"

As the world premiere of *Lilacs* approached, Mr. Hindemith was asked how many tickets he would like for the opening concert. "But Robert," Mrs. Hindemith intervened, "Paul has never been to the premiere of one of his works in his life."

When it was pointed out that for this particular work 200 amateur singers had spent thousands of man-hours in a labor of love and respect, he agreed that these human elements might indeed make a difference, but added wonderingly, "Do you really think you can make it sound better than I already hear it?"

– And when some days later he arrived at a rehearsal to hear the baritone soloist—strong in vocal muscle and stage presence—but straying too far from his appointed musical rounds, he exploded, "For the love of God, Bob, ask him what notes he *can* sing. I sure as Hell can write 'em!"

Like Whitman's "gray-brown bird," *Lilacs* is a sometime gray-brown piece. Fifty years ago it seemed to those of us so recently wrapped in the patriotic festoonery of "Praise the Lord and Pass the Ammunition!" and "Coming in on a Wing and a Prayer!" as somewhat dense, occasionally knotted, and not overly festive.

– But it ought to be said that *Lilacs* is not one of Whitman's normally extravagant expostulations. In the main, it is sensitive and thoughtful poetry, rich in imagery—but solitary in its sorrow.

– And Hindemith's grief is also thoughtful and private—as, perhaps, grief ought to be. Hindemith avoids every opportunity for excess. The few loud moments are transitory, and move quickly back to the pervasive and quiet acceptance of life's final darkness.

It is as clear as anything can be that in 1945 Hindemith used the death of Lincoln as a metaphor not only for the deaths of Franklin Roosevelt and his own students, but for all the heroic and wasted lives consumed in the holocaust of World War II. He must have known personally—on both sides of the conflict—as many distinguished artists, philosophers, educators, politicians and accomplished citizens of whatever activity as any man of his time. But by 1945 the world of Hindemith's closest companions must have been all but gone.

The whole of *Lilacs* is a hymn for those he loved. It has nothing to do with proclamations of national mourning, the public beating of breasts, but with quiet private grief and a lonely broken heart.

On the night of Good Friday, 1865—while attending a performance at Ford's Theatre in Washington, D.C., Lincoln was shot by John Wilkes Booth, and passed away the next morning.

Some of the sermons on that following Easter Sunday carry a pious " 'serves him right!" for being caught dead in such a "school of vice and corruption." (– 'Worse than a concert hall?)

"We remember with sorrow the place of his death," intoned Dewey Fuller in Boston. "He did not die on Mount Nebo, with his eye full of Heaven. He was shot in a theatre. We are sorry for that. It was a poor place to die in. It would not be selected by any of you as the spot from which you would desire to proceed to the bar of God." Six weeks later Phineas Gurley of New York Ave. Pres. D.C. managed to add to the weight of his grief, "It will always be a matter of deep regret to thousands that our lamented President fell in the theatre. Multitudes of his best friends—I mean his Christian friends—would have preferred that he should have fallen in almost any other place.

Good Friday—The shooting.

Saturday—The death.

Easter Sunday—Eulogies begin—and *Monday,* the embalming. (Professional critics of the latter vary from "frozen face" to "same sad look"—the embalmer traveling with the train through the next two weeks to make periodic "improvements.")

Tuesday—Lincoln lies in state in the East Room while outside gathers "the largest mass of people that ever thronged the White House lawn."

Wednesday—Funeral service in the East Room: Cabinet members, Supreme Court justices, brand-new President, 600 dignitaries, General Grant; no Mrs. Lincoln, but Robert and young Tad, weeping.

A casket six-feet six-inches long by eighteen inches wide at the shoulders leaves the White House in a black hearse drawn by six gray horses to the sound of muffled drums to rest in the capitol rotunda. Sixty thousand spectators watch a parade of forty thousand mourners.

Thursday—At ten o'clock, doors open for special viewing by wounded soldiers from the hospitals. Before midnight, twenty-five thousand walking wounded file by.

April 21 to May 4—The casket travels by special train from Washington, D.C., to Springfield, Illinois, for burial; Lincoln lies in state—for public viewing—in places like Constitution Hall, Philadelphia; City Hall, New York City; the Court House, Chicago.

Behold a cortege seventeen hundred miles long, night and day for two weeks: In Newark, "a square-mile of mourners," in Richmond, Indiana—whose population must have been countable in the hundreds—ten thousand people stand bare-headed at three o'clock in the morning as the train passes.

Not one mile of the one thousand seven hundred miles unattended—whatever the hour. Bonfires, children on fathers' and grandfathers' shoulders, cities and citizens draped in black. – On several railroad divisions the same engines and engineers that had brought him to Washington four years before.

In a country of thirty million people, a land which stretched from the Eastern to the Western seas, seven million mourners line the funeral route. – Nearly one out of every four living persons.

At the various stops for formal viewing, one-million-five-hundred-thousand mourners file past the face of the dead President—one-twentieth of the population of the just-barely-maybe re-United States.

Here is a land and people torn by a civil war so recently concluded that its ending has not yet been formalized, so bloody that the president of the winners says sending troops to McClellan is like "shoveling fleas in a barnyard," so ruinous economically that a century will pass before the losers can sense recovery. – And here lies one man, revilement and ridicule a few short hours behind him, but already missed so deeply that the vanquished general, a reluctant but gifted leader of secessionist armies, declares he "surrendered as much to Lincoln's goodness as to Grant's artillery."

What is the breadth of love and grief which keeps one-fourth of a wounded, exhausted nation standing at parade-rest for twenty-one times twenty-four hours? Isn't that an all but incomprehensible "long, black trail?"

– Lincoln saying, "Don't it seem strange to you, that I, who could never so much as cut off the head of a chicken, should be elected into the midst of all this blood?"

– Whitman and Hindemith saying, "When Lilacs last in the door-yard bloom'd . . . I mourned."

April 3, 1986

Amis –

"The whistle keep' a-blowin', but the train done gone." – But not without leaving its "long black trail." Certainly, most of us will never again read Whitman's *Lilacs* without hearing in our mind's ear Hindemith's voices.

Deepest thanks and warmest congratulations upon (particularly) the decisive performance of the *Death Carol*. I cannot remember another occasion over the past forty years wherein a piece of this dimension and difficulty was "set down" on a "first take."

There could be a few knotty (naughty) spots in the Schmitt *Psalm*, but we can look forward to duck-souping Fauré, Beethoven and Berlioz.

R

LEOŠ JANÁČEK

Glagolitic Mass

December 30, 1974

Friends,

Janáček's *Glagolitic (or Slavonic) Mass* and Samuel Barber's *The Lovers*, in addition to providing us with more intriguing and singular musical fare than we have faced for many months, raise provocative questions regarding the texts and the "purposes" of choral music.

The *Glagolitic Mass* should lead us (particularly those of us involved one way or another with church music) to consider the tangle of shadowy relationships which make it so difficult—but invigorating—to isolate out-and-out secularity from inner and outer religiosity. And *The Lovers* ultimately will require each of us to reach some sort of participative decision as to what constitutes (at the minimum) "good" or "bad" taste, or (at the unlikely maximum) "porn-" or "connubiography" in the public performance of music.

Janáček's *Mass* (1927) departs from both musical and religious tradition in a number of ways. In the latter instance it shuns the Latin liturgical text and uses one based upon "the ancient glagolitic (or 'cyrilian,' so called according to the alphabet used) rite, brought to Moravia in the ninth century by the Saints Cyril and Methodius, and extinct in the churches of that country since the fifteenth century." Its vocal writing is almost without exception "rhetorical" (speech-like) in pitch and rhythm. Other than repetition and sequence almost none of the prevailing musical forms or idioms are employed or, if used, are relatively unimportant, to the purpose or definition of Janáček's musical language. The *Mass* would appear to have been intended for performance in the open air rather than the interior of a church; and James Goodfriend writes that "for all its flaming ardor, (it) was not intended to be a religious work, but a *national* one. 'I wanted to portray the faith in the certainty of the nation, not on a religious basis, but on the moral strength which takes God for witness,' said the composer in a magazine interview in 1928." (How about that: Big Who is witnessing for little whom?)

" 'To every word the folk utter is attached a fragment of the national life . . . therefore the melody of their speech should be studied in every detail.' These fragments gathered from the market-place, the harvest-field, the village green or the drawing-room, are 'invaluable for individual characterisation.' With these veristic tendencies, and a nature which shrinks from no logical issues, Janáček has forged a tone-speech which expresses itself in swift, eruptive figures, close-knit and elliptical. His idiom is the same for his instrumental as for his choral music. It is instantly penetrating. There is no spinning out of the lyrical material, no time spent upon musical dissertation; the dramatic climaxes are driven home and clinched with breathless rapidity. The phrases—vocal or instrumental—whether they follow each other continuously or are broken by pregnant pauses, whether they are urgent with passion or languid with sorrow, tensely emotional, or all but quiescent—are always natural and convincing. The fact that the diction is rooted in the Moravian dialect need not trouble the hearer, because, in spite of the strongly localised accent and lilt, it is all emotionally intelligible. What actually disconcerts listeners who cannot think and feel spontaneously is this refusal to dally with the emotional crises, or to indulge in musical commentaries. Erwin Schulhoff says of Janáček's music: 'It is so strenuous, intuitive and unfabricated that it compels us not merely to lend an ear, but to live in it for the time being.' "

(Rose Newmarch, *Grove's Dictionary of Music and Musicians,* Macmillan Company, 1942.)

After initial but more than cosmetic study of Samuel Barber's *The Lovers,* there is no doubt in my mind that musically and textually this will be understood and heard as an enormously sensitive expression—lyric, tender, mature and autumnal—of, apparently, physical aspects, but, in reality, the prevailingly deeper "introspects" of male-female love.

I was first introduced to the poetry of Pablo Neruda by South American friends—who felt certain he was the principal poet of our hemisphere now—which title many consider his due—but I had never come across the poems chosen by Barber.

In the total atmospheres of both text and music I find a rare, earthly beauty and an exceptional and pure love (though I admit to questioning after first glance at the "specificity" of one or two phrases, their possible acceptance by a Thursday night audience).

At any rate, these works should provide a provocative and instructive six to seven weeks, for the technical problems also are new and numerous. I figure our next rehearsals to be—with appropriate drills and exercises in pitch, rhythm and enunciation—the most strenuous of our octannual pursuit of Orpheus and/or Eros through the preserves of Puritannia.

R

October 3, 1990

Friends—old, new and in-between:

Janáček's *Glagolitic Mass* would not be nearly so difficult to *mass*ter were it not for two factors: (1) the execrable condition of the choral parts from which we are asked to sing, and (2) the difficulties of a Slavic language (extinct for, roughly, 1,000 years) for those without a Slavic tongue.

(Aside: Isn't "execrable" execrable? Absolutely Latrinish?—An onomatopoeia not of sound but of meaning. End Aside.)

There's not much we can do about Item (1). Were they available, it would have cost about $8,500 to purchase complete piano/vocal scores for the entire chorus. What we *can* do is isolate and *mass*ter one element at a time: pitches, rhythms, enunciation, dynamics, tone color—and, finally, "cue-ings" which may yield security (if not serenity) to entrances.

As regards Item (2), we all owe a massive missive of thanks to Jane Potter for her help with the enunciation problems of this text.

In 1953 the Collegiate Chorale scheduled for Carnegie Hall what we were assured was the American premiere of Janáček's *Mass*. (Later, we found that there had been an earlier performance by the "Friends of Music" in New York—though what forces were involved or if, indeed, it had been accompanied by an orchestra were not specified.) For our performance I attempted a setting in English of the ancient Slavic text, feeling, first, that ecclesiastical Latin would be thoroughly against the grain of Janáček's motivation as well as his prosody; and, second, that there wasn't enough time or expertise in greater New York to identify and subdue all the problems of language. The translation was not altogether a disaster, but it certainly did not represent the music as Janáček had conceived it.

Also on that program was Hindemith's *Lilacs*—which many of us know, respect and love. I can remember being infuriated at the reviews. So overwhelming was the impact of Janáček's *Mass* that scarcely a mention was made of *Lilacs*.

For performances with the Cleveland Orchestra and Chorus in 1965 we enlisted the aid of special linguists from Cleveland's uniquely large Slavic population, in particular the wife of one of the orchestra's bassoonists and a Slavic priest.—There were just enough Slavs in the orchestra chorus to make every rehearsal a nightmare of conflicting opinions.

What Ms. Potter is doing is "winnowing" some of these conflicting theories and practices, thus saving each one of us years of exhaustive labor and frustration—leaving us only enough exhaustion and frustration to blight those years left to us. Ain't that nice?

'See you Monday,

R

GUSTAV MAHLER

Symphony No. 8: "Symphony of a Thousand"

January 9, 1991

Dear Associates –

Now, isn't that a fitter salutation (than the "Dear Troops" of last week) to the forces drawn up (and quartered, eighthed and twelfthed) to probe and conquer the sandy fastnesses (and cragged, pinnacled slownesses) of Mahler's "Symphony of Six Hundred and Seventy"—all this on a day Congressional arguments begin as to the windom or losedom, the rightdom or wrongdom of war on who-knows-whose block?

Among this week's Adjunct Mail is an informative translation of the *Veni, creator spiritus* which serves as text for Part I of the *Symphony*—in the translation and lay-out of Deryck Cooke (noted Mahler-scholar who, from fragmentary sketches, "constructed" Mahler's *Symphony No. 10* for today's performances).

The text deserves far more than a first-reading or casual study. Your pleasure in rehearsals and performances will be tremendously enriched as it becomes substantially memorized. Twice-through daily will bring that familiarity quickly and, up at least to the Gloria/Doxology, offer minimal affront to anyone's orthodoxy (other-doxie?).

According to contemporary reports Mahler did not have a complete and authoritative text of the hymn in front of him as he began writing. However, stimulated by remembered text and, of course, the "general import" of its major invocations, the music apparently spewed forth in an enraptured eruption. Mahler's wife, Alma (-Mahler/-Gropius/-Werfel)—the latter two among those who came to bat in later innings) has the following account:

"After we arrived at Maiernigg (in the summer of 1906), there was the usual fortnight during which, nearly every year, (Mahler) was haunted by the spectre of failing inspiration. Then one morning just as he crossed the threshold of his studio up in the wood, it came to him—'*Veni creator spiritus.*' He composed and wrote down the whole opening chorus to the half-forgotten words. But music and words did not fit in—the music had overlapped the text. In a fever of excitement he telegraphed to Vienna and had the whole of the ancient Latin hymn telegraphed back. The complete text fitted the music exactly. Intuitively he had composed the music for the full strophes."

Most scholarship, I would think, regards this account as somewhat simplistic; but it certainly is true that in the large section of Part I which some analysts regard as the "Development Section" of a Sonata-Allegro form (Nos. 19 to 64) there are evidences of other considerations taking precedence over textual clarity and particularized expressivity. For instance, certain lines of the hymn are omitted from Mahler's setting; in others, word-order is reversed or scrambled; and musical motifs which in the "Exposition" are used for certain texts, are here given a new and different text. This is not necessarily a limiting or denigrating assessment of the music. All great composers have set differing texts to identical music. – And, not infrequently, text is illuminated thereby.

The principal difficulty for me lies in the fields of tempi as they may be related to specific texts or musical motifs. Mahler indicates so many tempo qualifications—without identifying them metronomically—that it is difficult to know from his "a tempo" marks, for instance, whether one is to return to a Tempo I, Tempo II or *Tempus fugit.* Consequently, there are enormous differences in tempo relationships and actual speeds in all comparable performances of this movement. It is as though there were substantially no "tradition" or "style."

This, of course, is remarkable in that the work was written in this century, at a time wherein Mahler also conducted both the Metropolitan Opera Company and the New York Philharmonic Orchestra and could have been heard here and in Europe by people no older than our grandparents and, in the case of a few of us, by our parents. Item One: get text-oriented.

Item Two: As regards rehearsal next Monday: we will be assigned our specific responsibilities in the two four-to-eight-part Choruses, and be seated accordingly.

In 16-voice writing, individual vocal and musical responsibility begins to be very acute—even in the 200-voice choir. In terms of vocal range and dynamics—and occasional harmonic progression—this is a beast of a piece. Our rehearsal procedures are calculated to "save" voices; but the success of the performance chorally will depend upon each person's ability to sing the work in solo-quartets or solo-octets—which, I suppose, we'll have to get down to testing ASAP—or earlier.

See you Monday.

Peace,

R

May 3, 1978

Dear, dear!

'Great to be back with you! ('Except I'll never again hear so chamber-like a large chorus as in your Schubert *Grand E-Flat Mass*.)

Now, on to Val-hollow (and a big smoocher fur die entire motherin' Welt!). – We'll clean up the doethe-Goethe final act this week-end, and pull it all together on Monday night. Right?

Right!

RS—and yours

List'ners rave and rant and holler,
Zounds the sounds! for Gustav Mahler!
Jung at heart hail Sigmund's kin,
"Wolfgang's out and Gustav's in!
Spartan hearts are infantilish,
Those on sleeves are much more stylish!
Rupt your rapture! (not unlikely)
Muzzle mind, and 'sic 'em psychly!"

Mean- and erst-while singers panic:
Tessitura sic tyrannic!
'Cry to heav'n for what they must have
To navigate the eighth of Gustav.
"Half the tempo! Down an octave!
Twice the – ! Up the – !" Quel concoctive!

Still and all (as sometimes happens) –
Once the notes are stripped of scrappin's –
It's rather fun, and not unsunny,
To bathe in pools of aural honey.
So, grieve not, Gus! Our new Apollo!
Where you lead us we will wallow!

September 19, 1972

Dear Friends –

I write with great happiness after last night's rehearsal on the Mahler *Symphony No. 2* to reaffirm my statement that this can indeed be a year of remarkable achievement for our chorus. Last night's sound was gorgeous.

I will contrive for next week a sheet of rhythmic exercises, the practice of which—both in warm-up sessions and at home—can make such rhythmic problems as we faced Monday night responsive to "Standard Operating Procedure." In the meantime make up your own exercises of counting and hand-tapping two against three and three against four—and enjoy.

Also, if you are not skilled in German, check the text against the enclosed transliteration or another person who is experienced; read the text aloud five times a day (5 minutes—or less).

Tenors (and Altos who sing some tenor parts): Check your notes within the unfamiliar Tenor Clef (Middle C on line four).

Everyone: We can still accept a few persons in each of our men's sections—*if they are musically experienced and responsible.* Help us find them, and thus keep our chorus maturing.

All choral conductors: We are planning a series of workshop and seminar sessions on Choral and Rehearsal Techniques. Register with Miss Eddie at the next rehearsal if this is of interest.

Affectionately,

R

Pronunciation Guide for Mahler *Symphony No. 2*

ü: Form lips as if to say "oo," but say "ee."

kh: Form mouth as if to say "ee" and push strong breath through in place of the "ee."

October 11, 1972

Friends:

I doubt that one can ever do
A too-neurotic Mahler Two.

There's sure a lot of things that must have
Harassed and distressed poor Gustav.

Imagine all the drools and dribblings
From eleven simp'ring siblings.

Snotty brats from wall to waller
Would drive a saint from mal to mahler.

And so he makes the chorus wait
An hour and ten, and sing but eight.

And even then, if one can hear it,
No-one has the proper spirit.
From whisper to whimp –and bang to holler
– The only way to go! with Mahler!

(Still—if I could figure Why- or how-for
I'd ersteh'n a little aufer.)

R

FELIX MENDELSSOHN

Elijah

Sketch of orchestra and chorus positioning for Mendelssohn's *Elijah*

September 27, 1994

Friends—long-time, short-time and (one can hope) about-to-be:

First of all—the very deepest thanks of all the Shaws for your thoughts, concerns, wishes, remembrances, greetings, cards, letters, flowers, plants, food and errands-run during the late summer weeks of Mrs. Shaw's critical illness. – For whatever combination of sciences, services and mysteries, there are at the moment unquestionable signs of improvement and reason for hope. Thank you.

I am looking forward to being with you next week for rehearsals of Mendelssohn's *Elijah.*

It has been a fascinating experience this summer to return to *Elijah*—and, in particular, its problems of performance in English—after some fifty(!) years of edits, re-edits and rumination.

I suppose everyone would agree that, strictly from the choral point of view, *Elijah* is an absolute miracle of a piece when it is engaged with Old Testament dramatic action, but somewhat less successful when it preaches a Victorian missionary moral. Contrast "Hear our cry, O Baal" (No. 12) and "Behold, God the Lord passed by!" (No. 34) with "Cast thy burden upon the Lord" (No. 15) or "He that shall endure to the end" (No. 32). Setting aside Felix's conversion to Christianity—which apparently was consummated for him *a priori* and *in absentia* by his grandfather—it seems to me that Mendelssohn is at his *contemplative* and *doctrinal* most convincing in the great arias: "If with all your hearts" (No. 4), "Lord God of Abraham" (No. 14), "Then shall the righteous shine forth" (No. 39), and "It is enough" (No. 26); though, even this latter is the core of a dramatic situation, rather than one of the sermonizing texts.

It should be noted here that Mendelssohn was the Classical-Romantic explorer and performer of the then-forgotten works of J. S. Bach, in particular Bach's *Passion According to St. Matthew.* He was undoubtedly deeply moved by the presence, in the Passions, of the Lutheran chorales. (His No. 15, "Cast thy burden upon the Lord," is clearly a direct descendant of Bach's procedures—complete with fermatas—and situated by Mendelssohn to serve a similar function.)

It is clear to us now that, though his intents and procedures were similar, Mendelssohn's performance venues and his musical materials were different enough to dilute any "homage to J. S. Bach" he may have had in mind. In the first place Bach's "audience" was a *congregation* of *believers,* and his Lutheran tunes and texts were the common property of both congregation and musical preceptors. Whether or not the chorales were sung by the congregation, they were sung on *behalf* of the congregation; and this introduced into any performance of Bach's Passions also a unique and over-powering play between Narrative-Time (Scriptural then-and-there) and Performance Time (here-and-now). What occurs psychologically in any performance of Bach's Passions is that the listeners interrupt to say, "We also are witnesess—not to the event, but to the meaning of the event; and we feel thus and so about it." – Not only do "we feel thus and so," but "we all feel thus-and-so right now," and "we've felt this way as long as we've known these words and these tunes."

Mendelssohn's audience was not a congregation of believers in a house of worship, but paying customers, very probably, of a minority upper economic class. His "chorales" were not, then, impulsive and commonly bonded responses to a religious drama, but further sermonettes and homilies delivered by angelic mini-hosts of angels in very proper Victorian measures and nuances—at their worst a sort of Hallmark get-well card.

Elijah is a long piece. In spite of its popularity one seldom hears it uncut. My experience through the years has been largely one of attempting to find inner and outer excisions (cuts within movements and a few of whole movements) which would keep the piece at unrelieved "genius level" all the way through. (One early "rule of thumb" was to cut everything that didn't sound as though it could have come out of *A Midsummer Night's Dream!*) The most minimalistic and brutal of these Marine-hairstyle performances was at the invitation of the CBS Symphony in the 'forties to do an *Elijah* for one of their weekly symphonic broadcasts: three minutes of spoken program notes, 56 minutes of musical time, and 60 seconds of station-break.

Traditionally, *Elijah* encompasses about two hours and fifteen minutes of musical time (plus intermission), or roughly 60 minutes longer than present Symphony Hall practice. This can be shortened some ten-or-thereabout minutes by tempo adjustments and rapid transitions. – And there is one major dramatic sequence which some of us feel can be cut without lethal injury: the subsidiary story of Elijah, the Widow and the Widow's Son (Numbers 6, 7, 8 and 9). (If, also, one begins the cut from measure 74 of No. 5, the narrative line of Elijah's introductory Curse and the Famine is perhaps even strengthened.) What one loses here dramatically, however, is an introduction to Elijah's personal tribulations and motivation, and musically, the initial appearance of the soprano soloist who, other than "Hear Ye!" has little to do for the remainder of the evening. With this cut, and a few others, recent performances have brought together two "Acts" of about fifty minutes each; and, until recent study, I have felt that the deletions actually strengthened the work, certainly that they gave it greater dramatic flow and thrust for contemporary audiences. (– Which should have been a warning, not a rationale.)

For—as for now—I'm not so sure.

The conclusion of the work (particularly Numbers 40 and 41) had always seemed to me somewhat extended, and textually obscure, inappropriate or unnecessary. Part of the problem—as also with other *Elijah* textual fragments—arises from the occasional obscurities in the King James version of the *Bible*. No one doubts the timeless beauty of the King James translation, nor should anyone doubt its very special propriety and authority with reference to Mendelssohn's *Elijah*. – But, as beautiful as it is, it is also occasionally obscure—even misleading; and both the American Standard Revised version and, especially, the New English Bible clarify and enrich many Old Testament texts—both narrative and lyric.

With a double cast of soloists—to separate and to clarify dramatic roles from cantata/sermonettes, and with quartets and octets of angels added to choruses of the false, the faithful and the tell-tale-tellers, and with the light thrown into obscure textual corners by new Biblical scholars, *Elijah-Entira* might even seem as short as that *Elijah-Instanta* amputation of a half century ago.

Think *Kings I & II, Psalms* and *Isaiah,* but sing *A Midsummer Night's* Madness and Magic.

'See you Monday,

R

October 3, 1994

Friends –

I have just re-read the remarkably informative preface to the *New Novello Choral Edition* of *Elijah* edited by Michael Pilkington; and I am prompted to write an addendum to last week's letter as it relates to textual matters and motives as well, also, as the differences between the purposes of our performing edition and the *Novello* edition.

For years those of us who have performed the Bach Passions together have been grateful for—and astounded at—the preface by Arthur Mendel to the G. Schirmer edition of *The Passion According to St. John*. In addition to providing the most authoritative musical text and an improved English translation of the work, Mendel gives us in a 50-page preface what seems to me the most succinct, complete and well-reasoned advisement on Bach style and performance practice that exists in the English language.

I mention this primarily to emphasize the gratitude and respect I feel for the (1991) *New Novello Choral Edition* of *Elijah* edited by Michael Pilkington. The performance practices of Mendelssohn's Classical-Romantic symphonic music are not so lost in historical antiquity as Baroque custom. The completion of *Elijah* and its first performance, Mendelssohn conducting, were commissioned by the Birmingham (England) Festival of Music, and Mr. Pilkington's principal attention is therefore directed to the assembly of the text, the translation into English and the inevitable musical adjustments which resulted.

I hope deeply that any of you who may look forward to conducting *Elijah* will turn to this edition for historical background, details of Biblical sources and fascinating fragments of correspondence between Mendelssohn and his librettist while the work was in progress.

This edition from which we are working is, of course, not calculated to serve historical or musicological ends. Its purposes are very limited and entirely practical. Our rationale is that choral singing (like all musical performance) has a whole series of specific disciplines for which the composer of the work cannot and should not be held accountable. In concerted vocal music a good many of those are disciplines of enunciation—the metric allotment and placement of the sounds of speech. – But there are also completely *musical* adjustments of duration, accentuation, articulation, dynamics, balances, tonal color and tempo—and their interactions—which must be meticulously and unanimously executed if music's community of utterance is to be achieved.

If these disciplinary details are prescribed by a conductor only during rehearsal, 200 singers will notate them 150 different ways, and the remaining 50 singers won't write—or remember—anything at all. Under these conditions rehearsal time is doubled, music's high purpose mongrelized and lives wasted.

– So, the first function of our edited scores is to detail the various informations noted above—enunciative disciplines, musical durations and articulations, sectional balances, dynamics, etc.—in order that our disciplines are unanimous, consistent and accumulative, and allow the chorus of the many to become the heart of the whole. There are, also in the present edition, some departures from the original English text—though fewer than those which were in our editions of some years ago.

There is every indication that Mendelssohn took a very serious and detailed interest in the translation prepared for him by William Bartholomew, and the letters between the two of them form some of the most stimulating aspects of Mr. Pilkington's preface.

I want particularly, this week, to quote to you an exchange between Mendelssohn and the Rev. Julius Schubring, the original librettist (whom Bartholomew translated)—along with the designates of King James.

Last week I had a sentence or two which referred to the dramatic-narrative Old Testament texts as inspiring music superior at least in eloquence to the "sermonizing" or "moralizing" texts. And I referred also to the *Widow's Scenes* as being possible to omit from a performance sequence—without, I suggested, unduly harming the essential story-line of the first part of the oratorio. (In nearly 50 years of hearing and performing *Elijah,* I've heard these movements [6–9] only on recordings.)

"Lo and behold!" my joy this week to run across the following exchange between Mendelssohn and Schubring (noted by Pilkington, but quite forgotten in 1993 when I began thinking toward this series of performances and the recording).

Schubring to Mendelssohn, 31 October 1838:

"I have sought throughout—although it is not always possible—to introduce pieces, not merely suitable to the particular situation in question, but such as might awaken an echo in the hearts of the hearers. . . . The thing is becoming . . . an interesting, even a thrilling picture, but far from edifying the heart of the listener. . . . Therefore you must carefully consider whether . . . you prefer to turn away from church music (i.e. music which refreshes, consoles) and create a tone picture. . . . If not, we must diligently set to work to keep down the dramatic, and raise the second element, and always aim at this."

Mendelssohn's reply is dated 2 November (2 days later—bless his doctrine-prickin' heart):

"I figured to myself Elijah as a thorough prophet, such as we might again require in our own day—energetic and zealous, but also stern, wrathful and gloomy: a striking contrast to the court rabble and popular rabble—in fact in opposition to the whole world, and yet borne on angel's wings. – But if I might make one observation, it is that I would fain see the dramatic element more prominent, as well as more exuberant and defined—appeal and rejoinder, question and answer, sudden interruptions, etc. . . .

"The omission of the passage of the Widow, and also of the raven is decidedly most advisable; and also the abridgement of the whole commencement, in order that the main points may be dwelt on to one's heart's content. . . .

"The dramatic element should predominate, as it should in Old Testament subjects. . . . The personages should act and speak as if they were living beings . . . and the contemplative and pathetic element, which you desire, ought to be entirely conveyed to our understanding by the words and mood of the acting personages."

Go get 'em, Felix! *Illegitimi non carborundum est.*

R

WOLFGANG AMADEUS MOZART

Mass in C Minor

October 6, 1987

Friends –

'Must say, first of all, thanks for the note-learning and note-teaching that's been done in my absence. Still, I'm sure it was satisfying to you—as it was to me—to have all the music and all the people back together again. – While it compounds the problems of articulation and simultaneity, and introduces new problems of balance, it's the clearest demonstration I know of the principle of the "whole being greater than the sum of its parts."

Somehow, all the *extra*-meanings of music—those which defy adequate verbal expression—arise out of music's *wholeness* (which has the same word root as *holiness*), and even then emerges more fully as the wholeness becomes a more *perfect* wholeness.

Every measure of the *C Minor Mass* is an undeserved miracle, but I was struck again last night by two details: First, the entrance of the chorus after the solemnity of the opening five measures. Here are three measures of an arching and receding C minor chord, with voices entering as from distant "corners" of the earth (or the "hidden recesses" of the human mind) in waves of sound which, as they present no structural material, never will be heard again. – Overlapping waves of longing and urgency (which are actually interruptive) before the "substance" and architecture of the piece can really be presented. – What an extraordinary prominence to grant to the basic universal human cry. ("Help!—Won't *some*body help?")

Second: When the "Jesu Christe" comes (p. 56) before the "Cum Sancto Spiritu," it really enters not as we have experienced it in rehearsal (as an intro-duction to the fugue which follows), but textually as a continuation of the "Quoniam" and musically as a bridge to the "Cum Sancto." (Correctly punctu-ated, "Altissimus" in ms. 529 and "Christe" in ms. 547 both should be followed by commas.)

– But the point is not to correct punctuation. The point is not even that the three movements can really be performed without pause or breaking tempo (the half-note of "Quoniam" equalling the eighth of "Jesu" equalling the half-note of "Cum Sancto").

The point is the freshness, youthfulness, energy, enthusiasm, vitality, radi-ance and sense of victory in the six measures of "Jesu Christe." It comes after an E minor trio which also is confident and energetic, but without pause it bursts like an instant sunrise into a C major choral salutation in the most-rooted of four-part settings at very nearly the most emphatic of vocal sonorities. – And, it's all over in thirty seconds.

Now, everyone has to father his own ortho- or hetero-doxy, but what an heroic figure Mozart presents for our consideration!

Let's get the "Osanna" as clean as the "Cum Sancto" begins to be.

R

October 4, 1966

Isn't it astounding how vast a difference there is between even a computer-like vocal return of the information to be found in a line of printed music and the creative collaboration to which a great composer summons us.

In surface ways only "nothing" could be simpler than most of the music of the *Mass in C Minor*. – But how incredibly complex and difficult it is.

I'm not speaking now of the emotional, intellectual ponderings and prob-ings it provokes. There are these, to be sure.

But how does one really get the opening three choral measures to "sound?" – So that the successive soprano, alto, tenor, bass arcs are realized—rather than a blob of vocal silly putty?

How do we relate the two subjects in the *Kyrie* so they do not blur but comment on each other? How do we contrive the inside phrasings of the *Cum Sancto Spiritu* and establish the over-all dynamic force and flow so that we don't envelope ourselves and our listeners in four minutes of choral smog? How do we get two subjects to profile through the *Osanna* maze?

And of "simpler" things—where does how much of a crescendo happen for how long within what beat before the diminuendo takes place how fast?

These and a score of other questions per measure have to receive practical answers—if the work is finally to be sounded (in both senses).

It occurs to me that in this life those who have the most to say must leave the most unsaid. Here is a man who probably was the most literate musician in the history of music and he's had to leave most of it uninscribed. (I can't see this as a valid argument for tape music—just because it's a permanent ineradicable one-man show.) The point is that Mozart sends out a call for help. In direct propor-tion to the far reaches of his creative imagination are the delights and require-ments of our own creative participation.

In terms of sandpaper we're getting down to triple-O, and in terms of granite to linseed and pumice.

R

'Sorry about the snafu with the how-to-make-three-out-of-four-women's-sections, I had it all figured—I thought. I never could score satisfactorily with women in bunches. Here's the final, irrevocable and straight scoop for the three-part women's divisions in the Mozart *Mass:*

Alto: Numbers 301–360 inclusive,
Soprano II: Numbers 361–120 inclusive.
Soprano I: Numbers 121–480 inclusive.

FRANCIS POULENC

Stabat Mater

October 15, 1991

Friends –

This may be one of those "this-may-be-more-than-you-want-to-know-about-it" letters—but we may not meet again until performance week; so I write in brief concerning aspects of Poulenc's *Stabat Mater* which might be more accessibly approached during rehearsal.

Most of you will remember with enthusiasm Verdi's setting of the *Stabat Mater,* and would credit its evaluation in *The New Grove's Dictionary:* among the 19th century settings "the greatest is undoubtedly Verdi's (1898) . . . (who) was able to achieve a deep sincerity of utterance (as he did also in the *Requiem*) without renouncing a style perfected through years of experience in the opera house. . . . As in *Falstaff* and *Otello,* the expressive points are made with the utmost economy and there is no textual repetition. The result is probably the shortest setting of the *Stabat Mater* in the 19th century, and Verdi's example has been followed by most 20th century composers . . . Szymanowski's . . . Berkeley's and Poulenc's settings are outstanding."

You will recall that Verdi's setting was "non-stop" and mostly single-tempo—though it had clearly defined sections as regards dynamics, melodic structure and textual drama which influenced and qualified tempo—so that he was able to achieve variety *with* momentum.

Verdi's *Stabat Mater* performs at slightly over 12 minutes, Poulenc's at nearer to 33. Verdi's is a single movement work; Poulenc identifies 12 separate movements. Verdi's setting has no vocal solos; Poulenc's has significant soprano solos in movements VI, X and XII.

However, their orchestras are very much alike. – And both use the chorus—for the greater part—*rhetorically.* That is to say: *usually* the chorus—or (occasionally) a section of it—declaims the text unanimously, rather than imitatively or contrapuntally. Moreover, both are gifted writers for the human voice: Verdi, with a gigantic command of operatic *aria;* and Poulenc, with some of the most beautiful *songs* of the twentieth century.

Their works seem—to me—to differ mostly in two regards. The first is the use of *sequence.* Time after time Poulenc will repeat the final measure or measures of a two-measure or four-measure phrase for musical or textual emphasis. If he repeats it melodically or rhythmically it frequently will reach a new harmonic destination ([16] ms. 3–8). When he does not repeat text, he still is using the effect of musical reiteration to accumulate rhetorical emphasis. One of the grandest examples of this we reached late in last night's rehearsal (2 ms. before [47] through [48]). Both of these examples indicate an emotional insistence familiar to our century in the poetic public utterance of, for instance, a Martin Luther King, Jr. As *musical* "utterances" they are almost as far as possible removed from the arias or duets of J. S. Bach, wherein the entire musical form bears the emotional weight of the text, rather than the rhetorical and sequential repetition of a word or two, or a measure or two. Thus, it is not only Poulenc's choice of 12 movements—as against Verdi's choice of a single movement—which makes his setting longer than Verdi's. It is also his language of musical sequence and rhetorical repetition.

This is not to say that economy of time in textual setting is proof of excellence in musical composition. (You may recall that in Bach's *B Minor Mass* it takes him three movements and twenty minutes to set three words: *Kyrie, Christe* and *eleison.*) It simply is necessary that we understand Poulenc's musical language in order to achieve its honest performance. Except for Movement VIII, a beautiful *a cappella* motet, his reliance on homophonic repetition of text, rather than polyphonic development, means that we have to be *exaggeratedly* careful of *all the sounds* of speech. We cannot hide in a multiplicity of simultaneous texts, wherein "meaning" is to be found in the over-all musical design. Here we must speak with unanimity and faultless declamation.

The second major difference to be found in the two *Stabat Maters*—to me— has to do with harmonic density and texture. Except for three and one-half measures—wherein he writes two tenor parts—Verdi writes only for conventional SATB chorus—with frequent use of unison chorus, or unison men or women.

Poulenc does occasionally use unison vocal sections ([1] and [21]), but generally his textures and his harmonies are dense, and allow—or encourage— surprising harmonic movement.

The most primitive traditional harmony builds chords by adding to a given note the third and fifth notes above it. If one adds to these—as Poulenc frequently does—the 7th, 9th, 11th and even 13th notes above, one has a chord of seven notes—which is all the notes "they is" in a conventional scale (the octave being a repetition of Note #1). Now, consider two things:

First, fluency of motion from one chord to the next rests in large measure upon notes which the two chords may have in common. If one has seven notes to choose from, there are a lot of new and strange places one can go.

Second, clearly there are low and high limits to the human voice and, also, good melodies may range at least over an octave and a third. (A tough one, like our national anthem, will "free-range"—as the menu says—over an octave and a fifth.) Therefore, if one tries to give a melody some profile, and still desires to enrich its harmonies by chords of the 7th and 9th, the accompanying notes may find themselves pretty closely jammed together. – And since, also, in *all* voices, pitches in the middle to upper range can be sung many times louder than pitches in the lower to bottom half of the vocal range, it is a major problem to achieve enough *low* choral tone to balance a high melody—and even more difficult to balance one doubled by the soprano and tenor voices.

In Poulenc's *Stabat Mater* we can not merely reinforce the highest—or principal melodic—voice, allowing the orchestra to provide the fundamental harmonic matrix. From his 1937 a cappella *Mass* onward Poulenc has provided a richness of choral textures even in his works accompanied by symphony orchestra. To get that texture to sound through the color-range-dynamic capabilities of a twentieth-century symphony orchestra, I believe, never has been done. Even recordings do not reveal it; and, by placement of microphones and manipulation of dials, one would think that could have been possible. (Decades ago we did the U.S. premiere of the work in Carnegie Hall and, as I look at that old score and its editings, I realize very well indeed that we did not come close to a proper performance. – 'My fault.)

Actually, last night's rehearsal for the first five-sixths of it was beginning to show some of the necessary disciplines and sonorities, and I should not have been so cheerless at our breakdown on Movement IX. 'Sorry.

As with many of you, I believe that this chorus should "begin to rehearse" where other choruses "stop." We set our own standards—and they should get higher and higher with each and every work.

'See you—one of these days.

R

SERGEI RACHMANINOFF

The Bells

October 11, 1995

Friends –

Sorry to miss you last Monday night—partly because I have some revisions for the Rachmaninoff text of Movement III which, I think, will facilitate its singability and heighten its drama—but, also, because I just miss you.

Below, find the textual changes. They are written below your printed sylla-bles; and there should be no problem writing in the few, simple changes. Have your music neatly and clearly marked for Monday night's rehearsal. (We cannot afford time to do it there.)

Rachmaninoff *The Bells,* Movement III

Measures, Vocal Part

43–46 (S-A-T-B): Hear them, hear them/Lis—ten, lis—ten

79–81 (A-T-B): How be—seech—ing

84–87 (S-A-T-B) How des—pair—ing

91 (A-T-B): 'neath the/Thru the

93–94 (S): How be—seech – ing/How des—pair—ing

99–100 (S-A-T-B): In af – fright/Streams the fright

115 (B): In af – fright/Streams the fright

124–125 (T) In af – fright/Streams the fright

138–139 (B only) In af – fright/Streams the fright

138–139 (T & A) Keep the text: "in affright"

142 (A) Keep the text: "in affright"

142–143 (B) in af – fright/Streams the fright

180–182 (S-A-T-B) ruth-less con-fla-gra-tion/fi—e—ry dam-na-tion

215–216 (S-A-T-B) flick-'ring/sear—ing

218 (B) flick-'ring/sear—ing

327 (S-A-T-B) war—ring/ghost-ly

Thank you.

Now, it has been rare indeed, in recent years, that we have had to add to projected rehearsal time for our symphonic appearances. – But, I think you will agree that with this program some additional hours are needed to meet our standards of performance and recording.

Ann Jones, Nola and Norman suggest that, rather than a completely new and extra rehearsal, we add a half-hour to our regular remaining Monday night rehearsals, and that rehearsals with orchestra (Tuesday, October 31, and Wednesday, November 1) be called for 7:00 o'clock, as is our normal schedule for performance nights.

It seems to me that—given sufficient home-study—this could work.

Thank you again. Start an anti-hurricane prayer-group today.

R

January 13, 1983

Dear ᴀꜱᴏᴄiates:

(How's that for an acronym coming home to its roster? 'Doesn't presume as much as "dear friends," either.)

You certainly can learn a lot of notes in a short time when you put your minds and best habits to it!

Structurally, I think it would have to be admitted that Rachmaninoff's *The Bells* is closer to a whirlwind romance than an arranged marriage.

He's so finger-lickin' nimble harmonically that he can disappear into one dark corner of the keyboard forest one instant, only to reappear a moment later having passed completely through the mirrors of chromaticism.

It's a musical kaleidoscope of sonorities, colors, haste, waits, rovings and Russian-soullogisms, related to its national counterpart—Stravinsky's *Psalms*—much as odd is to even and Cain to Abel. What a paroxysm of incompatibility to wed them, for three wild nights in February at least, to Mozart's heavenly-bodied *Sinfonia Concertante*! Such match-missing surely should have been saved for the day of the Fool next April or the Year of the Leap a twelfth-month hence.

In addition to right notes—on which a beginning was begun Monday night—the two elements which will make *The Bells* absolutely irresistible to Atlanta's uniquely sophisticated audiences are, first, a convulsion of declamation, a rage of enunciation, a veritable fury of text. While the words do not in every instance fit their assigned notes as naturally as a shell its egg—being an English translation of a Russian adaptation of an American poem—they are, by and large, great words, and can survive both impeccability and ecstasy.

The second channel of resistless enticement will be available to us only as we are able to forget—or master—the vocal decorum descended from puritanical mortifications through Southern gentilities and summon forth (as the saying goes) deeper throats. – A gorge of growling, a surfeit of shrieks, a hullabaloo of howling, a veritable Babel of ululation.

Have you had enough?

Well-ordered choral performances of *The Bells* are recorded by the London Symphony Chorus under Previn and the St. Louis Symphony Chorus under Slatkin. For excess of animal vitality and essence of Poe, you may want to listen to the RSFSR Russian Chorus and the Moscow Philharmonic under Kondrashin.

Spasseba bolshoi,

R

Vespers

May 14–15, 1993

Opening Remarks at Spivey Hall

On this season's overview of Nineteenth Century Choral Music, we brought you in October the male choruses of Franz Schubert, representing, roughly, the first third of the century; in January a rather comprehensive selection of motets, waltzes and songs for mixed voices of Johannes Brahms, representing the mid-century through the 'seventies and early 'eighties; and tonight we are privileged to undertake Rachmaninov's "All-Night Vigil." Those of you who have baby sitters who expect you home before dawn may wish to step outside for a few moments to make a phone call. (Lest you be frightened by the title, be apprised that the 15 musical numbers take but 65 minutes in the singing.)

Though written during the early years of World War I (1915), with the restrictions which Rachmaninov imposed upon himself to insure their suitability for liturgical performance, their musical idiom clearly "looks backward"—to the 500-year-old orthodox Znamenny chant as clothed in the loving 19th century language of "the last great representative of Russian Romanticism."

It is indeed strange that these magnificent works were all but unknown by American musical enthusiasts until recent years. We knew the *Cherubim Songs* of Bortniansky and Tchaikovsky, the *Carol of the Bells* of Leontovich, and *Heavenly Light* of Kopylov, and a few others; but Rachmaninov's giant masterpiece lay in American obscurity until an Angel Records executive brought Shvesnikov's remarkable Melodya recording to the United States in the 1970's.

Ranging from unison voices to eight and twelve parts, and moving from simple chant through variation to improvisation, the *Vespers* sometimes can be a complex work to put together, but it speaks so directly and simply to the heart, that one of the recurrent difficulties in rehearsal is that we become so emotionally touched—that it is next to impossible to continue singing.

Do not be ashamed if at times your eyes fill with tears (it's good for you).

And it almost certainly is best if we withhold applause until the *Vespers* are complete. We will not be insulted if even then you do not applaud.

The melodies of the bells—sketched by Norman Mackenzie—are built upon the ancient chants; and are calculated to give the singers' voices and postures occasional rest, and the listeners a few moments for reflection, or a glance at the general sentiment of the upcoming text.

For me, it would be sad if the listener became so involved matching the Russian text word by word with its translation that one missed the almost unbearable poignancy of the music.

As the college year approaches its close—and before beginning this evening's concert—it is absolutely imperative that we take a moment to thank the retiring president of Clayton State College, Dr. Harry Downs, under whose creative guidance and hospitality these concerts—and this chorus—came into existence.

Dr. Downs, your co-workers and deputies simply could not have been more hospitable or helpful. Every visit to the campus has renewed our gratitude to you for making it possible for us to study, enjoy and perform the wonderful works of Durufle, Ives, Britten, Paulus, Schubert, Brahms and Rachmaninov that have been our concert fare.

If we may, though it be informal, may we dedicate this evening to the pleasures and accomplishments of your retirement in fond hopes that you keep very much in touch with these programs you so handsomely initiated.

FRANZ SCHUBERT

Mass in E-flat

January 25, 1989

Friends –

The Schubert *Mass in E-Flat*—his last of six—while offering page after page of extraordinary beauty and rare textual illumination, offers also in its contrapuntal writing some of his most abrupt, difficult, possibly even "unconvincing" and "over-extended" modulatory passages, as well as a host of interpretative problems which center mainly around tempo and tempo relationships.

We'll begin today with the *Kyrie,* and I'll try to fill in the later movements as we go along.

KYRIE

Because of textual sequence ("Kyrie eleison . . . Christe eleison . . . Kyrie eleison") almost any *Kyrie* falls naturally into an A-B-A musical form. Schubert's is no exception.

A

    1–10, Introduction
    11–48, "Kyrie" Block A (38 ms.)

B

    49–88 "Christe" Block B (40 ms.)

A

    89–126 "Kyrie" Block A (38 ms.)
    127–164 Codas (#1 and #2) (38 ms.)

Let me call your attention first (in a single-tempo movement) to the numerical balance of the three main choral blocks. (They are even more closely proportioned if one considers that ms. 49–50 belong to both A and B.)

This symmetry certainly is somewhat diminished by the fact of a 38-measure Coda (in two almost equal parts) and a 10-measure Introduction. In particular, the Coda, a developmental extension of "A" material, almost forces the movement into *four* equal blocks and—what is more important—adds to the emotionally *ruminative* quality of the work.

Sources of perplexity for the performer lie in the tension that exists between the harmonic movement (which is really very slow—sometimes remaining unchanged for matters of four complete measures—which therefore wishes to hurry) and the melodic and accompanimental motives (which move in quarters, eighths, triplet-eights, and even sixteenths—therefore suggesting a more considered, leisurely pace). The bass motive in the first 17 measures, in particular, suggests weight and solemnity; and the triplets underlying the *Christe* suggest majesty. For me, the proper tempo is one which is "just a little too slow" (quarter-note = 88–92?).

There are two other matters which intrigue me. The most conventional modulations and/or changes of key for succeeding sections of a musical composition are those which proceed to the dominant or sub-dominant tonalities before returning to the tonic. Schubert loves to juxtapose tonal relationships based on thirds. For instance, at the end of the *Christe* (m. 77) he has arrived at a D major tonality reaffirmed by a double plagal (IV–I) cadence (ms. 71–78). He follows this immediately by a B-flat seventh eight-bar period, a major third (or flat 6th) below his D major in order to recapitulate in his original key of E-flat.

In miniature the same thing happens in m. 8: measure 7 is an E-flat second inversion, and measure 8 is a C-flat seventh chord (the A-natural doubling as B-double-flat), a major third (and a flat 6th) below the E-flat tonic. Such changes force an abrupt change in function of the notes which the chords have in common, and account in great part, it seems to me, for the emotional stab or flow of energy which they provoke.

Note, also, that the *Christe* (m. 49) which begins—expectantly—in B-flat major (dominant of E-flat) hurls itself through a rapid succession of dominants to C major (E-flat, B-flat, F and C) in measure 57; it then substantially repeats the process (quasi C minor, G minor-major, and D-A-D) before its Schubertian fall to B-flat seventh in measure 81.

This kind of information surely is more than many of you really want to know. The point, however, is that after a rapid series of energetic and majestic modulations based on fourths and fifths, a modulation based on a falling third relationship has a startling emotional effect. It is quieting, ruminative, somehow inward and retrospective.

We will see that these third relationships grow more and more significant—and complex—in later movements. (We even may find that in the fugues of the *Gloria* and *Credo* they become *too* persistent and *too* complex and diminish the proportions and effectiveness of these forms.)

But first—we'll get them right before we judge their worth!

The words that come to mind for the *Kyrie* of Schubert's *Mass in E-Flat* are contemplation, meditation . . . the sweet and gentle sorrows of human existence, spurred by a somewhat ominous and persistent pedal motif . . . arching to more impassioned and extroverted cries to the more approachable *Man*/God . . . and subsiding to the original contemplative sadness . . . twice reconsidered and re-examined in a coda which fades into silence.

'See you Monday,

R

IGOR STRAVINSKY

Symphony of Psalms

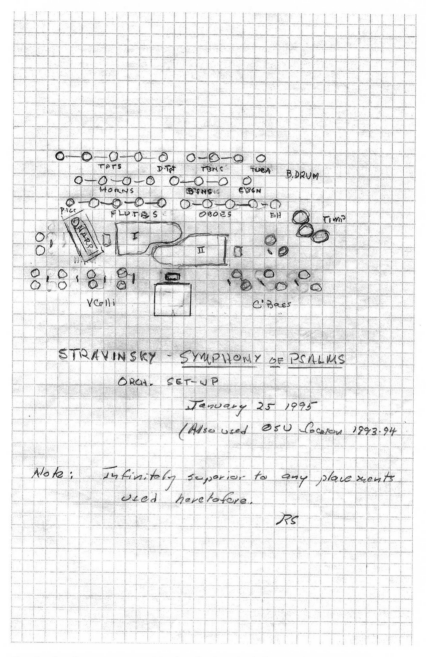

Sketch of orchestra stage positioning for Stravinsky's *Symphony of Psalms*

February 24, 1993

CBDNA Seminar
Ohio State University

Mr. Kirschhoff – Ladies and gentlemen of the CBDNA – Fellow students –

Good afternoon.

The Secretary of the Music Director Emeritus of the Atlanta Symphony Orchestra has a standard line she uses to ward off unwary program organizers like Professors Casey and Kirschhoff, who scheduled this satellite event in your otherwise heavenly procedures: "Mr. Shaw," she says, "only opens his mouth to change his socks."

In general, conductors talk at length only on three occasions: One, during rehearsals—to the scarcely restrainable delight of professional musicians; two, to committees composed in the main of patrons and matrons of a certain age, whose children have left home and thus allowed them to assume responsibility for the rest of mankind; and three, to convocations like this of professionals, educators and students who have gathered together with others of their species as much perhaps for self-protection as self-enhancement.

Their instructions were that we should spend the better part of the next hour in a consideration of Stravinsky's *Symphony of Psalms:* its musical nature and materials, and its preparation for performance.

So far as its preparation for performance is concerned, my advices are very brief: get someone like Craig Kirschhoff to prepare the orchestra and someone like Jim Gallagher to prepare the chorus. – And, also, accepting one's own proper share of responsibility, be painstakingly and laboriously clear about what information one may have accumulated through the years concerning matters of tempi, balances, articulation, color, dynamics, textual concerns and—of course— structure.

I did have the pure and immense privilege of preparing the chorus on three occasions on which Mr. Stravinsky conducted the *Psalm Symphony*—those with the CBS Symphony, which was Bernard Herrmann's orchestra in the '40's and '50's. On one occasion, also, I prepared the chorus for a recording of his *Mass* for voices and 10 wind instruments—with a wind ensemble conducted in the same early days by Joseph Fabranini for RCA-Victor.

I can recall from those occasions two or three principal impressions. Because we knew it to be a very special occasion in our musical lives, these impressions were also discussed by members of the chorus and there was a remarkable consensus.

First: though the hand and arm gestures were precise, specific and sharply angled—one had the impressions that he was conducting with his ears. He was listening to music, not "making" it. – Scarcely "instructing" it. (The "worst seat in the house" is the podium. How difficult it is to "hear" and "direct.")

Second: from his face and his gesture one could catch little of expressive musical plasticity or of personal emotional involvement. – No compelling swelling or receding of sound, but severity and side-by-side stark contrast. – In moments of textual joy or sorrow, nothing of the actor's art of communication, and not a hint in the countenance but a listening—and a hearing. – For one felt he was hearing both inside and beyond the sounds which anyone would hear—or even beyond those present in the room.

I should like, if I am able, to discuss three matters which relate to the *Symphony of Psalms* and, following that, say some things concerning the nature of music and the arts and the responsibilities of people in our profession to them and to our time and humankind.

> Concerning Stravinsky's *Symphony:*
> First: its general structure.
> Second: One thing we can infer about Stravinsky's musical language—from this work.
> Third: Given these understandings, what we should do about preparing the score and the parts.

> Number One: General (large-scale) Structure
> Though Stravinsky did not wear his religion on his sleeve or bumper-sticker, nobody else chose these texts. We are obliged to consider first what *he began* with.

MOVEMENT I

> Psalm 38, Verses 13–14
> "Hear my prayer, Lord, and my asking for pardon.
> With thy ears receive my tears.
> Do not remain silent. For a new-comer am I to you.
> And a stranger like my fathers.
> Forgive me that I may be soothed (cooled)
> Before I go away and am no more."

> Let me list the individual events which catch my eye and ear.
> 1. Begins in A minor; ends in G major—no big shock
> 2. What an A minor!

– Piano chord states its delight
– Left and right hands inverted
– Presence of 2 thirds
1st hint of the importance of minor 3rd

3. Immediately subsequent arpeggios

B-flat 7 and G7
– No common tone with BG7—far removed
– Common tone of 2 arpeggios: D, F (minor third)
– Note that G7 is a group of thirds when in root position.

4. Dual (opposite) articulation of Ostinati

Second hint of Piano Articulation ("Decay")

5. Chorus enters as a chant: 2 notes only

Phrase: 2 ms. + 2 x 1 ms.

6. Soprano has Chorus chant augmented both as to pitch and to time.
7. Descending Oboes: 4 Beats + 5 beats + 6 beats
8. Ostinato in Augmentation and Diminution
9. "B" section introduces wide skips

– Voices
– Horns

10. (ms. 4) Ostinato against much contrasted Theme 'A'

MOVEMENT II

"Waiting (expectantly) I waited for the Lord,
And He inclined to me, and he heard my prayers,
And He led me out of the lake of misery, and out of the dregs of mud.
And He set my feet upon a rock, and directed my steps,
And He has put in my mouth a new song,
A hymn to our God.
Many will see, and will fear,
And will hope in the Lord."

Things which catch my eye and ear.
1. ms. 1 "Enchainez" (French) "Linking"

– Makes final chord of Movement I A dominant to C minor

– And Movement I a "prelude."

2. ms. 1–4 and almost entire Fugue Theme a direct quote of Movement I Ostinato.

3. ms. 1–4, How displacement metrically affects harmonic implications

4. ms. 1–7, How it suggests by tempo and repetition "waiting patiently"

Let me digress for a moment:

Should it be true that what men have called "God" is the "Creative Principle," the "Creative Force" (no longer anthropomorphic, no longer a "He-God," "She-God" or "It-God," but a "that which creates"), then whether or not we feel that Stravinsky wrote a "religious," a "sacred" piece of music is of no matter. Even, whether Stravinsky thought he wrote a sacred symphony is of no matter. He was a part of "that which creates." And if the Judaic-Christian concept/myth/metaphor that man was made in the "image of God" have even poetic truth, then its "reverse" is equally true, or, as Robert Bridges has it in his Testament of Beauty, "both these truths are one."

That fugue subject just flat-out "waits patiently for the Lord." And, occasionally, words and music can hint at an "attitude" or an "idea" or a "hope" common to both but beyond the capabilities of either to "hint at" or "aspire to."

Further impressions:

5. What begins for 2 measures so securely as a *double*-fugue becomes, in triumph of creativity over scholarship, an enormously moving Second Fugue with only fragments of Fugue #1 as questing, tentative reminders of the original meditative mists which opened the movement.

6. The stretto exposition for unaccompanied voices accumulative rising sixths (Soprano), m. 2 (Alto), m. 3 (Tenor) and the cadence into B-flat have to be some of the most beautiful vocal writing in this century.

7. The accumulative impact of repetition and alternation of the principle motives (now given "ostinato" recognizability) and the thrust of the B-flat and G minor tonalities into E-flat major.

8. The use of the second and the sixth of E-flat major to enrich the E-flat ending, but also to lead it naturally into the C major/E-flat tonalities of the Third Movement.

9. The 3-octave unison ending of the chorus which will develop enough of the 2nd partial to make one think an entire section is singing B-flat.

MOVEMENT III

"Alleluia
Praise the Lord in His sanctuary
Praise Him in the Firmament of His power
Praise the Lord
Praise Him in His excellent powers.
Praise Him according to the multitude of His magnitudes.
Alleluia.
Praise Him with timpani and chorus
Praise Him with strings and organ
Praise Him with cymbals well-sounding
Praise Him with cymbals of jubilation
All ye that have breath, praise the Lord.
Alleluia."

Events which catch my eye and ear:
1. Piling-up of overlapping ostinati

1.   F1/Piano/Vc/CB 3 beats only
2.   Women's Voices: parallel thirds: 12 beats
3.   Horns: 8 Beats
4.   Men's Voices: 8 Beats

2. The presence of the B-flat no surprise: a resultant from the low C of the modern Contrabass with its extension.
3. Chant Theme: the omnipresent third—but major.
4. New CB/Vc ostinato—no doubt feels related to Movement I VC/CB ostinato even though different intervals.
5. Doubling of Piano/F1/Ob/Tpt/Vc

a—to use ictus of piano
b—spaced with rests to achieve maximum accentuation.

6. Further ostinatos—Repeated phrases: Winds and Strings are quasi-ostinatos, Timpani and Keyboard—carefully contrived.
7. Chant now in voices: Stravinsky willing to implode/explode text to achieve a primitive, pre-historic, pre-Biblical atmosphere of praise to the "Unknown." (Indian prayer from American prairies.)
8. A quasi-"B" Bass melody against an ascending chant—*very* much in the manner of Movement I.
9. Overlapping ostinatos: particularly S/B 2 ms., phrase against A/T 4 ms., phrase.

10. Wonderful appearance of the stately "grave" motto—at a moment of seemingly irresistible forward thrust.

11. Heightening hysteria (Ezekiel Saw de Wheel!) of the Cadenza with the addition of the Horn.

12. Subsiding of Chant—preparation for D major fugue by F-sharp Bass triads.

13. Articulation of Fugue

    – Indicating Stravinsky's attitude toward "passing"-tones and "passing"-metrics.

14. The most beautiful peroration in all of 20th century music—full of ostinato fragments—and one real one in Timpani and Pianos.

15. The closing of our Time-Space

    – Occasionally one can hear the B-flat in the final chord in an evocative acoustic.

We were to consider still what might be—from a study of the Symphony of Psalms—cardinal elements (or principles) of Stravinsky's musical language and performance practice. I think now of four.

First: In terms of sonority, there is a very special quality to Stravinsky's "ictus"—the initiation of pitched sound—and its decay. Time after time after time he doubles an attack by wind or string sonority with the percussive attack of the piano doubling the identical notes. Time after time he will double a legato melodic passage or ostinato with a second identical instrument playing the same notes but with a stopped or staccato articulation. In the final three measures of *Psalms* he writes commas between the choral statement of Do'mi'num. He writes rests between the syllables of vir//tutibus, sanc//tis and e//jus. His most frequent dynamic markings could well be *sfp staccato*.

It may be fair to attribute this affection for the sforzando and its subsequent decay to Stravinsky's regard for and long acquaintance with the piano. But even that does not account altogether for the difference between how his orchestral music sounds with piano as a part of the orchestra and how other commendable composers, reaching to imitate, fail to integrate the keyboard sonorities into the orchestral fabric. With Stravinsky, it all fits.

He constantly struggles towards an articulation which allows even the smallest metric units an independence of articulation. A nineteenth century legato or a vocal portamento is simply foreign to his language.

Think of the opening of Movement II: the initial notes of the fugue subject are separated by commas, but even the notes which follow—slurred by twos—must have a shortening of the second note (as though it were staccato) to phrase correctly; and even the later 32nd notes demand their "space in time" as inviolate.

Thus, perhaps, Stravinsky does not so much divide time as he multiplies it. He accumulates time. His larger units are molecular accretions of tiny particles—atoms—of time.

Number Two: This means that qualities of tempo must be absolutely inviolate. There can be no personal monkey-ing around with tempo, once it is correctly stated.

He did not always perform his works according to his original tempo markings. None of us should hold him to this. – But within his capabilities as a conductor—and they were many—once he had established a tempo he held it.

As in the Second Movement fugue—the beat is 32 to a measure—and any infraction or departure is instant chaos.

Think again how difficult it is to slow down the three measures which precede 20 in III to allow the Soprano fugue subject to enter entirely naturally and inevitably.

Number Three: A third aspect of Stravinsky's composition depends also upon this inviolability of tempo. It is the abiding and recurrent presence of short thematic fragments, many of which become so repetitive as to become ostinatos. We have noted time after time in each of the movements the presence and use of these fragments, their varying durations, placed in motion, offer a kaleidoscope of harmonic permutations. It may signal their importance to note that the opening 4-note theme of Movement II—in addition to its use in the fugue occurs no fewer than [????]

A fourth principle, it seems to me, is the absolute avoidance of any sentimentality.

For example, in the first movement at #4 and at #7, I had edited for the Oboe I a slight crescendo in ms. 1 and a slight diminuendo in ms. 2, followed by a 2-beat crescendo and a 2-beat diminuendo in measures 3 and 4, simply to suggest that while ms. 1–2 were a 2-measure phrase, measures 3 and 4 were 2 1-measure phrases.

The players, hospitably trying to please their guest conductor, obliged with slightly two much crescendo and slightly too much diminuendo. – And the phrases instantly became César Franck (another good French composer). We had to remove any editorial amendment as unsuitable and harmful.

For whatever reasons inherent in his music, and no matter what disturbing (to conductors) inferences we may draw from it, Stravinsky's music would seem to be at its best when offered chastely—without the intrusion of a second and "interpreting" personality. As conductors, we may be allowed to worship with the listeners—but we must not be seen to do so. And in no way must his vision be refracted through our "aura."

In retrospect, I have the sense that his near-scowling impassivity while he conducted was to remove *himself* from that which he knew to be his *better self.*

Isn't that a provocative picture of *The Creator?* – Removing himself from his creation (perhaps, even, unsure of the whence it came)—scowling in awe. "What hath God wrought?" – On the Supreme One gazing in fear at man: "My God! What have I done!"

There was a third matter; and it had to do with the preparation of materials—the orchestral and vocal parts.

Mr. Szell used to say to the Cleveland Orchestra, "Gentlemen, we begin to rehearse where others leave off." – And at least in one sense it was true, for the orchestra played from George Szell's own parts: and each part was so carefully edited with minute crescendi and diminuendi, with qualifications of dynamics to achieve balance, with nuances of tempo, with articulations and bowings that—were an orchestra and every player in it capable of reading all the information at sight—a first reading for the Cleveland Orchestra equalled a performance for most orchestras.

No conductor has the ability to direct each instrument's every nuance of balance, articulation, dynamic or dramatic color, but the guide to all these matters—or, at least, the guide to the player's creative participation in all these matters—can be put in the performer's part. This is hours upon hours of a conductor's preparation and of a staff of librarians' time. – But it accomplishes three extraordinary things: One, it saves hundreds of man-hours of rehearsal time (thousands, even, a season). Two, it invites the creative effort of the player to listen for the reasoning behind the editing. And three, it signals that the players' first accountability is to the composer and his score—not to the conductor.

Everyone will understand that Beethoven's responsibility is not putting into the score all the nuances of performance. His responsibility is to write his Tenth Symphony. We are the ones who must do the nitty-gritty work which will allow the machine to run, the flower to bloom, the worm to become a butterfly.

Do not let a single composer's dynamic mark to go by without indicating precisely when it decays or blooms—how far, for how long. If the mark is forte, should it be mezzo-forte, poco forte, sforzando forte, *fp, fmp, fmf*? Should it be marcato forte, sostenuto forte or forte cantabile? If it is a quarter note, is it staccato, semi-staccato, marcato, sostenuto, slurred or separate?

Surely, one can over-mark. One will find how much marking helps and how much gets in the way—but we are losing our chief tool to excellence of performance if we leave these questions to be discussed at rehearsal. They are the means by which a large orchestra becomes a chamber music group, by which an amateur symphony chorus becomes an expert madrigal ensemble, and by which we conductors cease to stand between the composer and the audience.

March 2, 1983

Thoughts After Your Extraordinarily Beautiful Performances of Stravinsky's
Symphony of Psalms

> When I was almost a young man, singing in the choir of the
>   First Christian Church on the northeast corner
>   of "A" and Vine in the little Southern California town
>   of Ontario,
> I must say our God was magnified each and every Sunday morning
>   according to an entirely different scenario.
>
> Even the words of something so obviously foreign to God and man
>   as *Symphonie de Psaumes*
> Could only have interested a Deity bedizened by jewels, gold,
>   marble, incense and the generally idolatrous customs
>   of a small group of scribes and Pharisees
>   who wore dresses and lived with each other
>   and maybe even women on the other side of the world
>   in a place called Rome.
>
> And, so for the music of his symphony, there certainly was
>   no way you could expect the God who gave us
>   Plymouth Rock, Chautauqua and the Boy Scouts of America
>   to respond to anything so inappropriate and
>   absolutely appalling,
> Certainly not the God of something as comforting and beautiful
>   as Softly and Tenderly you know Who's Calling.
>
> But, now that I'm somewhat older and have been exposed
>   to several different varieties of religious experience
>   —intellectual, aesthetic and emotional,
> It becomes a little easier as time goes on to distinguish between
>   those aspects of worship which are still humbly seeking,
>   and those which are largely self-promotional.
>
> And, I want to say to somebody, even if it's only in a
>   chorus weekly-letter,
> Year by year Stravinsky's kind of God is sounding better and better.
>
>   Alleluia, you-all-ya,

R

GIUSEPPE VERDI

Requiem, Quattro Pezzi Sacri

January 10, 1990

Friends –

When it comes to a "Final Four," who even comes close to the record of Verdi?

Andrew Porter, writing in the *New Grove Dictionary,* dismisses the *Ave Maria* as "slight," but acknowledges that the four as a group "form no unworthy end to Verdi's career."

I must say that I find the *Ave Maria* not only fascinating as an exercise in meticulously contrived accidentality—but genuinely and almost innocently expressive.

It seems to me that there are three major performance problems: the first and most obvious is that of keeping the performance "in tune": staying on a C major base of C = 523.3 while accommodating to the constant switching of harmonic polarities occasioned by the affluence of accidentals (something like 135 on the first two pages). For singers, A-sharp simply is not B-flat; and in theory, at least, if we sang the wrong sequence of "just" intervals vs. "tempered" (keyboard) intervals, we could stray so far from C major—and from each other—that we'd never find our way home.

A second performance problem is that of balancing the *cantus firmus* of the "enigmatic scale" against the emotional and melodic expressivity of the three other voices. So long as the whole-note scale is in the Soprano part (Verse IV) it is relatively easy for the listener to distinguish it; and when it is in the Bass voices it also has a natural focus; but when it is in the inner voices it is in danger of being lost. – At the same time, even when the major expressivity of the piece is harmonic, it is not necessarily the enigmatic scale which provides the critically expressive note. – And, equally true, the fragmentary melodies which appear in all three of the "concertizing" voices are inescapably geared most expressively to text. Somehow we have to achieve a balance which allows one to "see" (hear) the skeleton without removing one precious ounce of aphrodisiac flesh.

– Which leads to a third performance problem: that of *tempo.* Almost all performances of the *Ave Maria* are taken at a tempo considerably below the metronome marking of the composer. – Given the facts that a large symphonic chorus is particularly appropriate to the scale and instrumental forces of the *Te Deum,* and reasonably proper for the *Stabat Mater,* and since, also, the composer did not specify a smaller chorus for the *a cappella* pieces, the very bulk of the symphonic chorus argues against headlong flight and acrobatics. Moreover, it does take a certain amount of time to savour (let alone, tune) the chromaticism. – But, if the *Ave Maria* can be taken at or near Verdi's indicated tempo (quarter-note = 84) the piece has the chance of becoming an airy, buoyant madrigal, its burden of chromaticism levitated to artlessness, warmth and even geniality.

Concerning the four-part women's chorus, *Laudi alla Vergine,* more in later letters; but, at the moment, I doubt that there have been very many pieces of *a cappella* music which make the women's chorus sound so sumptuous. – Absolute essence of female vocal beauty. It's an extraordinary listening experience. One does not miss accompanying forces: – no need for bass-ier instruments or voices, – no need for interludes or introductions. – Just absolute rightness, completeness and elegance.

Porter calls the *Stabat Mater* Verdi's "Passion" (both in dramatic narrative and in modulation), a 'Dies Irae,' a 'Libera me' and an 'In Paradisum.' All of the Verdi "cliches" are there (oom-pah accompaniments, "panting" vocal articulations, etc.) and all of them are exactly right, as though invented just for this occasion.

The *Te Deum?* 'Ready for this? Verdi "rated them (*Quattro Pezzi Sacri*) highly, gave detailed instructions for their first performance (Paris 1898), and wished to have the score of the *Te Deum* buried with him."

No one came off well at last Monday's rehearsal. Verdi and Beethoven, of course, worst of all. – But, also, your conductor, who became so de-mented at the slowness of the learning process that he forgot the second of his axioms of rehearsal technique, namely: go slowly enough so that *no*body has the chance to memorize a mistake. (Part of his problem is that the more time he spends on rehearsal preparation—a lot last week—the more impatient he is to get to the "heart" of the music. Regard how knowledge in the very young lies in inverse ratio to wisdom.)

Part of the chorus's eternal problem is that, in any group of 200 singers there is such a diversity of musical expertise, if one scales rehearsal techniques and procedures to the capacities of the slowest member of the chorus, two-thirds of membership is going to leave town. – And this year, in addition, we have what I hope may prove to be a temporary problem: it is that one entire section of our chorus—which has a uniquely beautiful natural sound, possibly more beautiful than any of its forerunners—is slowing down the learning process of the other three sections. For the nonce this section will remain nameless—but, if it weren't for the nonce . . .

R

March 19, 1987

Department of incidental intelligence:

Bel canto (Italian: "fine singing").

"Few musical terms are as loosely used or open to as many different inter-pretations. Generally understood as indicating the elegant Italian vocal style of the 18th and early 19th centuries, the term did not enter the musical vocabulary until somewhat later. . . . Musicians began using the term only towards the middle of the 19th century, when a weightier vocal tone came to be prized, and less emphasis was placed on a light florid delivery. Among the reasons for this change in singing styles were an increase in the size of the orchestra, an expan-sion of the interior space of opera houses and concert halls, and the darkly dramatic subject matter of many 19th century librettos. . . .

"Rossini's concept of a *bel canto* singer involved three requirements: a natu-rally beautiful voice that was even in tone throughout its full range, careful train-ing that encouraged effortless delivery of florid music, and a mastery of style that . . . could only be assimilated from listening to the best Italian exponents."

– Owen Jander: *The New Grove,* 1980.

If any piece of music deserves fine singing, the Verdi *Requiem* is it. – And, obviously, a beautiful singing sound, "even in tone throughout the full range," with an "effortless delivery of florid music," in spite of a somewhat "weightier vocal tone" ain't soup for ducks.

I hope I'm not just seeing early daffodils—but some nice things happened at last Monday's rehearsal, both tonally and musically. If you will spend some time on the notes of the *Sanctus* and *Libera me* fugues, we can turn our full attention on Monday nights to the united and less trivial pursuits of beauty and beast-liness—in exemplary proportions.

Grr.

Cabaletta:
Verdi kept by his desk
    A composing machine –
(The recent invention
    Of mean-well Joe Green.)

As quick as a flash
    Or ahbrahcahdahbrah!
He put in a mass –
    And out popped an opera!

Canzona:

His operatic plots, it's clear,
  Were frequently intended
As parables of social wrongs
  And how to get them mended.

If he were writing wrongs today
  We'd call him humanistic:
He'd not a womanizer be,
  —But might be womanistic.

Ladies: Please mark the following text elisions in Verdi's *Laudi alla Vergine* –

Measure 3, beat 4: tu-o
Measure 4, beat 3: yo
Measure 7, beat 1: yoo
Measure 14, beat 1: yo
Measure 16, beat 1: leh-ee
Measure 20, beat 4: su-o
Measure 24, beat 3: su-ah.
Measure 27, beat 3: tu-o
Measure 29, beat 4 (S1): cu-ee
Measure 36, beat 1: yo
Measure 38, beat 1: o-ee
Measure 42, beat 2 (A1): o-ee
Measure 42, beat 3 (A1): ah-ee
Measure 54, beat 2: yah
Measure 57, beat 4: su-ah
Measure 61, beat 1: tu-ah
Measure 67, beat 4: eh-ah
Measure 67, beat 4 (A1): eh-ah
Measure 71, beat 2: yah
Measure 71, beat 4: ee-eh
Measure 78, beat 4: eh-ee
Measure 80, beat 2: ah-eh

WILLIAM WALTON

Belshazzar's Feast

April 5, 1984

Dear Group –

Re-studying Walton's *Belshazzar's Feast* has awakened a new respect for it. It's such a successful "mothuh" that one's first or youngest hunch is that—like a Hollywood score—it can't be quite as "serious," let's say, as Stravinsky's *Symphony of Psalms,* Bartók's *Cantata Profana* or Hindemith's *Lilacs.*

Of contemporary symphonic/choral literature, only Britten's *War Requiem* and Orff's *Carmina Burana* have enjoyed so ecstatic a popular reception.

Certainly it is true that the afore-mentioned works of Stravinsky, Bartók, Hindemith and Britten have textual psycho- and socio-logical and, perhaps, philosophical significances uncontested by *Carmina* and *Belshazzar.*

But, *Belshazzar* is one smart piece of writing: in its cyclical use of materials, its proportions of slow to fast to faster and of quiet to loud to louder, its contrasts of textures, colors and sonorities, and its achievement of dissonance without too great a sacrifice of melodic logic, it's the work of a very gifted professional composer—and "they ain't too many of 'em."

Britten is, of course, the century's greatest selector of texts for music. – And the twelve movements he has written to clothe the facets of his symphony to Spring range far and wide over the century's vocal and choral styles. He jumps back and forth and around semi-tone clusters, "artificial" scales, nearly electronic "loops" of motivic imitation and multiple tonalities—somewhat as though the work were an experiment, rather than a conclusion.

I think it's going to sound a lot simpler to the audience than it does to us. – And, besides, with *Belshazzar* everybody gets a new bat and glove on their way out of the ballpark.

Thank you for your rehearsals of the past weeks. I wish it were possible for me to be with you every time—feeling ready and randy. It's not only that I'm so damb dumb—though that's a big chunk of it; it's also that what began less than two decades ago as a part-time orchestra has grown so in size, tempo, density and duration—and occasional flavor with man and the Great Unknowing—that there's just more of it than there ever used to be.

You have almost all the notes of *Belshazzar* in the mind. Mostly what remains there is getting them in the voice (big, big voice) and up to tempo.

I look forward to working with you on the Britten. It has some fascinating problems in intonation and balance. Affectionately,

R

PART IV

PREACHING THE GOSPEL (OF THE ARTS)

The musical values that orchestrated Robert Shaw's career began at a young age. Though seminal in his youth, these basic tenets were developed, questioned, and fully explicated throughout the decades of his service to and in music.

The lectures and addresses reveal the passion of an amateur, the zeal of an evangelist, and the depth of a philosopher. Ever the raconteur, Shaw accents the main themes with anecdotes. But one element is constant—he makes everyone within the reach of his voice or the sight of his words think about music.

Shaw was by profession a conductor; he was by calling a minister who believed that "it is no less a divine miracle that the arts (flesh) become word (spirit)." He still teaches those who will hear him that the music we teach is a sacred trust because great art illumines and enlightens our humanity.

The speech to the MTNA delegates in 1955 outlines a cantus firmus that is richly embellished in the Norton Lectures at Harvard. The same theme of humanism seen through a divine spectrum of mystery, awe, and wonder is woven into the lectures at churches and schools—even commencement addresses!

It is this very passion leaping off the page that Robert Shaw brought to the concert hall. Thorough preparation aside (and at times Shaw was relentless in pushing his forces), his "sacred" task was to allow the music to speak to the listeners, and in so doing to enlighten their humanity.

February 14, 1955

Speech delivered at MTNA National Convention in St. Louis entitled "Music Is Order" Printed in September–October 1995 issue of *American Music Teacher* magazine

Mr. Stout and Members of the Convention—Musicians, Teachers and Friends—(I hope, for all our sakes, that these terms are not mutually exclusive):

The Gold Room is not completely unfamiliar to me. I must plead guilty to having been here once before some ten years ago under similar circumstances, and to having contributed at that time, in the carefree folly of youth, to its slide from its nominal standard.

I couldn't tell you which is the more embarrassing at the moment: the remembrance of past foolishness or the premonition of its imminent recurrence.

There are two differences between the present occasion and that earlier one. The first is the difference of auspices. That one was in conjunction with a conference of Music *Educators,* and this one I understand is with a convention of Music *Teachers.*

On the flight out I was trying to figure the difference between the two, but since arriving I have noticed the agendas abound in "critico-analytical orientations" and "Diagnostic and therapeutic implications" – and it has rather knocked my theories into a mortar board.

TEACHERS VS. EDUCATORS

I had it figured that a teacher was one who taught that which he knew, while an educator was a person who was so well qualified that he could teach anything—even that which he didn't know. Education, in essence, is the science of getting there first—without necessarily anything at all.

The reason Education is necessary is because some people just don't want to learn anything. A person who wants to know something can be taught. But a child who doesn't want to know anything at all has to be *educated.*

It's a little bit like the TV commercial I heard the night before last. You remember there used to be those "How-to-fix-it" books. Well Gimbels last night was giving away a book titled "What to fix—and how to fix it." (That's the *educational* point of view.)

The second difference (and the first one begins to look a little faded to me) is that this time I was asked not only to "demonstrate" but also to "make a speech." It was in Boulder, Colorado—and I've got witnesses to prove it.

Some of you folks get chances to make speeches all the time, but in the life of a performer this is a big thing. The eyes get bigger than the butterflies in the stomach; and the mouth, which always was large enough to accommodate the foot, now handles both of them nicely—with room enough to walk around in. You could invite a few friends and have an invitational track meet. (In educational circles these are known as *seminars.* In political circles I believe they're called *hearings.*)

I suppose part of this desire to have an audience for one's own incomparable logic and wit is the shame of being a conductor. I've never quite recovered from Hindemith's reply to a reporter in Chicago who asked him a few years ago if he were giving up his composing in order to concentrate on conducting: "All my life," he said, "I've struggled to be an honest musician—and now you want me to be a conductor." (It was at a time when he was at Tanglewood and this made Koussevitsky very unhappy.) – But you notice how just every one of them is doing it: Hindemith, Stravinsky, Thomson, Copland, Bernstein, Foss, Barber. I tell you—you get enough musicians in this field and there's going to be no room for conductors at all! And the conductors are going to have to go some place.

So another reason I was content (content? – I was ecstatic) at the prospect of speaking is that I can read the handwriting on the wall; and I, too, want to become an educator.

Now I want you to know that I'm not completely without experience in this line. I've had a whole arm in some of the most progressive educational experiments in the history of American music. Some of these institutions were so progressive they weren't even accredited. I remember the courtly superiority with which Koussevitsky dismissed the faculty discussion at Tanglewood over the possibility of accreditation: "Credit? . . . Vas is credit? . . . It is a credit to come to Tanglevood."

– And I was there at the launching of the "Literature and Materials Rocket" when it took off from Morningside Heights. I can only speak for the time I was there—but it hadn't come down when I left.

Most important of all—since I was here 10 years ago—I've—uh—acquired some degrees. My Bachelor of Arts was awarded to me in a Manhattan mailbox by Charles Addams (with a major in English literature).

DOCTORATES

– But that was small punkins. Since then I've been *doctored*—not once—but twice. I admit I had witnessed and even contributed to this embalming process in the big city. I'd seen the factories where they turn out Muss Docs, and Docs of Ed, and Docs of Ad, and Docs of Muss Ed, and Docs of Muss-Ed-Ad . . . I'd seen enough of this to wonder how anyone possibly could escape coming off the assembly line stamped *Campbell's* or *Kleenex* or *Hadacol* or *Fragile This Side Up.* I'd heard all the boys say, "Look this is just part of the game. You've just got to sweat this out. It's not a business of trying to be creative . . . Just try to stay sane."

But my Doctorate was free as the air—completely unearned—like Salvation by Grace, or Original Sin with the Fun Thrown In. This is a degree of great beauty—because it has no meaning. What it says is: "This man may be a fool or a criminal but we don't know . . . We got no line on him . . . And we're taking no chances. He's gonna join . . . Whap."

It was a very impressive ceremony—there was only one slight hitch. Either the President of the college was so intent on finding something nice to say that he overshot the mark, or else somebody had slipped something into the chapel water, because, as he concluded the obituary he finished up with, "and by the authority vested in me by the faculty and trustees of the college, and in accordance with something or other I hereby confer upon you the degree of Doctor of—*Divinity.*"

POISE

Well, there was a minor low-pressure area in the chapel as everybody drew wind at the same time. – But I wasn't at all surprised. Judging by what I'd just heard it was the least they could do. I just looked around to see who was going to get it. The faculty, lined up behind the President shoulder to shoulder, grew bolder and bolder, and finally got across the fact that somebody had made a "boo-boo." – But the President wasn't at all concerned. He muttered right back something like, "Divinity-Schmivinity . . . MusicSchmoosic . . . Who the devil's gonna know the difference?"

Since that time I have been a second time similarly, but I must say more straightforwardly, doctored. Last June, at a regular commencement of Pomona College, I was commenced along with some two hundred fifty or three hundred candidates—some deserving and some honorary. The salutations, addresses, the announcements of prizes—all were over; and people had settled down to the tedious business of watching the parade of graduates to the platform to receive their union cards. The routine is familiar to everyone. The entire graduating class is lined up Indian file in alphabetical order at one side of the stage, and all the diplomas are lined up in reverse alphabetical order on the other side of the stage; in the middle stands the President, and between him and the pile of diplomas stands the Dean or Secretary of the Faculty. At a given signal the assembly belt begins to operate and if a president of a college isn't on his toes or somebody steps out of line, Zowie! The platform is a backlash of robes, diplomas, mortarboards and whimpering seniors. In most circles the mortarboard is the clue to the whole thing: for once you become a Bachelor of Arts, you may wear your tassel on the right side. In barbershops, baseball parks—everybody will say: "You can tell him alright! There goes the old . . . BA!"

– So the Secretary of the Faculty reads the name on the diploma to the President. Now the President has a pretty good idea that it isn't Marianna Peppersmith at all. In fact, it looks a good deal more like Joe *Pepperschmidt*. Still, with the gowns and all—one can be mistaken; and he knows what can happen if he gets one bolt behind on the assembly line. So he looks Joe straight in the eye, calls out "Marianna Peppersmith, Bachelor of Arts," reaches out with his right hand to shake Joe's hand, extends the diploma with his left hand and with a third hand that comes from goodness knows where reaches up, gets a grip on Joe's tassel and flips it. This is the reason for Joe's four years of struggle—to get his tassel out of his left eye and into his right eye. Parents beam. It's a beautiful ceremony, and a highly significant moment.

– But at Pomona these moments had dragged into minutes, and the minutes into quarter-hours before suddenly the break came, and with it a roar of laughter and applause. Few of us caught the name, excepting perhaps his parents, but someplace down among the rrs or esses or tees, as the President of the college reached up to flip the tassel, it stood straight up and it wouldn't be brushed down, not forwards, backwards, left or right. It had been wired. In all fairness to the President it is to be reported that he put up a short but vigorous tussle with Joe's tassel. – But he lost. And the boy walked calmly across the stage, serpentined the front of the auditorium and stood solemnly with the graduated part of his class—to the cheers of those bored of education.

PUBLIC DOMAIN

Once you get to be an honorary doctor your name and address become the property of all sorts of advanced cultural services: alumni societies, literary guilds, Record of the Month Club, Fruit of the Month Club, Animal of the Month Club, Bird of the Month Club, Bath of the Month Club, Bird-Bath of the Month Club. Now, it's a strange thing about telegrams and telegraph agencies. People send wires and they are *phoned* to their addresses; Western Union has a specially trained crew of people who do nothing but read other peoples' telegrams. They have a special formula for those received in the evening: they are filed away—hoarded—and along about six-thirty or seven in the morning they hold what they call a "Western Union Wake"; phones all over town begin to ring.

I staggered out of bed on a cold morning a few months ago and ran downstairs to get to the phone just in time to see my wife hang up the receiver.

"Who was it?"

"Western Union."

"What did they want?"

"Had a telegram."

"What did it say?"

"Don't know—I told them to mail it."

"Mail it!"

"Settle down, it couldn't have been important; it was addressed to *Doctor Robert Shaw*."

Somehow in our generation we are obligated to rewrite the old proverb. "A little knowledge is not really so dangerous as a lot of education." For given sufficient degrees, we are liable to confuse ideologies with ideas, measuring with thinking, and organization with action. We have more and more of the science of teaching, and less for our teachers of the teachings of science. It may well be that our advanced curricula in education are so occupied with methods that we can recall only rarely and with difficulty the body and fervor of our faith.

> Years ago—
> the fable goes—
> they took a dog
> for an experiment in
> educational psychology
> graduate level.
>
> Every day before they fed the dog
> they'd ring a bell.
> This went on for several hundred
> years.
>
> Then one day
> they just rang the bell—
> no meat—
> and the dog drooled
> just the same.
>
> His stomach had been what they
> call conditioned
> to the ringing
> of a bell—
> A sort of audio chewing gum.

The day they wait for
   is the day when the dog drools
   and behold
   the bell rings.

There are some wonderful lines in T. S. Eliot's *The Rock:*

". . . The endless cycle of idea and action,
Endless invention, endless experiment,
Brings knowledge of motion, but not of stillness:
Knowledge of speech, but not of silence;
Knowledge of words, and ignorance of The Word.
Where is the life we have lost in living?
Where is the wisdom we have lost in knowledge?
Where is the knowledge we have lost in information? . . ."

– So, if I talk to you for a while about some of the things which (so it seems to me) music is and does, it is a calculated risk. (Music is not only a dubiously productive conversation piece that wouldn't stop us in a conference of music educators; but it's a matter very difficult to discuss—which is a lot worse.) However, there may be certain understandings which are essential, and which may be at least hinted at.

First, to state it as simply as possible: Music is Order in Sound and Time.

Music is Order. Order is the contradiction of Chaos. In order lies sanity. It is a wholeness—which has the same Anglo-Saxon word-root as holiness.

I asked Bernard Rogers once how he composed, and he replied that he sat down to a piece of blank paper with an eraser, and when he had erased everything that wasn't essential he had a piece of music.

Stravinsky almost denies the existence of what the uncreative call "inspiration"—as though music could spring full blown out of a dream. He calls himself an "inventor" of music. A fortuitous accident—a sound unexpected but rigorously observed—may cry for development, but that development is an exercise of the intelligence and the *will* to *fabricate*. Order is in this connection not so much the work of an "artist," as the work of an "artisan."

ORDER AND CHAOS

One of the most striking juxtapositions within my recent memory occurred a few years ago in New York where were performed within a week or two a contemporary orchestral composition called *Ideas of Order* and the Haydn *Creation,* the opening movement of which is entitled "A Representation of Chaos."

There could be no doubt in which of the works were the greater ideas of order, and in which lay the greater confusion. Music is Order.

Music is Order in Sound: in *pitch,* in *color,* and in *amplitude.* These facts are familiar to us all. Western music orders *Pitch* first of all by prescribing (and with quite considerable justification in physical and psychological science) that out of the seemingly limitless world of auditory experience only twelve tones (together with their duplicates at the octave) are legitimate building materials; and it further proposes certain rules of preferences of traditional behaviour for relating those twelve tones. Music orders *Color* by traditionally recognizing only three basic instrumental devices for initiating sound waves: the vibrating elastic surface (timpani or wood block), the vibrating stretched string (piano or violin), and the vibrating air columns in a wood or metal pipe (pipe organ, saxophone or trombone). However, by prescribing what sort of mechanisms are to initiate the vibration, western music in the last 340 years has enormously augmented its palette and the potential complexities of its orders. Undoubtedly electronic devices will find their way, into legitimate musical service (– Though I am constrained to observe that the way to lick the liquor problem in this country is to put electromoronic cocktail calliopes in every bar.) So absorbed with *Amplitude* has western music become that it has produced in the symphony orchestra the biggest, loudest, most varied musical instrument the world ever has seen.

I am moved to make three editorial comments in passing. In musical composition, just as in other areas of human affairs, no amount of bellowing, bullying, bluffing—no amount of stamping and storming, of pushing people around—can obscure for long the absence of genuine ideas and the indifference to truth. ("Do you swear, Senator, to tell the truth, the half-truth—and nothing but—?") Bach can say more with two flutes than a Mac-Dowell can with a whole New York Philharmonic.

I conducted a performance of the Berlioz *Requiem* last year—and will do another in San Diego this summer—and if any music in the world has megalomania this is it: 4 brass bands, symphony orchestra of 200, 14 percussionists with 4 bass drums and 18 timpani, and a chorus of 400 to 500. – The champion heavyweight composer of the world. Now the bands are supposed to be stationed at the four corners of a cathedral, but there's only one cathedral in the United States that could hold these forces and an audience too. (And that was 300 miles away, and not completed yet.) So we performed in a field house, a hockey rink. (Actually, if any piece of music can justify these outlandish forces, the Berlioz *Requiem* is probably the one of sufficient genius to do so.) One of the major problems was to arrange things so that the conductor occasionally was visible to a quorum of the executants. The planners of this performance seriously considered setting up a television system of communication—particularly with the brass bands. It was all a little bit like the Mount Rushmore National Monument in South Dakota: God's aesthetically impoverished peaks, ennobled by four gargantuan life-defying figures—Washington, Jefferson, Lincoln and Teddy Roosevelt. Do you know how long Teddy's mustache is? Forty feet, from here to here. Isn't that a lot of lip? The Bach *St. John Passion* take 1/10th the forces of the Berlioz *Requiem*—but so many times the heart and so many times the mind. The "Benedictus" of the *B Minor Mass* calls for only 1 violin, 1 cello, 1 tenor—and three impossibly great human beings.

– Which is the subject of the second editorial in passing. The great music of the world has been written for people no less than instruments. – And even if the world's greatest violinist makes a recording of the Bach *Double Violin Concerto* by himself, recording the two solo parts on separate tapes and superimposing those tapes in an electronic mixing room—no matter how perfect the performance, something's gone out of music. Bach wrote his music for two human beings, not for solo engineer.

The third thing I want to say about sound is that its vitality and communicative power depend upon an almost umbilical relation to the physical ecstasy of the human cry. Unless a performer is somehow resonant to this essential sound of man and his earth (the voices of growing things—page Thoreau at Walden Pond), unless he is painfully conscious in his memory, experience, and imagination of these sounds of growing things, he's in no position to create or recreate music.

INHIBITIONS

We lose too much of essential human qualities in the civilizing process. We are a web of inhibitions . . . And a musician must be one to whom something is more important than himself.

One of the most beautiful stories I know concerns a certain African tribe in which, at the time when the boy passes to manhood he must go off into the jungle by himself—there to indulge in an orgy of dancing and shouting and wailing and sobbing. He must leave the village—for his sounds would make the people in the village ill.

Kathleen Ferriers and Eileen Farrells and Toscaninis and Walters are great because they find the basic and, finally, simple human sound in what for the rest of us are mazes of complexity.

Music is Order in Sound.

What is not so familiar a part of our understanding is that Music is also Order in *Time*. Unlike sculpture, painting, even in many respects the drama, music is not a Space-art, but it is essentially a Time-art. Its material is Time. Time is its "clay," its "canvas." It is the purpose of music to give shape and meaning and beauty to Time. Music exists from Now to Somewhen; and it establishes its own consciousness and consequences in Time.

There are two aspects to this Timeness of Music; and it is something of a paradox that music can hold them both, for they are in fact contradictory. The first is the basic element of cycle, of recurrency—the here-it-comes-again-ness which we call Rhythm. By it we assume that Time is divisible, can be fragmented into equal portions. A whole series of terms group around this assumption: pulse, measure, beat, meter, tempo. (Tempo is a silly kind of idea when you get right down to it, for it attempts to measure the speed with which Rhythm [and Sound?] moves through time . . . Not speed through *space*—that would be simple—but at what pace can one pass through how much time? How fast can one live how long?)

RHYTHM

The whole field of Rhythm is the most complex of music's ideologies. The major theorists of our time admit their failure to arrive at a convincing system here. Rhythm is the total consequence of pulse-patterns, of groupings ordered as to duration and accentuation.—And its principal and most provocative assumption is that Time is divisible. Actually, almost all our day-by-daily life turns on this wheel: four seasons per year, two high tides per day, thirteen full moons every twelve months—breakfast lunch dinner bed breakfast lunch dinner dead the earth spins and the earth circles regular as clockwork grab the brass ring and ride get the beat baby it's cool, it's real cool.—It's also true. It's real True. For Toscanini, *tempo* was the heartbeat; and the steadier the *tempo*, the healthier the heart. Expression? Maybe a little; but don't spill any, and keep walkin'. The second aspect of Music's Time-ness says exactly the opposite, and is equally true. – For it is the experience of each of us that the hours are of varying lengths; that no two minutes are ever of equal duration, that this moment is endless . . . and already is gone. – Eternality within the instant: *life*-time, *this*-time, *next*-time.

It is the capacity of music so to order Time that its meaning is not to be found in its measure. The least pertinent question one can ask about the *Missa Solemnis* is how long it is. Ages of quietness are in the moments of musical *Praeludium* which precede the "Benedictus"; and 16 minutes by the clock of "Benedictus qui venit in nomine Domini" are a single breathless instant or an eternity of blessing.

It has to follow that every performance is a first performance, and every song a swan song. For this moment never has been shaped by this sound. New-time New-artist. This instant of life within the now become the past. Clay that vanishes as you shape it.

Music is Order in Sound and *Time.*

The second thing I want to say is that music has meaning. It is a distillation of the human spirit and a representation of truth. Now, this may come as no great shock to many of you, but I assure you it is an aesthetic position accustomed to considerable opposition.

All of us would grant that when joined with words music tells a story, ponders an event, or proposes an attitude. – But that music *without* text has meaning and is a representation of valid reality is a position more difficult to defend.

A friend in college who was trying to decide between a career in mathematics or music used to assure me that certain equations in higher physics had an emotional beauty quite as real as that induced in him by music. It's quite probable that not many of us (including myself) could share that enthusiasm. (He chose physics.) But I do get a hint of what he meant when I begin to explore the ideas and imagery inherent in some of the simple geometric patterns of our everyday life.

What, for instance, is the meaning of a circle? – Or of a wheel? – A Triangle? – Or a curved line curved just so? That is not so simple or unproductive as it sounds. For these things are not simply definitions. They are ideas and symbols of ideas, and their implications probe deep into the human spirit.

If it sounds silly—
    Take that circle again.

A circle means
    an infinite number of points absolutely the same distance from a certain point.

The first thing you face
    is the idea of Infinity
    It's a big idea—
    people haven't always had it.

Then there's the idea of
    —a Point.
    That's a big idea—
    it's the idea of One,
    the Indivisible—that's monotheism.

A Circle also means
   no beginning
   and no end.
   That's Forever—
   Eternality—
   Everlasting.

Now one more thing—
   set that Infinite Indivisible
   Eternal Circle in Motion
   —a Wheel, no less,
   Let it move—
   Point after infinite circumference point.

How long, then,
   before this infinite number of points will begin to repeat themselves?
   —And if they do—
   if the wheel really goes
   only once around—
   can the points really be Infinite?
   Can Infinity repeat itself
   on into Infinity?

Or what about that axis point?
Does it turn 'round too?
—Because if it does, then part of it's up
while the other part's down
or part of it's facing East
while the rest
faces West.
—And anything that can face two ways at once
has two or more sides
—and is no Point.

The axis, then,
   cannot really be said
   to move at all.

And at the center of Infinite Motion—we have Infinite Un-motion.

If it sound silly—
   take that circle.

My greatest good fortune in music has been my friendship for the past ten years with Julius Herford—a German pianist and musical thinker of prophetic perception. Many of you now know him (or *of* him) through his work at Tanglewood, Juilliard and, more recently, the graduate divisions of Union Theological Seminary, the Westminster Choir School, the Summer Workshop at San Diego and his numerous lecture-recital sessions throughout the United States.

It is Mr. Herford's great genius to understand form in music as the source of its spiritual energy. Factors of proportion are factors of meaning. Pattern is not simply two plus two—or perhaps two plus two is a far more significant thing than our childish memorizations testify. Formlessness is not the same as fracture or distortion of form; for these are new elements of order and elements of energy which have meaning only in relation to the pre-existing form from which they sprang.

Form in music is a symbol, and it symbolizes something to which we can give the name only of spirit. When we have recognized the devices and tabulated the relationships we will not have explained it away. It exists in spite of our understanding. At some point deep in human consciousness pattern will answer pattern, and that will be no crisp intellectual gymnastic, but a warm and moving awareness. What we call emotion is, surely, a part of it. Tears, laughter, and a tensing spiritual temper are assuredly within the mandate of Form.

There is a very remarkable book, now available in a pocket edition, written by an English mathematician, J. W. N. Sullivan, and called *Beethoven, His Spiritual Development.*

It is Mr. Sullivan's argument that within the past few decades the mechanistic theory which had ruled men's thinking for some 300 years—namely, that scientific method and matter-of-fact are infallible and unexceptionable—has been severely shaken; for science has been able to provide knowledge of structure, but not of substance.

– And that, therefore, matters-of-*value*—elements of our experience which science has ignored because they were not measurable—are not thereby proved to have no bearing upon the nature of reality.

A work of art may indeed be a "revelation." The "higher consciousness" of the great artist is evidenced not only by his capacity of ordering his experience, but also by having his experience.

BEETHOVEN

"Beethoven lived in a universe richer than ours, in some ways better than ours, in some ways more terrible. And while he does not communicate his experience to us, he does communicate his attitude towards it. And we recognize his universe; we find it prophetic of our own. It is indeed our universe, but experienced by a consciousness aware of aspects of which we have but dim and transitory glimpses.

"The reason that our reaction to a work of art cannot be adequately described is not that some unique and isolated faculty *is* involved, but that art is not superfluous, that it exists to convey that which cannot be otherwise conveyed."

All of music is an attempt at communication between human hearts and minds; at the very minimum the creator reaches out to and through the performer, and both of them reach out to the listener.

One of the primary assumptions of music is that human beings can and should understand each other with reference to the whole produce of the human mind and heart possessing that which we call aesthetic or spiritual value. Even were its subject matter the disintegration, imminent and desirable, of the human species—even so, just at that point at which the creative understanding acts to produce a work of art, it affirms that man is one of a community of men upon whose understanding—of himself and his ideas—the meaning of his own existence is predicated. Art is at once exhaustively personal and inescapably social.

– Which leads me to the third thing I want to say about music: it is that the great music is the people's music—the most human and universal music. Music is great not because certain self-appointed Custodians of Art with a capital A have decreed it so, but because it calls out to something deep and persistent in the human thing. Music is great because it carries something so native and true to the human spirit that not even sophisticated intellectuality can deny or destroy its miracle.

POPULAR MUSIC

Popular music is not the people's music. The people think so little of it that they tire of it in six to sixteen weeks. They demand a new tune to dance to, to trade small talk above, to make what some call love by.

There is music which is calculated to make us forget—and there is music which allows us to remember . . . to remember our humanity and whatever individual conscience may ascribe to divinity.

It is not primarily a matter of raising the standards of musical taste. It is primarily a matter of providing adequate opportunity for the exercise of inherent taste. One falls in love by being at the right place at the right time for long enough. If there is no place where the people can meet Bach or Beethoven, how can the people be expected to love them? If Bach is not sung, he is not met.

November 9, 1981

Lecture on "The Conservative Arts"
Memorial Church, Harvard University

Professor Gomes, Professor Forbes, Ladies and Gentlemen—Good Evening.

It has occurred to me more than once that the conductor has certain things in common with the preacher, the politician and the professor: chief among them a strong sense of caution and a high regard for the quick cover-up—cowardice and camouflage. The preacher has the psalmists and prophets—as well as the anxieties of his congregation—to compensate for his clouded vision. The politician can hide behind his party's slogans and platforms. The professor can fall back upon textbooks, libraries, last year's lectures and—if all else fails—the Socratic method. And the conductor has the inexhaustible bounty of the real creators—the composers—as well as the ministrations of instrumentalists who, in fact, make the music, to deck the hall behind him with beauty.

In the very worst sermon, political address, classroom lecture or musical performance, something of value may happen. You can muddle or muffle the words of Isaiah, Lincoln or Galileo, but they will not be silenced. – And in any major musical score there are so many possibilities for error that no one man can make them all.

But a conductor who takes to the lectern or pulpit in a church of this past and presence is a fool and doubly damned; for he has abandoned the costume and jousting stick which normally enable him to ward off the perceptive mind, and you now regard him face to face.

It is entirely possible that this willingness to risk double jeopardy by assenting to the William Belden Noble Lectureship is closely connected with a geriatric compulsion to make retribution for too much of a life-time spent in the field of conducting.

Just six months short of 35 years ago I entered this Memorial Church on the first—and only other—occasion, at the invitation of the 1947 Harvard Symposium on Musical Criticism, to conduct with the Collegiate Chorale and members of the Boston Symphony the premieres of Aaron Copland's *In the Beginning*, Malipiero's *La Terra* and Paul Hindemith's *Apparebit Repentina Dies*, works commissioned by the symposium for that event.

Just two years *prior* to the Harvard Symposium, the Collegiate Chorale had commissioned Mr. Hindemith to write a major choral-orchestral work, which only a very few weeks later became *When Lilacs Last in the Dooryard Bloomed—*"A Requiem for Those We Love" (and, I think, one of the musical benchmarks of this century.) – And just two years *after* that symposium, Mr. Hindemith began his Charles Eliot Norton lectures, whose published title became *A Composer's World.*

As regards the superiority of singing or playing over conducting—everyone's great teacher is Paul Hindemith. In *A Composer's World* he informs us that conducting first began at the end of the 13th century when one member of a vocal quartet in a church in Périgueux, France, undertook to signal the other three members when to engage in basic organum, that is, singing in parallel motion to the Gregorian melody at the interval of the octave or the fifth to achieve a more ravishing and undoubtedly less spiritual sound.

Note first that this early conductor actually participated in the production of sound. "If one of them sings incorrectly," Hindemith quotes Elias Solomon, seven centuries later, "he whispers into the singer's ear, 'you are too loud, too soft, your tones are wrong' as the case may be, but so that the others don't hear it. Sometimes he must support them with his own voice, if he sees they are lost." Note finally that this occurs not only at rehearsals, but also at performance.

(*Today's* conductor talks at length only on three occasions: one, during rehearsals—to the scarcely restrainable delight of professional musicians; two, to committees composed in the main of matrons of a certain age whose children have left home and thus allowed them to assume responsibility for the rest of mankind; and three, to convocations such as this of students, instructors, friends of the family or innocent bystanders—victims of a runaway ecumenicalism, assembled to watch an out-of-town dog so old his tricks have come 'round again.)

Hindemith, however, did not limit his observations on conducting to historical information. While he was writing "Lilacs," he also was traveling by train from city to city, conducting programs of his symphonic works with major orchestras. In Chicago he was asked by a reporter if this meant that he was giving up composition to become a performer. "All my life," he said—in his wishy-washy way—"All my life I have struggled to be an honest musician, and now you want me to become a bloody conductor!"

When I asked Mrs. Hindemith how many tickets they might like for the world premiere of "Lilacs," she looked surprised. "But Robert, Paul has never been to a premiere of one of his works in his life!"

When I protested that involved here were two hundred amateur singers for whom this was an act of love consummating in a single hour thousands of man-hours of unpaid labor, he agreed that he might attend but added wonderingly, "Do you really imagine that you can sound it better than I can hear it?"

At the intermission of the first full rehearsal, when the soloist, strong in spirit and vocal flesh, but weak in the tonal disciplines of time and place, had strayed too far for too long from the composer's appointed rounds he finally exploded, "For the love of God, Robert, ask him what notes he can sing! I sure can write 'em!"

Now, some may laugh, but others of you are engaged in some creative or productive aspect of the arts. At least the soloist was doing something. All the conductor was doing was marking the passing of the *status quo ad infinitum et absurdum*. No wonder he didn't rate wrath. What he was doing made no perceivable difference.

I made up for myself then my own little Charlie Brown ladder of goals—only, of course, my ladder went down instead of up:

If you can't compose—perform.
If you can't perform—teach.
If you can't teach—administer.
If you can't do any of the above—conduct.

I'd like first to state—in as few sentences as may be possible—a position and an argument; and then move through some paragraphs concerning the pilgrimage which led to this position, and ideas encountered along the way; and conclude with a few words as to why and where in this world it seems to me that the arts and artists are needed.

The position and the rationale certainly are not unique with me. I use the personal pronoun only because I would not wish to dictate your thoughts or your forms of expressing it.

One, I believe that the arts are a "lodestar" of man's humanity. – More even than political or religious institutions, in today's world they guide and guard his intellectual and ethical sensitivities.

Two, if man is to continue to inhabit this planet and grow in wisdom and dignity, the arts cannot be separated from "the people." – I mean Carl Sandburg's "the people" and Abe Lincoln's "common man." In our funny, fuzzy world, the economic ability to rent a seat for a concert is no proof that any communication has taken place. And while the arts do address themselves to man's keenest and most discriminating intelligence, and while also a large part of mankind has yet to experience and become responsive to the transforming powers of a Beethoven *Ninth Symphony,* the arts still are the major tools capable of teaching, training and eventually lifting the mind of man to his potential and proper humanity.

And three, this is never going to happen if the consumers stay in one room and the artists in another. A "proscenium" is only an enlarged doorway, and unless the traffic is heavy and constant, we're all doomed. The supporters have to become artists. And the professionals have to become—or remain—lovers of art.

I am not speaking "figuratively." Government support and private philanthropy—however proportioned or politically fluctuating—will never be able to match institutional costs unless the good-will, administrative intelligence and promotional skills of the artists themselves are enlisted in the effort. And conversely, when groups of artists are concerned primarily with contracts, with "love for sale" and monies receivable, their intellectual, aesthetic and even digital sensitivities atrophy. They lose their reason for being.

The Atlanta Symphony Orchestra has been blessed from year to year with volunteer administrators who also are members of its Orchestra Chorus. This is not simply larynx and lip-service on a casual basis. During choral performance weeks this can command as many as twenty hours per week of rehearsing and performing; with associated anxieties, exhaustion, unbidden criticism and disrupted home schedules. But it is also, I think, the means by which false images are exorcised, and an integrity rather than a polarity in the arts community achieved.

Some years ago, as a prelude to the Alaska Festival of Music, I was invited to be one of the commencement speakers at the University of Alaska.

These ceremonies were on a Monday afternoon, and I had arrived in Fairbanks early enough to hear Sunday's Baccalaureate Address delivered by the chief chaplain of the U.S. Army, a full general, I believe. His advices to the graduating classes—in which there were a number of Master's and Doctorate degrees represented—were twofold. First, to the women he recommended that, now they had their education, it were best to forget it and settle down to the business of building a nest, pleasuring a man and raising young; and the implication was not to be missed that an education for women, especially one concerned with the liberal arts, need not be an insurmountable obstacle to the real business of life if one had a good forgettery.

Second, to the men of the classes he admonished that from the Alaskan mainland on a clear day you could see Communism forever, and greater honor was available to no man than to lay down his life ag'in it, and seemingly as quickly and as frequently as possible.

I had but recently returned from a tour of Russia with a chorus and chamber orchestra as part of our cultural exchange program. For six weeks we had toured a somewhat narrow north-to-south corridor, giving thirty concerts in eleven cities. The programs were made up almost exclusively of religious music—first, because that is the historical nature of the great choral repertoire, but also because their ministry of "un-theistic" culture had specifically requested Bach's *Mass in B Minor*.

The tour corresponded precisely with the sharp edge of the Cuban crisis, and where we might have expected to meet demonstrations or picketing there were only affectionate greetings of "bravo" and "thank you." There were near-riots preceding all *B Minor Mass* performances, due only to the throngs of people unable to gain entrance; and the night of its final performance, the work was broadcast in its entirety—including lengthy audience response—throughout the entire Iron Curtain complex. For three hours the only radio fare available to this "materialistic," "atheistic" audience was a monument of Christian creed, philosophy and art.

Gifts proferred in return for the pleasure they said they had received were abstract paintings in the manners of Mondrian and Pollock, and, even more poignantly, contemporary icons out of Mother Russia by El-Greco-esque twentieth century distortionists. (What a strange twist to find the avant-garde, the independent and rebellious young linked to religious expression. In my college days it had been considered hopelessly insensitive to be any less than agnostic.)

Here is a fraction of a review published in the *State Journal of Arts:*

"The spiritual life of modern man is infinitely complicated. His thinking, memory and aesthetic feeling are constantly developing. But still the human principles that are characteristic of man were and remain immutable. They rest on ideas simple and eternal as the world itself: truth, goodness, beauty.

"All this the music of Bach reveals to us in forms which are simple and majestic, clear and infinitely wise. The music sings of life. It uplifts us, forces us not only to rejoice and to grieve but, most of all, to think." "Atheistic materialism?" One could wish that Sunday's televangelism would show the same concern for the souls of men.

My point in passing is certainly not that the political and economic problems of the world are going to be solved by going singing. Economic and political problems exist and they have to be solved economically and politically. But I drew two conclusions from that experience, reinforced by similar tours of twenty countries in North Africa, the Middle East and Europe, and nine in South America.

First: a generous and lively exchange in the liberal and performing arts can accomplish some things: it can gain us time, and it can give us the hope that if we understand each other so warmly and naturally in these areas we may one day be able to compose political and economic differences.

One other thing occurred to me on the plane flying back. In general, the intellectual and moral climate of our times is agreeable to the proposition that man does not live by bread alone. (In any of the green-belted suburbia they have it that man does not live by grass alone.)

And it is precisely this interchange in the humanities—architecture, medicine, poetry, philosophy and music among them—which give life its measure and its meaning. These are the fruits which validate political and economic activity. Man does not live by bread, grass, economics or politics alone, but by adventures at the highest level of human intuition, aspiration and understanding.

All this and a good deal more became my answer on the morrow in Alaska to our chaplain's "dirty mind." It was titled "The Conservative Arts," finding a delight in the adjective such as Charles Addams might find in Valentine's Day— "Say it with fungus." – Or, as Arthur Hoppe expressed in a recent column, "raising one-half of a 'V for Victory' sign."

For, of course, what I had very earnestly in mind were the *liberal* arts—so called, tradition says, because their study in Roman days was accorded only to free, or liberated, men—and, even of these liberal arts, that portion of them which we designate as "creative," "performing" or occasionally "seven and lively."

Not surprisingly, I had to conclude to myself that "conservative" was not necessarily a dirty word. In spite of the contemporary cross—and back—fire of piosity and poison, Judased and prejudiced from either side, if "conservative" can mean literally "conserving, preserving," then the topic has made its point. "What do the liberal creative arts conserve?" Nothing—but humanity.

The argument, then, behind the title is that the arts, and probably in direct ratio as to how liberal and creative they are, are the preservers and the purveyors of those values which define humanity (and for some divine Divinity) and finally, in fact, may prove to be the only workable Program of Conservation for the human race on this planet.

I asked myself a series of questions:

What are the meanings of art? What is it trying to tell us of man? What is man trying to tell us of himself?

Second, what may be the function or influence of art in a world gone schizophrenic, paranoid, masochistic? Let's take the last question first.

The 'sixties and 'seventies have unfolded twin vistas: Outside—man and his societies teetering on the brink of self-annihilation; and Inside—helplessness; for, to quote the butcher, the baker, the candlestick maker, "I don't see what I possibly can do about it."

Governments, not for any lack of earnestness or endeavor, possibly even without malice, and for reasons which must be disturbingly unknown—even to themselves—engage hourly and horrifyingly in a juggling and counter-juggling of propagandas, munitions, monies and men uncertifiable even by the laws of average.

– And I asked myself parenthetically, "Is man really worth saving?" Certainly all those born only months ago are. And everybody's pre-teen child. And students in universities, none of whom has had the opportunity to merit the wind he inherits. But, in spite of Socrates, Bach, Jesus, Beethoven, Shakespeare, Lincoln, Buddha, Gandhi and a host of lesser saints, is it not possible to paraphrase the psalmist, "When I consider this earth, the work of my fingers, the horrors I have created, what is man that he is mindful of himself?"

Might it just be that man is not worth saving?

There came immediately another question, and it was really a half-answer. "Could it be possible that human life itself—unclassified—is a plus on creation's side? Not: is this life or that life worth saving? Not even: is it worth killing for? But, in view of the timeless, consciousless upward climb of warm mud to cold man, is the life-force in the man-thing of itself a value, and enough to save him from self-destruction?"

My lifetime has seen the table-stakes raised from trade-routes and development rights, through principalities and powers to man himself—absolute or obsolete—and the game is not the same.

Fact of life Number Two: the lonely sickness in each man's soul—familiar no doubt as well to kings, prime-ministers and senators as to students, teachers, musicians and bartenders—that there is, indeed, very little that "I can do about it."

> They say this world,
> Is smaller now
> —But not my world.
> My world is full
> Of hurricane and tide
> Of flux and flood
> Of thrust and space
> I never thought to face.
> And still no place
> To hide.

The jailor of Paul and Silas at Phillippi, originator of, "What must I do to be saved?" was panicked only by an earthquake at midnight, not by "How will you have your cities this morning, with or without people?" or "How do you like your children, crisp—or scrambled?"

Which of us, simply by accident of being born, and in personal as well as public affairs, does not find himself on a runaway rocket blasting a trackless blackness, speed and destination out of sight, mind and control? "What is man? And, can he be saved?"

It was my conviction then—as now—that an attention to the conserving, liberating arts might give us more than half-answers and some hope.

I have not listed or defined these arts first, because there is little uncertainty as to where in general they lie—certainly among the "Humanities" (a term which always has amused me by its implication that other branches of knowledge must comprise the "In-humanities") and second, because I have a suspicion that in the end art may prove to be as much an attitude as an aptitude and a point of view as well as a product. By "art," then, we know we mean the languages and produce of Beethoven, Shakespeare, Donatello, Bach, Dickinson, El Greco, Picasso, Melville—and a host of others.

What does this sort of art show itself to be? Why is it important? How can it help us? I find for myself four answers.

First: Art on this scale is the most pervasive, persistent, powerful affirmation of the life-force in the man-thing. Than sex it is stronger and longer—by centuries, and oceans. It is a true transubstantiation: pitch into sonata-form into spirit; paint onto canvas into tears; words onto paper across a proscenium into the heart of man. Essence inferred into substance achieved—in order to communicate that Essence. Ally through all time of the evolutionary thrust, it is finally the Flesh become Word.

Second, facing the bewildering profusions of matter and sensation, the Arts testify to man's ability to isolate and identify, then to relate and to order. Out of the countless and contrary, out of confusion and chaos, emerge in perfect sequence, symmetry and heart-breaking recognizability a G Minor Symphony, cathedrals at Chartres and Coventry, *King Lear* and "The Lord is my shepherd."

Matters of proportion—
    the relations of tone, timbre and texture
    of line, rhythm and tempo
    of expectation, continuation
    recurrence and closure
are not grandmother's eboned and
    polished clothing tree
    dunce-capped and slack-coated
    tall in the hall
    while love is made in the parlour—
They are root, trunk, branch and leaf—
    seed, sap and substance of Art's meaning.

Art is the achievement of Order.

The Third aspect of art's meaning I found eloquently stated in a book of an English mathematician, J. W. N. Sullivan, entitled *Beethoven, His Spiritual Development*. It is Mr. Sullivan's thesis that during the past few decades the mechanistic theories which ruled man's thinking for some 300 years have been severely shaken. Science has been able to provide knowledge of matter, but not of essence. Therefore, matters of value which heretofore have been ignored because they were not measurable, may still have something to say concerning the nature of reality.

"A work of art may indeed be a 'revelation.' The 'higher consciousness' of the creative artist is evidenced not only by his capacity of *ordering* his experience but also by the capacity of *having* his experience."

The reason that our reaction to a Beethoven quartet or a *B Minor Mass* cannot be adequately described is not that some unique and isolated faculty is involved, but that art is not superfluous. – The Arts exist to convey that which cannot otherwise be conveyed.

The Fourth mark of Art's meaning I find in the simple fact that it is unremittingly an attempt to communicate, to establish contact, to find kinship across even centuries and oceans. It does seem to me that political and economic configurations—their facets running hot and cold—are more frequently divisive than embracing. – And it is to the credit of art and the arts that, except for short periods when they have been subverted by politics or principles not their own—as in Hitler's Germany or Stalin's Russia—they have been a unifying force in the affairs of men, have been the open hand of man reaching for his brother, and have promoted understanding and affection rather than half-truth and no-trust. Art has burned neither heretics nor books.

But, to our shame, the Church named after the "Good Shepherd" and "Holy Comforter" has had a history of persecutions, inquisitions and crusades—in just one of which, in the year of our Lord 1212, and in a much smaller world, fifty thousand innocent children were "shepherded" to their deaths by sword, starvation and pestilence, and the few fortunate survivors "comforted" by being sold into slavery.

The arts may indeed be not the luxury of the few but the last best hope of humanity—to inhabit with joy this planet.

Now, this thinking is not very original but was years in the gathering, and I certainly have no hankering to discard or deny it. But I acknowledge that my primary impression of the past two decades is that of a beautiful aesthetic theory murdered by a set of ugly sociological facts. The taste of waste was already on the tongue before Kent State, but it was brought to a rare bitterness when I was asked to conduct a memorial service in a chapel on the lawn by the street where four weeks before the blood had been shed.

And I can assure you that it seemed relatively simple in the little communities of Southern California in the 'thirties, when he politicked on your campus or in your home, to see that a quite unparticular candidate for Congress was devious, and did not know wrong from left. What we did not know then in our youthful idealism, but what I think I've observed since, is that Lincoln was the exception and Nixon the rule. But need he have become the ruler had not the arts of communication been so much at home 'mid the homilies, and the pleasures and palaces, of the market-place?

How *do* the arts in bloody awful fact fit into our contemporary American Society? Who supports them? Are they supportable?

Well, that support is not as minimal as it might appear to museums, ballet companies, symphony orchestras, opera associations, independent colleges, and less densely populated states.

Can anyone among us even roughly estimate the total investment of Commerce and Industry in those visual arts which dominate periodicals and most printed communications—including junk mail—or in the cinematographic, athletic or musical arts which rule television?

In the field of personal amusement and entertainment what are the take-home profits of Country and Western or Rock and Roll recording artists and companies? – Or of their personal appearances? What is the cost of one week of one Las Vegas gambling casino show, or of one Academy Awards evening?

– And where does Religion meet the Arts? Its very own task forces would prescribe that the gospel crusade with anything less than a choir of 4,000 "Just-as-I-yammers" is not merely undeserving of prime-time, but has only one foot in the stadium. Organized religion has learned well the lesson that from a T.V. studio or on the road a lot more apples are merchandised by serpents than by penitents.

And the greatest of all sponsors and employers of the communicative arts is an Eisenhower-identified industrial/military/political complex which, by appropriate aesthetic computations and manipulations only occasionally identified as propaganda, can lead one man to a white marker in Southeast Asia, and another to a White House at the Southeast corner of Maryland, and convince many more than half the people that that's a fair shake.

What has now become of the affetuoso sentiment that the arts are the lodestar of man's humanity?

They were to be the affirmation of the life-force in the man-thing. They were to resolve Order out of Chaos. They could indeed provide a "revelation" of man's nature and destiny. They could assure human kinship across centuries and oceans.

Here, of course, I arrive at my present predicament: Were these to be things which the Arts could be *used* to do? Or were they to be the very nature of the Arts? Somehow, by acquiring the disciplines necessary to "make" a poem or a song or a play or a picture, could man become in-formed—*inwardly formed* by something: trial and error, mass and proportion, self-doubt and self-respect, earthly matters and textures and mixes—to find his is-ness and his relation to others?

Is this asking too much of the arts? Did they never carry this lodestar of potential and responsibility? Certainly farthest from my intentions was the thought of asking the arts to be judged by any contemporary political or social ethic—even my own—or to prove themselves in dutifully censored works.

Are the arts, then, simply tools of communication available to thief and fraud no less than saint?

Is there any less hanky-panky in the American Federation of Musicians than there is in the National Council of Churches or the Federal Bureau of Investigation?

Did Picasso's *Guernica* accidentally inspire the French Army of Resistance, or moth-ball the Spanish Freedom Brigade?

How many lives at Auschwitz were saved when the SS community chorus suddenly burst into Beethoven's setting of Schiller's "Alle menschen werden bruder!"

When the opposing trenches in "No-Man's Land" of World War I sang "Silent Night – Heilige Nacht" on Christmas Eve, how many lungs blistered by mustard gas were instantly healed?

Could Abraham Lincoln have shortened the Civil War by crooning "Tenting Tonight" from a Goodyear blimp?

The faith of our founding fathers, as of the entire Age of Enlightenment, kept generations from sleep at night for fear of missing the perfectability of man. Certainly, this was the flavor of the academic air in the orange groves east of Los Angeles between Mt. San Antonio and Laguna Beach in the 'thirties.

But, "Vanity . . . vanity!"

The 'sixties and 'seventies have reminded us that institutions and skills and even men themselves are no less capable of inhumanity than of humanity. They have reminded us that the "office" or the "calling" will not invariably ennoble a man or make him great. In any of us at any moment—even in those of us who would be happy to know ourselves as artists—the Scales of Manhood may tip towards humanity or inhumanity.

It is possible that there may be some cause for hope in the long tale of Creation—which most of us now call "Evolution." Man may be, in a sense, *becoming*. But for anyone aware of himself or a Thou or an Other, at this infinitesimal instant in the fleeting panorama of a "life-time," the underlying certainty is the certainty of struggle.

For me it has become abundantly clear that instant and unmeritable salvation in an inexhaustible hereafter is a terrifying evasion of the Christian ethic, as also of man's responsibility to himself and his heritage.

There was a memorable professor of philosophy in Southern California in the 'thirties who was president of the Western Philosophical Association—which meant that of the Western Hemisphere—Hartley Burr Alexander. Because he was a Christian philosopher, his books bore Christian titles: *Truth and the Faith* and *God and Man's Destiny*. In the latter book he had a chapter on "The Honour of God," and I love these sentences:

"I cannot see God as a burning, all-powerful glory, with evil dissolved before Him, undisturbed and actionless, for life and our own crying hearts belie this. There can be but one open understanding of the procession of the stars up from their unguessed abyss, . . . of the laboured emergence of earth's habitable forms, and of the affliction-attended discoveries of the fruits of the tree of knowledge. – We are in some sense mounting. – But each age is like a stricken field where many are fallen and the waste is heavy, and there is no utter assurance, not even for God himself, that a triumphant quiet will be as an end. . . .

". . . Yet can we rest with this assurance: that here within the narrow circles of human days, there is always and uncompromisingly a baser and nobler course, and it is for us to choose the nobler. Only so are we keeping faith . . . with our own honor; God can do no less with the truth that is his."

I suspect that in the long run—if there is a long run—the arts will be seen to be the lode-star of Man's humanity—even more than religious or political structures—for some of the reasons I listed earlier, and for three more which lean upon me now.

In the first place, it is clear that a commitment to the creative process starts the human animal on an endless, thorny and lonesome road of self-discovery, away from the comforts, blurred objectives and compromises of institutions. "Forty days and forty nights" is a Biblical metaphor for what is really a lifetime of wilderness and solitude. But the more deeply man delves into himself, the more surely he understands—and the more knowingly and tenderly he returns to—his fellow-man.

In the second place, the Arts are concerned not with the consumption, sale or other exploitation of earth's material wonders—not even with their recycling—but with their reincarnation. They propose not a mounting monopoly of a medium of exchange, but the sweet, quiet exchange of truth and beauty themselves.

I parenthesize:

Our inch of time witnesses an historically unique peril. For the technological explosions in the *means* of communication have cracked, warped and shrouded the *essence* of communication. "Image-Making" and its accoutrement of logos, commercials, testimonials, campaigns and conventions, entertainments, propagandas and public relations are elements of *control*—

and therefore of separation and division. Their avowed intention is to force a predictable response. They are the absolute antithesis of communication—the meaning of which originally was a "coming together—the way of, the fortress for."

And in the third place, in a time and a society whose values are geared to the biggest, the fastest and mostest, whose gaze is fixed desperately upon the future—as far at least as the next election or life after death or prosperity, whichever should happen to come first—the Arts offer an historical perspective. For their concern is with originality—meaning, that which has origins. Thus the Arts lead man to consider and build upon his own beginnings—his essence and his potential.

Of course, the Arts are capable of being subverted.

But, I suspect that their subversion has largely been exercised by those who have learned to manipulate a few of their surface skills rather than by those who have voluntarily undertaken the relentless and unremitting rigors of their disciplines. And I also suspect that the finest of the Arts—symphonic music among them—have too complacently accepted a comfortable elitist and Ivory Tower status. Scarcely believing their own gospel, they have not proved to be irresistible missionaries. For this reason alone the dedicated and skilled amateur symphony chorus is a critical—even essential—colleague of a healthy professional symphony orchestra.

For, finally, the simple truth is that every man is an artist—whether he wants it or not.

The only question is whether he's enough of an artist to fulfill his humanity—and to fill full his short mortality.

The understandings of the spirit are not easily come by. It takes a creative mind to respond to a creator's mind. It takes a holy spirit to receive the Holy Spirit. – And "just as I am" is not nearly good enough.

There's no freeway to Truth. There's no easy on, easy-off approach to Beauty.

You scratch and scramble around intellectual granites; you try to defuse or tether your emotional tantrums; you pray for the day when your intellect and your instinct can co-exist, that the brain need not calcify the heart, nor the heart o'er flood and drown all reason.

But in the struggle lies dignity and a tolerable destiny. (The alternatives to life aren't all that attractive anyway.)

So while we're here, let's hold fast to the liberating, conserving arts. – For Man in all his glory is clothed only by such as these.

– And without them there soon could be no body to clothe.

November 10, 1981

Lecture on "Worship and the Arts"
Memorial Church, Harvard University

Professor Gomes, Mr. Ferris, thank you. Ladies and Gentlemen—Good evening.

From the time the Noble Lectureship was visited upon me—as now I am visited upon you—I have been not a little apprehensive that I failed to qualify for its initiatory purposes, which propose (among other and splendid goals) that "The object of the Founder of the Lectures is to continue the mission of her husband, whose supreme desire was to extend the influence of . . . (Jesus as) the Way, the Truth and the Life . . . (and) as the inspiration to Christian Missions for the conversion of the world."

Certainly, it is a charitable and Christian act to set out in search of the sheep which is lost; – but it is quite another matter, having found him, to put him in the pulpit.

So that you can appreciate how far back it is possible for one man to have slid, you should know that for three generations the Shaws and Lawsons—both of whose names I bear—have been ministers, chaplains and missionaries in the service of an evangelical denomination removed from Congregationalism chiefly by water rites and Welch's grape juice. This edifice, however, by my father and grandfather, would have been mistrusted as either Episcopalian or Unitarian. Our biases—to match our abilities to discriminate—were scarcely theological. In the age-old confrontation of reason vs. the heart as the road to salvation, we'd have been numbered among the "feelers."

(I had but recently been told that "Gloria in Excelsis" was Hebrew for "Bringing in the Sheaves.")

From infancy "church" in our family was no sometime thing, but a seven-day, twenty-four-hour shift. Indeed, for a season fifteen years ago, and another period thirty years prior to that, I used to find myself in the very critical condition we face today—somebody out there and me up here.

This, of course, was when I was much younger—and infinitely wiser.

For, from a lectern or a pulpit one may begin with the incidental, but must end with the essential. One rummages through life's attic of preferments, accidents, and re-runs, the hopeless chest of experiences accepted and avoided, to see if there be anything other than grief worth, as they say, "sharing."

Some nights ago, when I'd been readin', writin' and wrestlin' for hours, trying to link some reasonably valid questions with some possibly valid answers, I was consoled by the memory of a *New Yorker* cartoon of twenty years ago wherein a kindly, worn woman of a certain age has her hand on the shoulder of her minister-husband; "Come to bed, dear," she says. "They can't all be Sermons on the Mount."

I take as my texts for this evening's homily four verses from the contemporary scriptures according to Charles Ives, and five from the Gospel according to John.

Charles Ives' sentences are to be found in a post-face to his privately published volume of 114 *Songs*. In a pungent 3,500-word essay which he randomly and randily entitled: " . . . The Circle of Sources . . . The Truth about Something . . . (or) How to Write Music While Shaving . . ." he asks these questions: "Is not beauty in music too often confused with something which lets the ears lie back in an easy-chair? Many sounds that we are used to do not bother us, and for that reason are we not too easily inclined to call them beautiful? Possibly the fondness for personal expression—which self-indulgence dresses up and miscalls 'freedom'—may throw out a skin-deep arrangement which is readily accepted at first as beautiful—formulae that weaken rather than toughen the musical-muscles. But if a composer's conception of his art, its functions and ideals, even if sincere, coincide to such an extent with these groove-colored, tried-out progressions in expediency, so that he can arrange them over and over again to his delight—has he or has he not been drugged with an overdose of habit-forming sounds? And as a result do not the muscles of his clientele become flabbier and flabbier until they give way altogether and find refuge only in platitudes—the sensual outbursts of an emasculated rubber-stamp?"

The familiar opening verses of the Gospel according to John seem to me even more provocative in the translation of the New English Bible of the Oxford and Cambridge University presses.

"When all things began, the Word already was. The Word dwelt with God; and what God was, the Word was. The Word, then, was with God at the beginning, and through him all things came to be; no single thing was created without him. All that came to be was alive with his life, and that life was the light of men. The light shines on in the dark, and the darkness has never quenched it."

Let me suggest to you the questions which this evening's title suggest to me. Be sure that I presume no ministerial certainty for my answers. I speak to you as a lay member of the larger religious community concerned, as surely all of us are, with man's nature and condition as a brother—or sister—of Man, and a son—or daughter—of God.

I ask myself three questions:

What is the Nature of Worship?

What is the Nature of Art? And . . .

What, then, are the responsibilities of the Arts to Worship (and the Church); and what are the responsibilities of the Church to the Arts?

First—what is the Nature of Worship?

". . . from the Anglo-Saxon W-E-O-R-T-H plus S-C-I-P-E . . .

ship: a suffix embodying a quality or state,

preceded by *worth:* that quality of a thing

rendering it valuable or useful;

excellence, eminence, virtue."

Therefore: worship—the state or quality of worth.

From that: the courtesy or reverence paid to that which is worthy.

From that: divine worship—divine honor to divine worth.

Under what conditions does Worship occur? When and where does it take place? What are the attitudes and states of being which allow it to happen?

For me, its absolute minimum conditions are a sense of mystery and an admission of pain.

> What wondrous love is this
> O my soul
> O my soul . . .
> What wondrous love is this
> O my soul?
> What wondrous love is this
> That caused the Lord of Bliss
> To bear the dreadful curse
> For my soul
> For my soul . . .
> To bear the dreadful curse
> For my soul?

> Amazing grace . . .
> How sweet the sound!
> That saved a wretch like me.
> I once was lost
> But now am found,
> Was blind, but now I see!

> Through many dangers, toils and snares
> I have already come;
> 'Tis grace has brought me safe thus far,
> And grace will lead me home.

Sometimes I feel like a mournin' dove
Sometimes I feel like a moanin' dove
Sometimes I feel like a morning dove
A long ways from home.

Sometimes I feel like a motherless child
Sometimes I feel like a' eagle in the air,
Sometimes I feel like I'm almost gone,
– A long ways from home.

These words are miracles to me—of ungraven images and boundless mystery; their melodies, shaped and worn by life-times and Niagaras of tears, are as perfect as anything I know in music.

This is not nostalgia; their saintliness and humility is the acquaintance of my later years. In my youth I was accustomed to a shoutier, sweatier fare:

Oh, there's power . . . power
Wonder-working power
In the blood
  (In the blood)
Of the Lamb,
  (of the Lamb)

Oh, there's power . . . power
Wonder-working power
In the precious blood
Of the Lamb.

I was sinking deep in sin
Far from the peaceful shore,
Very deeply stained within
Sinking to rise no more—
When the Master of the sea Heard my despairing cry,
From the waters lifted me—
Now SAFE . . . AM . . . I.
Blessed assurance, Jesus is *mine!*

Strangely, even these—as I recall them, and viewed through the blurring of time—seem somehow superior in poetic plausibility and common decency to the sanctimonious swill that, by the miracle of electronics, begins early every Sunday morning to violate the potentials and purposes of what is called the Lord's Day from Gethsemane Gardens, Florida, Crystal-Christ-o-rama, California, and Salvation-City, Virginia.

In the great folk-hymns and spirituals of the eighteenth and nineteenth centuries there is a directness and dignity, a fervor of utterance, and a humility which invoke man's nobility, and to me, a spark of divinity.

His voice as the sound of the dulcimer sweet
    Is heard through the shadow of death.
When Jesus wept,
    a falling tear
    in mercy flowed
    beyond all bound.

O tell me where the dove has flown
    and where he builds his nest . . .

Broad is the road that leads to death,
    and thousands walk together there.

Swing low, sweet chariot,
    Comin' for to carry me home.

My Lord, what a mornin'
    When the stars begin to shine.

This little light of mine
    let it shine
    let it shine
    let it shine.

Ev'ry time I feel the spirit
    movin' in my heart
I will pray.

Angel, oh angel
I don't want to be buried
    in the storm.

There is a balm in Gilead
    to make the wounded whole.

Occasionally, of course, mystery and pity will find a contemporary voice: Robert Frost, writing, "Dear Lord, forgive the little jokes I've played on Thee, And I'll forgive the great big one on me."

Dylan Thomas, in his *Child's Christmas in Wales*, writing of finding breast-up on the snow always on that icy morning "by the post-office or the swings . . . a dead bird . . . perhaps a Robin, all but one of its fires out"; and of receiving books that "told me everything I needed to know about the wasp . . . except 'Why?' "

The princess of cynicism, Dorothy Parker, caught weeping:

The night that I was christened . . .
It's a hundred years or more . . .
An old hag came and listened
At the white church door,

A-hearing her that bore me,
And all my kith and kin,
Considerately for me
Renouncing sin.

All the time she huddled
In a dim, grey cloak,
Stood there and muttered,
Spat and spoke,

'I give you sadness,
The gift of pain,
The new-moon madness,
The love of rain.'

And little good to lave me
In their holy silver bowl
After what she gave me,
'Rest her soul.'

"Nobody knows the trouble I've seen. Who is that a-comin' yonder on a cloud?"

Pain and mystery.

There must be little in our national life so frightening as the self-righteous alliance of evangelism and show business that can send a Southwestern Conference football band marching through Buddhist Japan, complete with twirlers and rangerettes, to save souls for Christ. – Or the Sunday Spectaculars of bigotry and contempt for men's minds so proudly exhibited by televangelism: Christianity pre-packaged and pre-digested in a succession of monologues and commercials; with the exciting new chapter of the romance of that lovable 33-year-old Trail Boss "everybody knows" and Big Daddy in the skies. These have to be a flat-out denial of Christ's compassion for the souls of men.

The witticism about the Unitarian praying "To whom it may concern" is really only about half-a-laugher, but totally disturbing. Hartley Burr Alexander in "God and Man's Destiny" concludes: "This is faith's humility, and the fountain of its prayer, never more feelingly uttered, as in the name of the souls of men, than by an Indian of the American prairies, 'A man from the earth am I . . . have compassion upon me, Whoever, from above, you the Supreme.'"

> So, musing all my days with uneasing wonder
> and encountering many phases of many minds,
> I grew, as all things grow, in the pattern of Self;

writes Robert Bridges in his *Testament of Beauty.*

> 'til stumbling early upon the mystic words, whereby Jahweh revealed his secret being to the Jews, and conning those large letters I AM THAT I AM, and reading there that man was made in God's image knew not yet that God was made in the image of man; nor the profounder truth that both these truths are one, no quibbling scoff—for surely as mind in man groweth so with his manhood groweth his idea of God, wider ever and worthier, until it may contain and reconcile in reason, all wisdom, passion and love, and bring at last (may God so grant) Christ's Peace on Earth.

Mystery and a sensitivity to pain surely are irreducible conditions for worship.

A second thing can be said about worship: it is that, though all of us on occasion have experienced in solitude what we felt to be a sudden flash of divine goodness and beauty, in a very important sense and a fellowship.

The chief prophet of this undertaking is Martin Buber, a German-Jewish philosopher, theologian and mystic, familiar, of course, to this gathering, who is of such contemporaneity that Dag Hammarskjold, shortly before he died, recommended him for a Nobel prize.

If I understand him correctly, the thesis of his books *Between Man and Manhood* (Now, you understand, of course, that Buber uses "Man" and "Manhood" generally—and not sexually. And so must I—regretting that our language betrays such bias and imprecision.) and *I and Thou* is that man finds his being and its relationship to "the Other"—that Outside Mystery which some call God—only when he is confronted with, addressed by, and responsive to another human being, a *Thou;* that the *I* and the *Thou* and the *Other* are inextricably inter-twined and interrelated ("all one Body, we?"); that this "revelation" happens not in isolated retreat from the world, but in day-to-day living; and that it is this communion which identifies man's manhood, and is of God.

That is to say: the Lord our God is One, but it takes two to find Him.

Words sometimes cripple thoughts, and these are further obscured by being in translation, but hear these sentences:

"Man's threefold living relation is, first, his relation to the world and to things; second, his relation to men; and third, his relation to the mystery of being (which the philosopher calls 'the absolute' and the believer calls 'God,' and which cannot in fact be eliminated from the situation even by a man who rejects both designations).

"A God reached only by renunciation"—of one or two of these elements—"cannot be the God who has made and held together all that is. The way can only be a 'communion,' and no essential relation to this God can stand outside of it."

And then he says a remarkable thing: "I have given up the 'religious,' which is *nothing but* the exultation, the ecstasy; or it has given me up. I possess nothing but the everyday out of which I am never taken. The mystery . . . has made its dwelling here where everything happens as it happens. I know no fullness but each mortal hour's fullness of claim and responsibility. Though far from being equal to it, yet I know that in the claim I am claimed, and may respond in responsibility, and I know who speaks and demands a response."

Worship is a "communion."

A third thing can be said about worship: this celebration of the worthy is also approachable on a formal, ritualistic and ceremonial basis. It is a healthy thing for the larger family of man—communicants with whom one does not have a daily contact—to come together with dependable frequency to consider divinity's wonders and man's relation to them and his fellow man.

It will surprise no one to suggest that a coming together of this size and occasionality must provide a number of elements of worth, harmonious and supportive of one another, and so conceived and fashioned, that this wider communion of men makes possible a deeper understanding of God.

This is where the Arts knock on the church door: outside, trying to get in; or inside, trying to get out.

Precisely because it is occasional and structured, "Worship" itself becomes an Art, or a confluence of the Arts, or at least similar to the arts in that it has a certain amount of Space and Time in which to contemplate and to proportion Truth and Beauty.

'Small wonder that formal worship invokes the rhythms of sight and sound as well as of reason—not only as stimulants to quicken the perception, or as unguents for life's abrasions, but as factors of worth themselves.

– Which leads us to our second major question: What are the meanings of Art? What can the Arts tell us of Man? What is Man trying to tell us of himself? Or of his Mystery?

These questions were the main attention of yesterday's talk. Will you forgive me if I for a moment recapitulate their arguments?

First: The arts are the Flesh become Word. That "the Word became Flesh" is familiar doctrine. – But what about the reciprocal miracle? The daily possibility of Matter becoming Spirit? Paint onto canvas in one century turned into tears six centuries later? Words onto paper today flung into a theatre tomorrow to change a life the year after? Little spots of ink transfigured into a miracle of symphonic sound joining thousands of listeners and performers in a rare community of Brotherhood? Art is the Flesh become Word.

Second, facing the bewildering profusions of matter and sensation, the Arts testify to man's ability to identify and to isolate, and subsequently to relate and to order. Out of confusion and chaos, emerge a Vittoria "O vos omnes" and "Swing low, sweet chariot," *Don Giovanni* and *Our Town*, "In the beginning was the Word" and "This is my letter to the world—that never wrote to me."

Third, the arts provide for the exchange of ideas and values otherwise incommunicable by languages of numbers, symbols, alphabets or grunts. "A work of art may indeed be a 'revelation.'" They exist to communicate that which is otherwise incommunicable.

And fourth, across boundaries of time, space, chance and malice, the Arts are the open hand of man reaching for his brother, and his earnest good will. Separate from Church and State, unstructured and individual to the point of anarchy, alone, of the great ethical-social-intellectual movements, they have been free of the intolerances, excesses and downright inhumanities which seem eventually to beset human institutions.

What is it in the nature of the Arts that allows them to offer their communicants such hopes of maturity and survival?

First: the discomforts and disciplines of creativity, which lead, all but ineluctibly, to self-knowledge and otherly-love.

Second: the spiraling reincarnation, rather than the waste or exploitation, of this earth's wonders.

And third: a link with history—past and future, and with the origins of originality.

The Arts, then, are not merely worthy hand-maidens of worship; but, given creativity on the order of a *Missa Solemnis* or a *St. Matthew Passion,* surely they are themselves unqualified and unparalleled acts of worship.

There was one other question—though a double one. The first part of it was, "What are the responsibilities of the Arts to Worship and the Church?"

First, it seems to me that we have to agree that only the best is good enough. One does not sharpen his sensibilities to excellence by stuffing his ears with mediocrity, however sanctimonious. One does not gain strength for the terrifying stresses of virtue by gorging his muscles on fraud and hanky-pank. A God of

Truth, Goodness and Mercy is not honored by laying last night's Top-Forty or Disco Derivatives on His altar. Man may indeed laugh himself all the way to the bank—but God is not mocked—nor is he worshipped.

This raises a few questions: on what grounds and upon whose authority are we to decide what is worthy and what is worthless for worship? May not one man's *Passion Chorale* be another man's *Old Rugged Cross?*

I suggest to you that the dilemma is more apparent than real, and that it can be solved by common sense, plain every-day good manners and a healthy combination of humility and industry which, however, lays upon no-one the obligation to matriculate at a School of the Arts.

Let me lay before you four criteria which may help this evaluation.

The first is that of *motivation.* Let's say right out that purity of purpose dignifies. Not every continent-straddling, world-striding evangelist is an Elmer Gantry. Though, if we were completely frank and had the wry wit of our grandfathers, we might observe "that too big a load of success and too much horse power will tear the heart right out of a clutch of humility in no time at all." Similarly, 10,000 "How great Thou artists" are not irretrievably doomed for chanting softly and tenderly in Yankee Stadium.

I can recall returning to my father's little yellow brick church when San Diego was still half-Navy and half-wetback, after my second exposure to the Bach *Passions* and *Cantatas* (the one that "took") to hear my mother and grandmother sing together "There were ninety and nine that safely lay—in the shelter of the fold." – And I discovered I could still cry.

But how much greater an experience it would have been had we been able to study and rehearse and perform competently together—as a service of worship—Bach's *Passion According to St. Matthew.* We'd still be crying.

Purity of purpose dignifies . . . But not all tears attest to equally deep springs of sorrow.

But what of that cancerous explosion whose purpose is not so pure? "Positive pop puts Christian radio in mainstream," was the headline in the *Atlanta Constitution's* Sunday Arts Section. "It's one of the fastest growing formats in radio today." "It reflects bigger budgets and a move to pop professionalism, countering the sincere amateurism that marked the early years." And these lines that lay it right on Madison Avenue: "There would have been a market ten years ago if there'd been a product." "To cross over into the secular market-place, you've got to take the cross over."

Jesus looked around and said to his disciples, "How hard it will be for those who have riches to enter the Kingdom of God." (Mark 10:23)

"And making a whip of cords, he drove them all, with the sheep and oxen, out of the temple; and he poured out the coins of the money changers and overturned their tables. And he told those who sold the pigeons, 'You shall not make my Father's house a house of trade.' " (John 2:15–16)

A second criterion must be craftsmanship. Music is a craft, and it has rules and standards—and within comfortable limits these are knowable. There is handsomely constructed music, and there is cheaply constructed music. We do not ask that every building be an unassailable masterpiece; but it ought at least to have the mortar, brick, foundations and girders specified in the contract.

Great text and great music do not meet in Las Vegas or on Madison Avenue.

The contemporary plague of that most popular *How Great Thou Art* cannot for long obscure the fact that it is more appropriate to show-business than it is to worship.

Great text and great music meet on the planes of purpose and craft, where music's edifice on its own terms is as honest and serviceable, and as beautifully proportioned, as the text it seeks to illumine.

In the third instance, art and music worthy of worship will have historical perspective. It will have *origins*—which may, in time, even lead to originality. This criterion is very close to what we mean by "style," and it adds to *motivation* and *craftsmanship* the incalculable increments of *heritage* and *tradition.*

Note that this does not preclude, but embraces the rich legacy of folk-hymns, carols and spirituals: those tunes and texts, lovingly turned and polished by generations of unintentional composers—nameless amateurs who loved their God and sought to praise Him.

These, the late Haydn masses, and requiems by Brahms, Berlioz and Britten, and, perhaps, even Charles Ives' *Psalms* are really the *people's music.* "Pop" is not the people's music. The people think so little of it that every 6 to 10 weeks they have to have a new tune to dance to, to trade small talk above, to go up an elevator with, to make what some call "love" by. The real people's music is passed from generation to generation. Music worthy of worship will have a heritage.

And then—once in a very great while—we may come across a sculpture, a building, or a piece of music which is indeed a "revelation," evidence not only of the creator's capacity to "*order* his experience" but, more importantly, to "*have* his experience."

And that is the fourth and final criterion—the creative miracle of "revelation": a cathedral at Chartres or Coventry or St. Mary's in San Francisco, Bach's *Mass in B Minor,* Stravinsky's *Symphony of Psalms,* Britten's *War Requiem.* – For, of course, the revelations themselves begin to set standards. *We* do not set them. – Exposure becomes acquaintance, and acquaintance becomes "communion"; and finally we begin to understand what an act of worship really is . . . and what it asks of us.

Jesus was asked, "Which of the commandments is the first of all?" And he answered, "The Lord our God, the Lord is one; and you shall love the Lord your God with all your heart, and with all your soul, and with all your mind, and with all your strength."

We never were told that it would be easy.

Nor did he say, "all your heart, most of your soul, and—let's see—about 'half' your mind."

The truth is that worship should be a heart-wrenching, soul-searing, mind-stretching and generally exhausting experience. One should not be required to check his mind at the door, should someone get him to the church on time.

What, finally, shall we say is the Church's responsibility to the Arts?

I've not yet thoroughly developed this thesis: – At present it's little more than a hunch, and perhaps I over-value it because it's a recent idea, and they don't come all that frequently.

It seems to me that any institution—and churches run the same risks as symphony orchestras, banks, universities, divinity schools and governments—any institution runs the risk of becoming "set in its ways," rigid in its policies and doctrine, hard in the arteries and soft in the head.

My hunch is this: that in a world growing denser in population, and poorer in sources of energy, we inevitably will have stricter political and economic organization—more controls—in order to provide food, housing and occasional comforts. In this sort of world the creative arts will loom as the finest flower of a maturing, creative mankind.

– But, even more importantly, for me at least, the arts may provide the day by day confirmation of a Creator's hand still at work in the lives and affairs of men.

If the Christian Church can accept the doctrine of "eternal life"—and most of it does—does it not follow that *this* life is somehow a part of *that eternal one* (eternity being indivisible and having no beginning and no end); and, therefore, LIFE in the universal, eternal sense—of which we are only a very small part—must still be a "becoming?"

I am not arguing Genesis vs. Evolution. (What's a few million years to the Infinite?) I am simply suggesting that if there is a Judeo Christian Creator/God—a God of Life and Love—He somehow/somewhere/somewhen must be about his business: Living and Loving.

However we may view Creation up to this moment, it strikes me as contrary to both reason and faith to attempt to argue that it is concluded. If so, when? – And, if so, then God indeed is dead. – Or no longer God.

Surely, it is at least short-sighted of a Christian "majority"—even if occasionally "moral"—to raise up an eternal, omnipotent Creator—and not give him anything to do since Day Six. Surely an almighty, everlasting Creator must be somewhere lasting and creating. – And if, indeed, generic man was made "in his image, after his likeness . . . male and female" (not hetero-, homo-, bi-, but BOTH! simultaneously! Talk about equal rights!) . . . – if, indeed, man was made "in that image," given a Timeless, Boundless Creator, what better place to see the Creator at work than in those who were made "in that likeness."

To me it follows that the Church, if it wants to keep in touch with the Creator, must provide a home for all that is—and all who are—creative, lest the church itself wither and drift into irrelevance.

Basic to the responsibilities of a Church in the Christian tradition is the presentation and interpretation of ancient evidences of God's creative presence and process.

But, is it not also equally important to recognize and identify—wherever they occur—the Creator's continuing manifestations and processes, and celebrate the fruits of a Holy Spirit still at work in today's fleeting fraction of Time's continuum?

To refer again to Charles Ives, and to substitute about a word and a half: "Is not "*worship*" too often confused with something which lets the ears (mind) lie back in an easy chair? Many sounds (or ideas) that we are used to, do not bother us, and for that reason, are we not too easily inclined to call them "*worshipful*"? Possibly the fondness for personal expression may throw out a skin-deep arrangement, which is readily accepted at first—formulas that weaken rather than toughen the muscles. But if worship, its functions and ideals, even if sincere, coincide to such an extent with these tried-out progressions in expediency, have we or have we not been drugged with an overdose of habit-forming sounds? And, as a result, do not our muscles become flabbier and flabbier until they give way altogether and find refuge only in . . . platitudes . . . ?

"When all things began, the Word already was. The Word dwelt with God; and what God was, the Word was. The Word, then, was with God at the beginning; and through him all things came to be; no single thing was created without him. All that came to be was alive with his life, and that life was the light of men. The light shines on in the dark, and the darkness has never quenched it."

I am not qualified to speak of the historical currents, tides and shapes of Christology. – But in my time it does seem to me that Christianity has become so preoccupied with the door-prizes attendant upon the divinity of Christ that it has not nearly fathomed Jesus' humanity.

What of Christianity's mind-boggling, seldom credited metaphor? What if the "Son of God" were in truth the "Son of Man?" What heresy lies hidden behind this scriptural identity? What does it mean that he who is hailed as

"Redeemer/Intercessor/Messiah/The Way/The Truth/and The Life as an infant was seen as Emmanuel/God with us?" Is there any possibility that the emphasis upon the God-hood of the Son of Man, to the exclusion of the Man-hood of the Son of God—like the concept of a concluded, unalterable Creation—affords a blanket of endless bliss in preference to a hair-shirt of responsibility? Knowing that the gospels do, in fact, attest to Jesus' awareness of his very special relationship to what he called "the Spirit" and "the Father," have we been slow to understand, or unwilling to credit, the language and the confidence with which he reached out to touch the souls of those around him—as, also, the soul of Everyman through Alltime?

"Whoever receives this child in my name receives me; and whoever receives me receives the One who sent me." (Luke 9:48)

(What if that were taken literally?)

"My daughter, your faith has made you whole." (Mark 5:34)

"You are the salt to the world. . . . You are light for all the world." (Matthew 5:14)

" 'The seed sown on rock' stands for those who receive the word with joy when they hear, but have no root in themselves. . . . " (Luke 8:13)

"A pupil is not superior to his teacher; but everyone, when his training is complete, will reach his teacher's level." (Luke 6:40)

"Why do you call me good? No one is good but God alone." (Mark 10:18)

"In truth, in very truth I tell you, the Son can do nothing by himself . . . I cannot act by myself; I judge as I am bidden . . . my aim is not my own will, but the will of him who sent me." (John 5:30)

"You cannot tell by observation when the kingdom of God comes. There will be no saying, 'Look, here it is!' or 'there it is!' for in fact the Kingdom of God is within you." (John 5:19)

"When the time comes, the words will be given you; for it is not you who will be speaking: it will be the Spirit . . . speaking in you." (Matthew 10:20)

"I am not myself the source of the words I speak to you; it is the Father who dwells in me doing his own work. . . . In truth, in very truth I tell you he who believes in me will do what I am doing; and he will do greater things still. . . . " (John 14:10, 12)

". . . The light shines on in the darkness, and the darkness has never quenched it."

So if, in truth, "in very truth," there be that great Indivisible, Incomprehensible, Omnipotent and Eternal Audience of One—what joy the Great Whoever must have watching the Creative Principle take hold in his "Likenesses" and continue his never-finished tasks of Creation.

May 14, 1986

Friends—

This week I've been preparing a commencement address for a school of church music; and, in addition to ideas concerning the special nature of the choral art, particularly as it relates to amateurism and professionalism (the attentions of several of these past letters), my mind and words kept turning to the most hilarious, mirthless fable I've read in years.

Malcolm Muggeridge is a former editor of the English humor magazine *Punch,* and a British TV lecturer, journalist, commentator and interviewer with a vast and not infrequently indignant audience. In 1976 he was invited to give the series of "London Lectures in Contemporary Christianity," later published as *Christ and the Media.* Starting from the premise that "the media in general, and TV in particular, are incomparably the greatest single influence in society today," he charged that this influence is "largely exerted irresponsibly, arbitrarily and without reference to any moral or intellectual, still less spiritual guidelines whatsoever. . . . "

. . . that TV's umbilical dependence upon instant action and constant sensation precludes even the most fleeting moments of reflection or contemplation, and, consequently, all the normal processes of thought which are essential to value judgement.

. . . and further, that TV's hypnotic attraction, together with its seemingly infinite economic potential, must inevitably re-channel even the most sensible and selfless of human souls into careers of corruption.

I suppose it's true that this decade is the first to face the fulsome, ripe and foulsome flush of the Electronic Church. The word "flush" comes to mind with what possibly is a Freudian wistfulness, for certainly there are not enough sewage-disposal plants in the world to handle even American TV's Sunday morning effluence. (– One need no longer look at pornography on TV. There is something worse.)

In the first of his lectures, in a wonderful flight of fantasy, Muggeridge extends the New Testament temptations of Christ to a fourth and final one.

"The first temptation, it will be recalled, was to persuade Jesus to turn stones into bread, thereby abolishing hunger and coping with the population explosion. . . . The second was to induce him to jump off the top of the Temple without coming to harm, thereby achieving celebrity and publicizing his message. The third was to accept the kingdoms of the earth from the Devil, thereby acquiring the requisite power to set up the Kingdom of Heaven on earth.

"Jesus turned down all three offers, recognizing that to provide unlimited bread would lead men to believe that they could live by bread alone; that seeking celebrity would induce men to see themselves as gods and worship themselves; and that accepting the kingdoms of the earth would substitute Caesar for God, and render his entire ministry meaningless."

Now comes the fourth temptation: Jesus is offered his own world-wide network: The Jesus H. Christ Broadcasting Company—with exclusive rights to the Dead Sea Video Tapes and Everlasting Life News; with studios in Crystal Cathedral, Orange County, California, and an inexhaustible Loyal Majority of listeners safely locked into computers in Lynchburg, Virginia.

And Jesus turns it flat down. Instead he entrusts his message to twelve nondescript, unknown, unevenly literate, impoverished, but committed live listeners. – And there follows, however slowly at first, the most awesome explosion of communications in the history of mankind.

For the next two thousand years "the greatest artists, poets and musicians dedicate their genius to celebrate that message; cathedrals are built to enshrine it, religious orders to serve it; mystics spend their lives exploring it. It is the source of the brightest and most far-reaching hopes of the human mind. Its sheer creativity extends to every field of exploration, from the expanses of space to the tiniest particles of matter."

That is the heritage. – Now, consider what arcs across Sunday morning skies from satellite to homesite in "His" name.

I have a grieving suspicion that, in the church bearing that name, except for a few isolated and unamplified voices, it may already be too late for ministers of "The Word." Sniffing larger congregations and bigger budgets, they've taken Jesus' injunction "Go ye into all the earth" to include the electronic highways of the heavens.

– But it might not be too late for ministers of music. Every day they can turn to the more recent, but no less holy, manuscript-ures according to Vittoria, Schütz, Bach, Brahms—and perhaps even Ives, Penderecki, Fauré, Durufle and Stravinsky.

Might it be possible that the arts, in return for having been given a home for centuries upon past centuries, at this moment of peril to the Christian religion, could halt the pervasive appeal to man's mediocrity and hypocrisy, might even restore worship to a consideration of God's mystery and man's dignity.

I keep hoping that in one of those colossal coliseum crusades, when the world's greatest gospel singer since "Cowhands for Christ" rides in to sing "How Great Thou Art!" a still small voice from the hundred-and-fifth row, accompanied perhaps by a string quintet and an oboe, will begin to sing quietly—for only twelve people to hear—Bach's *Cantata 56,* "Ich habe genug . . . " which is roughly translatable, "Enough already!"

'See you Monday,

R

March 9, 1982

Reflections and Excursions on "Orchestra and Chorus"
Trinity Church, Atlanta, Georgia

Dr. Keiser, Rev. Williams, Drs. Bonkovsky, Saliers and Peck, Ladies and Gentlemen—Good evening.

Tonight's topic, by all odds, ought to have been the easiest to flesh out on paper. Clearly, every lecture series should present at least one lecture with the subject of which the speaker may be presumed to have had personal experience.

I fuzzily recall a halting conversation over tea and cookies in their Paris living room with Alice B. Toklas some years after Gertrude Stein's death. I had been given a letter of introduction by Thornton Wilder, and Miss Toklas had granted visitation rights, though within a few moments it must have been clear to her that she was entertaining a young Californian whose mind was remarkably uncluttered by books or museums. (William Schuman put it more positively thirty years later, "Lord! Bob, were you dumb!")

In retrospect it seems to me that Picassos and Post-Impressionists were mounted three and four high on every wall and stair-well; and photographs of Hemingway, Miller and Fitzgerald filled all the spaces in between. "Gertrude," she said, pointing to a snap-shot, "Gertrude always said that if Ernest had had the courage to write about what he *was* rather than the hero he *wanted to be,* he could have been a fine writer."

What I had in mind some months ago, when these topics were set in semantic cement, was first, a comparison of the choral and orchestral instruments as they have appeared to me—their musical disciplines and aesthetic/intellectual/psychological characteristics; and second, "excursion" into more speculative areas—amateurism vs. professionalism, populism vs. elitism, participation vs. consumerism, government support vs. private philanthropy and, ultimately, a consideration of "where we are, whither we are tending and what we may be able to do about it."

I take my cue from the five-year-old whose names and parenthood I happily but wonderingly share. Realizing, just as he was about to be delivered to the schoolhouse door, that he had completely forgotten to bring his free-choice artifact for the morning's major event, he turned to his mother, "Come on in, Mommy! You're my show-and-tell!" – Just because some things may be obvious, let's not *overlook* them.

What are the *similarities* between the choral and orchestral phenomena? First, of course, both are musical instruments.

Music, among the arts, is distinguished principally by the fact that it exists in Time, rather than in Space. It has certain *metaphorically* special attributes: Harmony—the simultaneity of sounds—seems a kind of space; and ranges of audibility—high to low, soft to loud, and even bright to dark—seem at least metaphorically spatial.

Conversely, others of the arts do have temporal attributes: Poetry, for instance, some of whose rhythmic and reiterative elements are so dominant that we describe them as being "musical." Drama, for another, which certainly has acts *I* through *V*, and hours normally Two through Four to deal with events and ideas both momentous and ageless.

– However, the theatre's proscenium *is* a "frame," and everything within it a picture. In the 1930's and '40's that picture became so realistic, and the frame so insulative, that Thornton Wilder could say, "The trouble with the American theatre is that a man can pull a gun on a Broadway stage and shoot another man, and the other man is the only man who dies . . . nobody in the audience dies."

Even sculpture—among the specifically visual arts—can have captivating temporal qualities. It may very well be that the final fascination of *mobile* sculpture is not motion through space, but change through time. In the Carpenter Center at Harvard there's a water-mobile (which sounds as though it ought to have been invented by Peter Wabbit), eight stainless steel goblets swinging from Ferris Wheels within Ferris Wheels, filled and spilled randomly as they move by steadily falling water, which must offer nearly infinite permutations of balance and form in a single plane, and also something of the hypnotic spell of the ocean's ebb and surge against the land.

But *time* is very specially Music's continuum. Music exists from Now to Somewhen. Its purpose is to organize Sound through Time; by prescribing simultaneity and succession as to pitch, color and amplitude, it accomplishes a communication of pattern and proportion and a variety of emotional states, some of them, no doubt, intentional.

It is this *when*-ness that carries music's *paradox*. On the one hand it rests upon the assumption that Time is divisible: that this moment—or fraction of a moment—"metronome-marking x to the minute" is exactly equal to another moment ten minutes and a whole development from now.

Actually, our world and our lives turn on wheels of cycle and recurrency.

Sunrise and Sunset
High tide and low tide
Summer, Autumn,
   Winter, Spring
Family planning
   for fish, mammals and sand-fleas.
– Or pick a war from One to Ten,
There's plenty more,
Boys will be men!
Here we go 'round and 'round again.
Grab the brass ring, baby,
And get the beat
It's cool, real cool
And true, – so true.

For Toscanini, tempo was the heart-beat. Expression? Maybe a little, but don't spill any—and keep moving.

We stop—we "take" Time—to fix intonation. But—rhythmic ensemble must be fixed "on the move." – Or, rather, while we're all *living* at a precise and artificial rate of life.

The paradox in Music's use of Time arises in that it seeks by the artifice of Time's *fractioning* to stimulate emotional responses which are supremely indifferent to Time's *measure*. In Beethoven's *Missa Solemnis* a fifth of an hour of "Benedictus qui venit in nomine domini" passes in a contemplative stasis all but unique to Western thought. – And just forty seconds of the final *presto* of "Gloria in excelsis Deo" will buffet, tumble, and stomp upon one's chest, leaving the listener gasping for air.

I often have wondered if the reason that even confirmed symphony-goers so resent the new and unfamiliar repertoire (when they and others will run to the new show at the museum, or the new play at the theatre; or to the new book at the library) is that somehow a very personal life-tempo and life-timing is being disturbed by someone else's unfamiliar time.

It is not the single, isolated sound which disturbs the lover of familiar classics. No single instant in music is that shocking. It's that which precedes, or that which follows which seems disordered.

What happens behind a picture frame, a proscenium or within the covers of a book were "*once* upon a time"—somehow not really affairs of ours. But, "*my life*-time being disordered," by some unfamiliar sequence, is another matter.

So, choral music and orchestral music are Time-Arts rather than Space-Arts. And this leads to further similarities.

It means that musical structure; score study and musicological research are the same for vocal as for instrumental arts.

The Bach of the *Suites* and of the *Cantatas* is one and the same Bach. The *Ninth Symphony* and the *Missa Solemnis* employ a single musical language—though one would seem to be trying to make a religion of humanism, and the other to make humanism of a religion.

It means that all technical *ends*—though not always the *means* thereto—are the same.

Matters of pitch are right or wrong.

Matters of rhythm, meter, tempo and duration are precise or imprecise.

Matters of loudness are proportioned or disproportioned.

Articulation is just or unjust.

Color and Textures are appropriate or inappropriate.

These are music's technical considerations, and they are the essentials of the interpretive process—which is not nearly so mysterious as those of us who are mystified by it would have you believe.

There is one other great temporal similarity between the choral and orchestral processes; and it lies in the fact that both are *performing* arts. They are arts of the *where* and *when;* and their miracle is that a *St. Matthew Passion* or a *Missa Solemnis* can reach across oceans and centuries to "this rehearsal tonight" or those vesper hours next Sunday evening, to a fourth-generation Californian or a sixth-generation Scarlett O'Hara, and to audiences in Anchorage or Odessa, and command their presences and unite them.

Music has no being unless it is sounded. And every sounding, rehearsal or performance, is the psalmist's "new song"—new time, new place, new people, changed even from last night's rehearsal. And, by the same token, every sounding is also a "swan-song"—this moment's farewell, this span of time forever past, with its passing accounted in beauty or in error. (How special this makes even rehearsals!)

What then are the *differences* between the choral and instrumental apparatuses?

The most apparent one is that, in general, the chorus deals with words, with human language, and the orchestra does not. In this respect *only,* the chorus is enormously more complex and more complicated than the orchestra. Instruments initiate sounds by setting in motion vibrating surfaces or solids (percussion), vibrating columns of air (brass or winds) or vibrating strings (harp or violin). In each instance, the agent for initiating the vibration is basically a very simple tool: a mallet for percussion, a vibrating reed or lip for winds, a taut and frictive ribbon or a plucking finger for the strings.

But, for a moment, bring to mind the size of the standard unabridged dictionary; and realize that, theoretically at least, it is conceivable that any first syllable in that dictionary could be asked to initiate a musical phrase, which could be followed by any other word-forming unit at random *ad infinitum;* and, further, assume that ours is a double chorus of eight parts, each with its independent text, and that upon us rests the obligation of beginning together, proceeding together and ending together. It ain't easy.

Some of us who love choral music are sensitive to hearing it described as "monochromatic" or even "color-less." – But, think, for a moment, of the hundreds upon hundreds of different sounds of speech, and the thousands upon thousands of their possible sequential permutations. Truly, with proper care, the chorus can be an extraordinarily color-full instrument.

The other aspect of choral word-life to be noted is how fortunate the chorus has been in the "natural selection" of texts appropriate to community utterance. The "popular" song, for instance, is almost unexceptionally a lyric of personal "romantic" love—and absolutely ludicrous in the throats of 200 singers. On the other hand, the successful and durable choral-work will have a text which joins people happily, even nobly together in work, play, or religious or civic fervor.

Probably the most unnerving difference—or change—to a choral musician moving directly to the orchestra is the virtuosic velocity of first-rate instrumentalists and the speed with which they can rehearse. It is astonishing, is it not, that a fine symphony orchestra of one hundred-plus independent—even antagonistic—minds can perform as many as 10 to 12 different pitch or articulation functions per second precisely and simultaneously. The conductor is not doing it. He may be marking only every twelfth note. – Or worse, he may be making it *im*possible for the players to do it. But, if it is done, the players do it.

Furthermore, the orchestra is an instrument of extreme range and density, the octaves above and below the limits of the human voice calling for continuing education in pitch recognition.

Moreover, the dynamic range of the orchestra is beyond the possibilities of most vocal ensembles.

And, also, though we talked for a few moments of the color which enunciation can bring to choral performance, one must admit that vibrating surfaces, solids, strings and columns of air do a mighty acoustic kaleidoscope make. Though every musical instrument, in some respect of construction or performance, seeks to imitate some aspect of the human voice, man has built a machine that can fly higher, lower, faster and louder than he can sing.

These complexities and dexterities bring into clear relief one other great difference between choral and orchestral skills. It is that, while instrumental facilities are achievable (and aesthetically tolerable to listeners) only after years of practice and exercise, the human voice and pitch perception are relatively freely bestowed and unearned, like Salvation by Grace and honorary degrees— or Original Sin with the fun thrown in. A better singing product is assured if these talents are taken seriously and educated; but what an extraordinary gift it is to be granted at one's first choral rehearsal—the privilege of singing the bass part of a Bach chorale or, if the voice has not yet changed, the children's ripieno phrases folded into the opening chorus of the *St. Matthew Passion*. "In the beginning" . . . the very beginning . . . the chorus encounters "the Word" – the "Unspeakable Word."

If we turn now to aesthetic sensibilities and comprehensive intelligence, the *dis*similarities begin to blur. The conservatory training of the professional instrumentalist almost certainly will provide him with disciplines beyond those of the school – or Sunday-chorister. – But aesthetic sensibilities are enriched also by the *liberal* arts; and it is entirely possible—though hopefully infrequent—for one to concentrate so thoroughly on educating the fingers that other areas of intellectual, aesthetic and ethical awareness are retarded or crippled. One would have great difficulty in naming a professional orchestra which in intellectual range and depth could outsmart the student Glee Clubs of Harvard, Oberlin or MIT.

A few weeks ago, an Atlanta music critic handed me a series of questions which were directly in the line of this evening's attentions. The critic at first referred to Gunther Schuller's now renowned address to the students at Tanglewood:

". . . Today the term 'professional symphony musician' often elicits images of musicians who are embittered, disgruntled and bored, who have come to hate music (and particularly to loathe new music), for whom a rehearsal is an excruciating agony, at best a necessary evil.

"This cynicism is spreading like a cancer through our orchestras. – I know of only a handful that are not in an irreversibly malignant state—creating an environment into which it is downright dangerous for young people like yourselves to step, lest you also be infected. . . . "

The critic's question was "Is this true?" Well, certainly Mr. Schuller's remarks in general are too true of too many symphonic musicians. (Even one would be too many.)

But the blame for this condition is not the musicians' alone.

In general, the orchestral musician passes abruptly from a study period of fifteen to twenty years of the severest sort of self-discipline—a work schedule which would give Olympic swimmers pause—into a society that in most areas, and until very recently, has offered superior economic rewards to trades and occupations which do not require nearly the investment of time, effort, money and intellect that successful music-making demands.

Now, except in rare cases, no one *forced* the apparently gifted young child to undergo all that discipline. But the young musician has been led from childhood to regard his talent as a special one, and the arts in an historical sense as a "crown" of civilization—which somehow is a lot easier to prove about *past* civilizations than *present* ones.

For many young musicians it is a shattering awakening to discover that, even among the soloistic "best" in any generation, there are only a handful whom society elects to reward unstintingly. Even for those who seek ensemble rather than solo careers, it is discouraging to encounter the scarcity of employment opportunities, the uncertainty of regular work and an historically meagre compensation.

If one has the slightest insecurity in his own mind about *why* he chose the "arts," and what his intellectual, spiritual commitment is to them, he is indeed susceptible to becoming one of Schuller's "embittered, disgruntled, bored musicians . . . who have come to hate music."

Paul Hindemith's antidote for this was twofold: first, active participation with other musicians in musical projects for *non*-profit, chief among them chamber music. One of the healthiest aspects of trio, quartet and small-group performance is the opportunity to escape a conductor's musical dictates—to fly free. The second of Hindemith's therapies is association with students and young musicians for whom the arts are still a spiritual vision and a quest.

For today's symphony orchestras the remedies are not very obscure, though not easy to effect.

1. Create an atmosphere and working conditions which do, in fact, acknowledge the arts as a "crown of civilization."
2. See that every "artist"—even though he be a "section player"—has the opportunity, and the obligation, to perform frequently in a solo or chamber music fashion.
3. Establish audition and selection procedures that are as concerned about human sensibilities and artistic commitment as they are about digital dexterities.
4. See that volunteer administration and professional management have frequent and pleasurable contacts with performing musicians on occasions other than financial and contractual.

5. Don't let anyone—including oneself—forget that we are all in the *service* of a human excellence and creativity vastly superior to our own, and that we have a responsibility to make this beauty and excellence available to our entire human community—not just a narrow stratum.

It could very well be that the conventional symphony orchestra in our time is obsolete—or at least worthy of restructuring. What is desperately needed for institutional health and the happiness of its participants is a *Society of the Musical Arts*—whose members have the opportunity—and the obligation—to play not only symphony concerts, but also opera, ballet, oratorio, chamber music and recitals, together with a balance of teaching and coaching responsibilities which keep them in touch with many aspects of community life.

If great music is to enrich the life of a city it has to find ways of touching more than one-tenth of one percent of its citizens.

The choral art offers some interesting light herein largely because, I venture, it has remained substantially volunteer . . . amateur (from *amo, amare,* to love).

In the earlier parts of this century American choral music had three principal motivations: one, recreation and good clean fun (not bad as far as it went—which was mainly to the beer-barrel and back); two, special vocal methods (which had the result of making music a ribbon for the voice, rather than training the voice to become a vessel for the music); and three, worship (which is not suspect in principle, but, judged by the quality of the musical offerings laid on Sunday's altars, more often than not has assumed that the Creator of all Good Things was Himself Tasteless, Mindless and Couldn't Care-less).

Strangely, none of the musical arts in America has matured so tardily, but so rapidly, as the choral art. Literally hundreds of American choruses are offering entirely satisfactory performances of the most sophisticated and complex of choral and choral-instrumental scores.

Perhaps, just because it has been so closely associated with schools, colleges and universities, in many respects the choral art is in the vanguard of contemporary musical thought. The graduate degrees in Choral Conducting—performance as well as musicology—offered by the major schools of music in the United States are, in most cases, as strenuous, comprehensive, and more practical than their counterparts in Orchestral Conducting. More practical, because there really are jobs out there.

Statistically, the classical way to come to successful symphonic conducting is by way of opera coaching, which, in turn, depends upon pianistic facility. Of recent notable conductors of American orchestras only Koussevitzky, Toscanini and Ormandy are clearly outside this regimen.

Opera coaching has at least four advantages: one, its pianistic requirements ensure that the practitioner is always working with the full musical composition, harmonically as well as melodically; two, the opera coach is in daily contact with gifted, occasionally "great" voices—of which all instruments are in some respect imitative; three, the coach is exposed daily to ensemble necessities; and four, the coach is "in the wings" in the event of emergency opportunity, and it invariably arises.

Since there are so few opera companies in the United States—and so many distinguished choruses—it is not beyond the realm of possibility that the chorus will begin to provide to the American conductor, particularly if he has keyboard facilities, the training and the pathway to symphonic conducting which opera coaching has provided to the European conductor. Choral conducting does have advantages not unlike those of opera coaching:

1. The choral conductor is working with the entire musical composition. He faces all the *musicological* problems of style and structure, and all the *performance* problems of ensemble, intonation, balance, etc.

2. He is working with vocal sound. Instrumental articulation has its genesis in speech patterns; sectional orchestral intonation finds a paternity in choral unison; and such excellences as a "singing line" are vocally inspired.

3. From his beginnings the choral conductor also is working with an ensemble product. His is not a "solo" (or even a duo) performance. In most instances his collaborators are unpaid—or paid only in scholastic accreditation—and he has to learn day by day to merit his "followship."

4. The fact that the great body of the distinguished choral literature of the past 250 to 300 years has been written also for instrumental or orchestral collaboration also forces the serious choral conductor to deepen his orchestral knowledge, enrich his repertoire, and refine his conducting techniques to be more communicative to professional instrumentalists; he may, in fact, be standing "in the wings" when an emergency occurs.

5. The choral conductor is also in regular contact with a community of listeners. To aim one's performing style at the largest possible audience ultimately will degrade both performer and listener. – But in every audience there will be *some* listeners who really "hear," and who can guide towards an interpretative enrichment. Seldom will appraisal and guidance of this quality issue from the pen of professional critics, and never from the "standing ovation."

I parenthesize:

The evaluations of the public or of the professional critic are not really a proper concern of the performer. – That those evaluations are subject to manipulation (both favorable and unfavorable) is attested by the hundreds of "public relations counsels" accepted as a legitimate (if not auspicious) factor of the performing arts.

The performer not "in tune" with popular or critical tastes has two alternatives: if he has sufficient desire and ability he can *fashion himself* after the "In" image; or he can hire a *public image* constructed for him by press-agentry.

Obviously, both these devices put great strains upon integrity—the artist's relation to himself and his art. Since even the successful performer spends only a very small part of his life "in public," his relationship with himself conceivably is even more important than his relationship to an outer "image"—bought, assumed or thrust upon him.

The critical key to a choral conductor's transition to orchestra conducting is *keyboard expertise.* It prepares the choral conductor for the astounding speed of articulation which instruments possess over the human voice; and it enormously expedites score-study. The saving in preparation-time can allow a wider study of more music of more composers and, ultimately, may enrich one's historical and stylistic sensibilities.

Those without this keyboard wizardry had better be prepared to work harder and live longer.

The really striking thing about the major conductors, though, is how *absolutely different* they were in musical personality. Even with extraordinary coincidences of musical background and training, even sharing or succeeding one another with the same orchestras, their musical products were enormously dissimilar—a dissimilarity accountable only to the mysterious and precious uniqueness of the human "being": personality, intelligence, "soul."

For each of them, however, Mt. *Solemnis* was no less a demanding climb than Mt. *Eroica.*

– And, unlike most of those who daily wrote about them, only one or two of the ten steadily confused the depth of the ocean with the height of its splash.

How, then, are we to sum up the effects of professionalism and amateurism in the arts? If professionalism is seen to cause or inherit some strains—psychological or sociological—are they inherent in *professionalism* or *institutionalism,* or in both? If professionalism is seen to promote or allow higher standards of performance, should government support go largely (or exclusively) to the comparatively few, elite professional institutions—or should it be spread as widely as possible among "the people"?

By what standards, finally, are we to judge a nation's cultural accomplishment: (1) those of its elite professional institutions, (2) of its "popular," commercially profitable art-forms, (3) of its folk-art, or (4) of its amateur (voluntary) collaborative undertakings?

Charles Ives brings to our murkiness a delightful, flickering light:

". . . Our theory . . . stands something like this: That an interest in any art-activity, from poetry to baseball is better, broadly speaking, if held as a part of life, than if it sets itself up as a whole, – a condition verging towards atrophy of the other important values, and hence reacting unfavorably upon itself.

"Every normal man—that is, every uncivilized or civilized human being not of defective mentality, moral sense, etc.—has, in some degree, creative insight (an unpopular statement) and in interest, desire and ability to express it (another unpopular statement). There are many, too many, who think they have none of it, and stop with the thought or before the thought. There are a few who think (and encourage others to think) that they and they only have this insight, and that they and they only know how to give true expression to it. But in every human soul there is a ray of celestial beauty (Plotinus admits that), and a spark of genius (nobody admits that).

"If this is so, and if one of the greatest joys, and deepest pleasures of men, is giving rein to it, why should not everyone instead of a few, be encouraged to work where this interest directs—'to stand, unprotected, from all the showers of the absolute which may beat upon him—to learn to use whatever he can of any and all lessons of the infinite which humanity has received and thrown to him—that nature has exposed and sacrificed for him—that life and death have translated for him,' until the products of his labor shall beat around and through his ordinary work—shall strengthen, widen and deepen all his sense, aspirations and powers which God has given man."

The fact is that posing *professionalism* vs. *amateurism* and *elitism* vs. *populism* and *consumerism* vs. *performance-ism* are theoretical abstractions of true-to-life daily dilemmas; they will not disappear—and it may even be good that they do not disappear.

Robert Bridges in his *Testament of Beauty* writes:

" . . . We sail a changing sea
    through halcyon days and storm,
Our compass trembles in the binnacle . . .
and wisdom lies in masterful administration
    of the unforeseen."

And Martin Buber was quoted two days ago: "The mystery has made its dwelling here where everything happens as it happens. I know . . . only each hour's fullness of claim and responsibility . . . and I know who seeks and demands a response."

Our dilemmas change day by day and can only be faced practically and daily. And none of us must be foolish enough to think he can propose more than a temporary or personal answer. However theoretically desirable, it may be generations before the American people through their government can arrive at a program for support of the arts that will simultaneously reward excellence and encourage participation.

But to each of us is given his own back-yard. To each of us is given his own "hour's fullness of claim and responsibility."

I read with rue and wry in *New York Magazine* on the plane the other day a characterization of the Houston season of grand opera, which began, "Opera-going in these wealthy sun-belt cities is still essentially a *social* activity among the rich who foot the bills; and the decorative showiness of *bel canto* suits the audience's *nouveau riche* style."

But it was clear from Allison Williams's introductory words of Sunday morning that Trinity has been tending home-grown and vital art enterprises for more than two decades. Not only did Adele McKee supply us with an Ives *Psalm* on Sunday, she left us to swim for ourselves on the second verse of a hymn only moderately familiar. Many of us have seen highly innovative and successful theatre in the Trinity gym. The Westminster Chorale is on a singing tour of London. And the Atlanta Symphony and Chorus is about to perform a *Missa Solemnis* at a *World's Fair?* in *Knoxville?*

Each of us does have a back-yard. – And each of us must be his own gardener—his own artisan—his own artist.

The only question is whether he's enough of an artist to fulfill his humanity—and to fill full his brief mortality.

It takes a holy spirit to receive the Holy Spirit. It takes a creative mind to respond to the Creator's mind. – And, by Infinity's time, man ain't seen nuthin' yet.

"When all things began, the Word already was. The Word dwelt with God; and what God was, the Word was. The Word, then, was with God at the beginning, and through him all things came to be . . . All that came to be was alive with his life; and that light was the light of men.

"The light shines on in the dark, and the darkness has never quenched it."

October 11, 1987

"Creativity and Responsibility"
Fourth Presbyterian Church, Chicago, Illinois

Surely it cannot have escaped the attention of the residents of the north-central grain-, beef- and snow-belts that—just within the lifetime of color TV—the God of Abraham, Isaac and Old Glory has moved his headquarters to Dixie.

Mindful of the fact that O'Hare and Hartsfield are the two busiest airports in the world, I bring potential commuters the additional good news that, if we can trust our daily newspapers, and if Caesar does not allow him some amelioration of his present tax position, God is about to move his whole operation from Lynchburg, Virginia, to Atlanta, Georgia—electronics, electric fences, electioneering, and all.

We scarcely can believe our good fortune. "The city too big to hate" (a phrase Calvin Trillin called "the triumph of Babbitry over Bigotry") can almost overnight become "the city too paranoid to love."

Perhaps sensing that he might be needed in the days ahead, a cartoonist named Marlette arrived in Atlanta recently from the *Charlotte Observer,* bringing with him one of the classics of journalistic art. It shows a man dressed in a hunter's coat and cap, standing on a ladder at the edge of a roof covered with snow, and holding a smoking rifle. By the chimney a dazed reindeer is staring at an open sack, scattered presents, and the still form of Santa Claus, lifeless across the ridge-pole. "Hot damn! Edna!" the hunter calls to a woman leaning out of a second story window, "I got me a secular humanist!"

I have wondered many times, as I pondered the responsibilities of this day, if there is any greater need in our society than that of discerning the sanctity which abides in the secular, or of restoring to its rightful position of ethical and political authority the hopes and concerns of "Christian humanism" (a designation attributed to the founders of Presbyterianism by the writers of the Encyclopedia Britannica).

It was almost exactly one hundred years ago that Friedrich Nietzsche announced—in a manner however Teutonically clouded—that God was dead. It is a matter of record that this news reached Atlanta in something only slightly over three-quarters of a century, and that it was passed on with earnestness and dignity by a professor of the Candler School of Theology of Emory University, but, it must be admitted, with only minimal support from Southern Methodist congregations and clergy.

It is from this same university, now celebrating its one-hundred-fiftieth anniversary, and ascending rapidly in the esteem of the councils of learned men, that I have stolen this morning's title. "Creativity and Responsibility" is the Emory rubric for its anniversary year of seminars, lectures and special events.

I suppose that what they had in mind was to examine, in a series of scientific, philosophic and artistic fields, whether or not exceptional creative talent should acknowledge relevance or responsibility to the *status quo* of the human condition ("status quo" being roughly definable as "the mess we're in").

But, clearly, if that is what they had in mind, they have managed to telegraph the answer with their question. – For no scientist will view even the narrowest of fields of exploration as removed from all other fields—or fielders; the phi-losopher's commitment to wisdom already is the search for the appropriate human response to natural phenomena and events; and any artist is seeking *first of all* to communicate *some*thing to *some*body which otherwise may be incommunicable.

As regards "creativity and responsibility," therefore, I find in my mind only things which appear to be common-sense and—for me—true. – But, they are at least home-made and hand-written, and even a personal truth may be rare enough these days to risk its telling.

The idea of creativity has led my thinking first of all to a re-examination of the accounts of what is called "The Creation," from the myths of Egypt and Mesopotamia to those of North American Indians, Australian aborigines, and the accounts in *Genesis, Proverbs* and the *Gospel According to John.* In nearly all but that extraordinary poetic vision of John the vast and mysteriously seminal presence of timeless waters plays a fascinating role: "In the beginning" . . . void . . . darkness . . . "and a spirit moving over the face of the waters."

The accounts in *Genesis* are, of course, attributable to two different sources, linking very clearly about halfway through verse four of the second chapter. Conceivably, one could read this verse as a summary of the familiar seven-day sequence or as the titular sentence of the second account.

The cadenced litany of evenings and mornings in Chapter One of "light, firmament, land, seas, sun, moon and stars, all manner of grass, herbs and fruit, and every living creature that moveth"—this litany culminates on Day Six with the creation of human life. "Let us make man in our image," says God. (Had I ever before heard that plural? Let us? . . . Us who?) "Male and female," says God. (One likeness—both sexes . . . ? simultaneously? – And God gives the newly created likeness "dominion" over "all the earth" and "every living thing. . . . And behold, it was very good."

With the opening verses of Chapter Two God arrives at Day Seven; his labors ended, he rests from all the work that he has made, blessing the day and sanctifying it.

Then comes the abrupt change in sources, for Verse Five, wherein we might have expected an Eighth Day—or a Second Week—begins in the middle of a sentence about plants still unplanted and unwatered and says flat out that, "There was not a man to till the ground."

"But there went up a mist from the face of the earth." – And the second creation of man is poetically as rich as the first, for the "Lord God formed man from the (moist) dust of the ground . . . and breathed into his nostrils the breath of life; and man became a living soul." There follow immediately in quick strokes the creation and naming of the animals, the formation of Eve from

Adam's rib, and the treacheries, trespasses and punishments of life in a garden "Eastward of Eden."

The account of Creation in *Proverbs* VIII is fascinating because it stands in form and imagery—as, of course, it does in historical time—somewhere between the ingenuous (everything but artless) narrative of *Genesis* and the mind-boggling abstraction of "In the beginning was the Word."

It is not quite yet "the Word" that speaks through the eighth chapter of *Proverbs*. Rather, it is *"Wisdom"* who speaks. And it is worthy of note, I think, that insofar as Wisdom is personified in the verses which open the chapter, it's personified in the feminine: "Doth not Wisdom cry, and understanding, putting forth *her* voice?"

> The Lord created me at the beginning of his work,
> the first of his acts of old.
> Ages ago I was set up, at the first, before the
> beginning of the earth.
> When there were no depths, I was brought forth,
> when there were no springs abounding with water.
> Before the mountains had been shaped,
> before the hills, I was brought forth;
> Before he had made the earth with its fields,
> or the first of the dust of the world.
> When he established the heavens, I was here,
> when he drew a circle on the face of the deep,
> When he made firm the skies above,
> when he established the fountains of the deep,
> When he assigned to the sea its limit,
> so that the waters might not transgress his command,
> when he marked out the foundations of the earth,
> Then I was beside him, as one brought up *with him;*
> and I was daily his delight rejoicing before him always,
> Rejoicing in the habitable part of his heart
> and delighting in the sons of men.

For me the opening verses of the New Testament *Gospel According to John* are even more evocative in the translation of the New English Bible:

> When all things began, the Word already was.
> The Word dwelt with God, and what God was, the Word was.
> The Word, then, was with God at the beginning,
> and through Him all things came to be;

no single thing was created without Him.
All that came to be was alive with His life,
and that life was the light of men.
The light shines on in the dark,
and the darkness has never quenched it.

I dwell on the Judeo-Christian accounts of *The Creation,* first, because they are a familiar part of our heritage; if we are, indeed, to discover creativity's responsibility, it seems to me it will be seen to owe as much to the human past as to humanity's future. – But also, of course, to remind myself of how extraordinarily perceptive the early writers were about human nature—in particular the dichotomous qualities of good and evil and, inescapably, humanity's *un*finished state.

Most of all, however, I am struck by the distance in conceptual imagery between the Babylonian sources of the Hebrew accounts, two to three thousand years before Christ, and the incredible ideational leap of John's gospel as the ancient story met the "real, live" Greco-Roman world—alien, Gentile and even secular, all those bad things.

It does seem to me that it makes very little difference whether one's thought is colored by *Genesis, Proverbs* and *John* or by secular or planetary hypotheses, whether by cubits or light years. These seem to me to be but momentary symbols, not the substance, of meaning.

If, indeed, the human mind can move from *Genesis* to *John* in three millennia, and from a seven-day week to the Big Bang in five millennia, does anyone seriously doubt that from somewhere five millennia from now (should there be "world enough and time") both the seven-day week and the Big Bang will appear primitive and groping, however true to what we call human nature.

For some weeks of each year, our family lives in a little village in the southwestern part of France. At present the village has forty to fifty inhabitants, all living in stone dwellings that originally had only dirt floors and accommodated both animals and people. Though the Dordogne River and lush valleys are only one or two hours away by foot, and minutes away by auto, it is basically a terrain of high plateaus and severe canyons, of scrub vegetation and sparse grass suitable for the grazing of sheep rather than gardening.

We are told that men have been living in the caves of these ravines for forty thousand years or more, and we have seen some of their drawings. We are told that in this dry land their holy places were springs and underground streams, and that is not difficult to credit. – And we are told that in instance after instance Christian shrines, abbeys, monasteries, and churches have stood for two hands of centuries—stand today—on the sites once held sacred by primitive man. These founts now hold what is called "holy" water. For the love of God—why not?

As regards astro-, bio- or "theo"-physics I scarcely am even pre-school.

But, all my pondering of the facts or fancies—equally meaningful—of creation leads me to believe that the physical world which I can touch or see or theorize is not a Thing, but an Action. – Not a Where, but a When. Universe is not its name—Creation is its name. It is a great big no-thing of Becoming.

Surely, there will continue to be measureless eons of the Unknown in this drama. Whether or not the *still-to-be-known* is also a *Knowing*—which some today call God—is for each to say. If so, the *Unknown-but-Knowing* is *also* a *Becoming*. For me it is enough that human life, though not yet Creation's "crown," and imperiled at this very moment by aspects of its own humanity, is a part of the Action and on its forward edge.

At the age of eighty-five Robert Bridges completed his *Testament of Beauty*, in whose two hundred pages and four "books" of philosophical poetry are these lines:

> So, musing all my days with uneasing wonder
> and encountering many phases of many minds,
> I grew, as all things grow, in the pattern of self;
> 'til stumbling early upon the mystic words,
> whereby Jahweh revealed his secret being to the Jews,
> and coming upon those large letters I AM THAT I AM,
> and reading there that man was made in God's image
> knew not yet that God was made in the image of man;
> nor the profounder truth that both these truths are one,
> no quibbling scoff—for surely as mind in man groweth
> so with his manhood groweth his idea of God,
> wider ever and worthier, until it may contain and reconcile in reason
> all wisdom, passion and love, and bring at last—
> Christ's peace on earth.

Is the calling of the "Son of Man" the "Son of God" merely an inadvertance? What if the God-Man and Man-God were an attempt to say something not limited to Zero A.D. and Bethlehem of Judea? Is it frightening, or merely incomprehensible, that Buber's I and Thou and the Other should share the responsibilities of Creation, even perhaps be one with its "substances?"

– And, if we can accept that the universe is not a place but a time, might we not be able to move in our thinking to where we can understand creation not only as action but as a spirit? – even, the spirit of love? Could it be possible that God *is*—love?

Melvin Konner has written with explicitness and compassion about human genetic and biological restraints. He sees the human animal as a transitional creature like the archaeopteryx embedded in Mesozoic rock, "a bleep-poor reptile, and not very much of a bird." – A bleep-poor human, and not very much of a God.

The dinosaurs, he says, ruled this world for over a hundred million years, or "one hundred times the brief, awkward tenure of human creatures," and are gone "almost without a trace." – And humanity could do the same.

His hope is hinged to the fact that we are capable of knowing our danger, and that we conceivably could have a hand in the shaping of our destiny, could save this creature from a "protracted, dissolute self-destruction." That is: if we are "in the least capable of sympathy with the suffering of other human beings," and if we have "any sense of joy, order and beauty of life." He calls this complex of affections a sense of wonder, and I do not find it far from what I have called "Love."

There is absolutely no question: creativity does have responsibilities. We are in creation and of it—along with whatever Gods may be. Our plate holds all the creativity we can swallow, and ours is all the responsibility there is.

We know, almost without argument, in our inch of time, those attitudes and conditions which favor human survival, and those which imperil it. The axioms of survival are as simple and homely as folk-hymns:

— A sense of wonder at the blue-white orb of earth spinning in space.
– A sense of kinship with all human creatures, even those outside our kin or ken.
– Lack of fear of dissent and contradiction.
– Freedom of expression and movement.
– Affection for tradition, but willingness to break with custom.
– Spirit of play, as well as dedication to work.
– Hope and purpose on a grand scale.
– And a dozen more.

I have a suspicion that, viewed from Lynchburg, these counsels to human behavior might be seen as secular humanism or even non-theistic liberalism. Then—goody for them! Their god just fits his electrified fence.

It may very well be that in our time humanity senses its predicament as being so precarious that men, women and children are running for whatever shelter is available. Anyone who isn't worried ought to be. And, certainly, there is a plethora of placebo-vendors at the touch of a dial. But, by and large, the electronic church is merchandising a quick, slick and bogus solution instead of offering a slow, laborious but honest life-time share in the responsibilities of creation. – Which is, after all, where we now stand—hoping we have "world enough and time."

March 15, 1994

"Religious Emphasis Week" Address
Westminster School, Atlanta, Georgia

The Secretary to the Music Director Emeritus (Conductor Laureate) of the Atlanta Symphony has a standard response she gives to any organization rash enough to request his public discourse. "Mr. Shaw," she says, "only opens his mouth to change his socks."

To your considerable misfortune Mr. Clarkson's request was spoken and delivered in person—so here we are.

When I first went to New York to seek my "fort-I-an" Leo Durocher was manager of the (then) Brooklyn Dodgers; and the *New York Times* reported his tongue-lashing of a young ballplayer who had just made his third—and game-losing—error in center-field: "You stupid son of a So-and-So! You've managed to louse up that position so thoroughly that nobody will ever be able to play it again!"

I have the sick-at-my-tummy feeling that the same thing is about to happen to this lectern and Christian Emphasis Week.

Since Mr. Clarkson has mentioned the Kennedy Center Honors, let me just report to you that among the many wonderful things that happened—including beautiful hotel rooms, fabulous food, limitless limousines and White House hospitalities—it should be noted that it was a most decisive lesson in the Scales of Celebrity. If one is standing or walking any place within twenty feet of any combination of Gregory Peck, Audrey Hepburn or Lauren Bacall you are absolutely invisible. On a Celebrity Scale of 1 to 10, I would have scored Point Zero Zero Zero Three.

– And had it been—as it was this year—Johnny Carson or David Letterman, you'd have been caught in a complex of minus nines.

I have had more difficulty writing this speech than any article or statement I ever have written.

I suppose part of that excuse has to be attributed to the fact that Mrs. Shaw and I have a son attending school here. – I suppose it is still true that one of the reasons young people (kids) study hard or try to excel in extra-curricular activities is because they want their parents to be proud of them. – Well, let me just tell you that it "ain't" nearly the pressure that wanting your *children* to be proud of you is—in front of their peers and friends. That's pressure.

Moreover, scholastically, without exception, every contact I have had with Westminster has reinforced my respect and affection for the school, its faculty, students and programs. Dr. Pressly, the school's founder, has to be considered one of the real heroes of Atlanta's last half-century. Every adviser or teacher I've met has been not only a master of his subject, but sincerely, even selflessly, interested in the welfare of his students. And the personal and intellectual quality of my sons' friends I certainly did not meet until college years. And I would be embarrassed not to measure up to their standard.

Then, when the printed announcement of the week's activities came, I was disturbed by the title. I had been asked to address this gathering during *Religious* Emphasis Week, and this announcement specified *Christian* Emphasis Week; and, as will become clear as I continue, I had hoped there might be speakers representing other religions and other approaches to the "Sweet"—and bitter— "Mystery of Life."

The sub-title also gave me pause. "Music as Worship," together with the quotations from Psalms and Philippians and instructions from the Peachtree Road United Methodist implied that music could—if not "should"—be a servant in the ritualistic activities of Christian worship. Now, obviously, this is true. Not only music—but all the arts—can and should be used in formal worship.

– But, as I approach what surely are the final digits or teens of my earthly years, I am becoming increasingly convinced that the Arts—and certainly Music among them—are not "as" anything. They are not to be thought of as servants of a more exalted function. Great music is worship. The *Fine*-est Arts are worship.

Let me say that I'm no longer disturbed by a "Christian" Emphasis Week. I think every week should be a week of religious emphasis. Religion is the human attempt, both individual and social, to come to some understanding of the mysteries of Matter and Life and Time and one's responsible behavior thereto. Is there anything in self-conscious life more important than this? Don't we need every bit of information we can get? Should there not be also a Buddhist Emphasis Week, and a Judaic Emphasis Week? – And weeks for Zoroastrianism and Muhammedanism, and Hinduism and Greek Mythology, and let's hear it for Ancestor Worship?

For it seems to me reasonable that a fine educational institution (like Westminster) should examine with great care the moral and ethical teachings of all religions, together with their institutional histories. – To see, for instance, if there is any relationship between today's institutions and practices of Christianity and the words and actions of Jesus of Nazareth. And, as a third-generation, and occasional Christian, minister, I fear my conclusions.

Obviously, these conclusions and evaluations are a result of my own experience. You will have different experiences, and you will reach different
conclusions. – But, to be honest with you, since I have been asked—even if by
others in your names—I should present, for your examination, mine.

I'm a fourth-generation Californian, which is rare for a man of my age. I
can remember California before they paved it. We learned to swim—or drown—
in irrigation ditches, mountain lakes or the Pacific Ocean.

I was also a third-generation preacher in an evangelical sect called the
"Christian Church"—or, officially—the Disciples of Christ. Though not quite so
numerous as Baptist or Methodist churches, they were about the same in theological content and Sunday rituals. Like the Baptists, we practiced baptism by
immersion and observed weekly communion—but with Welch's grape juice.
Ours differed from these denominations principally in that we had no national
governing administration. Each church was totally autonomous.

In addition to being a preacher, my grandfather was also California president of the Anti-Saloon League—and probably therefore somewhat personally
responsible for Prohibition in California.

This must have been a conviction which reached Grandpa somewhat late in
life, for mother used to tell a story about a combination fishing-trip and religious retreat he went on to the High Sierras with the men of his church board.

As mother has it, Grandpa didn't say anything when they passed a bottle of
whiskey around the camp-fire the first night. – And though card-playing and
gambling clearly were "sins," he also was silent when a deck of cards appeared.
He watched quietly the first few rounds of poker and, when they passed him the
cards, he said he figgered he knew enough to deal the same number of cards to
each man. He played along with the bidding and, when it came time to "putup
or shut-up!" Grandpa laid down one-two-three-four-five aces, saying something like, "Go thy way, and sin no more." Nobody ever did figure how Grandpa
got 5 aces out of somebody else's deck of cards.

The fathers of some of my friends sold insurance or groceries or carpenter's
tools called hardware, or—if they were real wealthy—Model T Fords. Our
father—there were five of us—sold Christianity—and he was good at it. He had a
wife who was the best singer of gospel songs and spirituals I ever heard. Her way
with black spirituals was such that I have often thought she could have stood
with Marian Anderson on the steps of the Lincoln Memorial the afternoon
Miss Anderson was denied the stage of Constitution Hall in Washington, D.C.
by the all-white Daughters of the American Revolution.

For a minister's family in those days "Church" was not a week-end affair.
Every day there was something: morning family devotionals, church family
suppers, prayer meetings, Boy Scouts, weenie roasts, Capture-the-Flag, funerals,

weddings, Daily Vacation Bible School, Youth Choir, and three services every Sunday. Should a child by misfortune pass away in the town, the minister's family got the clothes. In our family there was always somebody the right size. Once there was an electric train; another time, a bicycle.

Our church received new members by what was called "confession of faith." At the conclusion of the pastor's sermon we'd sing the "Hymn of Invitation." And, at that time, any one who wanted to join the church could walk forward and be received into the membership by public declaration and acceptance of "Jesus Christ" as his or her "personal Saviour."

Well, you can see what a temptation that would be for a six-year-old boy! – Everyone looking at you as you walked down the aisle—the minister putting his hand on your head and praying over you. – The kids in your Sunday School class wishing they had the nerve to walk down there like that.

From the time I was eight years old I suppose I made that walk two or three times a year. My father would meet me down on the level of the congregation, below the pulpit, push me off to one side, saying something like what W. C. Fields used to say, "Go away, boy, you bother me!" – Or, "Come back when you're older, son."

Finally, I got to be twelve years old—the age at which Jesus was found teaching in the Temple—and I was admitted. I guess everyone figured—as with the kid who was going to inherit his dad's Ford Dealership—that one day I'd end up in the ministry.

—But college brought major surprises and one cataclysm.

Pomona College is only 107 years old, but since World War I it has qualified as one of the scholastically classy colleges of the United States. In my time it had about 1,000 students. It now has a half-dozen brother- and sister-colleges adjacent to it (with differing curricular emphases) in what is too smugly referred to as the "Oxford of the West," but it still will be listed on anyone's "Six to ten best colleges in the U.S."

There I had my first courses in "Comparative Religions," and had my first lessons in how, when and by whom the Old and New Testaments were written and assembled.

There I met my first Jew. I think that up to then I had figured the Jews were an ancient race who lived in a land called "The Holy Land" in a time called "B.C." And here was a living, brash, funny and exciting 18 year-old from some place called "the Bronx" in New York City who knew infinitely more about every subject (including my own religion) than I did, and who made every lecture course he attended a One-on-One debate with the professor.

I became a student Youth Minister in the town's Community Church and instituted a series of Sunday afternoon services of music and readings in the college chapel.

The cataclysm occurred when my father began suffering a series of variously incapacitating strokes, and I was asked to take some of his Sunday services.

I cannot remember the precise month, but the events are very clear. On a Saturday afternoon I would drive the 125 miles from Pomona College to San Diego where I would hole-up for the night in my father's church study, and attempt to pull together materials for the Sunday morning service and sermon.

On this occasion I was met by the president of the Church Board with the news that they had a very serious problem.

The brightest and most beautiful girl youth leader of the church was desperately ill in the hospital. I must come to the hospital at once, and if she were still alive Sunday morning we must have a special service of prayer for her recovery.

I did not know the young woman and I had not had a lot of first-hand experience with death. To my untrained eye that evening in the hospital, except for a few (and much too infrequent) spasms of breathing, she looked grey, drawn, and moribund. – But she made it through the night.

I have no idea what we had for a sermon that morning—probably something pieced together from the College Youth Services. The prayer was another matter.

I have a problem with public prayer. I can understand private meditation. I can even understand united congregational prayer. And I am sympathetic with the Quaker practice of congregational quiet and meditation until someone is "moved" to speak.

But I do not like to be prayed "upon"—with words which I have not chosen for myself. Nor do I like to pray "upon" others—with thoughts they may not be thinking, in manners which they might find uncomfortable, and for ends they might consider none of my business. – And I am particularly uncomfortable praying publicly to a God who by all customary Christian definitions is all-powerful, all-knowing, all-loving and whose eye is already "on the sparrow."

We had reached the place in our mimeographed Order of Worship where it spelled out *Pastoral Prayer,* and I began saying some of the things I have just said. I saw peoples' heads drop, glance up, and then drop again.

A few eyes already had closed. – Perhaps this was it.

I went on: if there is a God of limitless love and power then that goodness and power already is in motion. And what remains is the question of whether all *human* forces—medical, psychological, mystical—whether we all are doing all that is humanly possible to help this young girl win her battle.

By this time all heads were bowed. I may have said "Amen."

We dragged through the sermon, sang a final hymn (not a *Hymn of Invitation*) and the services came to an end.

I was at the front door of the church going through that frightful ordeal where the church goer says "Lovely service" and the minister says "See you next Easter," when a middle-aged man ran up the steps. " 'She made it,' " he said. " 'The crisis passed at eleven thirty-three!' " – Exactly prayer-time. – And the next Sunday there was a list "this long." – And the following Sunday I left the church.

I had enough sense to know that there are medical cures that by all the laws of medical science are absolutely inexplicable. (We count on that heavily in our family.) But I also had enough sense to realize that I would never be able to work within an institution willing to credit that I was in any way responsible for that cure.

I tried to wiggle my way back into the church just a few years later—but in a different function. A musical motion picture was made on the Pomona campus with Dick Powell and Fred Waring and a host of other radio and motion picture celebrities. I was doing choral work on the campus at that time, and was offered a position in New York which included forming choruses for network radio shows, Broadway musicals and World's Fair entertainments. This was the great era of the Broadway and Hollywood musical: the late Thirties and the Forties. It was the days of the Big Bands and the great love ballads of George Gershwin, Jerome Kern, Richard Rodgers, Vincent Youmans, Hoagy Carmichael, Cole Porter and Irving Berlin.

My personal interest, however, lay still in sacred music—music for worship. And, being young and completely impractical, I fantasized that if I could form an incredibly expert youth chorus of mixed voices, I could get the whole world of serious composers to begin writing music on sacred texts (on texts which they or I considered sacred) and we could draft a new service every Sunday night and put on a service of worship which eventually would result in a new liturgy appropriate to young people of our day and age.

We picked a Fifth Avenue Church whose minister at the time was the most famous minister in the United States, in books, in radio and in motion pictures.

We put a small announcement of auditions in the *New York Times;* we canvassed the past members of the New York All-City High School Chorus—a diamond-mine of talented people of college- or post-college-age who were still living in New York. We gave the strictest musical audition we could conceive. And we selected 200 voices out of the 600 auditioned. We were helped by the fact that times were tough and jobs were scarce. Certainly, some very talented folks joined in the hopes that it might lead to employment. Members ranged in age from 18 to 60 plus, with most in their twenties or very early thirties. We had every shade, shape and color of human flesh; and we had every species of human ideology, philosophy, occupation and religious custom.

We said we were "a melting pot that sings," and, by the end of the first rehearsal we sang louder—and better—than anything New York had ever heard.

But following the third rehearsal the minister called me to his study. "Mr. Shaw," he said, "our consistory has met and I have to inform you that you may continue to use our social hall for rehearsal so long as you have in your membership no Negroes, Catholics or Jews, and 50% of the remainder must be members of our congregation." – And so, of course, I left the church a second time—and 200 good singers left with me.

In all fairness, that story had a happy ending—nearly a half-century later. And I read a part of a letter I received in 1986—*only* so you can realize what a remarkable moral sense and mental acuity is possible for a man who was well into his 90's.

"I read in an airline magazine that you are retiring next year as Music Director of the Atlanta Symphony Orchestra.

"I have always regretted the many mistakes I've made in life, particularly my insensitive and stupid mistake in connection with the fine organization you were developing years ago at the church in New York."

There follow some flattering sentences, and he concludes,

"I have followed your . . . career with admiration.

"It is not necessary for you to be burdened with answering this letter. I just wanted you to know that I have ever been sorry about my lack of cooperation. I am sure you have long since forgotten all about it. But I never did."

Obviously, these events have shaped my relationship to Christianity and to the Church—and they may not line up with your experience at all . . . but perhaps it is time for the main question. What do—could—in fact, the finest of the Fine Arts have to offer to religious thinking—or Christian Worship?

I suppose all of us have a favorite cartoon. Mine of the moment is the work of Doug Marlette, who used to be with the *Atlanta Constitution*, but whose cartoon was published originally in the *Charlotte Observer*.

Mr. Marlette's cartoon shows a man dressed in a hunter's coat and cap, standing on a ladder and holding a smoking rifle at the edge of a roof covered with snow. By the chimney a dazed reindeer is staring at an open sack, scattered presents and the form of Santa Claus, lifeless across the ridge-pole. "Hot damn! Edna!" the hunter calls to a woman looking out a second-story window, "Hot damn! I got me another *secular humanist!*"

To me, these humanist-hunters really are man-haters who forget that *humanism* in its beginnings was intimately linked with the adjective "Christian," precisely because its Judeo-Christian heritage prompted a concern for the sanctity and potential of human personality. And the sad fact is that it is mostly *contemporary religious institutions*—principal among them the electronic church—which not only have managed to debase the term *humanism*—but humanity along with it.

For *the arts* and *human creativity* never have been more important. They are not simply skills; their concern is the intellectual, ethical and spiritual maturity of human life. And, in a time when popular religious and political establishments seem to have lost their visions of human dignity—or even propriety—they appear to me the custodians of those values which most worthily define humanity, which most sensitively divine Divinity, and, in fact, may prove to be the only workable *Program of Conservation* for the human race on this planet.

What are the meanings of Art? What can the Arts tell us of human life? What is the artist trying to tell us of herself—or himself? Or of mystery?

I find four answers:

In the first place the arts are the most persistent and powerful affirmation of the life-force in the human-animal.

I descend into one of the limestone caves near our farm-house in France to examine by twentieth-century electric light the drawings of bulls and bison, horses and deer sketched by one of my forbearers 25,000 years before Christ. Sketched in what degrees of darkness? With what kinds of tools? For whom to view?

The drawings snare no rabbits . . . harpoon no fish . . . grub no roots.

I am told that these early artists did not even live in this cave, but that it was a primitive temple, an offering of thanks, and sacred to their sources of food and life.

I note that a few of the animals are clearly male and wounded by arrows and spears, but most are female—and pregnant. And I ask myself if the mysteries of life and death *were less* or *more* mysterious than they are 270 centuries later.

At a museum in Milan I pause at a piece of Etruscan ceramic sculpture: a miniature human skull the size of my fist—with two fingers groping out through the eye-sockets. This is roughly only 2,500 years old, but I can't recall any painting, sculpture or poem of the last 77 years, 10 months and 15 days which so disturbingly evoked to me the human hunger for knowledge.

I recall the voices of my father and grandfather announcing from their pulpits on Christmas mornings that "the Word was made Flesh." And the reciprocal truth strikes me that it is possible for matter to become spirit. – That the Arts are the "Flesh become Word." And for me that is no less a miracle, and no less Divine.

Second, facing the infinite variety and complexity of earth's materials and the human sensory systems, the Arts testify to the ability of the human brain to select this and reject that, to relate and combine, and finally to achieve Order and Beauty.

Are there a billion/billion ways to organize the words of the English language? – but there was a Shakespeare, a Yeats and a Dylan Thomas even in my lifetime! Are there a trillion/trillion ways to organize simultaneous and sequential pitches? – but there was a Mozart—and a Stravinsky, Bartók, Hindemith and Britten even in my lifetime! How many miles of zeros would it take to number all of earth's building materials and the forms in which they might conceivably be combined? – but there was a Leonardo—and a Golden Gate Bridge in my lifetime!

Out of an infinity of substances and sensations, out of confusion and chaos emerge in perfect sequence, symmetry and breath-taking recognizability, *King Lear, The Magic Flute,* a cathedral at Chartres, "The Lord is my shepherd . . . " and "Do not go gentle . . . rage, rage, rage against the coming of the dark."

"When I consider the heavens . . . the wonders Thou hast created . . . What is Man that Thou art mindful of him?" – Well, not altogether "bad."

Third, the Arts provide for the exchange of ideas or values otherwise uncommunicable by alphabets, or numbers, or equations or grunts. The reason that our reaction to a Beethoven quartet cannot be described is that the Arts are not superfluous. They exist to convey that which cannot otherwise be conveyed.

Off-stage in an Anchorage High School auditorium a well-weathered woman of uncertain years waits for the students' programs to be autographed. This is at a time when Alaska has more light airplanes than automobiles, and more miles of unpaved landing strips than of paved roads, and she has just listened to the first Alaskan performance of Mozart's *Requiem.* "This is the only Mozart I've ever heard," she says, "and I don't speak no Latin . . . I had a child who died last winter. We kept her in a snowbank 'til the ground got soft enough last week. Thank you very much."

The truth is that it does not require a graduate degree in Musicology or Art History to what they call "appreciate" great art. What it does require is equal parts of modesty and vulnerability—and a preference for the small truth over the big lie.

And Fourth, across boundaries of Time and Space the Arts are an open hand instead of a closed fist. That painter in his cave at Lascaux had sharpened his arrows and his spears for food—not for piercing the infidel. His eyes smarted from the smoke of his pitch torches, not from the burning of heretics or books. His message is very clear: "The days of the hunter are numbered, but the years of the artist stretch on and on—as long as the mysteries of life and death. Good luck!"

To humanity's shame, even that church named after the "Good Shepherd" and "Holy Comforter" has had a history of persecutions and crusades—in just one of which, in the year of our Lord 1212, and in a much smaller world, fifty thousand innocent children were "shepherded" to their deaths by the sword, starvation and pestilence, and the few fortunate survivors "comforted" by being sold into prostitution and slavery.

What do we see around us?

Well, by now most of us have seen "Schindler's List," which celebrates in a magnificent manner how one man saved 1,000 Jews from extinction in the gas chambers and ovens of Hitler's concentration camps. But 6 *million* were killed by a nation of predominantly Lutheran and Catholic Christians. Undoubtedly, there were heroes among these Christians. One remembers that Pastor Niemueller spent two years at Dachau—and survived.

But Pastor Dietrich Bonhoffer was hanged just 30 days before the Armistice—when it was clear that the war was over—because he stood against the Nazi holocaust and was said to have heard of a plot against Hitler's life.

What shall we say of the Christians who shell the Muslims in Sarajevo? – Or the Protestants who blew up Catholic children in Ireland? – Or of a Jew who machine-guns Moslems at worship in a cave in Hebron?

Were the Ancestor-Worshippers who bombed Pearl Harbor less or more humane than the Christians who ushered in atomic warfare at Hiroshima?

What about those churches in the Southern United States who started "Christian" Academies when it became clear that their Sunday-School kids might have to go to Monday-School with kids whose black wouldn't wash off?

Historically, the Muslims had until the year 1100 a flourishing science of mathematics and medicine far ahead of Christian Western Europe, when it was abruptly stopped by the Sunna—the ruling council—because scientific thought led to "loss of belief in the Origin of the World and in the Creator." What might our world be today had their sciences and mathematics and medecine been encouraged rather than stifled?

Aristarchus in the third century B.C. already had figured the earth was a revolving sphere around the sun. His near contemporary Eratosthenes had calculated the circumference of the earth within 240 miles—and Hipparchus had reckoned within a few miles both the circumference of the moon and its mean distance from the earth. (This was 17 centuries before Copernicus.)

Joseph Campbell asks, "What might have been the saving in human terms (people burned at the stake) for instance, and where might now be the exploration of SPACE had the Christian emperor Justinian not stepped in and closed all Greek and Roman schools whose teachers were not 100% Christian and who refused to teach the Hebrew Genesis story of Creation (itself an embarrassment because it introduces in verse 8 of Chapter Two a story of Man's Creation diametrically opposed to the narrative of Chapter One)."

Where might the position of women be had not Judaism and Christianity made them bear the guilt of the events in the Garden of Eden? What kind of Schizophrenia is induced by holding up the Virgin Mary as (1) the model of Virtuous Womanhood, and (2) instructing girls to bear lots of children.

And, perhaps most subversive of all, what has been the frightful cost in wars and personal human misery of the Judaistic concept of the "Chosen People" as it blended into Christian cocksureness and missionizing insolence?

Might not the arts, indeed, be not the luxury of a few, but the last best hope of humanity to inhabit with joy this planet?

What is it in the nature of the arts that allows them to offer these hopes of maturity and survival?

In the first place it is clear that a commitment to the creative process starts the human animal on a thorny and lonesome road to self-discovery, away from the comforts and compromises of institutions. "Forty days and forty nights" is a biblical metaphor for what is more nearly a lifetime of wilderness and solitude. But the more deeply this lonely human being seeks a self-hood, the more knowingly and tenderly she—or he—returns to—other selves.

In the second place, the arts are concerned not with the consumption or sale of earth's material wonders—not even with their recycling—but with their reincarnation. They propose not a mounting monopoly of a monetary medium of exchange, but the sweet, quiet exchange of truth and beauty themselves.

And in the third place, in a time and a society whose values are geared to the biggest, the fastest, and the mostest, whose gaze is fixed desperately upon the future—as far at least as the next election or life after death or prosperity, whichever should happen to come first—the arts offer an historical perspective. For their concern is with originality—meaning that which has *origins.* Thus the arts lead us to consider and build upon our own beginnings—our essence and our potential.

The Arts, then, are not merely "handmaidens" of worship; but, given creativity on the order of a Brahms *Requiem,* a Stravinsky *Symphony of Psalms,* or a Bach *St. Matthew Passion,* they are themselves unqualified and unique acts of worship.

This, of course, raises the question of "quality." It seems to me that we have to agree that in the worship of the Great Whoever or Whatever only our very best is "good enough"—only because it's our best. A God of Truth, Goodness and Mercy is not honored by laying Saturday Night's Disco Spin-offs on Sunday's altar. One does not gain strength from the stresses of virtue by gorging on fatty fraud.

But, fortunately, the "revelations" do come along: a cathedral at Chartres, an address by a president at Gettysburg, a dream-sequence by a black preacher at a white marble presidential memorial in Washington, D.C., a *St. John Passion,* a Britten *War Requiem.*

And, even more importantly for me, at least, the arts provide the day-by-day confirmation of creation's hand still at work in the lives and affairs of men and women.

If the Christian Church can accept a doctrine of "eternal life"—and most of it has high hopes—does it not follow that this instant is somehow a part of an *eternal one* (eternity being indivisible and having no beginning and no end); and, therefore, LIFE in the universal, eternal sense—of which yours or mine may be only a very small part—must be part of a "becoming"?

I am not now arguing Genesis vs. Evolution. (What's a few million years to the Infinite?) I am simply suggesting that if there is a living, loving Creative Presence or Process—then He/She/It somehow/somewhere/somewhen must be doing exactly that: living and loving.

However we may view creation, it strikes me as contrary to both reason and faith to argue that it is concluded.

Is it not somehow shortsighted to raise up an eternal omnipotent creator— and not give him anything to do since day six? Should not an everlasting creator be somewhere lasting and creating? – And if, indeed, human life was made "in a Creator's image," given a timeless, boundless creator, is there a better place to see the creator at work than "in those likenesses"?

To me it follows that Christianity, if it wants to keep in touch with the Creator, must provide a home for all that is—and all who are—creative, lest Christianity itself wither and drift into irrelevance.

Is it possible that Christianity in our time may have become so preoccupied with the door-prizes attendant upon the *Divinity* of *Christ*—that it has not nearly fathomed the *humanity* of *Jesus?*

What if the "Son of God" were in truth the "Son of Man"? What heresies or truths lie hidden within this scriptural identity? What does it mean that he who is hailed as "Redeemer/Intercessor/Messiah/The Way/The Truth/and The Life" was in the beginning seen as "Emmanuel/*God/in/us*"? Is there any possibility that the emphasis upon the God-hood of the Son of Man, to the exclusion of the Man-hood of the Son of God, affords a blanket of endless bliss in preference to a hair-shirt of responsibility? Knowing that the Gospels do, in fact, attest to Jesus' awareness of his very special relationship to what he called "the Spirit" and "the Father," have we been slow to understand, or unwilling to credit, the confidence with which he reached out to touch the souls of Everyman through Alltime?

These are his words:

"Why do you call me good? No one is good but God alone." (Mark 10:18)

"Whoever receives this child in my name receives me; and whoever receives me receives the one who sent me." (Luke 9:48)

"My daughter, *your* faith has made you whole." (Mark 5:34)

"*You* are the salt to the world. . . . " (Matthew 5:13) "*You* are the light for the world." (Matthew 5:14)

" 'The seed sown on rock' stands for those who receive the word with joy when they hear, but *have no root in themselves. . . .* " (Luke 8:13)

"In very truth I tell you, the Son can do nothing by himself. . . . " (John 5:19) "I cannot act by myself. . . . My aim is not my own will, but the will of him who sent me." (John 5:30)

"You cannot tell by observation when the kingdom of God comes. There will be no saying, 'Look, here it is!' or 'There it is!' For in fact the Kingdom of God is (*already?*) *within you.*" (Luke 17:20, 21)

"I am not myself the source of the words I speak to you; it is the Spirit dwelling in me doing his work. . . . In very truth I tell you, he who believes in me will do what I am doing; *and he will do greater things still. . . .*" (John 14:10, 12)

"When the time comes, the words will be given you: for it is not you who will be speaking: it will be the Spirit . . . speaking in you." (Matthew 10:20)

– And when you write your own psalms, plays and poems, when you play or conduct your own symphonies, when you paint your own pictures and mould or chisel your own sculptures, – be sure that there are some of us who dearly wish we'd been able to hand you a better Christianity—and a better world—in which to work.

PART V

CELEBRATING THE RITUALS OF LIFE

As public figures, conductors celebrate the rituals of life for communities, cities, regions, and in some instances the nation. The diverse plethora of such occasions requires a compassionate heart and a breadth of understanding. Shaw had both, and these qualities were further enhanced by a compelling oratorical voice. Always present was his innate sense of timing.

These accounts are representative of hundreds more, and they reflect a public and personal side of a conductor who was physically and emotionally planted in a community. The humility of acknowledging all who made awards possible, of comforting the living while celebrating lives fully lived, of responding to letters with a disarming sense of humor, and the use of original verse are glimpses of the conductor's human-ness.

AWARDS AND CITATIONS

March 16, 1996

Remarks for Choral Celebration Concert

None of the members of the Atlanta Symphony Chorus is paid. They are 100% volunteer—or, as the saying goes, *amateur.*

The word "amateur" comes to us through the Latin *amo, amoris*—the English equivalent of which is L-O-V-E—and *am-a-tor:* one who loves.

In any concert season the members of the Chorus devote about 90 evenings a year to rehearsals, performances and recordings. They do this out of love—for the art of music—and its disciplines and joys. – You can imagine what strains that puts upon their everyday professional commitments—and their "home" lives.

Over the twenty-five years of the chorus's existence some 2,000-plus Atlantans—including, perhaps, a majority of Atlanta's music educators and church musicians—have availed themselves of membership in the chorus. – And I know of one member—a physician—who in 25 years has missed only one rehearsal and zero performances.

And right here one thing needs to be said very earnestly: the factor which draws most of this chorus together is the opportunity it provides to sing the incredibly rich, life-changing symphonic-choral repertoire with an orchestra of excellence—and commitment.

Earlier this season at a post-concert symposium I was asked by a member of the audience seated in Baltimore, Maryland's Symphony Hall: "Mr. Shaw, you've worked with both amateur and professional choruses and orchestras for over a half-century. – What are the similarities—or differences?"

Without, perhaps, sufficient thought I replied, "Well—it seems to me that the Arts, like Sex, are too important to leave to the professionals."

417

What the chorus joins me in saying to you this evening is that the *amateur spirit* in the Arts is not necessarily limited to those who do not receive a weekly paycheck.

The greatest musical amateurs in my life have been Pablo Casals and Rudolf Serkin—whose concert fees were the highest of the highest, but who lovingly poured them back into festivals and institutes for needy and gifted young artists.

The musicians of this orchestra chose an economically treacherous career precisely because of the "stars in their eyes"—and the "lumps in their throats."

This city cannot now—or ever—afford to be without their commitment to the most beautiful and distinguished products of humanity's cultural life.

Let us never, as a city, pursue a course which would dim the "stars in those eyes."

Let us rather—in times of crisis—re-invent our own commitment, and shore up the approaches to the bridge leading to the next quarter-century. – That our chorus may continue to sing with the disciplines of professionals, and our orchestra to play out of ever-livin' love.

'See you in the year two-thousand-and-twenty-one.

Spring 1982

On the Occasion of the 35th Anniversary of the Roger Wagner Chorale

Listen, my children, and hear you shall
Of Roger the Wag and the Master Chorale!

'Twas the Year of Our Lord nineteen-forty-and-seven
Not our very own lord—but Old Whatsie (?) in Heaven

The War in the West had suddenly ended
The Dove and the Droppings of Peace had descended.

The Wars of World Three were still decades away,
TV not invented—so what's for Today!

Poor Los Angelenos had no-what to thrill
Life wasn't worth living with no one to kill.

So Roger resolved as he grieved at their plight,
"I'll dry all those tears—if it takes me all night!

"My head's full of plans, 'cause my heart's full of pity
Especially for girls in all parts of the city.

"Boys are all right if they keep to their places,
but to counter for tenors, the Lord gave us better.

"We're fresh out of wars and the joys that they bring
Let's just choose up sides and let everyone sing!

"This week it's our country, next year the whole nation
What a helluva (marvelous) gimmick to deal with frustration!"

"Saint Roger!" (they whispered—his laddies and lasses)
Emerged overnight as the Shiek (Sheik, shrink?) of the Masses!

The land of the movies and Tourneys of Roses
Had raised up a man who could heal their psychoses.

A town (?) with skim milk and dried honey
Found singing was fun, but conductors were funny.

Dwell not on Buck Roger and how he behaved,
But not . . . all the money we saved (caved?).

And Hail to Saint Roger, let's give him his day
– Along with the Master Chorale of L.A.

January 4, 1989

Friends –

Dejected, blue? – 'life seem dull? – no challenges? – feel unappreciated?
Hear the good news!

– From the Office of the Governor, no less! Addressed to the Executive Director of the Atlanta Symphony, no less!

"It is a distinct pleasure for me to inform you that your organization has been selected to receive a 1989 Governor's Award in the Arts. The Atlanta Symphony Orchestra Chorus is among six recipients recommended to me by the Georgia Council for the Arts from the more than 60 recommendations submitted.

"Having concurred with their judgment, I hope that your schedule will permit you to attend the public presentation ceremony. . . .

"I appreciate the contributions you have made to the State of Georgia. I look forward to receiving your reply and to sharing the evening with you."

How about that! Six out of sixty—and only the fifteenth year of the prize! That makes us at least #90 on Georgia's mind.

Wall Street sets off on the Oregon Trail! The country club visits the country! The queen walks through the sweat-shop! Capitol Hill climbs the Ivory Tower! Virtue is not its own-ly reward!

You *all* really done fine!

All choruses, all repertoires, all performances. All '88.

RS

March 20, 1997

M. François Bujon de l'Estang, French Ambassador to the United States
To Mr. Shaw upon the award of the "Officier des Arts et Lettres" Medal
On Behalf of the Government of France
Atlanta, Georgia

Maestro,

Thank you for welcoming me this evening to the august halls of the Atlanta Symphony Orchestra, among musicians whose perceptive interpretation of Francis Poulenc has just afforded us a rare pleasure.

Some members of the audience, who came here this evening to share your passion and show their admiration, may not have had time to note in the program that, in this particular instance, the Ambassador of France would come up on stage. But let me reassure you: I won't sing!

I have come to pay the respects of the French community in the United States and of all my countrymen who enjoy, in France and elsewhere, the recordings of the Atlanta Symphony Orchestra and Chorus. I am also here to express the high esteem of the French government and to present to you, on its behalf, the Insignia of Officer of Arts and Letters.

The Order of Arts and Letters is the highest French decoration for those who have shown particular distinction in the cultural arena. This is precisely the case for you. Ever since your student days at Pomona College, you have devoted your time, energy and knowledge—in a word, your life—to teaching music, leading orchestras and promoting choral singing.

The American people and the entire world bore witness to your talent and to the quality of your instrumentalists and singers during the extraordinary celebration of sports and brotherhood that were embodied, true to the spirit of

Baron Pierre de Coubertin, by the Centennial Olympic Games. Before becoming music director of the ASOC some 30 years ago, bringing it international influence and acclaim, you directed the symphony orchestras of San Diego and Cleveland. Your career already showed great promise under the patronage of Arturo Toscanini, Leopold Stokowski and George Szell.

Throughout those years, you devoted your energies to a project of great importance to you: the promotion of choral singing.

At the end of the 1940s you founded a choir that built an exceptional reputation for itself, not only in this vast nation, but in the more than 30 countries where it performed.

With your permission, the Ambassador of France would like to emphasize here in Atlanta, as a sign of our friendship and gratitude, the value of your efforts to enrich French-American cultural exchanges, which are a basic and very dynamic aspect of the relations between our two countries. Indeed, we are grateful for the creation by the Robert Shaw Institute of a festival in France that became a benchmark, and which played a major role in giving choral music the status and quality it now enjoys in my country.

At this point, I certainly shall not fail to mention the prominent role played by your late wife, Caroline, who was always dedicated and supportive of your endeavors in France, a country which had adopted her and that she so dearly loved.

Maestro, America, as well as the whole world, has recognized your talent. You have received too many awards, distinctions and prizes to mention here. I will note only numerous grammies, a Gold Album for the first classical RCA recording to sell more than a million copies, the first Guggenheim Fellowship awarded to an orchestra conductor, the Presidential Medal of Arts, the Gold Baton Award of the American Symphony Orchestra League and the Kennedy Center Honors. President Jimmy Carter named you to the National Council for the Arts.

Music is a voyage to the shores of eternity. When your baton traces the first measures of the *German Requiem,* we shall follow you once more to that world of celestial harmonies where the philosophers of antiquity located the realms of the divine.

I thank you in advance, and herewith bestow upon you the much deserved Insignia of Officer of Arts and Letters, before an Atlanta audience that admires you greatly.

Robert Shaw, au nom. . . .

March 20, 1997

Remarks upon receiving the "Officier des Arts et Lettres" Medal
from the Government of France

Mr. Ambassador –

You are absolutely correct in recognizing that whatever cultural enrichment between our countries I may have aided is the collaborative product of instrumentalists and singers, some of whom are with us on stage at this moment, others who will shortly join them—and some thousands who for a half-dozen decades have been—to use two terms in unusual but authentic connotation – confederates and conspirators.

None of the critically sensitive elements of music-making are conductible. They are playable and singable by artists with skill and a conscience. – But this hand makes no sound whatsoever.

You are right, also, that Caroline Sauls Shaw brought to this family—in addition to wonderful sons—an entire nation of new friends, thousands of square miles of unique natural beauty and centuries of a matchless culture.

In her name, and in behalf of the Atlanta Symphony Orchestra, its choruses and its supporters, I accept with gratitude and eagerness—the recognition of your government and your country.

March 30, 1998

Remarks upon receiving the "Gift of Music" Award
Orchestra of St. Luke's Gala
The Plaza Hotel, New York City

Ladies and Gentlemen, good evening.

Nothing could be clearer than that St. Luke's Gospel has it exactly right in Chapter 1, Verse 52:

They have "put down the mighty from their seats, and exalted them of low degree."

To ensure that tonight's flagpole sitter gets the point, St. Luke admonishes five chapters later,

"Woe unto you when all men shall speak well of you, for so did their fathers of the false prophets." (6:26)

– And hammers it home with:

"There are the last which shall be first, and there are the first which shall be last." (13:30)

Some choice!

Surely the "gift of music" already has been given by the "boys and girls in the band."

It would not be unusual to find a single gifted musician who would forego the security of a major symphonic institution to preserve a status both professional and amateur ("amateur," of course, is the sense of "amo-amare," to love).

But that such a musician should find other "loving" professionals, sufficient to form an association as productive and lasting as The Orchestra of St. Luke's, is a miracle of modern art.

Theirs is the real "gift of music" to all the rest of us, and I am privileged to voice our thanks.

October 29, 1998

Pre-concert remarks upon receiving Proclamation from the Governor of Georgia
And Induction into the American Classical Music Hall of Fame
Atlanta, Georgia

Mr. Klingshirn, Professor Sapp, Representative Polak –

Please be assured of my very deep thanks for your presence here tonight and the honors which you have brought with you.

As I read the list of inaugural inductees I realized that though they date from the time of Thomas Jefferson, and only a handful are now living, I have met or worked with eighteen of the twenty-five. – Either this is a very young country— or I am a very old man.

One important thing must yet be said this evening:

If you grew up on the Coast of California, you learned to swim in the Pacific Ocean. – Which meant also that you learned body-surfing and surf-boarding.

You would paddle your board out beyond the breakers—and wait for the Ninth Wave. They were the big ones—such was the mystique. – And if you were lucky, you'd ride down-hill all the way to the beach.

It never occurred to you to say, "Mommy, look at the big wave I just brought in." – The boy didn't pull the wave. The wave pushed the boy.

Ladies and gentlemen of the audience:

For the past two-fifths of my life the orchestra and chorus on this stage have been this boy's wave.

And Ladies and Gentlemen of the Orchestra and Chorus:

The members of this audience—and their friends and co-workers—have been the winds and the tides which formed and hefted our waves.

(Don't anybody ever stop making waves—or this land will become an intellectual Sahara!) This ceremony—uncomfortable and embarrassing as it is—is as nothing compared to the public execution which is Mr. Dvořák's subject matter for the rest of the evening.

EULOGIES

November 23, 1963

Remarks preceding Cleveland Orchestra concert

Certainly in the blackness which engulfs us all, each man *is* his own small island of grief—inaccessible and mute. One would not invade this privacy. But no public gathering during these hours takes place but in the light of that darkness.

Days ahead will be full of political appraisal and eulogy—but among those of us engaged in the pursuit of the creative, performing or liberal arts, a special acknowledgement is in order.

We are accustomed to think of him in terms of abounding physical vitality and humor: a laughing father treading water while a five-year-old Caroline bomb-dives from the deck of a launch into the Atlantic Ocean, a driving young executive pacing the world's most critical office—clutched at the knee by a three-year-old John-John, or substitute at large for a game of touch football with the junior senator and the Attorney General.

This is entirely fitting—but how terribly unfunny a word like "vigah" can become in a few hours.

And it is pertinent to this place and this moment that we remember a president of the United States who felt it natural to honor poets, painters, architects, scholars and musicians at his inauguration.

Under whose auspices Shakespeare and opera were presented to the President's cabinet in the President's home.

At whose invitation Pablo Casals performed Bach solo suites in the White House.

Let us remember the president who accorded new dignity and responsibility to the scholars and artists of his country. For whom the life and creative produce of the mind and the spirit were unrivalled natural resources. Who held scholar-ship and the arts as the ultimate focus of man's good-will, and indispensible ally of freedom, peace and social justice.

There is not one of us who finds his employment or delight in gatherings such as these who was not enlarged by his living and diminshed by his dying.

Robert Shaw

April 7, 1968

Martin Luther King Memorial Concert
Westminster III

On this day of national mourning each man is his own island of grief—but certainly no public gathering is possible without reference to the darkness which engulfs us all.

You will wish to welcome and hail with your applause young Gregory Shatten who will perform the Mendelssohn *Concerto* as announced.

But I, for one, would deem it appropriate if you did not applaud Schubert's *Unfinished Symphony,* which will conclude this afternoon's memorial concert with unique propriety.

Alas also the music with which we will now begin.

Of all men who ever lived—and attempted to communicate with his fellow man by speech and writing or painting or drama or sculpture or music—it is entirely possible that none had a greater understanding of heroism—of the tragedies and triumphs of man's quest for freedom—than did Ludwig van Bee-thoven. His *Egmont Overture* details in almost literal fashion one man's struggle against tyranny—his assassination—and the eventual triumph of his people.

The Funeral March from his *Eroica Symphony* is the classic lament for the fall of truth and justice and love.

Listen now to the day's eulogies—according to Ludwig Beethoven.

April 24, 1988

Remarks at the Memorial Service for Peter Harrower

It seems to me
    that no one person should have the right
    – or the responsibility –
    in moments as precious as these
    to disturb—or perhaps even to focus—
    the myriad memories
    – and shadows of memories –
    which abound in this room.

They must be swirling above our heads
    and through our minds
    in kaleidoscopic constellations
    totally defiant of the speed limits of light.

Which of us, for instance, knows
    from whom he may have received
    that last fleeting instant of recollection:
    – the timbre of Peter's voice,
    – the smile which lighted his eyes just before it touched his lips,
    – the explosive crack of his laughter
    (an unforgettable lesson in breath support and vocal "placement")
    – the long moments it took him to stand all the way up,
    – his love affairs with tools, fish and meticulously miniaturized trees –
    as well as those with Irene and Julie and Richard
    – or almost anything vegetable that could be laid out in seasonal
sequence or planted in rows or squares.

At this moment I wonder if any spirit ever
    has set sail from these shores
    to those unknown
    with prayers more numerous or earnest
    for comforting breezes and safe passage.

I know that I never have witnessed
    an embarkation
    so lovingly and thoroughly prepared
    by wife and children and friends.

The truth is, of course,
    that Peter built this harbour
    of kindliness and sanctuary
    for others.
    But it became also his home port
    and the one from which he sailed.

Peter did not take either home or religion lightly.
    He knew, for instance,
    that Jesus was a carpenter.
    And he reasoned that it was a Christian duty
    to build kitchen cabinets
    and storm windows that worked.

There wasn't a music room, den, studio or workshop . . .
    by Peter's thinking,
    that couldn't use at least one extra cupboard
    – if only to hide "acts of God."

He loved tools:
    Somewhere in the world, he knew,
    there was the perfect hammer
    for each and every nail
    – And he had started his collection early.

Somewhere in the world
    there was a power lathe
    which could take redwood burl
    and mill it to a perfect sphere.

Somewhere there was a power saw
    which could tri-sect an angle.
    All one had to do was make the basement
    just a little bit longer –
    and there'd be room for them.

Look down at your feet –
    These common stools for common prayer are called kneelers.
    Be careful.
    Some of them are trustworthy,
    and some of them may be broken.
    They come unhinged,
    or their feet fall off.

Nine months ago they all worked.
If you came into the church on a quiet afternoon
you'd find Peter down on his knees,
his loins draped with the girdle of righteous restoration:
– fifty pounds of hammers, pliers,
screw-drivers, snippers and staplers,
hinges, hardware and left-overs,
keeping these kneelers safe for the kneeling.
He was St. Luke's lay kneeler-healer.

Painter, sculptor, set-designer,
  lighting engineer, sound technician
seamster/teamster, make-up expert, costumer, gofur
  – there was almost nothing
that Peter couldn't make with his hands
  – out of nothing.

He could create costumes
out of Kindergarten trash bins:
out of papier-mâché,
McDonald's take-home cartons
and Vidalia Onion sacks.

He could take cafeteria tables, tomato crates
and abandoned DeSotos out of kudzu jungles
on red-clay roads
and, with a little paint and cross-lighting,
you'd swear you were in a garret in Montmartre
or a sacristy in Venice.

All the tricks of make-up and cosmetics were his
  – but his own characterizations
were built from within
  – not applied from without.

He could come onto a stage
with the stilt-legged gait
of a child's stick-figure drawing
or slide his slinky way
  – all six to seven feet of him –
into a creeping kitchen about to ambush
a particularly treacherous ball of yarn.

This was his world of make-believe.

But, unlike almost all the others
    in his singing-acting trade,
    he was even more at home
    in the world of I believe.

He could break your heart
    singing the words of Jesus
    in the *St. Matthew Passion*
    – which, of course,
    had been Bach's intention.

    But Peter didn't think for a moment
    that he was Jesus of Nazareth.
    This was not a role to be played
    or robe to be worn,
    these were words themselves well-worn,
    known from youth—as they say—by heart,
    now to be cradled and pondered anew
    in his own heart.

One believed Peter
    because he accepted *that* responsibility,
    rather than the evasive substitution of sandals, beard, robe and
        make-up.

All growing things
    blossomed and bloomed for Peter:
    children and flowers; of course,
    – but also things that were "good" for you,
    like turnips and collards and squash.

I've heard it said
    that he used to sing to his plants,
    – even, occasionally, talk to them.
I asked him once about that,
    and he said he only spoke
    when spoken to.

As Jesus was a carpenter –
    his first apostle
    (– Peter knew this as well
    as he knew his own name –) was a fisherman.

According to Peter
    there wasn't a body of water in this world
    – from the reflecting pools of the Taj Mahal
    to a glass of Perrier –
    that God hadn't created to be fished in.

I've heard it said that,
    just as azaleas, elms and spinach
    would suddenly sprout
    when they heard his footsteps,
    fish would actually leap into his boat
    – though I never heard it from him

Students also flowered under Peter's care.
    "What makes the lamb love Mary so –?
    'Cause Mary loves the lamb, you know."
    "It was his kindness," they say.
    "– And the fact that he taught
    the whole person
    – not just the vocal machine,"
    another said.

For Peter, music was itself a value
    – not a vehicle for public favor
    or spectacular fortune.

Not every one of God's children
    was intended to star on the stage
    of the Mega-la-Scalaton Opera Co.

    Some were intended to sing
    only in their own showers.
    What was important was that they do it
    – and do it better.

We shouldn't forget that, just as Peter loved tools,
    fish, flowers and people,
    he also loved Italy.

    To an ex-bombardier
    Italy was incredibly beautiful –
    as divinely created and as hand-made.
    – For, as his dearest artist friend says,

"There isn't a thing Peter couldn't make with his hands
  – as a painter or sculptor."

So Peter loved Italy.
  And how lucky we were –
  that when he came back home –
  he brought it with him!

He was himself
  in his courtly, gentle way
  something of a Renaissance reincarnation.

And I have wondered in the past few days
  if someone like Peter
  might be enough
  – once again –
  to make God believe in Man.

I add to that "wonder,"
  and the one with which I began
  concerning the warm winds of our love,
  two others which fill me with awe
  – and a sense mystery.

I wonder how many marriages, which
  we may know—or know about—
  will ever match the mutual heroism and devotion
  of the last nine months of this one.
  Those days seem to me the holiest of sacraments, and,
  in the deepest of possible senses,
  a consummation.

My second wonder scares me even more.
  We are accustomed, are we not –
  to hear from time to time of the triumph of mind over disease.
  – Or, given an incurable disease of the body,
  of the heroic victory of the mind and the will
  over the afflictions, of organs and limbs,
  in order to effect a courageous and un-self-pitying close.

But here, you see, was a disease
  which attacked the very bastion
  of self-hood and identity –
  the brain, the mind.

And, so far as I could see
  (not, of course, sharing the final hours)
  even with the progressive atrophy of motor function
  and the wasting away of intellective process,
– So far as I could see –
  Peter still remained Peter.

The spirit—or whatever—
  was still Peter's spirit.
He could still love, for instance –
  right to the end.

Isn't that awesome? And holy?
– That there could be an is-ness beyond
  even intellect?
– And that is-ness
  the spirit of love and caring
  – Like Peter's?

I wonder if it could be enough
  to make God believe in man.

June 23, 1990

Couzou, France

Earlier in the summer, on the twentieth anniversary of the death of George Szell (Music Director of The Cleveland Orchestra from 1946 to 1970), a performance at Blossom Center (acoustical and architectural queen of American outdoor symphonic sites) with the Cleveland Orchestra and a revitalized Cleveland Orchestra Chorus.

Given these forces one would certainly have a right to expect a fine performance—and it probably was that. – But staggering to me was a sense of the unique emotional and intellectual state of the audience. I know that I never have been in a situation where the listeners (some 5,000) were so eager to listen and so capable of hearing. Mr. Szell's legacy still is alive in Cleveland. His audience returned through rain and cold to say their thanks. Somehow, it felt as though they sang it—and none of us will forget it. (Following are a few sentences of remembrances from that evening's program.)

GEORGE SZELL: A TRIBUTE

Even to himself, George Szell must have been something of an enigma. I often have wondered if he ever let his right hand (of command) know what his left hand (of compassion) was doing. Long after the act, one would hear rumors of his charity or personal generosity—but, to his face, one would not dare to accuse him of the indiscretion of sentiment.

His disciplinings, however abrupt, were tolerable—first, because they were not motivated by self-pity. (He was distressed not for himself, but for the composer.) Second, we knew that he clearly demanded many times more from himself than he required of us. And third, almost always, when the right arm of authority descended it was followed quickly and demonstrably by an improvement in the product.

It is not the function of a "conscience" to be comforting—and for many of us George Szell was the conscience of our profession. Above all was his insistent advocacy of the composer's prescription and intent, as versus a performer's personal "style" or "interpretation."

In direct line from this were judicious performance practices that favored structure over color, clarity over sonority, temporal stability over eccentricity, remote control over balletic ecstasy, and right notes over best wishes.

Always he elected elegance over extravagance. And, if asked to choose between the intellect and the emotions, he would have declared the mind to be itself the sun.

For me and, I think, for most of us who were privileged to make music in his time and presence, his recorded performances reveal a seldom-approached blend of solo instrumental virtuosity and ensemble disciplines. But even more remarkable is that which is missing: those emphases and excesses—some, perhaps, even unintentional—that too often in this age make up a performer's trademark or "image."

When it came to making music, George Szell's enigmatic sort of self-awareness was sufficient to eschew personal caprice and idiosyncracy. Earlier than might have been expected, those who came to watch him perform ended by listening to the music.

To the ends of our days we will be grateful.

LETTERS

July 21, 1961

– Flying well below the clouds on the world's favorite airplane, a friendly, bouncy DC-3 held together by a fresh coat of paint on the inside and riveted aluminum patches on the outside. Two hours from Lansing, Michigan, to Cleveland, Ohio. Two weeks ago by jet it was only seven hours from New York Idlewild to Anchorage, Alaska. Beethoven *Missa Solemnis* in Alaska (about time for a re-run in Cleveland) and within the past few days two Verdi *Requiem*s, the first at the University of Minnesota and the second last night at Michigan State University. The latter made particularly pleasant by renewed association with Howard Swan, head of music department at Occidental College, Los Angeles, teaching at East Lansing during summer sessions, remarkable choral conductor and rarely comparable man, and first meeting with Harold Taylor, ex-president of Sarah Lawrence College (a position held since he was thirty-years-old), distinguished, laughing maverick of U.S. higher education, and bearer of the season's happiest limerick:

> The latest report from the Dean
> About the Teaching Machine:
> – Oedipus Rex could have learned sex
> Without ever bothering the Queen.

Fortunately I held in my tight little right fist of reciprocity a most recent, but all-time favorite fan letter forwarded from RCA Victor this summer. Ah! unhappily without return address. How would you have answered this charmer?

February 12, 1961

Dear Mr. Shaw,

My husband and I are great admirers of your chorale music and have many sacred recordings which bring us inspiration such as no others can.

Yesterday I purchased your "On Stage" record (choruses from Broadway shows of past 30 years—RS) for a Valentine present for my husband. Because he has a heavy schedule of singing and directing this week-end and next week, I gave him the gift last evening.

I was very anxious to please him with it and hoped it would be something we could enjoy in romantic moods. It was perhaps the most *disillusioning* choice I could have made.

The numbers were well done and the selections were good but why did you have to arrange them in such a helter-skelter order. Just about the time a fairly romantic mood can be achieved, the chorus breaks in with some rouser like "Wintergreen For President."

And the "pièce de résistance" is your following the beautiful "Through the Years" (which my husband sang most beautifully at our marriage ceremony 13 years ago) with "Buckle Down, Winsocki." We have to jump up and turn it off before the last number.(!!!)

Please see if a recording can be made from this one with one side romantic and the other varied in content. My personal suggestion for order is as follows:

Side I
Yesterdays
Gone, Gone, Gone
September Song
Dancing in the Dark
All The Things You Are
Through the Years

Side 2
(This side I don't really care how you arrange.)

Hopefully yours,

Mrs. L——D——

– Now, what could ever destroy a marriage like that? I suppose I've read the letter twenty-five times—and it gets sweeter and funnier every time. By now I even laugh at the date.

– And now to the business of the letter. Victor asked me this summer to remake an old album called "Great Sacred Choruses." It contained the best-known and most-loved oratorio choruses: *Hallelujah Chorus* from Handel's *Messiah; He Watching Our Israel* from Mendelssohn's *Elijah; The Heavens Are Telling* from Haydn's *Creation;* etc.

It occurred to me that, since the COC had done most of these choruses at some point in the past five years, you might care to make this record—with, of course, the Cleveland Orchestra and the original orchestrations rather than organ reductions.

There have been a number of problems to surmount: exclusive contracts, credits, time, place—and royalties, for instance. I suggest, with regard to the latter, that the royalties, which normally (and hopefully and rightly) would accrue to the Cleveland Orchestra Chorus, be used to establish a scholarship fund for singers in the Cleveland area.

Does it sould like a fun idea? It does to me.

April 16, 1981

Dear People –

A few weeks ago at the ACDA Convention in New Orleans I made reference in a public rehearsal of the *Missa Solemnis* to what I felt was the superiority of Beethoven's act of worship over most of what arrives over my TV set any Sunday morning that I'm fool enough to hope for better.

I received a letter of dismay and moderate outrage from one of the successful Sabbath Masters of TV Music asking me to clarify the content (or discontent) of my ad lib remarks. Most of you are aware of my chagrin with the state of "music for worship" in the contemporary (Christian) church. (One of these days you may receive the full "Religion and the Arts" epistle written last January.)

One of the compelling reasons for our existence—to my way of thinking (which adds vehemence to my way of feeling)—is that, surrounded by social and religious institutions whose tastes and standards are indistinguishable from those of the market-place, it is increasingly difficult to make a "musical offering" worthy of the Creator of All Things Good and Beautiful.

And I quote:

"I write hurriedly—but none the less sincerely—because your concern about my comments at the ACDA convention is undoubtedly sincere and shows no taint of 'anger' or 'self-justification.'

"My 'comments' were made during a rehearsal of the *Missa Solemnis* specifically to the performing choruses—not primarily to the assembled auditors, though I may have turned around for a moment.

"They were completely extemporaneous—but undoubtedly representative of my concern (for more than forty-five years) for the quality of music used in Christian worship.

"I have no idea what I said. It could have been said too strongly. – But it would have to have been an extemporaneous paraphrase of things I have said over the past four decades, and stated most recently and formally at an organ dedicatory service in Atlanta this winter, a copy of which 'sermon' is enclosed.

"I certainly did not have *your* church in mind. To my memory, I never had heard on TV one of your televised services. I don't think they are available in Atlanta.

"Here we get things out of (is it?) Coral Gables, Florida; Tulsa, Oklahoma; and some place now in Virginia where the religious right has established its rites.

"When I think 'discouraging words' about Southern California's religious manifestations I think *Forest Lawn*—which I find the vilest corruption of Jesus' simple lovingkindness, and man's mortality.

"Similarly I find the 'Show-Biz' techniques of Sunday morning Florida and Oklahoma to irretrievably be-foul what might be the aspiration, intellectual distinction and basic human decency of the act of 'worship.'

"To me they make of 'the Creator of All Things Good and Beautiful' a god—or mammon—who is Tasteless, Mindless and Couldn't-Care-Less.

" – What I was trying to emphasize in New Orleans was the shattering difference between the 'God' of Beethoven and the 'God' of the Sabbath-Spectacular available—at least in the South-East on TV.

"Since I don't have *any idea* what you offer as music for worship on Sunday morning you will have to answer your own questions about what to do to 'improve' it (or whatever your concern is).

"I do find one sentence that really scares me: 'These are selected to be used to have the broadest possible appeal and outreach to the television constituency.'

"I find nothing in the life of Jesus to show that he ever was interested in the 'broadest possible appeal.' His selection of only twelve, his 'temptations' and his death are testimony to the opposite.

"Eventually, I suppose, the question of what materials are suitable for worship has a theological *crux* (or, even, dilemma.) If one is only concerned with getting human 'souls' into a posthumous, y'all come 'heaven,' then any sort of drugs (including aesthetic) should be acceptable.

"If, however, God is also a 'Holy Spirit,' 'indwelling' in man, then—so it seems to me—those of us in the 'religious arts' have a responsibility to see that worship 'elevates' the human spirit and intelligence and soul. I am uncomfortable with a religion which brings God down to the level of Madison Avenue, Nielsen Ratings, Oscars, Emmies and Grammies.

"The logical sequel to 'The Making of a President' is 'The Making of a Christ.' "

End quote.

'See you ASOCs Monday night –

Love,

R

December 7, 1973

To Mr. Robert D. Thorington of Montgomery, Alabama

Dear Mr. Thorington:

Thank you for your letter of November twenty-sixth. It was the first information I had received concerning the incident.

I have since made inquiry of our management personnel and the offending members of our orchestra, and everyone admits to a serious breach of concert etiquette—for which one can only offer apologies.

Surely, someone among our principal players, assisting conductors or stage personnel, should have spotted the distraction prior to concert time, and had it removed. (After thirty-five years of touring, of appearing in nearly every concert auditorium of the United States, I cannot believe I should have missed the television's presence and potential hazard.)

I find only one mitigating circumstances in the entire affair, and it is, as reported to our Peter Stelling by your Dr. Campbell, that the TV set was brought to the hall by a Mr. Schnell (the local stage manager?) "for his own entertainment." If, therefore, it was positioned on an elevated light platform off-stage and tuned to the game, it seems to me as naive to expect orchestra brass players to avoid looking at it would be to expect a troop of Boy Scouts marching past a nudist colony to look only at their Scoutmaster—(or vice versa).

As I write and conclude my apology, I see three errors:

1. The set shouldn't have been backstage.
2. The set shouldn't have been "on."
3. No one should have looked.

No. 1 is not the players' fault.
No. 2 appears to be a fault shared by everyone.
No. 3 is only the players' fault.
Or,
Errors:
Home

1–100%
2–50%
3–0%
Visitors
1–0%
2–50%
3–100%

(I'll just bet the present administration in Washington would settle out of court *fast* for a balance sheet like that.)

Since you have undertaken, understandably, to insure that the orchestra does not return to Montgomery, we will not be privileged to make appropriate amends there. I hope, however, that if you should again visit Symphony Hall in Atlanta, you will allow me to apologize in person backstage.

Sincerely,

Robert Shaw

CC:
Mr. Oliver Roosevelt— *The Birmingham News*
Mr. Joseph Walthall—Pres., Atlanta Symphony Orchestra, Players Association

1974

Note. In the score for his 1812 Overture, Tchaikovsky calls for the firing of military cannons. Like most orchestras, the Atlanta Symphony often simulates cannons by setting off explosive charges during the performance. At a 1974 concert in Symphony Hall, things got a bit out of hand and smoke from the explosives set off the fire alarm backstage. When the audience emerged after the concert, they found fire engines lined up outside and firemen with hoses at the ready. Time *magazine got wind of the story and asked Robert Shaw for a statement. His response:*

"As the smoke cleared and firemen in full asbestos regalia appeared march-ing down the aisles, it became apparent that what I had mistaken in the din of battle as a premature entry of the chimes had been an over-eager automated smell-all and tell-all that didn't know its brass from principal bass."

January 25, 1980

It is difficult to assay the motivation of a letter which begins with the most personal of salutations—"Beloved Robert"—(after only a single casual meeting) and concludes with a list of multiple addresses. – So, for the first time, I shall answer a form-letter.

I find it thoughtless and presumptuous of you to accept a five-minute exhortation—however passionate, sincere, and ruminative—as a complete posi-tion paper on "professionalism vs. amateurism" in the choral arts.

It reminds me of people in the early days who figured they had the exclusive handle on what was known, evidently, to everybody but its originator as the "Shaw technique" of choral conducting. "It is based," some said, "completely on Enunciation." "No, on Rhythm!" others reported. "No, on Phrasing!" "On Dy-namics!" "On Tone!" – And so on and on . . . while, from what I could figure, all I was doing was sewing up the next rip in the gunny-sack. I headed only towards what seemed to me needed fixing; and, obviously, that varied from situation to situation.

Against some four days of closed deliberation—as well as two-thirds of a life-time of work and thought—to neither of which you were a witness, you are in the position of postulating a man's position upon the five minutes of rhetoric which you did witness.

With equal passion and sincerity I could have cried out for support of professionalism in the choral arts (as I have done for more than four decades)—had that been remotely necessary. – From my point of view, I simply was heading for the hole in the gunny-sack.

You may not be aware that years before there was an RS Chorale there was an NBC Chorale, CBS and ABC Chorales, an RCA Victor Chorale and a Fred Waring Glee Club, all of which I formed and conducted, and all of which were fully professional.

I quote from a speech which I wrote in those years, and which I have delivered at least once a year in one form or another since that time: "Payment, or the amount thereof (for making music), is neither final proof nor sliding scale of either professionalism or amateurism in art. The fact is that our greatest—

and, probably, most highly paid—artists are great precisely because they have managed to preserve an amateur's love for their art. Rudolf Serkin happens to be paid, but that is not the reason he plays."

I can think of no reason why it is important for you to have this information, but you're welcome to it: for over ten years I have petitioned the board of the Atlanta Symphony, "passionately, sincerely"—and unsuccessfully, to support a professional chamber chorus along with its volunteer symphony chorus and professional orchestra. The board has had other priorities, and I respect them. I respect also the fact that they are spending $75,000 to bring their volunteer symphony chorus to Carnegie Hall for a three-day *Festival of Requiems* during Easter week this year.

That I am not a member or promoter of either APVE or ACD is nobody's business but my own.

Now, let me get to the hole in the gunny-sack. At the meeting of the Choral Panel in Washington I was concerned about three things.

First, I was concerned that the clear intent of the *Statement of the goal of the National Endowment for the Arts* be sustained by the Choral Panel's actions: namely, "the fostering of professional excellence . . . *and equally* to . . . create a climate in which—they may be *experienced* and enjoyed by the widest possible public." The lucid majority of the subsequent qualifying paragraphs deal almost exclusively with the latter of these goals.

Second, I was concerned that a unique opportunity, available to the choral art as though by a marvel of the moment, be not defeated—perhaps for my lifetime—by allegations or indictments of privateering and self-interest. Hy Fain, the extraordinary and visionary executive director of AGMA in its early days, never would have allowed a professional choral movement—in the persons of a very few directors—to create, nourish and antagonize an adversary of 16,000 choral conductors, each of whom had loyal adherents of 100 or more singer-citizens. Have you considered what a million-and-a-half personal letters to Congressmen or the Endowment Staff could do to the Choral Program—or, indeed, the entire National Endowment?

And third, my greatest concern was that the very special qualities of the choral art—its unique amalgam, cross-pollination and transfusion of amateurism and professionalism, by means of which I feel it might summon and inspire all the arts in our country—be given a chance to work their miracle.

It is clear to anyone with long experience in the professional performing arts in the country that, *as presently institutionalized,* they place intolerable strains upon the dedication and devotion—the amateur spirit (amo, amare: to love)—which prompted their choice as a "means of life" in the first place.

To some of us, the survival of the symphony orchestra in the United States depends upon our ability to transform that institution into a "society of the musical arts," in which its member artists are not unremittingly under the daily discipline and dictatorship of one or a troika of directors, but who rather rotate through the repertoires of opera, oratorio, ballet, symphony and chamber orchestra and—more importantly—solo chamber music and teaching, and thus have the opportunity to express themselves as artists and human beings, and hold fast to their original vision and their happiness.

Upon this last matter I *am* writing a more extended "position paper," for I find it my chief concern as I try to relate the arts to today's society.

I have one more comment to make, and it is in answer to your denigration of the Atlanta Symphony's performance of the Mahler *Symphony VIII* a year and a half ago—which you did not hear.

As to the choral forces: Florida State University and Ohio State University are among the largest schools of music in the country; their choruses are in the care of absolutely superb choral technicians (who could give cards and spades to well over 99% of the choral conductors in the United States—of whatever persuasion or renown—and still walk away winners) and their students are, in the majority, "graduate" and professional trainees. Of the Atlanta Symphony Chorus, two-fifths of its 200-plus members are music professionals in one field or another. The children's chorus was large and well-trained.

As to the instrumental forces: I spent twelve years with the Cleveland Orchestra during George Szell's years, conducting as many as 80 concerts per year, seldom less than 20 of them subscription or touring programs. I am not unfamiliar with technical instrumental excellence. – And the Atlanta Symphony, by any standards, is a *very fine* orchestra:

– But nothing in my previous life in music prepared me for the effortless fluency or the shattering sonority of this occasion. I had no idea musical sound could be so incomprehensibly huge and so unutterably beautiful. We had most of "the 1,000" hoped-for, and they were all skilled.

If you weren't there, don't knock it.

For forty-five years I've been making a living conducting choruses, occasionally successfully; for thirty years I have been conducting symphony orchestras; sometimes that has been successful.

If you can admit that the recordings and tours of 40, 30, and 20 years ago were not without performance standards, let me simply report to you that compared to the technical securities and stylistic properties of the present Atlanta Symphony Chorus, those early efforts now appear, to the person who conducted them, as blind, ineffectual gropings.

It is very clear to me now that my principal teachers in my struggle to find essential choral techniques have been the members of the Collegiate Chorale, and the Cleveland and Atlanta Orchestra Choruses. There are some notable differences to be experienced between building an instrument and standing in front of one.

In like fashion, the past thirteen years of building the Atlanta Symphony have been chorally instructive beyond any possible foresight—as they inevitably refined expectations and techniques of articulation, rhythmic cohesion, tempo, balance and tonal palette.

Michael Korn said to me a year ago at Westminster Choir College, when he was enlisting my support of the APVE, "The trouble with you, Mr. Shaw, is that you make an amateur chorus sound like a professional one." Howard Swan used to say exactly the reverse.

Well, not without tears, sweat—and a hell of a lot of technique—which finally, maybe, is beginning to arrive. (I could have used it thirty years ago!)

If ever you'd like to participate in that learning process, you'd be welcome in Atlanta. – But, please do not feel obliged to answer this letter. I should find it difficult to respond further.

Robert Shaw

February 16, 1987

To Mr. John Kenna of Hughes Springs, Texas

Dear Mr. Kenna –

Thank you for your letter of 29 December.

All of us are shocked and saddened by having "shocked and saddened" you.

Your criticism of the pronunciation of the word *Israel* has been gratefully noted.

The pronunciation of *Israel* which you find so disturbing is probably just an "old Southern custom," left over from the Civil War; and should be stamped out—like the Republican Party or the playing of "Dixie."

If we can't handle Israel, think of the trouble we're going to have when we get to doing all the Arab music!

Sincerely,

Robert Shaw

VERSE

August 5, 1943

To Collegiate Chorale

This should begin with a lot of things all adding up to thanks to Gordon Berger who (I heard clear in California) has done a wonderful job as director of The Collegiate Chorale the past few weeks. People wrote things like "musician-ship, authority, modesty, humor"—which certainly indicates a heavy and happy debt of thanks. Very, very.

– I should waste Sydney's time with a 6-stencil diary of two weeks in the land of the milked and honeyed!

    So –
    Gather, my children, and don't be late,
      On next Monday night at precis-e-ly eight,
  Dragging his tired little own one as well,
  Robert the Rober will multi-tales tell –
  Of concerts, rehearsals and singing sans ending
  Of serious classes—the "science" of sending,
  Of Schumann for scholars and hymns for the masses,
  Of hostesses, co-eds, and MGM lasses,
  (The last, I regret, is pos'tively reeking
  Of cough-up-the-sleeving and tongue-in-the-cheeking.)
  But –
  Gather, my children, and man your defences,
  You'll need them for Robert tile A-manuensis!

December 5, 1556

> 'Would some God the giftie bear us
> To hear ourselves as others hear us,
>
> Or angels send with vocal radar
> To guide us through the fugues of Credar.
>
> A lot have thought about the Gloria,
> "It might confuse, but never boria."
>
> – While those whose souls indulge a sweet-tooth
> Can graze for days on Benedeectuth.
>
> Just three rehearsals left—so watch 'em:
> – Agnus Dei, dona pacem!

R. S.

October 28, 1959

> Lines in praise of practically nothing:
>
> Ah! quel dommage!
> My French is a state.
> Toujours too little
> And toujours too late.
>
> Toujours trop lentement,
> Jamais tout de suite.
> I get all my shieus
> Tangled up in my feet.
>
> It comes with a O,
> And goes by with a whoosh
> And me with mes pieds
> Walking 'round in ma bouche.
>
> Or toujours la speed,
> Mais jamais control.
> Je parle Français
> Comme une vache Espagnol!

Mal de my tummy,
And mal de ma tête.
Vive la France!
But I wish I was dete.

Lines in praise of somethings practical:

Among the host of things there are no substitutes for are absolute intonation and beautiful sound. The most extraordinary beautiful sound is of little use to music unless it functions in perfect relation to other true pitches. And absolute pitch is a good beginning, but only that. From then on only beauty will suffice.

It seems to me that we made some progress in these directions Monday night. And that's not easy.

R. S.

November 28, 1978

Friends –

Well-well-well
Good! Good! Good!

If you can keep your note when all about you
    Are losing theirs and blaming it on you;
If you can trust your ear when others doubt you,
    And simply go ahead as though you knew;
If you can count, and not get tired of counting,
    And "doo-doo-doo" 'til it comes out your ears;
If you can see the maestro's pressure mounting
    But never show you wish he'd act his years;

If you can "brighter-darker-higher-lower"
    And stifle every urge to scream or yell,
But goon "louder-softer-faster-slower"
    Nor wish "he'd go——!" or think, "Am I—in hell!"
If neither snow nor rain nor indigestion
    Can stay you from your weekly rack of slats;
If you can phrase the necessary question
    Without implying the conductor's bats;

If you can give up job and home and family,
    And drive 200 miles 6 times a week,
Trade name for number and—ad nauseamly—
    Adore your idjit digit like a freak;
If you can tremble if you're late one minute,
    And feel great guilt when awful seems to worsen,
You've won the crock! my friend, and all that's in it!
    And—which is more—you're now a choral "person!"

With apologies to Backyard Tippling,

R

January 6, 1981

Bread and Butter Letter No. 0.999999999

Dear People –

What a wonderful Christmas Festival!

Women-wise, the Ceremony swang like angels;
and man-wise, Ce matin was thrice-kingly.

Refrain (please!)
Ce matin—an' the livin' is easy
Fish are freezin'
'N the prices are high.

Santa Claus has come and went –
That which we hadn't, has been spent.

Daddy's back behind the plow –
Trees are in the gutter now.

Time to get back on a diet –
'See you all on Monday niet.

R

P.S.

'Twas a perfect end to Autumn.
So thank you from the Bautumn.

February 10, 1981

Dear People –

"Not to worry! –"

Upwaltzing like Leviathan
from wet of winter's waking,
Hope held Monday's face in
Tuesday morning's hands.
"All is not lost!" she prettied,
"See, the day dawns grey
– for Hindemith,
Muckly
– for Bruck'ner!
The omen's a 'go!' man!"

Hot doggery for augury! – sez I. – And if you'll read the *Apparebit* text once per day each day every day between now and Monday, I'll guarantee to have us singing all the right notes at the right dynamic levels by the end of Monday's rehearsal. How's them apples for temptations?

R

November 21, 1981

Little Miss Snippett,
Tip-toeing through Tippett,
    Was frequently put on the spot –
Providing occasion
For resuscitation –
    And, Lord! what a lovin' she got.

The heart of the matter
Is: Life with a Hatter
    Is Mad as a Rubik's cue-ball.
No child of our time
Ever had it so prime.
    We're very darn proud of you all!

C and R

November 25, 1981

Two Totally Unrelated Sexlets

I

> Now I lay me down to sleep,
> And pray Big Tongue my tongue to keep.
> I did the very best I could –
> If not superb, at least 'twas good.
> > When up to your ears in Anglification,
> > Remember this: "Less regimentation!"

II

> Christmas comes but once a year,
> And lasts but thirty-seven days.
> Thanksgiving lights the tree with cheer,
> And Twelfth Night ends it in a blaze.
> > I think that I shall never see
> > More needles fall from one damn tree.

R

P.S. Thanks for the week that was.
> – And thank you also for last Monday night,
> which was very fluent and pleasant.
> Next Monday night, ladies come at 7:30 and men at 8:00.

November 7, 1995

Dear Thanks-receivers –

Be assured of that! You certainly have earned all the Pilgrimy Puritantalizing alimentary enticements your bodies can metabolize.

List not to girth-removers and watchers of weight. Stoke up! The season of Jolly Consumerism is around yon corner. You done good. Betterness will surely follow.

Unrelenting thanks!

R

– A chorister's version:

Wild Notes—Wild Notes!
Though one with thee –
Wild Notes bring naught
But misery!

Futile—the pitch –
To a heart in shock –
Throw out the life-line!
Get me a Doc!

Growing an ulcer –
Beat after beat –
(Could one but find one –
Life would be sweet!)

Cancel the Compass –
Chew up the Chart!
What I need most is
Another heart!

Mooring's amouring –
Tell me I'm wrong –
Does anyone know
"Love's old sweet song?"

November 9, 1989

Well –

Come, now! Don't be coy or balkish,
'Tis the season to be mawkish!
Though the *Mass* was perfect, nearly,
Sing we must, and eke sincerely
Yuletide jingles and commercials,
"Peace on Earth!" (and our rehearsals)
Knowing Truth to be elastic
And the world redeemed by plastic.

Gird your loins and mind your morals,
Rest ye not on last week's laurels.

(Credit, as we witness sadly,
only comes when one does badly.)
Forego work and school and Cupid
Even though I-ta-i-poop-ed!
Stop whatever you are doing,
'Time for Be-te-le-he-mooing!

R

November 4, 1992

Friends –

The nicest thing about going away is coming back home. You have achieved wonderful things with your preparation of the Brahms *Requiem.* – This, in spite of the fact that it was a dozen years ago when last we performed it. – A landslide of votes of thanks to Ann Jones and Norman Mackenzie for their care and their skills.

Twelve years ago we were involved in preparing a trio of Requiems and I found today among more erudite files of comment and scholarship the following doggerel, dated April 22, 1980.

INTROIT

Berlioz, Verdi and Brahms
Were a trio of psingers of psalms.
What Berlioz wanted he never quite got,
And Verdi went "oom-pah" as often as not,
While, as for Brahms' love-life, it wasn't so hot.
But nothing impaired the musical chahms
of Berlioz, Verdi –
of Berlioz, Verdi –
of Berlioz, Verdi and Brahms!

November 16, 1994

So –

Listen, my children, and you shall hear
How thanks-y'all-giving came early this year.

I

Ms. Bonney flew over the ocean,
Half-widow, half-angel was she,
Shifted sands with high-tides of emotion
– But left each bar clean as can be.

II

Choose a moment of silence –
    – Could anything chill it
Like "It is enough . . . ?"
    Wringing tears from a stone.
Could anyone enter that silence . . .
    . . . fulfill it
Like Richard the Clement –
    And one of our own!?!?

III

– Lest-uh we forget-uh
    Marietta.
If—as one goes through life—
one finds that she
cannot always be the heroine
– or even heroinnier –

    Is it possible that the next best thing
is to become a supercalifragilisticexpialidocious sinnier?
    Certainly, life must hold something better
than being no belle at all –
    – Even if it's just-uh being Jezebel of the Baal.

And –

IV

How about Thomas ('Tain't never 'nuff!) Hampson?
Singeth Delilah-t'fully—looketh like Samson!
   Donkey field-mouse!
   Mair-see baw-koo!
   Grah-thee-ahth!
   Grahtseeahs ahdjeemoos teebee.

R

January 4, 1989

In 1916 had I known
What lay in store for '88
I wonder if I'd been as prone
To line up at the starting gate.

But now the 90's are in view,
And after them? – Lord, who'da thought!
Let's meet again and hoist a few
At good old oughty-oughty-ought!

You,
Too?

R

454

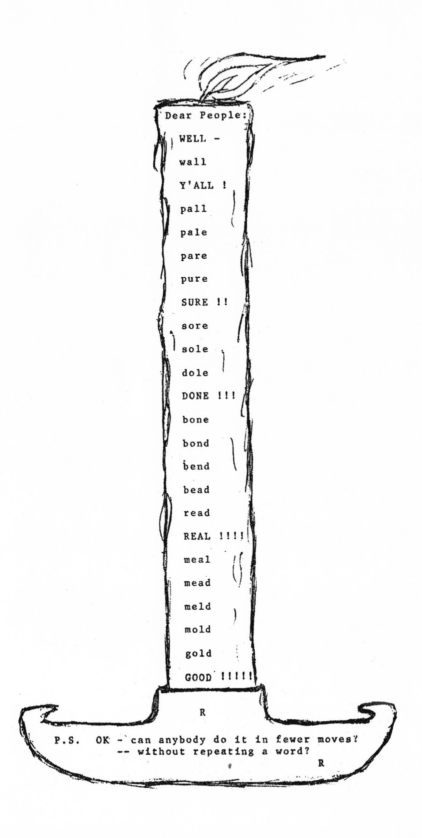

Dear People:

WELL -

wall

Y'ALL !

pall

pale

pare

pure

SURE !!

sore

sole

dole

DONE !!!

bone

bond

bend

bead

read

REAL !!!!

meal

mead

meld

mold

gold

GOOD !!!!!

R

P.S. OK - can anybody do it in fewer moves?
-- without repeating a word?

R

INDEX